Asian Universities

Asian Universities

Historical Perspectives and
Contemporary Challenges

Edited by

Philip G. Altbach & Toru Umakoshi

THE JOHNS HOPKINS UNIVERSITY PRESS
Baltimore & London

© 2004 The Johns Hopkins University Press
All rights reserved. Published 2004
Printed in the United States of America on acid-free paper
2 4 6 8 9 7 5 3 1

The Johns Hopkins University Press
2715 North Charles Street
Baltimore, Maryland 21218-4363
www.press.jhu.edu

Library of Congress Cataloging-in-Publishing Data

Asian universities: historical perspectives and contemporary challenges/
edited by Philip G. Altbach and Toru Umakoshi.
p. cm.
Includes bibliographical references and index.
ISBN 0-8018-8036-X (hardcover : alk. paper)—ISBN 0-8018-8037-8 (pbk. : alk. paper)
1. Education, Higher—Asia—History. 2. Universities and colleges—Asia—History.
I. Altbach, Philip G. II. Umakoshi, Toru, 1942–
LA1058.A85 2004
378.5—dc22
2004010444

A catalog record for this book is available from the British Library.

Contents

Preface

This book grew out of an earlier effort to consider Asian universities within a common framework. Both projects have drawn on the past as a way of understanding the present and future. A first attempt to bring together researchers from a variety of Asian countries to think about Asian higher education in 1989 resulted in *From Dependence to Autonomy: The Development of Asian Universities,* edited by Philip G. Altbach and Viswanathan Selvaratnam. The present volume provides both an expansion and an update of that earlier effort, although our focus here is on the present and future more than on the past.

This project was a collaborative effort of the Center for International Higher Education at Boston College in the United States and the Study Group of Asian Higher Education, which received financial support from Japan Foundation Asian Center, and the Center for the Study of Higher Education at Nagoya University in Japan. The collaboration proved to be a fruitful way to organize a research project. We appreciate the assistance of the Toyota Foundation with core funding for this project. The Center for International Higher Education at Boston College is supported by the Ford Foundation.

We are especially indebted to our research group, which met for a discussion of the project themes and papers in Nagoya in December 2002. This discussion was useful in analyzing themes and stimulating ideas for the chapters included here. The Nagoya meeting was coordinated by Toru Umakoshi. The discussions at Nagoya were summarized by Edith Hoshino, who also provided editorial assistance for the book.

Introduction

Philip G. Altbach & Toru Umakoshi

Asian universities are undergoing a dramatic transformation. This book focuses on change in the context of both the historical traditions of Asian academic systems and the challenges of contemporary realities. Although this volume is not a reference book in the traditional sense, it does provide data concerning the academic systems of an important group of Asian countries. The chapters, which are analytical in content, examine the past, present, and future of higher education. *Asian Universities* does not analyze all Asian countries but rather presents in-depth discussion of key Asian nations that reflect the realities of Asian development at the beginning of the twenty-first century.

We have organized this book around central themes in Asian higher education development. The two Asian giants, China and India, together representing about one-third of the world's population and both with expanding academic systems, are included because of their global importance. Japan, South Korea, and Singapore are countries that have attained high levels of socioeconomic development as well as sophisticated academic systems, and thus may provide models to other Asian nations. Malaysia and Thailand are both middle-income countries that have invested heavily in higher education and have achieved significant results. The Philippines and Indonesia face significant economic challenges but have nevertheless built large academic systems. Finally, Cambodia and Vietnam have low per capita incomes, have experienced war and political turmoil, and have only recently embarked on the expansion of their academic systems. This mosaic of Asian realities provides the organizing principle of this book and a useful overview for Asia and the rest of the world.

A significant portion of the world's higher education expansion is taking place in Asia—a trend that will continue in the coming decades. China has recently overtaken the United States in having the largest postsecondary system in the world. Most of the countries in this book are still expanding their academic systems. The challenge of massification is very much part of the Asian situation. Simultaneously, the steady and potentially falling enrollments in Japan and South Korea provide a different reality that is useful to understand.

The forces that affect higher education worldwide are evident in Asia. Expansion has driven the growth of the private sector in higher education—Asia has some of the largest private universities. At the same time that massification is under way in Asian higher education systems, there is a desire to build "world-class" universities to compete with the best academic institutions worldwide. Further, the pressures of globalization affects Asian countries, from the exodus of well-qualified students and staff to the use of English for research and teaching.

While Asian universities have diverse historical roots and patterns of higher education development, the authors in this volume believe that Asian countries can learn from one another. Although no common "Asian reality" exists, there is much to be learned from specific Asian experiences. The differences among Asian countries are in many ways as great as the similarities. Distinct historical models, contrasting economic systems, varying approaches to language of instruction, disparate levels of wealth and stages of economic growth, and other factors are evident in Asia. These variations, as well as some common patterns of development, make Asia a unique region.

The idea that the past influences the present and the future applies especially to universities, where historical tradition plays an important role in influencing contemporary realities. Most Asian countries experienced colonialism, and the colonizers' academic ideas significantly influenced contemporary academic systems. Even in those countries that did not directly experience colonialism—Japan, Thailand, and China—foreign academic models were used in shaping universities.

Ultimately, this volume has a modest and important goal—to highlight the realities of contemporary higher education in the Asian context. We are convinced that a comparative perspective can help to inform analysis and ultimately result in more thoughtful policy.

PART I

Asian Perspectives

1

The Past and Future of Asian Universities

Twenty-First Century Challenges

Philip G. Altbach

Asia is notable for its size and its diversity. Asia accounts for a majority of the world's population and for several of the world's most dynamic and fast-growing economies, as well as some of the weakest. In higher education, Asia has not traditionally been a leader in research or innovation. In the coming decades, however, Asia will experience massive higher education expansion—indeed, a majority of the world's enrollment growth will take place in Asia. Further, Asian economies will increasingly demand university-trained personnel to ensure the success of sophisticated economies. Research and development will inevitably become more important to Asian countries.

This essay concerns higher education trends in Asia from India and Pakistan to China and Japan. While Asia's diverse academic systems do not lend themselves to easy generalizations, there are some common elements as well as shared experiences. We are seeking to understand the challenges that face Asian universities in the 21st century, when institutions will need to be part of the international knowledge system and play a central role in meeting national educational needs. Universities are part of the global system of science and scholarship while at the same time being rooted in their own societies. The coming period will be one of considerable potential and looming problems for higher education in the region.

This essay will look at both the potentials and the challenges in broad terms, for it is impossible to fully analyze all of Asia in this essay (Postiglione & Mak, 1997). The focus will be on such topics as expansion, competition, and quality, as well as the role of research and the links between higher education and society in the Asian context. The central reality of the past several decades as well as the coming period for most Asian countries is expansion and coping with the effects of massification on higher education. Although much of this analysis revolves around the implications of expansion, several Asian countries face declining populations and the accompanying problems of likely contraction of the academic system. Between 1980 and 1995, enrollments in developing countries increased from 28 million to 47 million—a significant part of that growth taking place in Asia (Task Force, 2000, p. 27). Asian higher education will continue to expand rapidly, in large part because some of the largest Asian countries—such as China and India as well as Vietnam, Cambodia, Pakistan, Bangladesh, and several others—now educate relatively small proportions of their young people at the postsecondary level and face immense pressure to meet the popular demand for access and the economic needs of modernizing economies. Vietnam, for example, educates around 6 percent of the university age cohort, while Cambodia has half that proportion in higher education (Task Force, 2000, pp. 104–107). India educates around 10 percent. China has recently boosted its enrollment rate to 15 percent and now has the largest number of students in postsecondary education in the world—having recently passed the United States in total enrollments, although the United States is educating well above half of the relevant age group.

Academic institutions have always been part of the international knowledge system, and in the age of the Internet they are increasingly linked to trends in science and scholarship worldwide. All Asian nations—even the largest and best developed, such as Japan, China, and India—remain largely peripheral internationally (Altbach 1998, pp. 133–146). The major Western universities retain scientific and research leadership. As Asian universities grow in stature, they will need to become able to function in a highly competitive academic world. All of the elements of academic life, including research, the distribution of knowledge, the students, and the academic profession, are part of an internationally competitive marketplace. Without doubt, the immediate future holds considerable challenges for Asian higher education, as it does for higher education in the rest of the world.

HISTORICAL PERSPECTIVES: COLONIAL AND POSTCOLONIAL PATTERNS

Contemporary Asian higher education is fundamentally influenced by its historical traditions. No Asian university is truly Asian in origin—all are based on European academic models and traditions, in many cases imposed by colonial rulers, and in others (e.g., Japan and Thailand) on voluntarily adopted Western models (Altbach & Selvaratnam, 1989). The fact that all Asian universities began as foreign implants has played a central role in how academic institutions have developed—with regard to academic freedom, institutional autonomy, the relationship of the university to society, and other factors.

It is significant that no Asian country has kept, to any significant extent, its premodern academic institutional traditions. Most Asian countries had pre-Western academic institutions—the Confucian academies in China, the traditional *pathashalas* or *madrasahs* in India, and similar institutions in Vietnam, Cambodia, Thailand, and elsewhere were largely destroyed or abandoned as Asian countries began the process of modernization beginning in the 19th century. In India, for example, British academic practices came to dominate the system, although traditional patterns were never entirely eliminated (Ashby, 1966; Basu, 1989). Today, there are a small number of institutions providing education in traditional fields, such as ayurvedic medicine, but they are largely organized along Western lines.

The imposition of academic models by the colonial powers has had a profound impact. The British academic model was imposed on all of the countries that were under British colonial rule, and it remains a powerful force in such countries as India, Pakistan, Bangladesh, Sri Lanka, Malaysia, Hong Kong, Nepal, and several others. Even where the British model has been largely jettisoned, such as in Singapore, elements of it remain evident, and ties with the United Kingdom remain strong. Because of the extent of British colonial rule in Asia, the British model is probably the most important foreign academic influence in that whole region.

Other European colonial powers also exported their university ideas to Asia: the French in Indochina (Vietnam, Cambodia, and to a lesser extent Laos), the Dutch in the Dutch East Indies (Indonesia), Spain and, after 1898, the United States in the Philippines, and Russia in the central Asian republics that were part of the Russian Empire and then the Soviet Union. Japan began its role as a colonial power at the end of the 19th century, and it had an active higher education policy in Taiwan and Korea, its main colonies. It is worth noting that, with the exception of the Americans in the Philippines, the other (European) colonial powers were not enthusiastic exporters of higher education. Even the British, in whose colonies higher education was the most developed, did not spend a great deal of effort or money in fostering universities. Indeed, the role of indigenous populations in establishing Western-model universities during the colonial era deserves more emphasis.

It is also worth noting that, with few exceptions, the colonial powers did not dismantle existing indigenous higher education institutions. Rather, Western-style universities proved more popular because they were tied to the colonial administration and to emerging economic interests. Indigenous schools were simply left to atrophy. An exception to this generally laissez faire approach was Japan, which had a more activist educational policy in Korea and Taiwan and actively repressed local institutions of higher education (Lee, 2004).

The European powers felt that the implantation of higher education in their colonies would introduce a subversive institution. They were correct in this assumption since Western-educated intellectuals produced by the universities were everywhere the leaders of independence movements, and the universities themselves were important intellectual centers involved in the development of nationalism and dissent. Perhaps the most dramatic example of the impact of Western-educated university graduates is Indonesia, where the very concept of the Indonesian nation with a common language was created by a small group of intellectuals trained both at home and in the Netherlands. Despite the reluctance of the colonial authorities, there was a need for small groups of Western-educated people, literate in the language of the colonial administration, to staff the civil service and provide midlevel administration. The pressure for expansion came almost entirely from local people seeking the opportunities provided by a Western academic degree, and in some cases the colonial powers permitted modest expansion to meet these demands.

The role of Christian missionary work in the development and expansion of higher education in Asia is also significant. Missionaries devoted much effort to establishing higher education institutions to foster conversions to Christianity. In much of Asia, the establishment of early academic institutions was due to missionary work. This was especially the case in India, China, and Korea, where Christian organizations were among the early founders of colleges and universities, although in most Asian countries missionaries had less success in converting people to Christianity. A significant exception to this rule is the Philippines, which is majority Roman Catholic as the result of centuries of Spanish colonial rule. The Spanish colonial authorities gave the Catholic Church the full responsibility for higher education. South Korea also has a large Christian minority. Missionaries generally had the support of the colonial authorities although from time to time, as in India, there were disagreements concerning higher education policy. In some parts of Asia, Christian universities and colleges remain an important part of the academic landscape.

There are important common elements in the European colonial model in Asia. In all cases, instruction was offered exclusively in the language of the colonial power. Universities in the British colonies functioned in English, in the Dutch East Indies in Dutch, in Korea and Taiwan in Japanese, in the Philippines in English, and so on. The widespread use of European languages in higher education has had a profound impact on the development of higher education. It has been difficult, in some Asian countries, to use local languages in higher education—Indonesia is an example of a country that made an early and effective shift from a European language (Dutch) to an indigenous language (Cummings & Kasenda, 1989). Neighboring Malaysia had more difficulty changing from English and is now restoring some English to the higher education system. South Asia retains English as one of the languages of instruction. The Asian countries that were not colonized—e.g., Japan, China, and Thailand— did not adopt European languages. Thus, in much of Asia, the impact of colonial languages on academic development has been, and continues to be, central to higher education.

The colonial powers placed restrictions on the academic institutions they established in Asia—government control was strict and academic freedom limited. The purpose of the colonial universities was to train a loyal civil service and a small number of medical doctors, lawyers, and others to serve the colonizers—not to establish universities in the full autonomous sense of the term. Thus, the colonial university did not have all of the characteristics of the metropolitan model. This historical tradition of subservience and of a lack of full autonomy and academic freedom created problems for the emergence of modern universities in postindependence Asia.

It is also important to examine those Asian countries that were not colonized. Japan and Thailand are the most significant examples. China, while never formally colonized, was strongly influenced by Europeans, and also by Japan, along the coast where higher education became the most entrenched. In all of these cases, the noncolonized Asian countries chose Western academic models rather than relying on indigenous intellectual and academic traditions. In the second half of the 19th century, Japan and Thailand established Western-style academic institutions after careful consideration. In the Japanese case, the new Meiji regime adopted the German academic model with some influences from the United States as the pattern for the new universities. After some discussion concerning the appropriate language of instruction, during which the minister of education advocated the use of English, Japanese was chosen as the medium of instruction. In Japan, Thailand, and China, governments established Western-style higher education to assist in the process of modernization and industrialization.

Upon attaining independence, no Asian country chose to break with the academic models imposed by the colonial powers. Other links with the universities in the former metropole were also retained. In the former British colonies, English was retained as a medium of instruction to varying extents. As mentioned, Malaysia, which moved to Bahasa Malaysia a few years after independence, has recently reintroduced English to some extent in its universities. Indonesia was the largest country to shift the language of education, introducing Bahasa Indonesia immediately following independence. Korea and Taiwan stopped using Japanese and moved to Korean and Chinese, respectively. In the decade following the 1949 Communist revolution in China, a variety of Western patterns yielded to the Soviet academic model (Hayhoe, 1996). For different reasons and at different times, China and the central Asian republics, once part of the Soviet Union, found the Soviet model to be inappropriate. China dropped it a half century ago, while the central Asian nations are now in the process of change.

As Asian academic systems have grown and matured, countries have not been inspired to develop new indigenous academic models. Rather, Asian countries have looked abroad for ways to expand and improve their universities. For the most part, the United States has provided the ideas and forms for academic development. There are several reasons for this "Americanization" of Asian higher education. The U.S. academic system is the largest in the world—the first to cope with the challenges of enrollment expansion. The United States also has the largest and most advanced academic research system. Moreover, many Asian academic and political leaders studied in the United States and absorbed American academic ideas during their student years.

Asian academic systems carry the baggage of their historical past. The legacy of colonialism linked universities to government and gave considerable power to governmental authorities over higher education. Even in countries without a colonial past, notably Japan and Thailand, the impetus for the establishment of modern universities came from government. Asian universities have shallow roots in the soil of their countries—the norms and values of academe are perhaps less well entrenched than in many Western nations. On this point, however, it should be remembered that German universities voluntarily succumbed to Nazi authority despite their rich historical tradition. Still, historical traditions play an important role in all social institutions—and no institution is more influenced by history than universities.

THE ASIAN ECONOMIC MIRACLE

Nowhere in Asia have the early stages of contemporary economic development been dependent on higher education. Even in those countries that have achieved impressive rates of growth and have joined the ranks of the industrialized world—Japan, Taiwan, South Korea, China and to some extent Thailand and Malaysia—development has not been based on knowledge industries or on higher education. The underpinnings of economic growth are varied. The typical pattern was industrialization based on an inexpensive labor force, with a basic education and literacy skills, and a reliance on exporting relatively unsophisticated manufactured goods or the products of heavy industry. In some cases, raw materials (such as oil and rubber in Malaysia) or agricultural products were added.

Significant investment in education did play a role, but the focus was on primary and to some extent secondary education to provide the workforce for the emerging industries with the appropriate literacy and skills. The countries that had the most success—Japan, South Korea, Taiwan, and in recent years China—invested heavily in basic education and achieved very impressive gains in literacy and other educational skills. The South Asian countries, which invested less in education and still have much lower literacy rates, have done less well economically.

Higher education was not emphasized during the initial phases of industrialization, and most Asian academic systems remained small, enrolling a modest percentage of the age cohort. The universities largely served the elites, and there was only limited demand from other sectors of the population. Governments invested little in higher education. In a number of countries, private universities became an important part of the system (Altbach, 1999).

As a middle class developed, as a growing segment of the population acquired some wealth, and as literacy levels and secondary schooling became more widespread, demand grew for access to higher education. For much of East Asia, these trends occurred in the 1980s and have continued today. Other parts of the region have moved more slowly. Moreover, in a few places, such as India, expansion was not directly linked to economic development. Universities and other postsecondary institutions were established to serve this growing demand, often in the private sector, given the frequent unwillingness of government to invest in higher education. Almost everywhere in Asia, university expansion was driven by demand from the increasingly articulate emerging middle classes and those seeking upward mobility in society. Only later, as governments recognized the role of postsecondary expansion in economic development, did the public sector invest significantly in higher education.

As countries such as Japan, South Korea, Taiwan, Singapore, and others developed, their economies became more sophisticated and wages rose, and they were no longer competitive with lower-wage economies. They realized that they had to develop more sophisticated industries and a service sector to remain competitive. In short, they were forced to move toward becoming "knowledge-based economies"—and higher education was seen as a key factor in national economic survival.

Investment in academic institutions and in a research infrastructure is taking place in many Asian countries, although the pace of investment and expansion varies considerably. Japan transformed itself first, starting in the 1960s, and it was followed by Taiwan, South Korea, Singapore, with Malaysia, Thailand, and others following somewhat later. Governments took more interest in higher education, and increased expenditures for both expansion and research. Although government expenditure on higher education in much of Asia remains modest by international standards, it grew during this period of expansion. Asia had the advantage of an active private higher education sector that paid for much of the expansion. Some Asian countries, including Cambodia, Laos, Burma, and to some extent Vietnam, remain at an early stage of economic development, with higher education still given a low priority.

One of the most interesting examples linking higher education to new economic policies has been Singapore (Tan, 2004). Singapore, which has had until recently no private higher education sector, kept enrollment rates modest in its two universities. As the country redirected its economic growth strategies to such high-tech areas as biotechnology, medical and financial services, and related fields, there was a recognition that a larger proportion of the population needed academic qualifications. Academic institutions have been expanded and a growing segment of the age cohort is enrolling in postsecondary education. Singapore is developing links with some of the best universities abroad, and for the first time, private initiatives in higher education are being permitted. Malaysia now has a national policy of encouraging high-tech development, and is linking this strategy with targeted higher education expansion.

The regional giants, China and India, after developing their economies in a fairly traditional pattern, now have elements of both "old" and "new" economic policies, and their higher education systems are adjusting in different ways to the new realities. While China has achieved much higher literacy rates and more impressive economic growth than has been the case for India, both countries are faced with the challenge of adapting their academic systems to meet the demands of growing numbers for access while ensuring that at least a part of the system serves the needs of a high-tech economy. Both countries show that it is possible to have at least a part of the higher education system operate at very high levels of quality and are involved with the international knowledge system. Such schools as the Indian Institutes of Technology and the key Chinese universities are examples of the best-quality academic and research institutions. India met the demand for access by permitting privately owned but government-subsidized colleges to expand, which has resulted in a decline in the overall quality of the academic system. China now seems to be moving in a similar direction, encouraging the private sector (which receives no government funding) to absorb demand for access and expanding enrollments in many of the public universities without commensurate increases in funding.

Higher education will inevitably become more central as Asian economies become more technology based, more heavily dependent on informatics, and more service based. Japan and Singapore have already been transformed into postindustrial information-based societies. China and India have moved partly into this realm, as have South Korea, Taiwan, and Malaysia. All these countries have recognized the importance of higher education in this transformation and are moving to ensure that at least part of the university system is prepared to function in the new environment. Japan's current structural reforms of the national universities are aimed in part at ensuring that higher education institutions will be prepared to play an active role in building the new economy. China is also in the process of ensuring that some of its top universities will have the training and research capabilities to assist in the economic changes needed for a research-based economy. Other Asian nations that recognize their role in a knowledge-based economy are, in different ways, developing university structures that can serve the new economic realities. Poorer Asian countries—Cambodia and Burma are examples—have yet to grapple with these changes. Still others, such as Thailand and in the future perhaps Pakistan, have yet to think seriously about higher education's role in a changing economic structure.

As much of Asia moves toward a more sophisticated economic base, universities will become more central to the economy, research will receive more attention, and closer links will evolve between the universities and the economy. While the initial phases of Asian economic success did not depend on higher education and technology, it is clear that the next stages will rely on the universities for both training and research. Japan, Taiwan, and South Korea have already recognized this, and China and Malaysia are adapting to current realities. Other countries will inevitably recognize the importance of higher education for the next phase of development.

THE CHALLENGE OF MASSIFICATION

The central reality of higher education almost everywhere is the expansion in student numbers that has taken place since the 1960s. Worldwide, between 1975 and 1995, enrollments doubled, going from 40 million to over 80 million. While growth has slowed in many industrialized countries, expansion continues in the developing nations, and will remain the main factor in shaping academic realities in the coming period. The pressures for expansion will be most significant in the countries that still educate a relatively small portion of the age group—under 15 percent—and in Asia this includes such major nations as China, India, Indonesia, Bangladesh, Burma, Vietnam, Cambodia, Pakistan, and others. Most industrialized nations educate from about 35 and to more than 50 percent of the age group—in Asia, only South Korea, Japan, and Taiwan have achieved this proportion, with Thailand, the Philippines, and Singapore catching up rapidly. These patterns of enrollment in Asia do not reflect the growing international trend to provide postsecondary education to "nontraditional" students—those who are older but have either missed out on an academic degree or who require additional skills for their jobs or professions. This so far underserved segment of the population will also demand increasing access in the coming years.

Expansion is an inevitable and irresistible force. Ever-growing segments of the population demand access to postsecondary education because they know that it is necessary for social mobility and for improved salaries and standards of living in most societies. Countries need larger numbers of university-educated workers to support knowledge-based economies. As more young people gain access to secondary education, they naturally gravitate to higher education, having gained the qualifications to gain entry to universities. In addition, as a middle class grows in size and in political influence, it will also demand access to higher education. Few countries have been able to resist the social demand for access, and none can permanently block it.

Almost all Asian countries are currently coping with the implications of continuing expansion. This pressure makes it difficult to focus on other things—improving quality, upgrading research, enhancing the salaries and working conditions of the professoriate, among others. The inevitable result of expansion has been the development of differentiated systems of higher education, with institutions serving different roles and with varying levels of support and prestige. The traditional university remains at the pinnacle of a hierarchy, but is no longer the main postsecondary institution. An overall deterioration of quality is also a result of massification. In most countries, there continue to be high-quality universities that maintain traditional academic standards and a commitment to research, but many of the institutions lower on the hierarchy offer an education that is more modest in quality—and in prestige as well. As in other parts of the world, mass higher education means a differentiated academic system, with major variations in quality, purpose, and orientation. Massification drags down the overall quality of the academic system as it creates a more diversified academic system.

The challenges are considerable. Two of the most important are funding the expansion and providing necessary physical facilities. The problem of funding is particularly acute for two reasons. Not only is it difficult to find public resources to support ever larger numbers of students, but there has also been a basic change in thinking in many countries concerning who should pay for higher education and other public services. Led by the World Bank and other international agencies, countries increasingly argue that higher education is mainly a "private good" serving the needs of individuals and less a "public" or social good. Therefore, the thinking is that the "user"—students, and perhaps their families—deserve to pay a significant part of the cost of higher education. This has led to the imposition of tuition and other fees for higher education in most Asian countries. Indeed, there may be no Asian country, with the exception of North Korea, that does not charge tuition. The two factors of a simple lack of sufficient public funds and a new perspective on higher education have combined to instigate a major rethinking of the financing of higher education as a private good in Asia. Even in countries that adhere to a socialist economic system—such as China and Vietnam— tuition has been introduced.

While it is not possible to fully analyze the nuances of the public vs. private good arguments here, it is clear that an effective higher education system will recognize that both are part of the academic equation. While it is certainly the case that earning a degree is a significant advantage to the graduate in terms of income and in other ways, it is also true that universities provide a considerable public good to society. Not only are there public benefits accruing from the individual graduate (such as a heightened civic consciousness and the ability to pay higher taxes because of higher earnings), universities provide other benefits to society: they are repositories of knowledge through their libraries and other databases and they provide the basic and applied research that can help with development.

THE PRIVATE SECTOR IN ASIAN HIGHER EDUCATION

Another central reality of massification is increased reliance on private higher education institutions (Altbach, 2000). Private higher education is the fastest-growing segment of postsecondary education worldwide. In Asia, private institutions have long been a central part of higher education provision. In such major countries as Japan, South Korea, Taiwan, the Philippines, and Indonesia, private universities enroll the majority of students—in some cases upwards of 80 percent. The large majority of Indian students attend private colleges, although these are heavily subsidized by government funds. The private sector is a growing force in parts of Asia where it was previously inactive—China, Vietnam, and the central Asian republics are examples.

In general, private universities are found at the lower end of the prestige hierarchy in Asia. There are a few exceptions of high-quality private universities, such as Waseda, Keio, and a few others in Japan; De La Salle and the Ateneo de Manila in the Philippines; Yonsei in Korea; and Atma Jaya in Indonesia. Generally, private institutions rely on tuition payments, receive little funding from public sources (although in Japan and several other countries some government funding is available to the private sector), and have no tradition of private philanthropy (in part because the

tax structure does not reward private donation to nonprofit organizations such as universities), and as a result are unable to compete for the
best students. However, the private sector plays a central role by providing access to students who would otherwise be unable to obtain academic degrees.

It is useful to disaggregate the Asian private higher education sector
because of the significant differences among institutions and the divergent roles they play in society. As noted, there are a few very prestigious
private universities in the countries in which a private sector operates. In
some cases, these institutions are sponsored or founded by religious
groups—largely but not exclusively Christian. Sophia and Doshisha in
Japan, Yonsei and Sogang in South Korea, Santa Dharma in Indonesia,
Assumption in Thailand, and De La Salle and Ateneo de Manila in the
Philippines are examples. These universities are typically among the oldest in their countries, and they have a long tradition of training elite
groups. Another category is the newer private institutions, often specializing in fields such as management or technology, established with the
aim of serving a key but limited market with high-quality academic degrees. The Asian Institute of Technology in the Philippines and its sister
institution in Thailand and the new Singapore Management University
are examples of such schools. These prestigious private universities have
been able to maintain their positions over time and rely largely on tuition
payments for survival.

Most Asian private universities serve the mass higher education market and tend to be relatively nonselective. Many are small, although there
are some quite large institutions, such as the Far Eastern University in
the Philippines, which has a large student population and was for a time
listed on the Manila stock exchange. Some are sponsored by private nonprofit organizations, religious societies, or other groups. Many are owned
by individuals or families, sometimes with a management structure that
masks the controlling elements of the school. This pattern of family-run
academic institutions has received little attention from analysts and is
important to understand as it is a phenomenon of growing importance
worldwide. Even in countries that do not encourage for-profit higher
education institutions, family ownership has become an established phenomenon.

The emerging for-profit sector is a growing segment of private higher
education in some Asian countries. In 2002, China passed legislation
that permits private higher education institutions to earn an "appropriate" profit. Two for-profit higher education patterns have emerged in

India: several quite large and successful postsecondary trade schools and a number of colleges (mostly focusing on professional and medical training) that charge high fees and are intended to provide a return on investment to investors although their legal status has come into question. While a number of Asian countries have not as yet opened their doors fully to for-profit higher education, there are already semi-for-profit enterprises operating, and before long this trend will prevail.

Many Asian countries have long experience in managing large private higher education sectors, while others are seeking to establish appropriate structures. The main challenge is to allow the private sector the necessary autonomy and freedom to establish and manage institutions and to compete in a differentiated educational marketplace, while at the same time ensuring that the national interest is served. In India, where the large majority of undergraduate students attend private colleges, these institutions are largely funded by the state governments, and are closely controlled by the universities to which most are affiliated. University authorities, for example, determine and administer examinations and award academic degrees, stipulate the minimum qualifications for entry, and supervise the hiring of academic staff. Japan and South Korea have a long tradition of rigidly controlling the private institutions—going to the extent of stipulating the salaries of academic staff, the numbers of students that can be admitted, approving the establishment of new departments or programs, and supervising the appointment of trustees. In recent years, these two countries have moved toward allowing private institutions more autonomy and freedom. Other countries have imposed less strict supervision.

As in other parts of the world, private higher education is expanding throughout Asia, and the countries that are moving toward a large private sector would be well advised to look at the experience elsewhere in Asia for guidance. There is a dramatically growing private sector in China, with more than 500 private postsecondary institutions, most of which are not accredited or approved by the government. Vietnam and Cambodia also have rapidly growing private sectors, as do the central Asian nations. The challenge will be ensuring that the emerging private sector is effective, well managed and serving national goals.

DISTANCE HIGHER EDUCATION

Of the world's 10-largest distance higher education institutions, 7 are located in Asia—in Turkey, China, Indonesia, India, Thailand, South

Korea, and Iran. These institutions have enrollments of more than 100,000 each. A variety of distance methodologies are used to deliver academic programs. These institutions, which are all public universities, were established to meet the growing demand for higher education, especially in regions not served by traditional academic institutions.

The potential for expansion of distance higher education is fuelled by a variety of trends. Access to technology is rapidly expanding in many Asian countries, which enables growing numbers of people to take advantage of distance delivery programs. Distance institutions can reach students in places without traditional universities—a relevant factor in much of Asia, where transportation is difficult and people lack the funds to relocate to study in major urban areas. Distance higher education, as developed in the Asian context and in most developing areas, is less expensive to deliver than are traditional academic degree programs. Distance higher education does not require the facilities needed for traditional academic institutions—a considerable advantage in the light of greatly increased demand and relatively limited existing universities.

While claims are made that Asian distance universities are providing an acceptable level of academic quality, there have been few evaluative studies. It is likely that foreign providers will seek to enter Asian markets, especially if the academic doors are forced open should Asian countries enter into agreements under the General Agreement on Trade in Services, a part of the World Trade Organization (Altbach, 2002).

TRENDS AND CHALLENGES

Asian higher education faces considerable hurdles in the coming period. While there are significant differences among Asian countries in size, historical patterns of academic development, wealth, and other factors, it is nonetheless possible to highlight trends that are common to most of the region. Since the problems are similar, it may be useful for countries to examine the experience of other Asian countries rather than always looking toward the West for answers to pressing questions of higher education development. The following issues seem to be of special relevance for Asian academic development.

Massification

The challenges of mass higher education have been considered in this essay. It remains a central reality for most of Asia (Japan and South Korea are exceptions, with their well-established academic systems and falling populations). Massification will place continuing strains on public funds, and at the same time will shape academic decision making. Massification requires differentiated academic systems able to serve different segments of the population and fulfill different purposes—with varying levels of funding and resources.

Access

Directly related to mass higher education is the question of access—providing higher education opportunities for all sections of the population able to take advantage of them. In most Asian countries, educational opportunities lag behind for women, rural populations, the poor, and some minority groups. It will be a challenge to provide access to previously disenfranchised groups.

Differentiation

Mass higher education requires a clear differentiation of goals and purposes among academic institutions so that resources are efficiently managed and the various purposes of higher education served. This means that there must be a coordinated system of higher education loosely managed by an authority that has both power and responsibility for a system of higher education. Such a management arrangement need not be under the direct control of the state but can be a joint effort by public authorities, the academic community, and others. Systems require clear definitions of institutional goals and responsibilities, as well as appropriate funding. The private sector should be treated as part of the national higher education system. Small as well as large countries will necessarily need to develop such systems because even small populations will need a range of academic preparation to meet the new economic realities.

Accreditation and Quality Control

Large academic systems require transparency in terms of quality of academic programs and institutions and assurance that minimum standards are being met. This is necessary not only to provide students with appropriate information about institutions but also to ensure that public resources are being effectively spent. It is sometimes argued that the market will ensure effective quality control. While the market might ensure the quality of some products, it will not be effective for higher education because the measurement of quality is complex and far from obvious to students or to employers. Accreditation and quality control arrangements can provide this information and can ensure that appropriate standards are maintained. There are many models available, and these can be adapted to specific Asian circumstances—some accreditation systems are supervised by government while others are the responsibility of the academic system itself, other nongovernmental organizations, or a combination of several stakeholders.

Research

Not all universities need to be focused on research—for example, most American universities are mainly teaching institutions—but almost every country needs some universities that engage in top-quality research in relevant fields or that at least are able to interpret research done elsewhere. This does not mean that countries with out the financial resources or infrastructure need to have a full-fledged research university, but all need to have at least some academic staff capable of interpreting and using research. Supporting research universities is neither easy nor inexpensive. Yet, for most countries, it is necessary, for research is at the heart of the modern knowledge-based economy. Further, only universities can engage in basic research since this requires a long-term commitment and resources that industry cannot support. While a few Asian countries adopted the Soviet-style "research institute" model, most have realized that universities can better serve as the basis of a culture of research.

The Academic Profession

At the heart of any university is the academic profession. Yet, in many countries, the professoriate is in crisis—inadequately paid and suffering from ever higher workloads and low morale. In order to attract the "best and brightest" to academe, appropriate conditions must be created. In many Asian countries, there is too little evaluation of academic work— an evaluation system is needed that combines attractive working conditions and accountability that ensures productivity by the professoriate. Current trends toward a part-time teaching force (as is common in Latin America) contribute to a lack of professional commitment to academe. Research-oriented universities especially need a highly motivated and well-trained professoriate. In many Asian countries, few university teachers hold advanced academic degrees. An essential part of ensuring the necessary conditions for teaching and research is the presence of an academic environment based on academic freedom and an appropriate balance between autonomy and accountability for the professoriate. The academic profession requires careful attention and support in a modern university system.

Globalization and Internationalization

Universities worldwide are becoming part of a global academic environment, and this has implications for Asian universities. Distance education and information technology are parts of globalization—students, staff, and academic institutions themselves are affected by the ease of communication and the access to information provided by IT. Academic programs offered through distance education from abroad will have some impact on Asian countries as well. These are new realities that will require careful planning and adjustment in each system. Students and staff are increasingly part of an international academic community. Asian students are by far the largest group of students studying abroad worldwide, and more Asian scholars now work outside their own countries. The flow of academic talent is from Asia to the industrialized West for the most part (although Australia and Japan are also attractive destinations for Asian students and staff). India and China are the largest "exporters" of students and probably of staff as well, and Malaysia, South Korea, Taiwan. Hong Kong, and several other Asian countries also send significant numbers of students abroad. There is also a need for Asian universities to incorporate knowledge from abroad—and again the bulk of knowledge is imported from the "metropolitan" academic systems of the West. Asian academic systems cannot insulate themselves from the global academic system and will need to adjust positively to it.

Transnationalization

Related to globalization is the trend for academic institutions and other education providers from one country to offer degrees or other academic programs in another country. Asia is already the largest world market for such transnational educational enterprises, and this phenomenon will grow rapidly. Malaysia is probably the world's largest transnational market at present. China has recently opened its doors to foreign providers, and other countries will no doubt follow down this path. In most cases, academic institutions from the industrialized nations, and especially from Australia and the United Kingdom, with the United States beginning to become involved, open branch campuses or develop partnerships or other arrangements in an Asian country. In some cases, distance methods are used to deliver all or part of the educational degree or other programs. The implications of transnational higher education enterprises are as yet unclear, for local higher education markets, quality, accreditation, and control of higher education.

CONCLUSION

Asian universities are shaped by their historical traditions and have to face the complex realities of the 21st century. They enter this new era from a position of some weakness. With the exception of a few Japanese universities, Asian academic institutions are seeking to catch up with their counterparts in the West in an environment where entering the "big leagues" is both difficult and expensive. Yet, many Asian countries have some features that work to their considerable advantages as well. Well-educated populations, traditions of scholarship, and a high respect for learning are part of virtually every Asian society. Asian countries also have the opportunity to shape their relatively new university systems to meet the needs of the 21st century in ways that the more entrenched universities of the West may have difficulty doing. What is clear is that universities are an essential part of the knowledge economies of the future. Unless they are able to build effective universities that can educate a growing proportion of the population while competing globally for research and knowledge products, Asian countries will be doomed to peripheral status.

REFERENCES

Altbach, P. G. (1998). Gigantic peripheries: India and China in the world knowledge system. In P. G. Altbach (Ed.), *Comparative higher education* (pp. 133–146). Greenwich, CT: Ablex.

Altbach, P. G. (1999). *Private Prometheus: Private higher education and development in the 21st century*. Westport, CT: Greenwood.

Altbach, P. G. (Ed). (2000). *The changing academic workplace: Comparative perspectives*. Chestnut Hill, MA: Center for International Higher Education, Boston College.

Altbach, P. G. (2002). Globalization and the university: Myths and realities in an unequal world. *Seminarium* no. 3–4, 807–836.

Altbach, P. G., & Selvaratnam, V. (Eds.). (1989). *From dependence to autonomy: The development of Asian universities*. Dordrecht, Netherlands: Kluwer.

Ashby, Eric. (1966). *Universities: British, Indian, African.* Cambridge: Harvard University Press.

Basu, Aparna. (1989). Indian higher education: Colonialism and beyond. In P. G. Altbach & V. Selvaratnam (Eds.), *From dependence to autonomy: the development of Asian universities* (pp. 167–186). Dordrecht, Netherlands: Kluwer.

Cummings, William K., & Kasenda, Salman. (1989). The origins of modern Indonesian higher education. In P. G. Altbach & V. Selvaratnam (Eds.), *From dependence to autonomy: The development of Asian universities* (pp. 143–166). Dordrecht, Netherlands: Kluwer.

Hayhoe, Ruth. (1996). *China's universities, 1895–1995: A century of cultural conflict.* New York: Garland.

Lee, Sungho H. (2004). Korean higher education: History and future challenges. In P. G. Altbach & T. Umakoshi (Eds.), *Asian universities: Historical perspectives and contemporary challenges.* Baltimore, MD: Johns Hopkins University Press.

Postiglione, G. A., & Mak, G. C. L. (Eds.). (1997). *Asian higher education: An international handbook and reference guide.* Westport, CT: Greenwood.

Tan, Jason. (2004). Singapore: Small nation, big plans. In P. G. Altbach & T. Umakoshi (Eds.), *Asian universities: Historical perspectives and contemporary challenges.* Baltimore, MD: Johns Hopkins University Press.

Task Force on Higher Education and Society. (2000). *Higher education in developing countries: Peril and promise.* Washington, D.C.: World Bank.

2

Private Higher Education in Asia

Transitions and Development

Toru Umakoshi

Until recently, Asia was being praised as "the growth center of the world," and some used to say that the twenty-first century would be the "Age of Asia." The myth of Asian growth, as trumpeted mainly by Western observers, thus caused the World Bank to publish a report entitled *The East Asian Miracle* (World Bank, 1993). Because of growth linked to different parts of Asia, many people were beginning to believe that a rich "united Asia" would emerge. However, since the currency crisis broke that dream into pieces there is now a prevailing pessimism that Asia is far from being united, lacking any philosophy of integration like the European Union, and that its basis for growth is still immature.

However, it would be practically impossible to make generalizations about Asia because of its diversity of ethnicity, religion, history, and social systems. In higher education, there is an extreme disparity between Cambodia and South Korea, for instance: the number of individuals in higher education per one hundred thousand people is 119 for Cambodia and 4,642 for South Korea. It would be impossible to discuss here all those specific cases; this chapter will discuss higher education in Asia as a whole.

According to statistics compiled by UNESCO, in the last fifteen years between 1980–1981 and 1995–1996, the higher education population rose in Asia more dramatically than in any other area of the world (UNESCO, 1999; 2000): South Korea had an enrollment rate of 52 percent in 1995 and reached the universal access stage as defined by the model introduced by Martin Trow (1973). Japan is shifting to the universal access stage; the Philippines and Thailand are at the mass access stage; and Indonesia and Malaysia are getting closer to the mass access stage. Even China and Vietnam, which are intensively working to establish a "market economy under socialism," are experiencing a rapid expansion in higher education. Controversy still exists over whether the expansion of higher education should be regarded as the result of growth in Asia or as having fueled that growth.

This chapter explores the major reasons for the rapid expansion in Asian higher education from a perspective that focuses on its private sector. Asia is home to the largest and most diverse private higher education sectors in the world. Several East Asian nations, including Japan, South Korea, Taiwan, and the Philippines, have 70 percent or more of their total enrollments in private colleges and universities. The large majority of undergraduate students in India are in private colleges, although most such institutions are heavily subsidized by public funds and are subject to oversight by the public universities to which they are affiliated. Indonesia has a rapidly growing private higher education sector, and China and Vietnam have recently allowed the establishment of private higher education institutions.

THE SPREAD OF THE J-MODEL

There have been two theoretical frameworks for clarifying Asian higher education expansion from a macroscopic viewpoint. One is the argument by Ronald Dore that poses higher education expansion as a result of the inflated importance of academic background in developing countries. In the Asian developing countries that became independent after World War II, political changes (democratization) preceded economic changes (industrialization), thereby paving the way for the rapid establishment of democratic educational systems based on political principles. Academic background, which had over time been recognized in advanced nations as a condition for entering the labor market, functioned right from the beginning as a requirement for entering the modern economic sector. As a consequence, competition over university admissions intensified to such an extent that university graduates were produced excessively in developing nations. Still, the competition over obtaining academic degrees did not calm down. On the contrary, it became even fiercer and caused "diploma disease" (Dore, 1976).

The other argument is the "dominance-subordination" model suggested by Philip Altbach. The root of Asian universities and, in particular, their academic systems and fundamental ethos (core principles, administrative organizations, the professoriate, personnel affairs, research organizations, curriculum, teaching methods, examination systems, etc.) had been developed by following the example of universities in the United States and Europe, regardless of whether the particular country had been their colonial ruler. Major international academic societies, scholarly journals, and academic publications (including textbooks), which serve as the infrastructure for academic research, have their respective centers in the United States or Europe. Accordingly, there is a "center-periphery" or dominance-subordination relationship in international intellectual networks. The more powerful the United States became as the center of learning after World War II, the more Asians went to the United States to study and returned home to further strengthen the dominance-subordination relationship (Altbach, 1982).

Both arguments are convincing. Regarding the first argument, however, the recent economic growth in Asia has been expanding the labor market, which has accommodated an increasing number of university graduates year by year. Thus it is no longer appropriate to view higher education expansion only from a negative perspective—that is, in terms of academic career inflation. Besides, in some countries university graduates are able to supply labor in a sellers' market. And, contrary to the second argument, some advanced universities in Asia are shrugging off their conventional status as subordinate to Western universities and becoming independent. With respect to the teaching function, Asian universities no longer have a dominance-subordination relationship with Western universities.

In order to clarify the current status of Asian higher education, approaches that differ from the conventional arguments are required. In his 1997 book, *The Challenges of Eastern Asian Education*, William Cummings proposes a new analytical method, called "the Eastern Asian approach" (Cummings, 1997a). While the target of his analysis is Asian human resources development, in general, the issues he raises may be useful in examining the expansion of higher education. Cummings developed the Eastern Asia approach by looking at the policies implemented in Japan—hence his term, *J-model*. Most of the core components of this model were established in Japan and thereafter spread to East Asian countries. From the late 1970s to the early 1980s, the J-model spread to Taiwan and South Korea and, from the late 1980s to the early 1990s, to Thailand, Malaysia, Singapore, and Indonesia. Cummings summarizes the core components of the J-model as follows:

(1) The state coordinates education and research, with a firm emphasis on indigenous values transmission and the mastery of foreign technology. (2) High priority is placed on universal primary education, while state investment at the secondary and tertiary level is limited primarily to critical areas such as engineering and the sciences. (3) Individual students, their families, and the private sector are expected to provide critical backup for the education provided by the state. (4) The Asian state in seeking to coordinate not only the development but also the utilization of human resources involves itself in manpower planning and job placement and increasingly in the coordination of science and technology. (Cummings, 1997a, pp. 275–276)

This model seems similar to the World Bank's analytical framework, which seeks the cause of "the miracle of East Asia" in "the role of strong government" (World Bank, 1993). It also recalls the opinion of an economist (Kojima, 1996), who referred to the Japanese economic development model that had been spreading sequentially to newly industrializing economies in Asia and countries in the Association of Southeast Asian Nations as the "Flying Geese Model." Cummings pointed out that while pressing ahead with strong government-initiated policies, Asian countries were tolerant of private sector initiatives unless they went against public goals. A factor underlying this approach was the fact that the national budget relative to GNP was significantly low in contrast to the situation in the United States and Europe. Consequently, financial resources for preschool education and higher education in many Asian countries have been largely dependent on families (private education expenses) and a private education sector. Cummings also notes that it is characteristic of Asian countries, unlike Western countries, to depend on their private sectors for over three-quarters of their research and development expenses.

As a matter of fact, the private sectors in Japan, South Korea, Taiwan, and the Philippines accommodate over three-quarters of the higher education population, which is unusual in any other area of the world.

VARIATIONS AND DEVELOPMENT

This chapter will nowdiscuss the role of private sectors in higher education expansion from a comparative point of view. Roger Geiger, who made an international comparative analysis of private higher education systems, classifies them into the following three categories based on the relationship with public (or national) sectors: first, the massive private sector; second, the parallel private sector; and third, the peripheral private sector (Geiger, 1987). Geiger argues that at the beginning of a higher education system of the massive private-sector type, a limited number of public-sector institutions of high academic standards served as the core of the higher education system. A private sector was regarded as merely complementary to the public sector. In accordance with the rapid growth of secondary education, the private sector began to play a major role in higher education expansion by providing opportunities for applicants to colleges and universities. Geiger regards Japan as the classic case in this category. Parallel private sectors of the second category are typically shown in countries having varied ethnic and cultural groups that are officially recognized—such as Belgium, the Netherlands, and other countries. While demanding uniform, high academic standards from those groups, the nation promises to provide significant financial support to particular groups that have chosen to create a private sector. A prototype of the peripheral private sector as the third category would trace its roots to France under the Napoleonic regime. The principle of higher education exclusively controlled by the nation collapsed when the Catholic Church was authorized to found a university in 1875, thereby allowing the emergence of peripheral private sectors. Higher education systems in many socialist countries fall into this third category.

The private sector in the United States, which is the largest in scale in the world today, does not fall into any of the three categories defined by Geiger. Therefore, he discusses it separately as a fourth category: the "American private sector." Until the middle of the nineteenth century, private institutions had been in the overwhelming majority in the United States. Today, out of over 3,000 higher education institutions, 1,800 schools are private—the legacy from that era. With the public sector expanding after the mid-1970s, however, the number of students enrolled at those private higher education institutions gradually decreased to less than a quarter of the total higher education enrollments. In other words, higher education expansion in the United States has been attributed mainly to the public sector.

When considering the role of the private sector in higher education expansion, it is certain that the most significant contribution has been made by private sectors in the first category (the mass private sectors). In Asian countries, however, the private sectors in the second and third categories have also contributed to a certain extent to higher education expansion. In his discussion of the transition of higher education systems from elite to mass and from mass to universal, Martin Trow did not include the private sectors' role in promoting the transition, perhaps because at the time he was not familiar with Asian higher education. Higher education expansion in Asia, even in socialist countries such as China and Vietnam, is impossible to understand without considering the role of the private sectors.

Cummings directs his attention to the role of private sectors in the expansion of education in general, observing that Asian countries have formed a "private educational empire" (Cummings, 1997b, p. 144). Regarding Japan, he observes that the hexagonal building of the Education Ministry, standing prominently at Kasumigaseki like the Pentagon, seems to embody every kind of authority and actually contains a massive private sector.

Cummings points out the factors that promote the private sector in Asian countries. In Japan, South Korea, and China—the countries with Confucian traditions—retired public officials founded small private academies. Long before modern schools were established, Islamic *ulama* and Buddhist priests taught at their respective schools. In recent times, with the separation of religion from the state and the introduction of modern schools in the public sector, indigenous entrepreneurs and various groups in Asian countries began to found private schools as alternatives to the public sector. In Japan, two private schools, Waseda University and Keio University, were established. In Korea, under Japanese colonial administration, private ethnic schools were founded as part of the anti-Japanese movement, and there was a drive to establish a "Korean People's University" (Chosen Minritsu Daigaku). In Indonesia, under Dutch rule, the Taman Siswa School was established by an indigenous ethnic group, and Islamic Muhammadiyah schools were founded by Muslim groups. It is well known that missionary groups from the United States and Europe made efforts to found private mission schools as part of their missionary work.

In terms of colonial education policy, the Japanese governor-general of Korea followed a policy of assimilation, when possible restraining the desire of Koreans to start private schools. As a result, Korean private schools became "authentic" institutions to the people. Countries on the European continent generally placed emphasis on the public sector, and accordingly their colonies followed the same policy. However, England and the Netherlands did permit a private sector to exist in their colonies because of their segregation policies (elite education at public schools and general education at private schools). As a result, postindependence Indonesia had been prepared in advance for private-sector expansion. In

Malaysia, which had been a British colony, the private sector was closed for ethnic and political reasons. Ethnic Chinese schools, in particular, were not authorized as regular schools. However, once government regulations were eased, the energy for establishing ethnic Chinese schools was ready to surge.

During the American colonial period in the Philippines, the United States adopted policies on primary education that were initiated through the public sector, although it also generously authorized the legal establishment of private schools. As for secondary and tertiary education, similar policies were adopted toward the establishment of Protestant schools, partly because the Catholic Church already had a firm foundation in the Philippines. Regarding the last factor—that is, foreign influences— Cummings looks at the example of Allied-occupied Japan and positively evaluates the occupation policy supporting the authorization of private schools and the deregulation of the employment by the public sector of private school graduates. Socialist countries such as China and Vietnam nationalized every educational institution modeled on the former Soviet Union lines, which resulted in the suppression of the existing private sector.

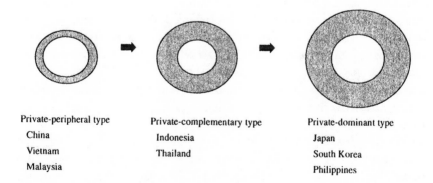

Private-peripheral type   Private-complementary type   Private-dominant type
China   Indonesia   Japan
Vietnam   Thailand   South Korea
Malaysia   Philippines

Figure 2.1. Transitional model of private-sector types. The shaded areas represent private sectors; the cores represent public sectors.

PRIVATE-SECTOR TYPOLOGIES

With regard to the role of private sectors as described above, this may be the time to propose a transitional model of the Asian private sectors. In accordance with the actual situations in Asia, the Geiger model mentioned above should be amended to some extent—specifically with regard to the parallel private sectors. The argument proposed in this chapter classifies the role of the Asian private sectors into three types: *private-peripheral, private-complementary,* and *private-dominant.* Each of these types is a transitional model. (See Figure 2.1.)

The Private-Peripheral Type

The first transitional stage is theprivate-peripheral type, which is found in countries where the government established key national and regional institutions that comprised the core of the system. According to the Trow model, the basic nature of higher education is elitism. Until fairly recently in these countries, private higher education institutions (the private sector) have not been authorized, and they only form the periphery of the public sector. China, Vietnam, and Malaysia fall in this category.

The Chinese public sector is divided into two levels: one level comes under the jurisdiction of central government ministries (including the Ministry of Education and other ministries and committees) and the other, under the jurisdiction of local and provincial governments. At present, higher education expansion is being carried out by the public sector, and major reforms are in progress based on the principles of "coalition, coordination, cooperation, and amalgamation" (Chen, 2000). *Coalition* means that central government ministries and local governments form a coalition to administer a university. *Coordination* means that universities individually administered by central government ministries are integrated so as to place a large number of institutions under the direct jurisdiction of the Ministry of Education and to expand their scale. *Cooperation* means interuniversity recognition of credits, and *amalgamation* means integration of universities and expansion in the scale of them. For example, in 1998, Zhejiang University—the principal university in Zhejiang Province—amalgamated with Hangzhou University, Zhejiang Agricultural University, and Zhejiang Medical University to create a new Zhejiang University, which was then shifted to the status of a coalition between the Ministry of Education and Zhejiang Province.

As part of the movement to develop a "socialist market economy" in the 1990s, the government in 1993 issued a new policy authorizing the establishment of private colleges and universities. The subsequent expansion in the number of private universities has been remarkable. As of 1999, only thirty-seven private universities had been authorized by the government to award diplomas, but it is said that the number of schools of all sizes claiming to be private universities has rapidly increased to around 1,300 institutions. It is anticipated that, in the near future, Chinese higher education will shift to the private-complementary type, in which public schools and private schools coexist.

Similar to the case of China, Vietnam is in transition to a market economy under the *doi moi* policy. The number of private universities has been rapidly rising, mainly in urban regions such as Hanoi and Ho Chi Minh City, since the policy allowing the establishment of private universities was first instituted in 1994. As of 1997–1998, there were fifteen universities, although each university is comparatively small in scale. The higher education expansion in Vietnam has occurred mainly in the national universities under the jurisdiction of central government ministries (the Ministry of Education and Training and other ministries) and through two open universities at Hanoi and Ho Chi Minh City and fifty-four colleges. Vietnam is also expected to shift to the private-complementary type of private sector in the near future.

Since its foundation as a nation, Malaysia had built a public-sector-oriented higher education system, and it had been cautious about expanding the scale. As of the early 1980s, the country had only five national universities. Since ethnic Chinese were not able to attend these national universities due to the policy of providing preferential treatment for Malays, many Chinese studied abroad at foreign universities. After the International Islamic University was established under the Company Act in 1983, the state began to emphasize higher education expansion, resulting in a boom in the establishment of new national universities, including Universiti Utara Malaysia, Universiti Sarawak, Universiti Malaysia Sabah, and Teachers University. The 1996 private higher education act resulted in the establishment of a number of private universities, such as Universiti Telokom (1997), Universiti Tenaga Nasional (1997), Petronas University (1997), and the Science and Technology University (1997). Furthermore, the University of Malaya (the core of the public sector) is on the way to incorporation. In Malaysia, the private sector is rapidly expanding toward the private-complementary type.

The Private-Complementary Type

The second stage is the private-complementary type and is represented by the cases of Thailand and Indonesia. In the beginning, the public sector provided the predominant core among universities, with the private sector on the periphery. In these countries the private sector then became the most rapidly growing part of higher education expansion, eventually complementing the public sector and becoming as large as, or larger than, the public sector. The basic nature of such higher education systems is close to the "mass type" in the Trow model (Trow, 1973).

Universities in Thailand are classified intoinstitutions of the conventional type and open universities. In Thailand, higher education expansion has been mainly attributed to national universities of the open type (e.g., Ramkhamhaeng University and Sukhotai Thammathirat Open University). These two universities enroll about 75 percent of students in the public sector. Meanwhile, private colleges have been spreading, not only throughout the capital area but also in provincial towns and cities, since the introduction of the 1969 private college act. As of 1995, there were twenty-nine private-sector universities and twenty-two public-sector universities. Private-sector universities enroll about 18 percent of the higher education population, and if the students enrolled at the two open universities are excluded, the number of students in the private sector is almost equal to the number of students in the public sector. Thus, the private sector in Thailand has been playing an increasingly important role as an actor in the expansion of higher education. The private sector contains about 8 percent of the graduate students in Thailand.

In the case of Indonesia,at the start of the second Five-Year Development Plan (1974–1975), the private sector (academies and colleges) served 48.5 percent of the higher education population. There were as many as 310 universities in the private sector, while there were forty-one universities in the public sector. About 20 years later—when the fifth Five-Year Development Plan ended in 1993–1994—the number of students enrolled in the private sector made up 65.5 percent of the total, and the number of private-sector schools had rapidly increased to 1,122. In the public sector, the number of schools increased by 10, to 55, and student numbers increased 6-fold in those 20 years. These rising student numbers were merely a result of the expansion of the scale of existing universities and the establishment of only a few new universities. In contrast, the number of students in the private sector increased 12-fold in the same 20 years, and the number of students per university has grown from about 360 to about 12,000 over the same period. The private sector in Indonesia is in transition from the second type to the third type, as will be discussed below.

The Private-Dominant Type

The third type is the private-dominant type. Historically, national universities in Asia have served as the core of higher education systems, but it is the private sector that has led the expansion. Japan, South Korea, and the Philippines fall under the private-dominant heading. In these countries, more than 70 percent of the higher education population is enrolled in the private sector, thus forming a private-dominant higher education system from a quantitative viewpoint. In view of the basic nature of those higher education systems, the private-dominant type is similar to the "universal access type" in the Trow model (Trow, 1973).

In the case of Japan, the private sectorserved 61 percent of the students enrolled at four-year colleges and universities and 87 percent of those enrolled at junior colleges in 1950—that is, immediately after the start of the new university system. For the subsequent 46 years until 1996, enrollments at four-year universities and colleges rose 11.6-fold, and enrollments at junior colleges rose 31.4-fold. During this period, the percentage of students enrolled in the private sector also increased to 73 percent at four-year colleges and universities and 92 percent at junior colleges. During the 10 years from 1965 to 1975, university attendance by the first postwar baby boom generation coincided with the period of high economic growth. Subsequently, enrollments at private universities doubled, increasing by more than 150 percent in the public sector. It could be said that the Japanese private sector has been making a more active contribution to the demand for higher education opportunities than the public sector. Regarding the number of graduate students, however, the private sector has consistently had a 30 percent share over the past 40 years, showing no significant change. National universities have so far served as the core of Japanese higher education and are maintaining their position by focusing on their graduate schools.

South Korea has already reached the universal access stage, having an enrollment rate in higher education of over 60 percent, as mentioned earlier. As of 1998, the private sector had a 71.6 percent share of the higher education population (61.5 percent at four-year universities and 96.3 percent at two- or three-year colleges). The percentage of private school enrollments has dropped a little from 80 percent, mainly because of the expansion of the (national) Air and Correspondence University, which accepts 314,000 students—about 16 percent of total enrollments at four-year universities. The postliberation higher education system in South Korea was developed through the establishment of Seoul National University and national universities in each province. However, in Seoul, there are a considerable number of private universities that are more prominent than the public universities.

These private universities were established on the foundations of the former private colleges that had not been allowed to upgrade to university status under Japanese rule. With significantly high social prestige, the private institutions serve as the core of Korean higher education together with the national universities. Further, a number of private universities were established to complement these core universities during the higher education expansion period in and after the 1980s. It is worth noting that many of them were established by huge, family-controlled industrial groups or large-scale corporations that had been leading participants in Korea's impressive economic growth. It is also typical of South Korea that owners of small businesses have been involved in different ways in the establishment of the junior colleges of technology that proliferated during and after the 1980s.

The Philippines should be viewed as another country in which the private sector has led higher education expansion. As of 1998, 1,030 institutions, or 80 percent of the total of 1,285 higher education institutions, belonged to the private sector, and 75.2 percent of students were enrolled at private institutions (Gonzalez, 1999). A number of private institutions were raised to university status during the colonial period. Subsequent to the involvement of the Catholic Church, Protestant missionaries were permitted to establish a university, and later private individuals (families) were also given permission. At present, the private sector of higher education in the Philippines is divided into religiously oriented universities (27 percent) and secular universities (73 percent). Secular universities comprise the mainstream of Philippine higher education. Specifically, the country permits the establishment of private higher education institutions to take various forms—from the initiatives of profit-making stock corporations to nonstock and nonprofit foundations. This approach was created during the colonial period under the U.S. colonial government, and it should be noted that an accreditation system was also introduced at the same time.

UNIVERSALIZATION AND PRIVATE SECTORS

As observed above, there is a wide range of Asian private sectors. Their founders vary from church-related groups or secular groups (profit-making or nonprofit) to private individuals. In scale, the private-sector institutions range from small-scale universities accommodating several hundred students to mammoth universities enrolling tens of thousands of students. In terms of purpose, a private sector can include short-cycle higher education institutions that provide vocational qualifications as well as universities complete with graduate schools for academic research. In terms of academic standards, institutions range from the bottom up to the top. It may well be that such diversification has provided the Asian private sectors with the flexibility to be able to adapt to different social demands. In the context of the universalization of higher education, the potentialities and problems of the Asian private sectors may provide some insights.

First, there is a strong possibility that the private sector will expand in China and Malaysia, which are at present still at the private-peripheral stage. Recent high rates of economic growth have increased the demand for a large and diverse workforce beyond what the public higher education sector can meet. Therefore, national governments have put an end to the state monopoly over higher education and shifted their policy to the accreditation of private universities. As occurred in the case of Thailand during the 1970s, the number of private universities in China and Malysia has been rapidly increasing. The institutions are now spreading not only in capital cities and nearby regions but also in provincial cities. As observed by Geiger (1987), these private universities are market-oriented. Their educational content is to a significant extent vocational. The fact that tuition fees in private sectors are higher than those in public sectors implies the emergence of an upper-middle class that can afford them. Another important characteristic is that most private universities are secular. As indicated in the case of the Philippines, non-church-related universities are more apt to expand than religiously oriented ones. If this trend continues, private sectors of the private-peripheral type are expected to shift to the private-complementary type.

Second, private sectors of the private-complementary type evolve from small colleges established in major cities to accept increasing numbers ofuniversity applicants resulting from the expansion of secondary education. To adapt to the expanding economy and diversified social demands, those colleges are transformed into universities specializing in specific fields of study. Some of them develop into private universities that are larger than many public-sector universities. As was the case during the university expansion period in Japan and South Korea, a private university is expanded either by adding scientific and technological departments to a private university offering programs in the liberal arts and social sciences or by adding liberal arts and social science departments to a university specializing in science and technology.

Private two- or three-year institutions are established to complement the public sector. Japanese junior colleges, 84 percent of which are private and whose female students accounted for 91 percent of enrollments as of 1998, have been performing a unique role of complementing four-year university education for women. Korean junior technology colleges were raised from vocational schools to two- or three-year higher education institutions in 1979. They have been serving as vocational and technical education institutions affiliated with local industries, thereby complementing four-year universities of science and technology. The junior technology colleges, in particular, have grown and now enroll 29 percent of the higher education population in Korea. They are committed to ensuring mass attendance at higher education institutions and serving as Korea's critical means of achieving universalization of higher education. It is noteworthy that 91 percent of junior technology colleges are private institutions.

Meanwhile, the public sectors did not stand by while private sectors of the private-complementary type were taking the lead in higher education systems at the mass-attendance stage. Owing to financial constraints, the approach the public sectors chose to take was to establish open universities and air and correspondence universities based on distance-learning methods. The two open universities in Thailand enroll 70 percent of the students in the public sector. The Air and Correspondence University of Korea enrolls 41 percent of the students in the public sector. These developments indicate that the Asian public sectors could not afford to establish new universities as a part of the move toward the mass attendance stage. The private sectors gradually expanded their scale to meet the demand for expansion of higher education opportunities—typical examples are the cases of Indonesia, South Korea, and Japan. It is certain that the Asian private sectors have the potential to advance from the complementary to dominant type, as higher education moves into the mass attendance stage.

Third, a typical example of the private-dominant type can be found in South Korea, which is in transition to universal-access higher education, with a current higher education enrollment rate of more than 70 percent. While the public sector has failed to keep expanding, private universities have continued to establish more branch campuses throughout the country so as to meet an increasing demand for higher education. Consequently, South Korea has reversed the assertion made by Cummings, as one of the characteristics of the J-Model, that higher education in science and technology as a national strategy was to be undertaken by the public (national) sectors. According to the statistics of the Korean Ministry of Education in 1998, the private sector in South Korea accounted for 73 percent of the schools for science and technology and 76 percent of the medical and pharmaceutical schools—higher percentages than for liberal arts schools (65 percent) and schools in the social sciences (71 percent). Moreover, elite private universities of science and technology—such as Pohang University of Science and Technology, which could get top marks in every aspect of university evaluation—were founded in provincial cities, and they are achieving a level comparable to that of the traditional private universities of high social prestige in Seoul (Umakoshi, 1997).

Through competition not only with the public sector but also among private institutions, the Korean private sector is building up a structure for dominating the higher education system in terms of quantity and quality. The 1997 higher education act created a new category, the "university of industry." These universities were positioned as prospective institutions for higher education in an age of lifelong learning. As is obvious, universities of this new type belong to the private sector. The universalization of higher education in Asian countries can be largely attributed to the energy of private sectors, as shown in the case of South Korea (Umakoshi, 1999).

CONCLUSION

The private-dominant type, the third private-sector transitional stage, faces some problems. The diversification of private sectors, which has been discussed above as a positive aspect of private higher education, has the potential to alter higher education systems and in some cases even to undermine them. Plainly speaking, the new private sectors might create a crisis for education and research. As higher education systems become more private-dominant, the achievement levels of students will diverge, making it harder to sustain consistent standards of quality. Academe will become more differentiated, with much greater variations in quality and status among institutions. Teachers' attitudes toward higher education institutions may differ as well, and their morale may suffer. The private sector depends in large part on part-time instructors, many of whom hold appointments in public universities. Although private sectors have thus far been developing in response to social demands, they have not necessarily been fulfilling what contemporary society needs in the truest sense. The relevance of private higher education should be reexamined. It must be remembered that these issues concern not just private sectors in higher education but also the entire higher education system.

REFERENCES

Altbach, P. G. (1982). *Higher education in the third world: Themes and variations.* Singapore: Maruzen Asia.

Chen, X. F. (2000). 1990 *Niandai Zhongguo Gaodeng Jiaoyu de Gaigoe* (Chinese higher education reform of the 1990s). Nagoya, Japan: Center for Studies of Higher Education, Nagoya University.

Cummings, W. K. (1997a). Human resource development: The J-model. In W. K. Cummings & P. G. Altbach (Eds.), *The challenge of Eastern Asian education: Implications for America* (pp. 275–291). Albany: State University of New York Press.

Cummings, W. K. (1997b). Private education in Eastern Asia. In W. K. Cummings & P. G. Altbach (Eds.), *The challenge of Eastern Asian education: Implications for America* (pp. 135–152). Albany: State University of New York Press.

Dore, R. P. (1976). *The diploma disease.* London: George Allen & Unwin.

Geiger, R. L. (1987). Patterns of public-private differentiation in higher education: An international comparison. In Research Institute for Higher Education (Ed.), *Public and private sectors in Asian education systems.* Hiroshima, Japan: RIHE, Hiroshima University.

Gonzalez, A., FSC. (1999). Private higher education in the Philippines: Private domination in developing countries. In P. G. Altbach (Ed.), *Private Prometheus: Private higher education and development in the 21st century* (pp. 101–112). Westport, CT: Greenwood.

Kojima, K. (1996). *Kaiho Keizai Taikei* (Open economic system). Tokyo: Bunshindo.

Trow, M. (1973). *Problems in the transition from elite to mass higher education.* Berkeley, CA: Carnegie Commission on Higher Education.

Umakoshi, T. (1997). *Kankoku no Daigaku Hyoka* (University evaluation in Korea). Report submitted to the Japan Society for the Promotion of Science, Tokyo.

Umakoshi, T. (1999). *Kankoku Koto Kyoiku ni okeru "universalization" no Shogeki* (Impact of "universalization" of Korean higher education). *Bulletin of the Institute for Higher Education, 7*(1), 55–67.

UNESCO. (1999). *World education report, 1998.* Paris: Author.

UNESCO. (2000). *Statistical yearbook, 1999.* Paris: Author.

World Bank. (1993). *The East Asian miracle: Economic growth and public policies.* New York: Oxford University Press.

SELECTED BIBLIOGRAPHY

Altbach, P. G. (Ed.). (1999). *Private Prometheus: Private higher education and development in the 21st century.* Westport, CT: Greenwood.

Altbach, P. G. (Ed.). (2003). *The decline of the guru: The academic profession in the third world.* New York: Palgrave Macmillan.

Altbach, P. G., & Selvaratnam, V. (1989). *From dependence to autonomy: The development of Asian universities.* Dordrecht, Netherlands: Kluwer Academic.

Clark, B. R. (Ed.). (1993). *Research foundations of graduate education.* Berkeley: University of California Press.

Cummings, W. K., & Altbach, P. G. (Eds.). (1997). *The challenge of Eastern Asian education: Implications for America.* Albany: State University of New York Press.

Hayhoe, R. (1996). *China's universities, 1895–1995: A century of cultural conflict.* New York: Garland.

Hayhoe, R., & Pan, J. (Eds.). (2001). *Knowledge across cultures: A contribution to dialogue among civilizations.* Hong Kong: University of Hong Kong Press.

Kaneko, M. (1989). *Financing higher education in Japan.* Hiroshima, Japan: RIHE, Hiroshima University.

Lee, W. O., & Bray, M. (1997). *Education and political transition: Perspectives and dimensions in East Asia.* Hong Kong: University of Hong Kong Press.

Malik, A. (1994). *Education, employment, wages, and earning: A case study of Indonesia.* Unpublished doctoral dissertation, University of Michigan.

Marsh, C., & Morris, P. (1991). *Curriculum development in East Asia.* London: Falmer.

OECD. (1974). *Policies for higher education: General report of the Conference on the Future Structure of Post-Secondary Education.* Paris: Author.

OECD. (1998). *Review of national policies for education: Korea.* Paris: Author.

Postiglione, G. A., & Mak, G. C. L. (Eds.). (1997). *Asian higher education: An international handbook and reference guide.* Westport, CT: Greenwood.

Sloper, D., & Le, T. C. (Eds.). (1995). *Higher education in Vietnam: Change and response.* Singapore: Institute of Southeast Asian Studies.

Tu, W. (Ed.). (1996). *Confucian traditions in East Asian modernity: Moral education and economic culture in the four†mini-dragons.* Cambridge, MA: Harvard University Press.

Yee, A. H. (Ed.). (1995). *East Asian higher education.* Oxford: Pergamon.

PART II

Asian Giants

3

Chinese Higher Education

The Legacy of the Past and

the Context of the Future

Weifang Min

Universities in China have undergone dramatic changes in recent years, including rapid expansion of enrollments, structural reforms, and quality improvement. Many of the national universities have the goal of becoming world-class institutions and have made significant progress. These changes in Chinese higher education have taken place in the context of an expanding Chinese economy, which has maintained an average annual GDP growth rate of 8 percent for the past two decades. The implementation of economic reforms and an open-door policy have helped the Chinese economy to become more integrated into the international economy. Chinese higher education has increased its degree of interaction with universities in other countries and now functions as part of the international academic community. To understand the challenges universities in China will face in the future, it is necessary to examine their historical development and current realities.

OVERVIEW

The current Chinese higher education system is one of the largest in the world, with more than 3,000 universities and colleges—including 1,225 regular full-time universities and colleges, 686 adult higher education institutions, and 1,202 new private universities and colleges. The system encompasses 13 million students and over 1.45 million staff members,

554,000 of whom are faculty members. The predominant public sector
enrolls about 12 million students and the recently developed private sector about 1 million students. The public sector consists of two major
components: regular higher education, which includes 7.19 million students, and adult higher education, which includes 4.55 million students.
Regular higher education institutions comprise universities with both
undergraduate and graduate degree programs and short-cycle (two- or
three-year) colleges without degree programs. Adult higher education
institutions include television-based universities offering a variety of programs, workers' universities for training and upgrading employees, peas-
ants' universities for training and upgrading farmers, colleges of management for training and upgrading administrators and Communist Party
cadres, educational colleges for school teachers and administrators, and
independent (private) correspondence colleges.

Table 3.1   The Chinese Higher Education System, 2001

Type of Institution	No. of Institutions	No. of Students
Graduate education institutions	728	393,200
Graduate programs at universities	411	371,600
Graduate programs at research institutions	317	21,600
Undergraduate education institutions	3,113	12,880,900
Regular[a] higher education institutions	1,225	7,190,700
Universities	597	5,212,000
Short-cycle colleges	628	1,978,700
Adult higher education institutions	686	4,559,800
TV universities	45	400,300
Workers' colleges	409	351,100
Peasants' universities	3	800
Management training colleges	104	153,900
Educational colleges	122	304,400
Correspondence colleges	3	15,500
University-run adult higher education programs		3,333,800
Private higher education institutions	1,202	1,130,400

Source: Department of Development and Planning, Ministry of Education of China, 2002.
[a]Regular higher education institutions comprise universities with both undergraduate and graduate
degree programs and short-cycle (two- or three-year) colleges without degree programs.

Adult higher education is provided in both part-time and full-time programs, some of which offer bachelor's degrees. They usually have no advanced degree programs. Table 3.1 provides statistics on China's higher education system.

In 2001, among the total enrollments at regular higher education institutions, students majoring in engineering accounted for 34.6 percent, in the humanities 15.5 percent, in management 14.2 percent, in the sciences 10 percent, in medicine 7.4 percent, in law 5.4 percent, in education 5.2 percent, in economics 5.0 percent, and in agriculture 2.6 percent. Engineering majors have accounted for the largest proportion of students since the 1950s and are still the largest single group at present. Currently, the number of students in management, law, economics and other applied fields is increasing rapidly, while enrollments in the basic sciences and the humanities are declining, in response to the labor market (Ministry of Education, 2002).

HISTORICAL PERSPECTIVES

Indigenous Higher Education

China's long higher education tradition evolved along with Chinese civilization. The earliest Chinese state was established in the Xia dynasty (about 2200 B.C.). From the beginning, Chinese culture attached great importance to education, as recorded in ancient Chinese writings: "To establish a nation state, education should come first." "A man without education cannot be a knowledgeable and moral man." These values and this belief system have exerted significant influence on Chinese people's character, thinking, and behavior for thousands of years down to the present time. For example, one of the current national policy goals is to invigorate the country through education and science.

Chinese higher education originated as early as 1100 B.C. during the Zhou dynasty and was called *pi-yong*. During the Han dynasty (206 B.C.–A.D. 220); higher education institutions were called *tai-xue*, which means "institutions of higher learning," and were attended by more than thirty thousand students during the dynasty's most prosperous time at its main campus in Changan, the capital city (Wang et al., 1994). During the Tang dynasty (A.D. 618–907) and afterward, Chinese universities were called *guo-zi-jian*, a type of higher education institution established for the children of royal families and senior officials. The content of learning was drawn mainly from the classical texts of Confucian teachings, which were also the dominant contents of the imperial examinations for senior civil service positions.

In addition to these ancient universities established by the Chinese state, which continued to exist until the late nineteenth century, private universities also flourished in ancient China. Confucius (551–479 B.C.) introduced private higher education in China during the Eastern Zhou dynasty, at a time when state institutions were becoming weaker. It was recorded that Confucius had more than three thousand students. It became fashionable to run private learning institutions during this time, and many leading scholars at different schools operated their own institutions. When speaking of ancient private institutions of higher learning, one must mention *shu-yuan*. These institutions started to appear during the Tang dynasty (A.D. 618–907), when they were first established in both the state and private sectors as places for collecting books. *Shu-yuan* were not places for teaching and learning initially but gradually developed into private academies or scholarly societies, as alternatives to official higher education institutions, eventually becoming a dominant type of private university throughout the country during the Song dynasty (A.D. 960–1279). *Shu-yuan* played an important role in ancient Chinese higher education and continued to function until the early twentieth century. As Ruth Hayhoe suggests, the *shu-yuan* of ancient China may have been similar to the medieval universities of Europe (Hayhoe, 1989). In short, indigenous higher education in China had a long tradition going back three thousand years, encompassing both public and private sectors of higher learning. However, constrained by feudalism, traditional Chinese higher education was only able to develop slowly.

Modern Universities and the European Model

Although the indigenous tradition had a significant impact on Chinese higher education, modern Chinese universities developed from the European model. This process involved a long and even painful interaction with the West after the Opium War in 1840, when the Western powers opened China's doors by gunboats. This opening made Chinese intellectuals aware of Western advancements in science and technology and of the backwardness of China, which they in their conceit viewed as the "Central Kingdom" of the world. The impact of the European university model on China worked through three major channels: the establishment of Western missionary colleges in China, the study-abroad programs for Chinese scholars and students begun in the late nineteenth century, and the modernization efforts of Chinese reformers.

As the Western powers gained the right of entry into China, the introduction of the Western university model on Chinese soil took place. Many foreign groups tried to create higher education institutions in China, including French Jesuit missionaries, American Protestants with the cooperation of British and Canadian colleagues, and German industrialists. By 1949, there were twenty-one universities run or subsidized by foreigners, including such influential institutions as Yenching University in Beijing and St. Johns University in Shanghai. Among the total of 205 higher education institutions in the country, foreign universities accounted for about 10 percent and enrolled about ten thousand students. The higher education models introduced by the missionaries and other foreign groups influenced the development of modern higher education in China, but they were "largely peripheral to the mainstream education reforms being engineered by a modernizing Chinese leadership. They did not look to missionary efforts for inspiration in their reforms, but visited or sent delegations to the nations whose educational institutions were of interest and modeled their reforms directly on foreign experience" (Hayhoe, 1989, pp. 36–37).

One of the important ways in which the European university model influenced Chinese higher education was the study-abroad programs for Chinese scholars and students. Seven years after the 1840 Opium War, three young students—Rong Hong, Huang Kuan, and Huang Sheng—followed their teacher, Samuel Robinns Brown, to the United States for university studies in 1847, the first Chinese to do so. Rong Hong received his bachelor's degree from Yale University and returned to China in 1854, becoming the very first Chinese person to have received a university education in a foreign country. Through the efforts of Rong Hong and others, in 1872 the Chinese government decided to send a group of 120 students to the United States, initiating the country's first official study-abroad programs. This was followed by programs that sent students to the United Kingdom and continental European countries. In the wake of increased Japanese influence in China, many Chinese scholars and students went to Japan, where they experienced the European university model with a Japanese imprint. In the late nineteenth and early twentieth centuries, more than ten thousand Chinese students studied in Japan. They would constitute a significant phenomenon in Chinese higher education. A large proportion of the returned students worked in the Chinese higher education system as teachers, researchers, and administrators, becoming a driving force in the development of Chinese universities.

One of the modernization efforts introduced in China after the Opium War was the movement to adopt the Western university model and to promote the learning of Western science and technology as a response to foreign aggression. From the 1860s to the 1880s, Western-style military and naval academies and foreign-language institutions were established in China. In 1898, as one of the major reform strategies, Capital Metropolitan University—the predecessor of Peking University—was established by the state. It was the first modern national comprehensive university in China and became a milestone in the development of the Chinese higher education system.

According to 1902 educational reform legislation, Peking University was regarded as the leading institution of higher learning in China, and it was expected to provide leadership for all schools in the country. However, in the context of the corrupt and weakened feudal Qing dynasty, modern Chinese universities were constrained from further development. Peking University achieved little during its first ten years. A new institutional environment and new leadership for Chinese higher education were needed. It was during the presidency of Cai Yuanpei that Peking University became the first truly modern Chinese university. Cai Yuanpei had studied in Germany from 1908 to 1911. After the Revolution of 1911, the provisional government established by Sun Yat Sen appointed Cai Yuanpei as the first minister of education in China. Drawing on his experiences as a student in Germany, he introduced the European university model to China through his involvement in formulating the 1912 education reform legislation. In 1917, after his return from his second period of studies in Germany and France, Cai Yuanpei was appointed as the president of Peking University (Hayhoe, 1989). As president of the university, he promoted institutional autonomy and academic freedom. He also emphasized arts and sciences, instead of ancient classics, as core curriculum areas, patterned after the Western university model.

In 1922, new educational reform legislation was implemented that reflected the greater influence of American university traditions. The American 6-3-3-4 schooling system—that is, six-year primary school, three-year junior high school, three-year senior high school, and four-year college—was adopted in 1922 as the basic system of teaching and learning. This schooling system functioned until 1949 and currently retains a strong impact on education in China. Since China suffered from continuous foreign invasions and civil wars before 1949, the economy was extremely backward, people were very poor, and higher education had developed slowly. By 1949, China had only 205 higher education institutions—124 public universities and colleges, 21 missionary universities and colleges, and 60 private universities and colleges (including short-cycle colleges), with a total enrollment of 117,000 students.

Soviet Influences in the Early 1950s

After the founding of the People's Republic of China, the central government took over and nationalized all higher education institutions. All private universities and colleges were brought under the jurisdiction of either the central or provincial government by 1952. During this period, missionary-based universities and colleges, which represented the foreign educational presence and influence in China, were regarded as perpetrators of Western cultural imperialism. Thus they were shut down and their academic components were merged into the public universities. For example, Yenching University's College of Arts and College of Sciences were merged to become Peking University; the Department of Education became Beijing Normal University; and the Department of Chemical Engineering became Tianjin University. St. Johns University's Department of Architecture became Tongji University; the medical programs became Shanghai Second Medical College; and engineering departments became Shanghai Jiaotong University.

After all universities and colleges became state-run institutions, the higher education system was then reorganized and restructured according to the Soviet model. The reorganization was based on the belief of the leadership that the higher education system, as one part of the superstructure of the society, should be integrated with the economic base of the country. Since China was engaged in building a socialist, centrally planned economy, it would need to change its higher education system accordingly. Thousands of Soviet experts were sent to China in all fields to assist the country in developing the planned economy. Large numbers of Soviet scholars came to teach at Chinese universities and colleges, and Soviet educational administration specialists provided assistance with structural reforms of universities. Many Soviet curricula, course syllabi, and textbooks were translated into Chinese and widely disseminated and used in China. As in the Soviet system, the policy objective in China was to bring all higher education institutions under the leadership of the government. National unified instructional plans were implemented at all colleges and universities throughout the country, so that the higher education system would closely serve the manpower needs of a centrally planned economy. Indeed, the reorganization following the Soviet model promoted higher education development in China and contributed to the industrialization and development of the centrally planned economy of the 1950s.

China's adoption of the Soviet model meant that specialized higher education institutions were established and that the Chinese higher education system became more departmentalized and segmented under different central-line ministries. For example, Beijing Agricultural University came under the jurisdiction of the Ministry of Agriculture, Beijing Forestry College under the Ministry of Forestry, Beijing Chemical Engineering College under the Ministry of the Chemical Industry, Beijing Metallurgy College under the Ministry of the Metallurgical Industry, Beijing Geology College under the Ministry of Geology, Beijing College of Mines under the Ministry of the Mining Industry, and so on. There were a total of about sixty ministries in the central government, each operating its own higher education institution. Existing universities and colleges also became more specialized. Some comprehensive universities became specialized engineering institutes, and their schools of arts and schools of sciences were removed. Some comprehensive universities retained their identities—for example, Peking University—although its Agriculture College was moved out to form Beijing Agriculture University and its engineering departments were transferred to other specialized technical institutes.

Along with the Soviet higher education model, the Soviet-oriented research system was also adopted in China with the establishment of the Chinese Academy of Sciences (CAS), which formed an independent national research system with hundreds of research institutes throughout the country. The major research function of the country was carried out by these institutes, which were separate from the Chinese higher education system. Large amounts of research funding went to the CAS instead of to the universities. The institutional structure of the Soviet research model, which separated research from the teaching of young people, significantly reduced the research capacity of Chinese universities, resulting in wastage of scarce human, physical, and financial resources. For example, while Peking University had a strong Department of Mathematics, the CAS established another large institute of mathematical research nearby in Beijing; and while Peking University had a strong Department of Chemistry, the CAS set up a research institute in chemistry next door to the university. Although since the late 1950s many Chinese scholars and professors have recommended closer cooperation between the Chinese universities and the CAS and better integration of teaching and research, the CAS is still functioning independently of the universities. When the CAS received a larger share of national research funding, research universities would get a smaller piece of the pie. The legacy of the Soviet research system has had a very strong impact on the Chinese higher education system, especially in terms of the development and strength of the country's research universities.

Among the far-reaching influences of the Soviet higher education model in China were departmentalization, segmentation, overspecialization, and the separation of teaching from research. These traits shaped the structure of the contemporary Chinese higher education system until the 1990s, even though they were criticized during the late 1950s and attacked during the Cultural Revolution that lasted from 1966 to 1976. They became the main targets of higher education reform during the transition from a centrally planned to a dynamic market economy.

The Great Leap Forward, 1958–1960

With the adoption of the Soviet model, the Chinese government had formulated and implemented the First Five-Year Plan for Economic and Social Development (1953–1957), which formed the basis for a national manpower plan. A higher education development plan was also implemented. Students represented products in a centrally planned economy, and the plan introduced national unified instructional plans, syllabi, and textbooks. It was a very rigid system. In 1958, after the completion of the First Five-Year Plan, the Chinese government launched a nationwide mass movement for economic development—the Great Leap Forward for Socialist Construction. The plan triggered the so-called Great Leap Forward in Higher Education, which lasted approximately three years. The policy objective was to increase significantly the number of universities and colleges and expand higher education enrollments to match the ambitious economic growth plan.

This great leap forward deviated somewhat from the rigid Soviet model. It reflected the impetuosity of the Chinese leadership with regard to economic and educational development but was also a reaction to the regimentation, overspecialization, and fragmentation of knowledge in the Soviet system. During the period, the number of higher education institutions increased from 229 in 1957 to 1,289 in 1960. Within 3 years, more than 1,000 new universities and colleges were established and total enrollments increased from 441,181 to 961,623. Such a dramatic expansion caused many problems for the Chinese higher education system in the 1960s, such as those of low efficiency and quality. These problems, together with the worsening of the Sino-Soviet relationship and serious economic austerity in the country starting in the early 1960s, led to a readjustment of higher education development policy. Accordingly, in 1961 the Ministry of Education cut down the number of higher education institutions and consolidated the newly established small universities and colleges. In three years (1960–1963), the total number of institutions had decreased from 1,289 to 407. From 1963 to 1965, Chinese higher education emerged from the period of hectic expansion and difficult reorganization, and by 1965 both the quality of instruction and institutional efficiency were improved.

The Cultural Revolution

Only a few years after the Chinese higher education system was put on track toward steady and healthy development from 1963 to 1965, the so-called Cultural Revolution broke out in 1966. It was a nationwide political movement that had a profound impact on Chinese higher education. Universities and colleges were attacked as places disseminating ideas that combined Soviet revisionism, Western bourgeois ideologies, and traditional feudalism. The Cultural Revolution negated almost everything in the existing higher education system, including Chinese academic traditions, Western academic influences, and the Soviet academic model. Universities and colleges were stopped from enrolling undergraduate students for more than four years, and no postgraduate students were enrolled for twelve years. The national college entrance examinations were abolished, and many universities and colleges were closed down. After 1970, some higher education institutions started enrolling "worker-peasant-soldier students" based on political criteria with no consideration of academic qualifications. Not only did the quality of instruction deteriorate, student numbers also declined dramatically. Total enrollments decreased from 674,400 in 1965 to 47,800 in 1970. These developments resulted in a serious shortage of well-educated specialized manpower. The reasons for the Cultural Revolution and its policy objectives were political rather than educational. The higher education sector was the most severely afflicted area in the society.

In the thirty-year period from 1949 to 1978, higher education in China was forced to undergo dramatic changes along a tortuous and circuitous path of development. The period included the takeover from the previous authority, nationwide adoption of the Soviet model in the early 1950s;

the Great Leap Forward and the educational revolution from 1958 to 1960; retrenchment, readjustment, reorganization, and consolidation from 1961 to 1963; and steady improvement of the system from 1963 to 1965. Finally, this period also included the unprecedented destruction and serious shrinking in size of the higher education system during the so-called Cultural Revolution from 1966 to 1976 and gradual recovery from 1976 to 1978. It is important to note, however, that the overall operational framework of Chinese higher education as of 1979 was still characterized by the central planning model that had been adopted from the Soviets in the early 1950s. This is the key to understanding the contemporary realities of the reform process that started in the early 1980s.

ISSUES AND REALITIES

From the 1980s up to the beginning of the twenty-first century, Chinese higher education has been characterized by a series of reforms. The economic transition, the fast-growing market economy, the rapid development of science and technology, and the increase in individual income levels and living standards stimulated increasing demands for higher education. Education was considered the strategic foundation for economic success given the growing recognition of the need for well-educated manpower, especially high-level specialized personnel. Priority was given to university development, and the Chinese higher education system has expanded quickly over the past twenty years. Total enrollments at higher education institutions in China rose from about 1 million in the early 1980s to about 13 million in 2001. Obviously, the structure of the old higher education system based on a centrally planned economy could no longer fit in with the new reality. Dramatic changes took place in the higher education sector.

The economic transition in China that began in the 1980s coincided with rapid advancements in science and technology, especially the revolution in information and communications technology, that have led the world into a new age of the knowledge-based economy. As knowledge-based institutions, universities have been called on to play a central role in economic development. Furthermore, the knowledge-based economy is international by nature. Capital, production, management, market, labor, information, and technology are organized across national boundaries, which has resulted in a strong tendency toward globalization. China's entry into the World Trade Organization (WTO) is a part of this process. Cross-cultural interactions, exchanges of students and faculty members, joint teaching and research programs, and academic communications, especially over the Internet, have formed an ongoing and irreversible internationalizing trend in higher education, providing further impetus from the outside world toward Chinese higher education reform.

Structural Reforms

While policies for economic transition and openness were being implemented, the structure of Chinese higher education in the early 1980s was basically unchanged from the one that took shape in the context of the centrally planned economy of the 1950s. It was in the context of central planning that the governance and administrative system of Chinese higher education originated and evolved. The central government instituted the national socioeconomic development plan and corresponding manpower plan, according to which the State Planning Commission and the Ministry of Education jointly formulated a higher education development plan that included the number and types of institutions and students needed, student quotas for each sector and each province, the distribution of student enrollments by field of study, and institutional enrollment quotas by discipline and specialty. According to the specific manpower requirements, higher education institutions devised their curricula. Students were usually trained in very narrow specializations. Graduate job assignment plans were designed by the government according to the manpower plan of each central-line ministry and province. The system was highly centralized, and universities, attached to governmental agencies, were simply part of the state-planned system. This centrally planned system continued to function all the way to the mid-1990s. In 1995, among the 358 national-level universities and colleges, 35 belonged to the Ministry of Education (State Education Commission, 1996), and 323 universities and colleges were under the jurisdiction of 61 central-line ministries, such as the Ministry of the Electronics Industry, the Ministry of the Metallurgical Industry, and the Ministry of Agriculture. The higher education system was compartmentalized and segmented in structure. Obviously, such a higher education system based on central planning could not fit in well with the new market economy.

As the economic sector has taken the lead in initiating reforms, dramatic changes have taken place in the human resources sector, which is closely related to higher education. In the newly developed market economy in China, it is market supply and demand rather than government planning that plays the basic role in resource allocation and utilization. The labor market plays the key role in determining human resources development and allocation. In such a system, higher education institutions need to gear their programs to meet the human resources needs of the labor market. This does not mean that all teaching and research should be shaped only by market forces, but it does mean that the human resources requirements for socioeconomic development, as signaled by the labor market, will be of primary importance to universities. The Chinese higher education system, which used to be part of the centrally planned economy, must be reformed.

The labor market now influences the wage structure of graduates by level and type of education, and thus the expected benefits of higher education as well as the demand for higher education opportunities. In terms of labor market performance, the relative competitive advantage of graduates with certain types and levels of education will serve as feedback to the universities. For example, if graduates in a given field are in oversupply, their competitive advantage in the labor market will be reduced. Student demands for this field will decline, and universities will adjust their programs and enrollment policies accordingly. This is exactly what is happening in China today. However, the market is not omnipotent—nor is it a panacea—and market failure also occurs from time to time. Thus, the state still has a very important role to play in this market-oriented environment.

The government uses a number of channels to influence, supervise, and coordinate the higher education system. Government actions range from setting the country's macroeconomic policies that will help to determine labor market needs and employment and wage policies in the public sector defining national priorities and funding relevant educational programs, to developing an accreditation and quality control system for higher education institutions, to establishing a legal infrastructure for both protecting and regulating the operation of colleges and universities.

The process of institutionalizing the new framework of higher education involves changes in governance and administration, the government/university relationship, the legal status of higher education institutions, university autonomy, and the focus on socioeconomic development and labor market demands. Much has been accomplished with regard to these reforms in recent years, and the new framework of higher education is now gradually replacing the old one.

As mentioned earlier, the national-level universities and colleges were under the jurisdiction of the sixty-two different ministries (State Education Commission, 1996), while the provincial universities and colleges belonged to the corresponding provincial-line departments. However, with the development of a market economy, after graduating from a university belonging to a specific line ministry, a student might well find a job in a completely unrelated field through labor market mechanisms. As more and more graduates found their own jobs in the labor market instead of through job assignments handled by the ministry, the manpower plan of the central-line ministries failed. The recent reforms have focused on restructuring the Chinese higher education system through mergers of universities or collaborative arrangements among higher education institutions that breach the existing boundaries between the different ministries.

Between 2000 and 2003, hundreds of universities and colleges were reorganized. For example, Beijing Medical University under the Ministry of Public Health merged with Peking University, which is under the Ministry of Education. Interestingly, until the early 1950s, Beijing Medical University was the medical school of Peking University. The medical university was separated from the comprehensive university and brought under the jurisdiction of the Ministry of Public Health in the 1950s when the Soviet higher education model was adopted. Similarly, in Hangzhou City, Zhejiang Province, Hangzhou University, Zhejiang Agriculture University, and Zhejiang Medical University, under different jurisdictions, were merged into Zhejiang University, which is under the Ministry of Education. Hangzhou University used to be the School of Sciences and Arts of Zhejiang University, Zhenjiang Medical University used to be the medical school of Zhejiang University, and Zhejiang Agricultural University used to be the agricultural school of Zhejiang University. These entities were all separated from Zhejiang University and brought under the jurisdiction of different ministries and departments in the 1950s, under Soviet influence.

Thus, in some cases, the current structural changes are, to a certain extent, a restoration of the university structure that existed before the Soviet model was adopted. From 1993 to 2001, 708 universities and colleges were reorganized into 302 institutions through the elimination of the line ministries' control over higher education institutions in China. The structure of the Chinese higher education system was changed dramatically.

Reforming the Curriculum

Changing the modes of teaching and learning is at the core of the reforms. Policies concerning curriculum and instruction evolved since the 1960s following the rationale of the centrally planned economy. This was a system in which students were enrolled, trained, and positioned as products of the centrally planned economy. Higher education was characterized by overspecialization. In the mid-1980s, before the period of reform, higher education in China was divided into more than 1,400 narrow specialties. For example, instead of a general program in mechanical engineering, there were specialties in light industry machinery, heavy industry machinery, chemical industry machinery, public works machinery, petroleum industry machinery, metallurgical industry machinery, agricultural machinery, mining machinery, and so on. Students were usually locked into narrow specializations, with little freedom to decide what to learn in school and what to do after graduation, which restricted their ability to respond to the new realities created by changes in technology and the economy. Even in a centrally planned economy this overspecialization resulted in a wastage of skills and expertise. For example, a survey of one hundred thousand college graduates in the late 1980s showed that more than 40 percent of them held jobs unrelated to their professional training (Guizhou Institute of Educational Research, 1988).

With the transition to a dynamic market economy under way, the rapidly changing needs of the labor market and advancements in science and technology stimulated a call for a more competitive and adaptive labor force. Therefore, it is imperative for China to implement reforms to broaden the specializations of students to increase their flexibility in the labor market. The reforms have emphasized expanding the knowledge base by changing the curriculum. Since the mid-1980s, fields of specialization have been broadened: for example, the overspecialized machinery programs have been folded into a more general mechanical engineering program. Interdisciplinary studies have been encouraged to provide students in the humanities and social sciences with basic knowledge in science, mathematics, and informatics. Likewise, students in science and engineering would acquire basic knowledge in the humanities and social sciences to help them understand how best to put what they learn at school in the service of the development needs of the country. The total number of specialties was reduced from more than 1,400 in the mid-1980s to about 200 in 2003. Further reforms in this direction are still under way. For example, at Peking University in Beijing, experimental classes have been created under the special "Yuanpei programs," in which students are enrolled not in academic departments such as physics, chemistry, or mathematics but rather in the general arts and sciences programs, with a much broader curriculum. After two years of studies in general education programs, students gradually become more focused on specific academic fields. This is a reversal of the overspecialization of the Soviet model.

Curriculum reforms were coupled with reforms in the teaching and learning process. The shift in emphasis went from the memorization of factual knowledge to the cultivation of students' ability in creative and critical thinking, problem solving, information acquisition and generation, and intellectual independence. The economic transition and the knowledge revolution dramatically changed the way of teaching and learning. Reforms in teaching and learning have not only encouraged students to acquire the existing knowledge, they are also encouraged to develop the ability to explore and anticipate what will happen in the future. Thus more heuristic and participatory methods of teaching were adopted. The current understanding in Chinese higher education is that young people should not be trained for short-term jobs but helped to develop the ability to cope with new challenges throughout their lives. Universities should not only educate the younger generation intellectually, but also tend to their moral, physical, and aesthetic development. Graduates should not be viewed simply as products but rather as well-educated members of future generations. These changes represent the mainstream of the current curriculum and instruction reforms in Chinese higher education. However, these reforms are unevenly implemented among different universities and colleges. In the leading national universities, new curricula and teaching and learning approaches were adopted more quickly because of their strong and more qualified faculty and better facilities, while in some of the local colleges in remote areas, reforms proceeded slowly because of inadequate human, physical, and financial resources.

Higher Education Finance

Stimulated by the soaring societal and individual demand for higher education, Chinese higher education enrollments have expanded rapidly over the past twenty years. However, the increase in state appropriations for higher education could not keep up with the growing costs, leading to serious financial constraints for universities and colleges. Although the cost of salaries and fringe benefits accounted for an increasing share of the total budget, faculty income was still relatively low in the 1980s and 1990s. There also was a shortage of nonsalary funding for the teaching and learning infrastructure, which resulted in understocked laboratories and libraries. Many universities lacked the necessary equipment and funds for upgrading obsolete facilities (Min, 1990). Obviously, without successfully tackling the financial constraints, the Chinese higher education system could not sustain a healthy development and upgrade its quality to meet international standards. Thus systematic reforms in financing higher education were implemented.

An effort was made to change the structure of government spending to benefit education. Despite the increase in state appropriations to higher education since the early 1980s, public expenditure on education in China remains relatively low by international standards. In the late 1990s, China was spending less than 3.5 percent of its gross domestic product (GDP) on education, as compared with an average of 6 percent in developed countries and 4 percent in other developing countries. A decision was made by the central government to increase appropriation to education at all governmental levels at a rate higher than the rate of increase of revenues. Allocations per student and teacher salaries were increased for direct teaching and learning purposes. The central government decided to increase allocations to education by one percent over the previous year continuously for five years between 1999 and 2003. Thus in 2003, the central government's budgetary allotment for education had increased by 5 percent. In the higher education sector, total government spending increased from 54.5 billion RMB yuan (U.S.$6.7 billion) in 1998 to 111.4 billion RMB yuan (U.S.$13.6 billion) in 2001, doubling in three years. Similarly, average teacher salaries increased impressively.

Developing a cost-sharing and cost-recovery system represents another major reform in the financing of higher education. Under the centrally planned economy, the Chinese higher education system did not charge students any tuition. It also provided students with free dormitory housing and stipends for food and other expenses, which amounted to about 20 percent of total recurrent costs. Chinese universities started to charge tuition and fees as one of the strategies to address their financial difficulties, gradually institutionalizing the concept that the expenses of higher education should be paid in part by those who benefit from higher education. At the same time, student loan and scholarship programs have been set up for students from needy families to address the equity issue. This policy became both necessary and feasible because of dramatic changes in national income distribution stemming from the transition in the economy. Along with the increasing willingness and capacity to pay on the part of students and their families, tuition levels gradually rose. At present, more than one-fifth of the total operational budgets of Chinese higher education institutions is covered by tuition and fees. In 2000, of the Chinese higher education system's 98.3 billion RMB yuan (U.S.$12 billion) in total recurrent expenses, 21.7 billion RMB yuan (U.S.$2.64 billion) came from tuition and fees paid by students.

One of the significant changes in financing higher education in China since the mid-1980s has been to allow universities to make use of their human capital resources and capacities in science and technology to generate revenue for themselves. This is one of the promising strategies for increasing the resources devoted to higher education. The revenue generated by universities themselves has increased remarkably since 1985, when higher education institutions were given the autonomy to do so. Universities generated funds through research contracts with industry, technical consulting work with businesses, training and educational services, and fund-raising activities. Many universities established foundations and development offices to seek contributions from alumni, other individuals, and businesses. Some universities, such as Peking University and Tsinghua University, even set up foundations as charitable corporations in the United States.

Chinese universities also generated revenues by incubating spin-off companies. For example, Peking University is home to the largest university-affiliated high-tech company in China—the Founder Corporation—which markets its innovations in computer-laser technology to the newspaper typesetting and publishing industry. In 2002, the company had a business volume of 14.5 billion RMB yuan (U.S.$1.8 billion). Although it was established outside the university structure as an independent legal entity, the Founder Corporation supported the university, providing research funding for the advancement of computer-laser technology and submitting a certain proportion of its net profit as royalties to the university. In recent years, 15 percent of Peking University's operational budget was supplied by its affiliated companies. Chinese universities also secure more and more of their research funding from the proceeds of their business ventures—increasing from 1.4 billion RMB yuan (U.S.$0.25 billion) in 1990 to 17.3 billion RMB yuan (U.S.$2.1 billion) in 2001. In 2000, of the 98.3 billion RMB yuan (U.S.$12 billion) in total recurrent expenditures of the Chinese higher education system, 57 percent came from state appropriations, 22 percent from tuition and fees, and the remaining 21 percent from revenue generated by the universities themselves. At present in China, some universities, such as Peking University and Tsinghua University, generate more than 50 percent of their total revenues.

Universities are also being encouraged to improve institutional management and thereby turn a relatively high-cost system into a more cost-effective one. This change was achieved by the internal reorganization of universities—rearranging small departments, broadening specialties, eliminating duplication in programs—to make more effective use of staff and physical resources. The teacher-to-student ratio was increased from 1:3 in 1983 to 1:16 in 2001. Arrangements were made for institutions or departments to share expensive equipment, faculty, and other resources. One cost-savings approach was to achieve economies of scale by consolidating small institutions into larger ones as well as by breaking down some departmental boundaries, as mentioned earlier (Min, 1991). The average enrollment at Chinese universities and colleges increased from less than two thousand in 1990 to over four thousand in 2001.

Promotion of the Private Sector

Although public higher education has expanded quickly, the unmet demand for higher education in China is still immense. Enrollments at higher education institutions in China comprised less than 3 percent of the college age cohort in the early 1980s, but that figure had risen to 14 percent by 2002. However, the demand for higher education is rising much faster than the rate of higher education expansion. Constrained by the limited resources available for higher education development, the Chinese government implemented policies to promote private institutions. In August 1993, an important document, the Provisional Stipulations for the Establishment of *Minban* Higher Education Institutions, was issued. *Minban* (non-state-run) universities and colleges are actually private institutions, as defined internationally.

The goal of this policy is to mobilize more resources from the private sector to accelerate higher education development. Since the early 1990s, local private institutions have mushroomed, financed by tuition fees, donations, and income generated by training programs, consultation, and technical services. Initially, Chinese private universities and colleges were usually small in size with flexible curricula. Their generally short-cycle vocational programs served as important complements to the public higher education system. However, the private institutions quickly grew and matured, some becoming very large and competitive. For example, Xi'an International University—a private comprehensive university established in 1992 in Xi'an City, Shaanxi Province—now has ten colleges and 21,000 students, modern teaching facilities that include a satellite digital transmission system, a multimedia computer network, a campus on-line network, a computer center, an audiovisual teaching center, and a considerable number of laboratories. Xi'an International even established international links with universities in the United States, the United Kingdom, Australia, and Canada. Currently, private universities and colleges number 1,202, and enroll 1.13 million students. It is important to note that when China adopted a Soviet-based centrally planned economy in the early 1950s, all private universities and colleges were converted into public institutions. During the transition from a centrally planned to a dynamic market economy, private institutions reemerged and have contributed significantly to the human resource development of the country.

Currently, there are over one thousand private universities and colleges, most with only two- or three-year study programs. To a certain extent, they are the equivalent of community colleges or trade schools in the United States. At present, only about 5 percent of these institutions have been officially accredited by the National Committee for the Establishment of Higher Education Institutions, and their diplomas are recognized by the Ministry of Education. In December 2002 the 31st session of the Standing Committee of the Ninth People's Congress adopted a new law to promote private education in China. This law gives private schools and universities the same legal status as public institutions and guarantees their autonomy. It also stipulates the evaluation procedures and legal guidelines that private institutions must follow. The legislation represents the official recognition that private universities serve the public interests. Private universities and colleges will be expected to grow more quickly, account for an ever larger proportion of higher education enrollments, and play an increasingly significant role in Chinese higher education.

World-Class Universities

The economic transition has been accompanied by dramatic technological changes. The rapid advancements in science and technology, the knowledge explosion, and the revolution in information technology have transformed the international economy. A country's capacity to generate, accumulate, deploy, and utilize knowledge and information becomes crucial for development. As knowledge-based institutions, universities play a critical role in a country's economic growth and social development. Universities are involved in knowledge generation, processing, dissemination, and application through their teaching, research, and service to industries and communities. Thus, if knowledge is the fuel of the new world economy, universities are one of the engines driving economic development in the twenty-first century (Castells, 1991). The Chinese government has, therefore, formulated policies not only to expand the higher education system but also to upgrade the quality of the leading national universities to world-class status. Increased funding was allocated to selected universities, such as Peking University and Tsinghua University. Special funding was also allocated to some other national universities to help them to upgrade and strengthen specific disciplines and academic programs. The rationale was that limited resources should not be thinly spread out but rather concentrated on some priority institutions or academic programs in selected universities.

As knowledge generators, world-class universities are usually also the leading research institutions. For this reason, the research function has been reemphasized in Chinese universities. In the early 1950s, when the Soviet model was adopted, research was separated from the universities, and the CAS was established to conduct research. Since the 1980s, there has been a growing recognition of the importance of combining teaching and research at universities, especially at the leading national universities with postgraduate programs. Universities were required to be both centers of teaching and centers of research. Integrating teaching and research is considered a major strategy to update curricula and improve instructional quality, as well as enhance research. At universities, both research and publication in international scholarly journals are being promoted as part of the effort to achieve world-class status.

World-class universities also need to establish worldwide contacts. China's implementation of policies of reform and opening up were based on the principle that no country can develop and prosper if it isolates itself from the rest of the world—especially in the information age. For Chinese universities to achieve world-class status, they need to be integrated into the international academic community. As reforms integrated China into the global economic system, Chinese universities also become more internationalized. Approximately 450,000 students and scholars have gone to study abroad in the past twenty years, more and more international academic exchange programs and joint research programs have been set up, and numerous international education conferences and workshops are held each year in China. With the introduction of information technology, especially computer networks such as CERNET (China Education and Research Network), which is interconnected with the Internet, the pace of international communication and collaboration in higher education has accelerated. Internationally oriented programs account for an increasing proportion of the curriculum. These programs—such as international studies, foreign languages, international relations, international economics, international business, international politics, history, and international law—have become very popular at Chinese universities. At the same time, more and more international students are coming to study in China.

To create world-class universities has been the ideal and goal of several generations of Chinese educators over the past one hundred years. When Cai Yuanpei was appointed as the president of Peking University in 1917, he certainly had such a vision in mind. In the current period of higher education reform and development, Chinese educational leaders in both the government and the universities have tried to realize this goal. However, being pragmatic in approach, they are aware that the limited resources mean the system can only afford to lift a small number of universities to world-class status in the near future. Thus, the Chinese Ministry of Education has made it clear that China will initially seek to promote fewer than ten universities in their struggle to reach world-class status, with top priority going to Peking University and Tsinghua University. It is expected that these leading Chinese universities will be able to serve as locomotives to help raise the standards of the higher education system as a whole in China.

Enhancing Faculty Development

Faculty are key to reforming the curriculum and the teaching and learning process, as well as to upgrading Chinese universities to world-class status. Great efforts have thus been made to strengthen the faculty. Of the 1.45 million employees in Chinese higher education, about 554,000 are faculty members. In general, the academic profession is well respected in traditional Chinese culture. However, the prestige of university teachers was destroyed in the mid-1960s during the so-called Cultural Revolution.

From the 1970s to the 1990s, the incomes of faculty members were relatively low. While basic salaries of university faculty were comparable to those of other professionals with similar educational qualifications, faculty remuneration was lower because of larger bonuses given to employees in companies, especially in joint venture firms. The government and universities have sought to raise faculty prestige and income with additional state appropriations and revenue generated by the universities themselves. From 1998 to 2001, the average annual income of university teachers in China doubled, going from 12,000 RMB yuan (U.S.$1,500)

to 24,000 RMB yuan (U.S.$3,000)—an increase that raised faculty sala-
ries above the average income levels in the country. The government also
spent 114.4 billion RMB yuan (U.S.$14.3 billion) to improve teachers'
living conditions. Fifteen billion square feet of new faculty housing was
built between 1994 and 2001 (Li, 2002). At present, the morale of university teachers is high in China, and the academic profession has become an attractive occupation for young scholars.

Currently, the Chinese higher education system is composed of full
professors, (9.5 percent), associate professors (30.3 percent), lecturers
(35.2 percent), assistant teachers (19.1 percent), and instructors (6 percent). (Lecturers are the equivalent of assistant professors in the U.S.
system; assistant teachers are the equivalent of teaching assistants, but
they are also full-time employees of the university.) At some of the leading national research-oriented universities, senior faculty members account for a much larger proportion of the total. For example, at Peking
University, senior faculty members including both professors and associate professors account for more than 70 percent of the total faculty. Among
faculty members, 46.4 percent are below the age of 35 years, showing
the effect of recent heavy recruitment of faculty due to the rapid expansion of higher education. About 39.8 percent of faculty members are
between 36 and 50 years of age and about 11.4 percent between 51 and
60. This latter age group is also relatively small, showing the genera-
tional gap of quality faculty that occurred as a result of the destruction of
higher education during the Cultural Revolution. Because the retirement
age for lecturers and associate professors is about 60 and for full professors about 63, only 2.2 percent of faculty are over age 61. Female faculty
account for an increasing proportion of faculty in China, increasing from
10 percent in 1950 to almost 40 percent in 2001 (Ministry of Education,
2002).

Traditionally, faculty members were trained mainly at domestic higher
education institutions, especially at national universities with graduate
programs. Since China did not have an academic degree system until the
1980s, only about 30 percent of all faculty members hold postgraduate
degrees. Along with the implementation of reforms and open-door policies, many internationally trained scholars with advanced degrees joined
the university teaching force, which improved the quality of faculty and
enhanced the international links with the world academic community.
As part of the current higher education reform, more faculty members
have been sent abroad for advanced studies. Chinese university faculty
have increased their international links through academic exchange pro-

grams, international conferences, study tours, and joint research projects with foreign colleagues and international academic and professional organizations. These activities play an important role in improving Chinese scholarship and in enabling Chinese scholars to contribute to academic development internationally.

TRENDS AND CHALLENGES

Chinese universities have undergone rapid expansion and dramatic changes. Enrollments have increased quickly. In 1998, about 1.08 million new students were admitted to universities and colleges, while in 2002 that number had increased to 3.49 million. It is anticipated that by 2005 total enrollments will reach 15 million and that the enrollment rate will exceed 15 percent of the college age cohort (Chen, 2002a). According to demographic projections, the college-age population will continue to grow quickly, reaching its peak in 2008. As a result, higher education will continue to face great pressure to expand, driven by the fast-growing economy, the rapid rise in family income and living standards, and the huge unmet demand from the 85 percent of college-age young people who currently are not enrolled in higher education institutions. This ongoing trend will lead to a series of challenges for the Chinese higher education system.

Maintaining and Improving Quality

The quality of higher education is always a major issue almost everywhere in the world, and Chinese higher education is no exception. Some of the leading national research universities that did not overexpand enrollments paid sufficient attention to improving quality while marching toward world-class status. Thus their quality level in both teaching and research was raised. However, the quality of many local universities and colleges was negatively affected by the rapid expansion of enrollments and overcrowding, which has made it difficult to sustain quality inputs such as the number of qualified faculty and staff, curriculum development and program upgrading, laboratory facilities, and library books. If these issues are not addressed properly, the quality of Chinese universities could deteriorate.

It is imperative for China to enhance supervision and quality assurance of higher education institutions, especially with regard to the accreditation and regulation of the newly mushrooming private universities and colleges. Since faculty quality is the key to quality education, serious measures need to be taken to improve and enhance faculty development. During the rapid expansion, large numbers of teachers were recruited and promoted. Some of them were short on academic qualifications and teaching experience, and some of the older generation of teachers were held back by social changes and unable to keep up with the rapid advances in science and technology. Thus, one of the challenges for Chinese universities is to develop in-service training programs to allow faculty members to improve their teaching skills and update their knowledge. Another task is to set stricter academic standards for faculty appointments and promotions and to attract capable young academics to join the university teaching force. A project entitled "Enhancing Higher Education Quality" was initiated by the Department of Higher Education in the Ministry of Education and was implemented in 2003 as part of a major effort to tackle quality problems in Chinese higher education.

China is a large country with a huge higher education system consisting of more than three thousand institutions; quality levels vary across institutions. The Chinese government has adopted various policies that gave priority support to certain key national universities. For example, the "211 Higher Education Project" initiated in 1995 gave additional special funding to one hundred selected universities. The "985 World-Class University Project," which was initiated in May 1998 during the centennial celebration of Peking University, gave more concentrated support to a smaller number of national universities to upgrade their academic levels to world-class status. As a result, higher education institutions in the future will be more differentiated, with a few national research universities at the top. The leading national universities should function as national "centers of excellence." They are expected to serve as the engines that drive the whole Chinese higher education system to a higher level. It will be a challenge for these key institutions to upgrade themselves and at the same time help to improve the quality of local institutions.

Regional Disparities

The Chinese economy has grown rapidly over the past 20 years, but the rate has varied greatly among different provinces across the country. For example, in 1980 the per capita GDP in Shanghai was 2,738 RMB yuan (U.S.$1,190), while in Guizhou it was only 219 RMB yuan (U.S.$95). By 2001, Shanghai's per capita GDP had risen to 37,382 RMB yuan

(U.S.$4,600) and was 12 times higher than that of Guizhou.

The increasing regional economic disparities were accompanied by regional disparities in higher education. For example, in 2001, for every 10,000 people in the population 169 were registered higher education students in Beijing; 112 in Shanghai; and 12 and 17 in Guizhou and Qinghai, respectively. The unmet demand for higher education in the underdeveloped provinces was huge. For example, in 2000, only about one-fourth of the young people who applied to higher education institutions and took the entrance examinations were admitted in some of the poorer provinces. Not only was the difference in quantity large, the difference in quality was even more significant. All the top-ranking national universities—such as Peking University, Tsinghua University, Fudan University, Shanghai Jiaotong University, Nanjing University, and Zhejiang University—are located in the economically more developed provinces and municipalities, while the less-developed provinces of Guizhou, Qinghai, Xinjiang, Henan, and Shanxi have no key national universities. The uneven development and growing regional disparities in higher education have become critical issues and have attracted the attention of the national leadership. One of the policies instituted gave high priority to developing the western part of the country. Each of the leading national universities in the more developed areas was required to twin with a university in a less-developed province and to provide substantial support to the provincial university. The assistance included helping them with respect to increased enrollment capacity, curriculum development, donation of equipment, and faculty development. To improve university management the national universities sent capable administrators and teachers to the twinned campuses and brought teachers and administrators from the provinces back to the universities in the developed areas for further training and upgrading. For example, Peking University sent an excellent administrator to its twinned university, the Xinjiang Shihezi University, to serve as vice-president, as well as providing teachers and equipment. These university-twinning programs have been in existence for two years and have been effective in reducing the regional disparity in higher education. However, given the very nature of the decentralized market economy, the uneven growth in GDP among different provinces, and the corresponding decentralized financial system—which was called "each province cooks its dinner on its own stove"—regional disparities will remain as one of the major challenges facing China.

Changing Patterns of Access

In China, the distribution of higher education opportunities and public investment in higher education used to be very unequal among different social groups. These inequities have lessened with the economic reforms and development and the expansion of higher education enrollments. For example, according to the 1991 City and Township Household Survey, college-age young people from the poorest 20 percent of households accounted for only 2.3 percent of higher education enrollments in China, while those from the richest 20 percent of households accounted for 55.6 percent of higher education enrollments. The enrollment rate for the highest-income families was 24 times higher than that of the lowest-income families. During the 1990s, access patterns changed for the better. In 2000, college-age young people from the poorest 20 percent of households accounted for 9.5 percent of total higher education enrollments in China, a significant increase from 10 years earlier. Students from the richest 20 percent of households accounted for 30.1 percent of higher education enrollments, a 25.8 percent reduction since 1991 (Ding, 2003).

In 2001, female students accounted for 42 percent of total enrollments, a higher percentage than before. The improved access is one result of the expansion of higher education, as well as the introduction of financial aid programs for students from low-income families. For example, in 2002, the Ministry of Education and the Ministry of Finance initiated a new national scholarship program with an annual allocation of 200 million RMB yuan (U.S.$25 million) that provides outstanding students from low-income families with stipends for living expenses. The program also stipulates that scholarship recipients should receive tuition exemptions from their universities.

Although access to higher education has improved to a certain extent, it remains a serious challenge for China. In 2000, the enrollment rate for the 20 percent of highest-income families was still three times higher than that for the lowest-income families. Furthermore, since the higher education system is becoming increasingly differentiated, more college-age young people from higher-income families are likely to attend the leading national universities than those from lower-income families, which creates equity issues within the system. This is another kind of access issue that China will need to tackle in the near future.

The Employment of Graduates

Before the 1980s, university and college graduates in China were treated like products of the centrally planned economy. They were assigned jobs upon graduation by the government, which determined where they should go and what they should do, in a top-down process. With the economic transition, the occupational prospects of graduates were shaped by the labor market. With the government no longer responsible for job assignments, graduates have to find jobs on their own. To do so, they must respond to the needs of a rapidly changing labor market. The rapid expansion of the higher education system meant that more than 3 million university students graduate each year—more than the labor market can absorb at once. Recently, it has become difficult for some students to find jobs upon graduation, especially those from local colleges and from overspecialized colleges—some of which are holdovers from the centrally planned economy. Unemployment will become a more serious issue in years to come as more young people graduate from universities.

The issue is mainly structural in origin. Among current higher education institutions, a large proportion still have highly specialized curricula. The students are locked into specialized fields, which makes them less flexible and adaptive to technologically induced changes in the workplace and to labor market needs in a rapidly changing economy. The result is often a mismatch between narrowly trained graduates and the manpower needs of the labor market. University graduates prefer to seek employment in large cities or the coastal regions, even though the job market is relatively tight, avoiding the remote areas in the interior that have a serious shortage of university graduates. To tackle the issue of unemployed graduates will require broadening fields of study, thereby increasing students' flexibility and adaptability. Universities will also need to establish closer links with industries and other sectors of society, as well as developing better communication and interaction between students and potential employers. More autonomy should be given to higher education institutions to adjust their enrollment patterns so as to reduce the mismatch between the supply and demand of university graduates.

Consolidating the Reforms

Chinese universities have just undergone a dramatic reform process. Restructuring higher education required eliminating excessive government control over institutions and granting universities more autonomy in the management of programs and resources (Communist Party, 1985). The ongoing challenge will be to deepen the reforms and consolidate and institutionalize the implemented changes. Extending greater autonomy and decision-making power to universities and colleges will make them more innovative, creative, and responsive in the development process. Another crucial strategy is to continue to multiply and diversify the sources for financing higher education. The structure of higher education needs to be differentiated by levels and fields of learning so that the system is better able to meet the country's social and economic needs. Another area requiring comprehensive reform concerns the faculty in the areas of appointments, promotions, professional development, and the introduction of more effective incentive mechanisms. The establishment and development of private universities should continue to be encouraged, and more effectively monitored, to expand the provision of higher education. Finally, it is imperative to construct and enact a legal infrastructure to better protect and regulate universities and colleges, while increasing institutional autonomy.

Facing the Challenge of the WTO

China's entry into the WTO will definitely have a strong impact on both the economy and the higher education system, bringing both opportunities and challenges. With the further opening up of the economy, the country will become more integrated into the global marketplace and face increased competition. Thus, Chinese universities need to produce a more qualified labor force in order to enhance the country's economic competitiveness.

Chinese universities will also be facing increased competition. In keeping with the educational commitments China made to the WTO, no restrictions will be placed on foreign countries' recruitment of Chinese students to study abroad, and foreign universities will be allowed to operate in China with Chinese partners. There will be more students and teachers flowing across national borders (Chen, 2002b). As a result, more high-quality Chinese students and teachers might be attracted to foreign countries or to foreign universities operating in China. It should also be noted that with the entry of more foreign companies into China, more high-level Chinese professionals may decide to leave the academic profession for higher-paying positions in corporations. Western thought patterns, values, and belief systems will accompany international trade and investment, resulting in new challenges for traditional Chinese values in education. China's entry into the WTO will further strengthen the trend toward internationalization in Chinese higher education. How to become an integral part of the international higher education community and at the same time keep their own cultural identity will also be a challenge for Chinese universities in the years to come.

CONCLUSION

The current reforms and future trends within Chinese higher education are the logical and inexorable consequences of the past. Just as the future will be shaped by current reforms and developments, the reforms since the late 1970s were the inevitable and logical responses to the failure of the centrally planned system adopted from the Soviet Union in the 1950s. The adoption of the Soviet model grew out of the international social, economic, and political context surrounding the founding of the People's Republic. It also should be understood that the Soviet model of higher education was implanted in China on a foundation built on several thousand years of Chinese cultural and educational tradition and more than a hundred years of Western higher education influence.

Recognizing the dysfunctional nature of the Soviet system and the changing international environment, in the early 1980s China made the historic choice to implement new reform policies and to open up to the outside world. The reforms have lasted for more than twenty years, leading China into the twenty-first century with the new characteristics and challenges discussed in this chapter. Some of these reforms and reorganizations are simply a restoration of the Western-influenced university model that predated the introduction of the Soviet system—such as the merger of Beijing Medical University back into Peking University and the consolidation of four universities into the new Zhejiang University. Some of the reforms are innovations generated by the demands of the current domestic and international context. It takes a dynamic perspective to understand current developments in Chinese higher education and the system's historical roots.

REFERENCES

Castells, Manuel. (1991, June 30). "University system: Engine of development in the new world economy." Paper presented at the Worldwide Policy Seminar on Higher Education Development in Developing Countries, Kuala Lumpur, Malaysia.

Chen, Zhili. (2002a, October 17). Historical accomplishments in education reform and development (in Chinese). *China Education Daily*, 1–3.

Chen, Zhili. (2002b, January 9). The impact of WTO on Chinese education and research strategies (in Chinese). *China Education Daily*, 2.

Communist Party of China, Central Committee. (1985). *Decision on educational reform* (in Chinese). Beijing: Beijing Foreign Language Press.

Ding, Xiaohao. (2003, February 7). "An examination on higher education equalities in China." Paper presented at the International Conference on Chinese Education, Teachers College, Columbia University.

Guizhou Institute of Educational Research. (1988). *Investigation of the effectiveness of the Guizhou education system* (in Chinese). Guiyang City, China: Author.

Hayhoe, R. (1989). China's universities and Western university models. In P. G. Altbach & V. Selvaratnam (Eds.), *From dependence to autonomy: The development of Asian universities* (pp. 25–61). Dordrecht, Netherlands: Kluwer Academic.

Li, Lanqing. (2002, May 10). "Implementing strategies of developing China through science and education and promoting higher education reform and development" (in Chinese). Paper presented at the National Conference for Educational Awards, Beijing.

Min, Weifang. (1990, October). The mode of expansion and cost-effectiveness of Chinese higher education (in Chinese). *Educational Research*, 129, 39–49.

Min, Weifang. (1991). Higher education finance in China: Current constraints and strategies in the 1990s. *Higher Education*, 21, 151–161.

Ministry of Education. (2002). *Statistical yearbook of Chinese education 2002* (in Chinese). Beijing: People's Education Press.

State Education Commission. (1996). *Statistical yearbook of Chinese education, 1995* (in Chinese). Beijing: People's Education Press.

Wang, B. et al. (1994). *Introduction to the history of Chinese education.* Beijing: Beijing Normal University Press.

4

Higher Education in India

Massification and Change

N. Jayaram

"Higher education in India stands as an immobile colossus—insensitive to the changing contexts of contemporary life, unresponsive to the challenges of today and tomorrow, and absorbed so completely in trying to preserve its structural form that it does not have the time to consider its own larger purpose" (Dube, 1988, p. 46). This is the way the system of higher education in India was depicted in the late 1980s. Since then, this "immobile colossus" found itself thrown into a vortex of change. The foremost among the events responsible for the change was the 1990 adoption by the government of India of structural adjustment reforms. Influenced by the World Bank–International Monetary Fund, structural adjustment has meant the gradual withdrawal of state patronage for higher education and a coterminous privatization of that sphere. However, with the government dithering about the long-term policy in this regard, higher education in India is now passing through a period of stunted growth. Based on an analysis of the history and contemporary realities of India's higher education, this chapter reflects on the scenario that is likely to unfold in future.[1]

HISTORICAL PERSPECTIVES

Colonial Beginnings

The foundation of India's present system of higher education was laid by the British colonial regime in the mid-nineteenth century (Ashby & Anderson, 1966, pp. 54–146). Initially, efforts of the Christian missionaries and the East India Company generated a protracted controversy between the "Anglicists," who supported a Western course, and the "Orientalists," who favored an indigenous direction. This controversy was finally resolved by William Bentinck in favor of the Anglicist orientation, barely a month after Thomas Babington Macaulay had penned his (in)famous *Minute* (on February 2, 1835). His policy was reaffirmed by Charles Wood's *Despatch* (of July 19, 1854). Upon the recommendation of the committee appointed on January 26, 1855, the first three universities were established at Bombay (now Mumbai), Calcutta (now Kolkata), and Madras (now Chennai) in 1857 (Bhatt & Aggarwal, 1969, pp. 2–11).

Modeled after the University of London (established in 1836), these pioneer universities consisted largely of affiliating and examining bodies with very little intellectual life of their own. All the universities established thereafter developed in an isomorphic fashion, patterned on the original universities. The British higher education implants in India were designed to serve the economic, political, and administrative interests of the British and, in particular, to consolidate and maintain their dominance in the country.[2] English was the primary language of instruction, as well as the exclusive medium of instruction in higher education.[3] The curriculum was biased in favor of languages and the humanities, and against science and technology (Jayaram, 1990, pp. 45–59).

It is not as if the British failed to realize the problems associated with such an educational implantation or its adverse consequences for the colonized society. Yet not until the early twentieth century, through the initiative of Lord Curzon, the viceroy of India (1898–1905), were efforts made to "rescue the original concept of the university from its corrosive narrowness." Several inquiries were undertaken during the last three decades of colonial rule, but "hardly any of their major recommendations were translated into university policy or practice" (Tickoo, 1980, p. 34).

Postindependence Policy Initiatives

The system of higher education inherited by India at the time of independence in 1947 was already a crisis-ridden legacy (Raza et al., 1985, pp. 100–109). In 1948–1949, the government of India created the University Education Commission (the Radhakrishnan Commission) to study the development of higher education and make proposals for its future expansion and improvement. The 1964–1966 Education Commission (the

Kothari Commission) was the first attempt in India's educational history to look comprehensively at almost all aspects of education and to develop a blueprint for a "national system of education."

The Report of the Kothari Commission (Ministry of Education, 1971) influenced statements issued in 1968 and 1979 on the National Policy on Education and, through them, the policies and programs adopted in the Fourth, Fifth, and Sixth Five-Year Plans (1968–1983). However, the educational developments in the country since the report was first published "show marked variations with those postulated by the Commission" (Naik, 1982, p. 6). This is partly attributable to the deliberately normative path chosen by the commission.[4] The Ministry of Education, in processing the report, obliterated it by treating in a piecemeal fashion selected aspects of what was conceived to be a comprehensive plan (Naik, 1982, pp. 31–32).

In 1985, the new Congress Party government proposed to embark on the complex task of "restructuring the system of education." Toward this end, in August of that year the Ministry of Education (since reorganized as the Ministry of Human Resource Development) presented to Parliament a 119-page document titled *Challenge of Education: A Policy Perspective*. This document highlighted higher education, since it "can provide ideas and men to give shape to the future and also sustain all other levels of education" (Ministry of Education, 1985, p. 6). The key policy measures contemplated included the delinking of degrees from jobs; the diversification of courses; a moratorium on the expansion of conventional colleges and universities; selective admission to higher education based on "scholastic interest and aptitude"; establishment of new centers of excellence; decentralization of educational planning, administration, and monitoring; and depoliticization of academia.

The Program of Action of the National Policy on Education (Ministry of Human Resource Development, 1986) was reviewed by the Acharya Ramamurti Committee (Ministry of Human Resource Development, 1991). The recommendations of the Central Advisory Board on Education, issued after considering the committee's report, were adopted by Parliament in May 1992. Still the nature of the problems to be addressed (Jayaram, 1991) attenuated optimism about the outcome. As with earlier reform initiatives, this policy also resulted in ad hoc, piecemeal tinkering with the system rather than its overhaul with grit and determination.

OVERVIEW

Definition and Scope

Broadly defined, the term *higher education* in India includes the entire spectrum of education beyond the twelve years of formal schooling. Candidates who are successful at the secondary school certificate (SSC) examination (conducted at the end of ten years of schooling) have the choice of two tracks of postsecondary education. The first track consists of several vocational, technical, and paraprofessional courses leading to a variety of certificates and diplomas. These courses vary in duration from one year, in industrial training or teacher training institutes, to three years, in polytechnics. Of these, only the three-year polytechnic course leading to a diploma is regarded as "higher education."

The second track, generally described as the "plus-two" stage, is a prerequisite for college-level education. This stage, which is of two years' duration, is offered in three different types of educational settings: colleges offering first-degree courses,[5] junior colleges offering this course exclusively, and some schools. It is organized and administered by a separate state-level body.

Candidates who successfully complete the plus-two stage can take up either a general degree course (such as bachelor of arts, bachelor of science, or bachelor of commerce) of three years' duration or a professional degree course—such as bachelor of medicine and surgery (5 years and 6 months), bachelor of dental surgery (4 years), bachelor of engineering (4 years),[6] bachelor of nursing (3 years), and so on. In both types of courses a postgraduate degree (master's degree) would entail two to three years of further education.

After the successful completion of any first-degree course (general or professional), a graduate can pursue a second-degree course such as bachelor of education, bachelor of library science, or bachelor of law. Since the mid-1980s, a five-year "integrated" degree course in law has been introduced by many universities. Another year of postgraduate education would earn the graduate a master of education, master of library science, or master of law degree. In all courses, further higher education leading to master of philosophy (one to two years) and doctor of philosophy (three to five years) is possible.

The post-plus-two level of education is imparted in colleges and/or university departments. Based on the nature of their management, collegiate-level educational institutions fall into four categories: private unaided institutions, private grant-in-aid (government-aided, privately managed) institutions, institutions managed by the state government (through the directorates of college-level education, technical education, or medical education), and institutions managed by the universities. While these institutions vary in the principles and practices of management, as far as their academic organization is concerned, they are all regulated by the university to which they are affiliated.

These institutions offer a variety of courses. If the level of instruction provided is a function of the type of institution (i.e., junior college, polytechnic, college, or university department), the quality of teaching is often a function of the basic facilities available in a given institution. This again is determined by the extent and nature of the resources the administrators can mobilize and their motivation.

Typology of Institutions

In terms of their structure, the largest number of Indian universities belong to the affiliating type. They have university departments that provide instruction at the postgraduate level and undertake research. A large number of colleges offering first-degree-level education are affiliated to these universities. A major task of such universities is to oversee the academic standards of affiliated colleges.

Universities of the unitary type, on the other hand, are self-contained and have no colleges. Most of them offer both undergraduate and postgraduate courses and undertake research. A few universities are in some sense a mixture of these two types. The territorial jurisdiction of the mixed type of university (e.g., Delhi University) is usually confined to the city in which the institution is located. In addition to affiliated colleges, this type of university manages its own colleges. As for their legal status and regulative responsibility, the universities are of two types: first, the central universities (established by an act of Parliament and regulated directly by the Ministry of Human Resource Development) and, second, state universities (established by an act of the state assemblies, and regulated by the respective state governments).

The 229 university-level institutions for which data are available include 131 conventional multidisciplinary universities; 70 professional/technical institutions offering programs in agriculture-related fields (34), in the medical sciences (15), in engineering and technology (21), and in law (1); 20 specialist institutions devoted to the Sanskrit language (6), regional languages (4), women's studies (5), population sciences (1), and music and fine arts, statistics, law, and journalism (1 each); and 8 open universities (AIU, 1997, p. x).

The government has conferred upon eleven university-level institutions the status of "institutions of national importance." These include the 5 Indian Institutes of Technology (IITs) and the institutions specializing in the medical sciences (3), statistical techniques (1), and the Hindi language (1). These institutions are empowered to award degrees that, according to the University Grants Commission (UGC) Act of 1956, can be granted only by a university. The 5 Indian Institutes of Management (IIMs), which are also national-level institutions, are not vested with the power to award degrees, though their "fellowships" are treated on a par with university degrees.

By 1998–1999, 38 institutions had been recognized by the central government as "institutions deemed-to-be universities" under the UGC Act. These institutions either specialize in some area of knowledge or are heirs to a certain tradition. They are not expected to become multidisciplinary universities of the general type.

Outside the university orbit are research institutes funded by the Indian Council for Social Science Research and research laboratories established under the auspices of the Council of Scientific and Industrial Research or those maintained by government ministries. While these institutions do not grant degrees, they are recognized as centers for doctoral research work, and many scholars working in them are recognized as guides for doctoral students at universities.

The concept of the open university that offers distance education constitutes yet another landmark in higher education in India. The open university seeks to cater to the educational needs of persons who for whatever reason could not obtain higher education or who wish to pursue their studies at their own pace and time. Introduced in 1962, this channel of higher learning in the beginning came under the control of the conventional universities. Besides the eight open universities, there are forty-one institutes or directorates of distance education functioning under conventional universities that cater to about five hundred thousand students.

Thus, in the context of India, the term *higher education* suggests too much homogeneity and glosses over the enormous structural and functional diversity within the system. Obviously, the institutions vary as to their objectives and sources of funding and the academic backgrounds, abilities, motivations, and commitment of their faculty and students. This chapter focuses mainly on the state universities and their affiliated colleges, which together employ the overwhelming majority (over 85 percent) of teachers and account for the greater part (about 88 percent) of enrollments.

ISSUES AND REALITIES

Introduction to the Crisis

At the time of independence, India had 20 universities and 636 colleges. During the next 5 decades, the country built up a massive system of higher education (Ministry of Information and Broadcasting, 1999). In 1998–1999, there were 214 (198 state and 16 central) universities, 38 institutions "deemed-to-be universities," 11 institutes of national importance, 9,703 colleges, and 887 polytechnics. The system now employs 321,000 teachers and caters to 6,755,000 students.

Behind the facade of impressive statistics on the expansion of higher education, however, lies the system's continuing crisis. Two decades ago, Naik (1982, p. 163) succinctly summarized the nature of the crisis as follows: "over-production of 'educated' persons; increasing educated unemployment; weakening of student motivation; increasing unrest and indiscipline on the campuses; frequent collapse of administration; deterioration of standards; and above all, the demoralizing effect of the irrelevance and purposelessness of most of what is being done."

It is, no doubt, simple to share the cynicism of critics of the system of higher education in India. Yet, given political developments of the past few decades, one has to concede that the socioeconomic cost of overhauling the system would be prohibitive. Also, the philosophical vision and political will required for such a task are sadly lacking. Viewed in this light, it is easy to understand why successive governments have been content with the expansion of the system with little major modification. This *expansion* is often mistaken for *development*.

Since a radical overhaul of the system is nowhere in sight, innovations in the system may be the only realistic alternative.[7] Optimistic academicians may even argue that such innovations are a precursor to change, evolutionary rather than revolutionary.

The Issue of Quality

The crisis confronting the system of higher education is not the same or even similar at all types of institutions or all stages of higher learning. In fact, contrary to the general drift in higher education, some institutions have maintained very high standards: the Indian Institutes of Technology (at Chennai, Kanpur, Karagpur, Mumbai, and New Delhi), the Indian Institutes of Management (at Ahmedabad, Bangalore, and Kolkata), the Indian Institute of Science (Bangalore), the Tata Institute of Fundamental Research (Mumbai), the National Law School of India University (Bangalore), and a few exceptional departments in some universities. Some affiliated colleges, too, have maintained high standards. Any good reputation that Indian higher education retains can be credited to these institutions. These are islands of excellence in an ocean of mediocrity (Jayaram, 1999, p. 118).

The vicissitudes of the crisis are most apparent at state universities in general, and at the undergraduate level in affiliated colleges in particular. By the early 1990s, fully 88 percent of the more than 4 million students in the country were enrolled in the conventional courses (the B.A., B.Sc., and B.Com.) at affiliated colleges.[8] It should be noted that this crisis now also encompasses the conventional postgraduate (M.A., M.Sc., and M.Com.) courses offered in the university departments. These courses are now performing an extended babysitting function. This state of affairs is understandable given the low unit cost of running these courses and the fact that students entering this stream pay little toward their education—far less than what students in private-sector primary schools pay. The unregulated expansion of this sector of education has been invariably identified as the main cause of its present predicament. As Reddy (1995, p. 19) aptly stated, "No university system in India seems to have a concept of its own optimum size."

What goes on in the name of higher education at many state universities or colleges has to be seen to be believed. At many institutions, the physical facilities are in so deplorable a state and the library and laboratory facilities so woefully inadequate that they have earned the sobriquet *academic slums* (Jayaram, 1999, p. 112). While the lack of resources is generally held responsible for the crisis—other problems do exist. For example, even prescriptions governing the minimum qualifications for the appointment and promotion of academic staff are violated; the guidelines concerning the minimum number of working days are not met;[9] the calendar of academic activities exists (if at all) only on paper; and the administrative function has virtually collapsed. All this has adversely affected the quality and standard of education imparted in India's colleges and universities.[10] One reason that the products of Indian universities are unemployed is that they are unemployable: students go out of the system with a certificate but with little systematic knowledge, practical skills, or linguistic ability.

The undue emphasis on certification rather than on the teaching and learning process—a proverbial case of the tail wagging the dog—has distorted the orientation of university education. Practically all that takes place in the university system is geared to examinations. Not surprisingly, a host of problems and scandals relate to examinations and certification. Indeed, many reforms in the university system involve examinations and certificates: weighting for internal and external evaluations, the grading system, continuous evaluation, the prevention of tampering with or faking marks cards—for example, the computerization of examination records, insertion of holograms on marks cards, lamination of degree certificates, and other innovations.

The Phenomenon of "Shadow Education"

The decline in the standards of formal education has fostered the phenomenon of "shadow education," or private tuition conducted through "coaching classes." With colleges being unable to teach effectively and students wanting to sharpen their competitive edge, parallel private tuition has become a vital and thriving sector.[11] The competition for admission into reputable institutions (like the IITs and the IIMs) and for prized courses (like medicine, engineering, and technology) is stiff, with the cutoff percentages for admission being high. For students, the alternative to government-subsidized professional education is to join private institutions that charge hefty fees. So, students appearing for various public examinations, including the School Leaving Certificate, the Pre-University Course, and national-level entrance tests invariably seek extra lessons or coaching.

Since most teachers involved in coaching classes are employed at colleges on a full-time tenured basis, private tuition raises the question of professional ethics. On the one hand, their being engaged in private tuition is a reflection of the substandard teaching the colleges are providing. On the other hand, since they know that many of their own students go for private tuition, they themselves do not take their teaching at the college seriously. Often the success of private tuition is attributed to the "leaking" of question papers by such teachers. In brief, private tuition seems to have caught the teachers and the students in a vicious circle.

Private tuition, given by individual teachers or by a group of teachers (coaching classes), is not a new phenomenon. It has now become institutionalized into a money-spinning enterprise. Institutes offering coaching classes even advertise in the newspapers and claim credit for the success of students in the merit lists of various examinations. Some reputed teachers have taken voluntary retirement or resigned from their college jobs to engage in this profitable enterprise. The dynamics of this dimension of education is seldom covered in discussions on the privatization of higher education (Tilak, 1999).

The UGC has always been critical of college and university teachers engaging private tuition but has been unable to do anything about it. State governments have been ambivalent about private tuition: while in principle opposed to it, many states have introduced special coaching classes for students belonging to the traditionally indigent sections of the population—the scheduled castes, scheduled tribes, and "other backward classes." Some states have formally banned private tuition and coaching classes, but find it impossible to implement this ban. Raids carried out by income tax authorities on the houses of some private tutors have not deterred teachers from engaging in private in private institutions. Teachers' unions are silent on the whole issue.

Supply and Demand

The structural adjustment reforms adopted in the early 1990s have had a significant impact on the demand structure of higher education—the expansion of conventional courses seems finally to have outstripped the demand for them by students. While generally the brighter students have always avoided these courses, even the mediocre ones now appear to be turning their backs on such courses. The latter invariably opt for professional courses such as medicine and technology, followed by computer science and business management. If they cannot make it to any of these courses, they would rather try their hand at some course with narrow but specialized job prospects such as packaging, plastic technology, fabric designing, or air conditioning and refrigeration, among others. The fact that good students are no longer taking basic science courses has seriously affected the academic programs of well-reputed scientific institutions such as the Indian Institute of Science (Bangalore), which has now come out with incentive schemes to urge meritorious students to take basic sciences at the graduate level.

The lack of a link between conventional courses and the job market seems to have become all too apparent to students and their parents.[12] At best, employers—not only in the private sector, but also in government—

use the conventional degrees as sieves for filtering the large number of applicants for the limited number of jobs. The unemployment situation, particularly among the conventional degree-holders, has worsened over the decades, with the government no longer able to absorb them in public employment (Jayaram, 1993a). Aggravating the situation is the economic liberalization program, which demands knowledge and skills generally not possessed by the conventional degree-holders. It is only natural that those who previously might have used the conventional courses as waiting rooms are either seeking early entry into the job market at lower levels, with the option of obtaining formal university qualifications later, or entering courses that carry better job prospects. Those who still seek conventional graduate courses are generally the leftovers and dregs or the first-generation students from rural and indigent backgrounds (the scheduled castes and tribes and other backward classes), especially those who are supported by financial assistance from the government.

While the demand for conventional courses has tapered off, the demand for professional and other allied courses has been steadily increasing, in spite of rising unemployment even among the professional degree-holders. Many educational entrepreneurs are unduly eager to offer such "moneymaking" courses in medicine, dentistry, nursing, engineering and technology, business management, computer science, and education. The latest scandal in the universities concerns the granting of permission to colleges to start these courses. Many of these institutions are inadequately equipped to offer any education, let alone professional education. The gross and brazen violation of the norms stipulated by such bodies as the Medical Council of India and the All India Council for Technical Education is a matter of serious concern.

To enhance their marketability and employment prospects, students taking professional courses try to specialize in a given field or obtain qualifications and skills in some sophisticated courses not generally offered by the universities. A glance at Indian newspapers reveals the number and variety of courses currently offered by institutions outside the sphere of the university system. These institutions, and the academic entrepreneurs who run them, seem to be extraordinarily sensitive to the range of knowledge and skills demanded by the changing market economy. They are also extremely flexible, both in the courses they offer and how they offer them. While the demand for skills and knowledge is their raison d'Ître, the maintenance of quality is their badge of success. As in any commodity market, one has to pay more for better-quality education.

It is important to note that in spite of, or essentially because of, their position outside the orbit of the university system, such institutions of higher learning have not only survived but even succeeded. Some of them have earned a niche for themselves in higher education, and even recognition from the academia and employers abroad. As statutorily established academic entities, Indian universities have never had to face competition, nor do they brook any competition either. With the liberalization of the economy and the state gradually relinquishing its responsibility for higher education the Indian university system is progressively becoming nominalized and marginalized. For its part, the UGC has been reduced to a mute witness to the gradual decaying of the university as a public institution. Whatever one's ideological predilections, it is now conceded that the future of higher education in India will be determined by the market economy and the private sector.

Ritualization of Distance Education

A reference to the concept and practice of distance education seems relevant here. In comparison to conventional university education, this mode of education can have better spread and coverage; its recurring expenditure is low and it is cost-effective; and it is flexible, both for the administration and for the students (Kulandaiswamy, 1993). Distance education was initially introduced by some universities as an innovation to provide opportunities for employed persons to pursue their studies and for those who, for various reasons, are unable to enroll in the regular courses. Its scope was later enlarged to encompass the concept of the open university. This mode is now institutionalized: almost every university has set up an office or directorate for this purpose, and states have begun establishing open universities. The Indira Gandhi National Open University (IGNOU), established in 1985, coordinates the activities concerning this type of higher education at the national level.

The concepts of open university and distance education are laudable, especially in view of their potential to increase coverage and equalize opportunities.[13] However, the way open university programs are run in most universities is far from satisfactory. The unrealistic aspirations and unfulfilled promises undermine many of the programs. The poor quality of the study materials, ineffectiveness of the contact programs, and lack of study-center facilities have virtually ritualized such programs. Not surprisingly, the failure rates are high for such courses. One wonders why universities would attempt to replicate what is more effectively being done by the IGNOU; the bitter truth is that they have found in the open university concept a "cash cow" to supplement their dwindling resources (Jayaram, 1999, p. 114).

Ineffective Quality Control

Within a decade of achieving independence, the state managers realized the need for an educational authority vested with the power to provide funds and to set and coordinate standards of higher education. Accordingly, the University Grants Commission (UGC) was established in 1956 by an act of Parliament. Modeled after the British UGC and established after World War I, the UGC in India is endowed with the responsibility of regulating academic standards. It receives money from the central government and is accountable to Parliament.

For its part, the UGC has undertaken several initiatives to provide significant support to help universities and colleges strengthen their teaching and research activities. Among other schemes supported by the UGC that deserve special mention are the Committee for Strengthening Infrastructure in Science and Technology, College Science Improvement Program, College Humanities and Social Science Improvement Program, the Faculty Improvement Program, and the Special Assistance Program. Financial assistance is extended to teachers to do research and to attend seminars, symposia, and workshops. Promising young teachers with a research proclivity are offered funds under the Career Award Scheme, and prominent senior teachers are given National Associateships. These schemes have, no doubt, injected a degree of vitality into a system that was becoming moribund. Nevertheless, the trend toward ritualization is too apparent to be ignored.

Though the UGC is expected to play a leading role in higher education, it is endowed with little power. Considering the inordinate number of universities and colleges it is required to oversee, the UGC has been virtually reduced to a fund-disbursing agency, incapable of enforcing its own recommendations (Singh, 1988). Also, given the diarchy in higher education—with the UGC exercising oversight and the state governments regulating it in practice—higher education has virtually remained an unbridled horse (Pinto, 1984, pp. 63–107). The data are not yet available on the efforts of the state UGCs (as in Madhya Pradesh) and the State Councils for Higher Education (as in Andhra Pradesh and Tamil Nadu) to address the issue of quality regulation.

The standards of academic performance in professional education are coordinated and regulated by statutory bodies such as the Indian Medical Council, the All India Council of Technical Education, the Bar Council of India, the Dental Council of India, the Pharmacy Council of India, and the Nursing Council of India; the Indian Council of Agricultural Research looks after agricultural education. The Central Advisory Board of Education is the national-level coordinating body for making general policies on education (Singh, 1993).

As a step in the direction of quality control in higher education, in keeping with the National Policy of Education (Ministry of Human Resource Development, 1986), in 1994 the UGC set up an autonomous body called the National Assessment and Accreditation Council (NAAC). Initially, the scheme of assessment and accreditation was voluntary, but the idea of an external institution doing this was not well received by universities and colleges. After all, for obvious reasons, the good ones did not need it and the bad ones did not want it. By May 2002, the NAAC had only succeeded in assessing and accrediting 261 colleges and universities. Not one of these colleges or universities is located in the backward states of north India. Now the scheme has been made mandatory, and nonaccreditated institutions will be denied developmental grants. Any institutions or be deprived of developmental grants. As of February 2004, 1,138 institutions (104 universities and 1,034 colleges) had been accredited by the NAAC. To what extent this will improve the state of affairs in higher education, even if indirectly, remains to be seen.

Constraints on Educational Planning and Implementation

An important constraint on the formulation and implementation of education policy for higher education is built into the very process of planning. In a quasi-federal polity like India, educational planning becomes a part of the overall national planning. Besides assuming the active participation of the constituent states, the national planning tends to be expenditure-oriented and overwhelmingly macro in perspective. Moreover, since higher education is the concern of more than one government department, the educational plan does not present a coordinated picture. Inevitably, all this has an adverse effect on the implementation of the plan.

Under the Constitution of India, education was largely the responsibility of the states, the central government being concerned only with certain areas like coordination and determination of standards in technical and higher education. In January 1977, through the 42nd Amendment, the central government was empowered to legislate on education concurrently with the states. Though the central government thereby established supremacy over education, the hopes of reform that this amendment aroused failed to materialize. With the gradual deterioration of the relationship between the center and some states, no government at the center can confidently take any bold steps in the realm of education.

The absence of a single machinery to look after higher education planning has often been noted. Responsibility for higher education is divided among various central government departments (e.g., education, finance, health, social welfare, and technology), with the state governments' involvement being only peripheral. The state governments pass the buck to the universities, which being totally dependent on state funding plead their inability to take on this responsibility. Even if state governments were able to draft an excellent plan for higher education, they can hardly be assured of its implementation given their dependence on the central government for funds.

The Decline of the Academic Profession[14]

One consequence of the rapid expansion of higher education, especially in the 1970s and 1980s, was the unprecedented demand for teachers. An increasing number of postgraduates churned out by the state university system found in teaching an easy employment avenue. The adverse consequences of the reckless manner in which teachers were recruited and allowed to function soon became evident. In its all India sample survey of teachers and students in higher education and members of the wider community, the National Commission on Teachers (NCT) recorded the "widespread feeling that no profession has suffered such downgrading as the teaching profession." This it found reflected in "the low esteem given to the profession and the unfavorable image of teachers held by parents, students and by the people at large." What is more pathetic, "even members of the teaching community have a low esteem of their own profession" (NCT, 1985, p. 21). The NCT's observations referred to the situation in 1983–1985, and there is no evidence suggesting that the situation has improved since then.

Studies on college teachers have invariably stressed the sad deficiency of academic preparation for and declining commitment to the profession. The NCT (1985) also bemoaned the fact that most teachers are simply making a living rather than following a vocation. This has, no doubt, a lot to do with the deplorable standards obtaining at the postgraduate level. More important, however, is the fact that for decades most master's degree-holders easily found employment in colleges, and even in universities, with absolutely no training in or orientation to teaching and with doubtful aptitude for that vocation.

To arrest this trend and to ensure proficiency in the subject and aptitude for teaching or research on the part of candidates aspiring to become teachers, the UGC introduced the scheme of the National Eligibility Test (NET), which is held twice a year. Many state governments have been permitted by the UGC to conduct a State Level Eligibility Test (SLET), which is treated as equivalent to the NET. The standard of the SLET has been so diluted in some states, that the UGC has been forced to withdraw the permission granted to the states concerned to conduct the SLET.[15] This seems to suggest that despite the laudable objectives with which the UGC introduces innovations, when it comes to implementation at the state, university, or college level, there is a tendency to scuttle those innovations.

The Academic Staff College (ASC), instituted in selected universities, has met a similar fate.[16] The ASCs were entrusted with conducting programs for properly orienting the people entering the profession of teaching and improving the knowledge and skills of those already in the profession. To instill a sense of seriousness, an element of compulsion has also been introduced: those entering the profession are required to attend an "orientation course" before they complete their probation period. Those in service are required to attend two "refresher courses" to become eligible for career advancement or promotion. As with all initiatives carrying an element of compulsion, the original objectives behind the establishment of ASCs have been set aside and the courses have been ritualized.

The structural adjustment reforms combined with the changing market forces have had a profound impact on academia. Not only have the prospects for employment in the academic profession become dim, but job security, which was once taken for granted in the academic profession, is becoming increasingly problematic.[17]

Most state governments have imposed an embargo on the recruitment of teachers. This has meant a freeze on the establishment of state-supported colleges, a drop in the number of permanent teachers in existing colleges, and redeployment of teachers through a policy of transfers. Besides, most governments have also introduced "voluntary retirement schemes" (giving incentives to teachers to retire early from permanent service), and some state governments have reduced or are contemplating reducing the retirement age for teachers.

The downsizing of the academic profession through freezes on recruitment, redeployment of excess staff, appointment of guest lecturers, and other measures is now a pan-Indian phenomenon. Moreover, it is not confined to the conventional liberal science colleges, but has been strongly advocated in technical education as well. However, in burgeoning fields such as computer science, information technology, and biotechnology, where the expansion has been most rapid, there is a dearth of qualified teachers. The problem of teacher shortage is most acute in medical education.[18]

Be that as it may, the academic profession does not have much achievement of which to boast. Most teachers do not avail themselves of the opportunities for professional development; the research output of teachers is low; outside of some universities and the IITs and IIMs, peer review or student evaluation of teachers is virtually nonexistent; and "self-appraisal" by teachers, as recommended by the UGC, has either not been introduced or is perfunctorily done and, as such, has seldom formed the basis of any action.

Interestingly, teachers' unions are no longer strong. Even the All India Federation of University and College Teachers Organizations (AIFUCTO) does not command the mass support it once did. The strike continues to be the predominant mode of protest of teachers' unions. Still, given how the government has dealt with strikes by much stronger unions of employees in other sectors during the last few years, teachers cannot take the material success of their strike for granted. Leaving aside all-India actions, even state-level agitations are running out of steam. It appears that whatever strength teachers' unions manifest is due not to any intrinsic qualities but rather to the soft attitude of the government toward them. It was only during the Emergency era (1975–1977) that teacher unionism was suppressed and their leaders jailed. But that period was the nadir of civil liberties in the country, when the darkness of the eclipse of law spared none (see Jayaram, 1992, p. 167).

Teachers have often blamed inadequate salaries and unattractive service conditions for the deterioration in the status of the academic profession. With the major revision of pay scales in 1998, following the Rastogi Committee Report, the teachers have obtained the best deal possible as regards salary. While the UGC pay package has been accepted in principle all over the country, there are significant variations in its implementation by different states. While some states have postponed the date of implementation, a few have not paid the arrears accruing from delayed implementation of the scales. Thus, the gross salary of different categories of teachers in terms of their institutional affiliation is not the same across the country. Even so, the increased gross salary of the teachers has brought practically every teacher into the income tax category.

Furthermore, to give adequate and suitable opportunities for vertical mobility to teachers at multiple stages in their career, the UGC has incorporated a career advancement scheme based on the professional development of teachers. While this scheme is well thought out, its effective implementation cannot be taken for granted, especially considering the experience of the now abolished merit-based promotion scheme.

Ironically, the improvements in pay scales and service conditions have come when the profession is in decline. Teachers are largely happy with the pay package, but they are also worried about the gradual withdrawal of state patronage from higher education.

TRENDS AND CHALLENGES

Decline of State Patronage

While public investment in education in India has always been inadequate for meeting the needs of "education for all,"[19] all along, higher education has been highly subsidized by the state (Tilak, 1993). Structural adjustment has meant a drastic cut in public expenditure on higher education: between 1980–1990 and 1994–1995, the share of higher education in development (plan) expenditure decreased from 12.6 to 6 percent, whereas the share of higher education in maintenance (nonplan) expenditure declined from 14.2 to 11 percent (Tilak, 1996). The annual growth rate of public expenditure on university and higher education, which was 13.1 percent between 1980–1981 and 1985–1986, had fallen to 7.8 percent between 1980–1981 and 1995–1996 (Shariff & Ghosh, 2000, p. 1400).[20]

Thus, the state, which had hitherto been the dominant partner in funding higher education, is finding it increasingly difficult even to maintain the same level of funding for higher education. There is no gainsaying the fact that financial constraint does not affect all sectors of higher education equally: invariably, nonprofessional courses are more adversely affected than their professional counterparts (Varghese, 2000, p. 22). Furthermore, the efforts to privatize higher education by encouraging private agencies to set up institutions of higher learning have enjoyed limited success in general education and nonprofessional courses. Thus, state universities and their affiliated colleges are the ones in financial crisis.

The gradual decline in state support of higher education has made it impossible to address the needed reforms within the conventional higher education system. The National Policy on Education (Ministry of Education, 1985) and its Program of Action (Ministry of Human Resource Development, 1986), and their review by the Acharya Ramamurti Committee (Ministry of Human Resource Development, 1991) were all prestructural adjustment reform initiatives. Neither the phenomenal fall in the demand for conventional courses in the B.A. and B.Sc. streams, nor the remarkable spurt in the demand for courses in such areas as computer science and information technology, biotechnology, and management studies, was anticipated.

Private Initiatives in Higher Education

The void created by the waning state funding for higher education is now being filled by two types of private entrepreneurial initiatives. First, there are the private colleges and institutes that are formally affiliated with a university. They offer courses approved by a university, and their students write examinations conducted by that university; the successful among them are given degree certificates by the university. While the institutions belonging to the minority communities enjoy certain administrative privileges granted by the Indian Constitution, in all academic matters the private colleges and institutes are governed by the university. Many of these private colleges get financial assistance amounting to from 80 to 85 percent of their expenditures; besides that, they are permitted to collect a small fee from the students to make up the balance. As such, these colleges must observe the grant-in-aid code formulated by the government. At the other end are the unaided private colleges that have to generate their own financial resources. They have much leeway concerning administration and the collection of fees from the students. Purely private universities of the American type are as yet an alien concept in India.[21]

The second type of initiative consists of the privately owned and managed colleges, institutes, and academies that conduct courses outside the purview of Indian universities. Typically, they offer courses in such areas as aviation and pilot training, glass technology, plastic technology, packaging, corporate secretarial training, marketing management, financial management, foreign trade, portfolio management, operations research, hotel management and catering technology, tourism administration, software marketing, computer applications, fashion design, and beauty aids. Unlike the diploma courses offered by the polytechnics, some of these courses offered by well-known institutes are accredited with professional bodies in the area, many outside the country.

Another educational innovation among the private initiatives is the concept of the "twinning program." This program involves collaboration between two educational systems, with both the systems taking responsibility for teaching and training of students and one of them holding the right to award educational credentials. The program may involve collaboration between an Indian institution and a system abroad (international educational collaboration), or between two systems of education within the country (intranational educational collaboration).

International educational collaboration is slowly gathering momentum. In India, it was originally devised as a way out of the governmental stranglehold on private institutions of higher learning and the enervating rigidity of the university system. Such international educational collaboration is not, however, confined to professional education. To meet the demand for high-quality first-degree education, especially in such areas as computer science, some private colleges have entered into twinning programs with universities abroad.

Such international educational collaboration involving twinning programs is significantly different from the more direct marketing endeavors of foreign educational establishments. Several universities—not necessarily well-reputed ones—in Anglophone countries including Australia, Canada, New Zealand, the United Kingdom, and the United States are enrolling Indian students for their educational programs. Often there is a distance-education component, but most of them have arrangements with respected institutes in the country for offering contact programs for students taking these foreign university examinations. Some of these universities even hold educational fairs in Indian cities to familiarize those interested in pursuing their educational programs.

All this necessarily implies opening the sphere of Indian higher education to foreign educational establishments. For more than a century, the well-to-do in India have been sending their children and wards abroad for higher education, with the most talented students obtaining fellowships from the Indian government or from foreign foundations. Given the globalization of higher education, such facilities are now being brought into the country. This is akin, no doubt, to the operation of multinational companies in industry and business, and as such, the phenomenon cannot be expected to be free of socioeconomic costs.

It is well known that such high-quality education involving multinational arrangements, often involving job placements, is expensive, especially as compared to the low-cost education offered by Indian colleges and universities. The concept of the twinning program is now taking root intranationally, too. Such programs have effectively combined the advantages of regular and distance modes of higher education. It is also significant that the educational institutions involved are putting their physical, material, and human resources to optimum use.

In light of these developments, it is unfortunate that the concept of autonomous colleges has not been put into practice to the extent that it deserves. In the light of the crisis confronting the university system, the need for liberating the better affiliated colleges from their bondage to the university can hardly be exaggerated. The National Policy on Education (1985–1986) recommended the granting of autonomy to selected colleges, and the UGC endorsed this recommendation. By 1990, 500 colleges were envisaged to be given an autonomous status; by 1996 only 113 colleges had been granted this status (AIU, 1997, p. xi). Vested interests among university managers and the politicians and bureaucrats of state governments have worked to ensure that this innovation remains virtually grounded.

The Uncertain Future

The structural adjustment reforms adopted by the government since 1990 have necessitated a policy of disinvestment of the public sector and open privatization in various spheres of the economy. For higher education, however, the government is hesitant to pursue this policy vigorously. Rather, a different strategy is in operation. There is now a moratorium on the establishment of new educational institutions (especially of the conventional type) in the public sector and an imposition of ceilings on student numbers in existing institutions. Academia is being downsized through a freeze on recruitment, reductions in the number of teachers, and rationalization of teachers' work. There is a proposal to introduce the contract system for hiring teachers in the future. At the same time, self-financing colleges (especially in areas of professional education) are being encouraged and the proposal to raise fees in public higher education institutions is on the anvil.[22] These measures, it is feared, will increase the cost of higher education and make it less accessible to the masses, and, given the government's inability to regulate the private educational institutions, adversely affect the quality of education (Kumar & Sharma, 2003).

Closely related to these trends is the internationalization of higher education referred to earlier. This is in conformity with the policy of liberalization of education as a service sector under the General Agreement on Trade in Services. As expected, in April 2004 India "opened up" the education sector, although the relevant legislation has yet to be enacted. Foreign universities and educational institutions (especially from Anglophone countries like Australia, Canada, the United Kingdom, and the United States) are likely to offer competition to the existing educational institutions in the country. It is feared that this might once again result in draining of resources from India as well as strong cultural and political influence by the foreign countries (see Kumar & Sharma, 2003, p. 607).

The lack of a coherent long-term policy perspective characterizes higher education in India today. Ad hoc policies and the multiplicity of actors—the central and state governments, the UGC, the All India Council for Technical Education, the universities and colleges, and the emergent private sector—dealing with the unfolding exigencies in higher education in different ways portend an uncertain future.

CONCLUSION

The conventional university system in India, confronted as it is with a systemic crisis, has proved itself to be incapable of introducing any significant educational innovation or implementing any effective educational reform. Given the mounting pressure for increasing accessibility and democratization, the trend in the universities is toward reducing everything to the lowest common denominator, or leveling down quality rather than raising it. The Indian university system is extraordinarily rigid and resistant to change. The impetus to change does not come from within the system. When experiments or innovations are introduced from outside, they are resisted; if enforced, they are ritualized. The fate of such innovations as the merit promotion scheme, faculty-improvement program, vocationalization of courses, semesterization of courses, curriculum development centers, annual reports, college development councils, academic staff colleges, and refresher and orientation courses is too well known to warrant elaboration. It is indeed ironic that higher education, which is expected to function as an agency of change, should itself be so resistant to it.

The void created by the paralysis and drift of the conventional university system is being filled by private entrepreneurial initiatives. Thus, significant educational innovations and experiments are currently taking place in institutions outside the university orbit and in the private sector.

In view of the rapid expansion of and increasing variety in knowledge and skills, there is enormous scope for educational innovations and initiatives. Private institutions have been more responsive to the demands of the economy and industry and the changing employment environment. They have also shown their ability to match relevance with flexibility in both costs and regulation. This does not, however, mean that all private institutions are necessarily good. Some of them are brazenly commercial establishments out to swindle gullible people looking for better-quality education at affordable prices.

Privatization of higher education is viewed as a fledgling but welcome trend—something higher education requires to sustain creativity, adaptability, and quality. The economic trail of liberalization and globalization demands it. Considering the chronic paucity of resources, gradually unburdening itself of the additional responsibility for higher education may be advisable for the government. Instead, it could better utilize the scarce resources for realizing the goal of universalization of elementary education and for improving the quality of school education.

Privatization of higher education, however, does not come without social costs. In a polity such as India's, where structural inequalities have been entrenched, privatization is sure to reinforce existing inequalities and to foster inegalitarian tendencies. This necessitates the social supervision of the private sector and effective measures for offsetting imbalances resulting from unequal economic capacities of the population. Thus, we again confront a dilemma: theoretically, how do we advance equality without sacrificing quality? Practically, how do we control the private sector without curbing its creativity and initiative? That is the challenge in higher education at the beginning of the new millennium.

NOTES

1. In writing this chapter I have drawn on my earlier work on higher education in India (Jayaram 1990; 1991; 1997; 1999; 2002).

2. British rule gradually supplanted the precolonial indigenous system of education consisting of *pathashalas*, *tols*, and *madrasahas* by stopping financial aid. The Indian urban elite, too, welcomed English education, as it was viewed not only as an avenue to jobs but also an instrument for social and political regeneration of India (Basu, 2002, p. 168).

3. It is significant that, in spite of the Education Commission's (1964–1966) (Ministry of Education, 1971, p. 527) emphasis on the need "to move energetically in the direction of adopting the regional languages as media of education at the university stage," English has not only persisted but is still the predominant medium of instruction. A review of the trends in the medium of instruction in higher education concluded that "a complete switchover to the regional languages as media of instruction at

all levels and in all courses is not a possibility in the foreseeable future" (Jayaram, 1993b, p. 112).

4. The report set forth eight premises: "(1) strong central and state governments that would be committed to educational development, (2) stable political conditions, (3) declining birth rate, (4) a growth of national income at 6 percent per annum, (5) a lessening of social tensions due to effective development, (6) a strengthened and revitalized bureaucracy, (7) a committed and competent body of teachers, and (8) a community of students dedicated to the pursuit of learning" (quoted in Naik, 1982, p. vi). With most of these premises remaining mere wishful thinking, the thrust of reform was expectedly doomed.

5. Following the 1986 Program of Action of the National Education Policy (Ministry of Human Resource Development, 1986), in most states this stage has been brought within the school system. In a few states, such as Karnataka, this has yet to be completed, as the existing school system is unable to take on the additional stage, and there is the problem of reallocation of teachers.

6. Those who have successfully completed a diploma course in the first track can enter the engineering course midway.

7. Introducing the volume on *Higher Education Reform in India*, Altbach and Chitnis (1993, p. 12) write: "We are not optimistic that systemic reform is possible in the Indian context. The system, having grown . . . to an immense size, leads a life of its own. To basically alter its direction or configuration would require unprecedented political will and the exercise of considerable power.... Improvements at the margin are probably all that can be expected."

8. In 1991–1992, those enrolling in undergraduate courses, mostly in affiliated colleges, accounted for 88.10 percent of the enrollments in higher education. While those enrolled in postgraduate courses constituted 9.50 percent, those enrolled in research (1.10 percent) and diploma/certificate courses (1.30 percent) formed only minuscule percentages. Coursewise, those enrolled in the arts (40.4 percent), science (19.7 percent), and commerce (21.9 percent) together accounted for 82 percent of the students in higher education. The enrollment in other courses was as follows: agriculture, 1.1 percent; education, 2.3 percent; engineering and technology, 4.9 percent; law, 5.3 percent; medicine, 3.4 percent; and veterinary science, 0.3 percent.

9. Indiresan (1993, p. 313) quotes a study conducted by the National Institute of Educational Planning and Administration (New Delhi) on the work ethos in colleges that found that the average number of working days to be as low as eighty-seven compared with the UGC–stipulated mandatory 180 working days.

10. Lacking any objective measurement of higher education standards over a period, it is understandably difficult to determine precisely the nature and extent of deterioration. Nevertheless, there is no denying that India's standards compare unfavorably with the average standards in educationally advanced countries. The Education Commission had drawn attention to this as early as in the mid-1960s (Ministry of Education, 1971, p. 66). No wonder, then, that degrees awarded by Indian universities are not regarded by many foreign universities as equivalent to their degrees. In fact, employers in India, including government agencies, are wary of these degrees.

11. More college teachers than university teachers are engaged in private tuition, and it is in greater demand for science and mathematics courses and in the English language.

12. Being aware of the disorientation of the conventional courses, the UGC had recommended the introduction of job-oriented courses at the first-degree level. Many universities have introduced a job orientation component in their undergraduate curriculum mainly to avail themselves of the funds provided by the UGC for the purpose. Thus, this UGC initiative has been ritualized.

13. It is important to note that while the expansion of the conventional university system has been described as phenomenal, in 1997 the system was estimated to cover barely 7.2 percent of the population in the relevant age group (ages seventeen to twenty-three); this was "well below half of the world enrollment ratio of 17.4 percent" (Kumar & Sharma, 2003, p. 605).

14. This section is an abridgment of a detailed analysis of the decline of the academic profession in India presented in Jayaram (2002).

15. As a screening mechanism, the NET is a step in the right direction. Nevertheless, inadequate academic preparation of teachers for discharging their professional responsibilities continues. Professions such as architecture, law, and medicine require their prospective recruits to undergo a specified period of internship. Even a high school teacher is expected to acquire the bachelor of education (B.Ed.) degree. To become a lecturer in a college or university, however, no prior training or experience is necessary.

16. By 1994, 45 ASCs had been started and 71,385 teachers had attended the orientation (27,675) and refresher (43,710) courses (Chalam, 1994, p. 43). While these numbers appear to be impressive, the functioning of the ASCs is far from being satisfactory (Indiresan, 1993, p. 317).

17. Only about 70 percent of university and college teachers have permanent employment with all statutory benefits. The others are either "temporary" (with no guarantee of continuation) or "ad hoc" (appointed against a leave vacancy for a short period) lecturers. Besides, new categories of teachers such as "part-time" lecturers (who teach for a specified number of teaching hours in a week) and "guest" lecturers (who help the college/department "to complete portions of the syllabus") have been added. Such teachers are paid on an "hourly basis," and they do not enjoy other privileges that go with a permanent or even a temporary or an ad hoc teacher.

18. In medical education other considerations inhibit qualified persons taking up teaching jobs. At the end of long years of study, the doctors holding M.B.B.S. and M.S./M.D. qualifications get the same salary as those who have a M.A./M.Sc. and Ph.D. in sciences and the humanities. Also, the service rules in the government colleges are archaic and despotic, and there are restrictions on private practice.

19. An international comparison revealed that in a list of 86 countries, India (with an expenditure on education of 3.8 percent of the gross national product [GNP]) ranked only thirty-second in terms of public expenditure on education as a proportion of GNP (Shariff & Ghosh, 2000, p. 1396).

20. It is significant to note that the government of India's discussion paper on "Government Subsidies in India" (1997) classified elementary education as a "merit good" and higher education as a "non merit good" warranting a drastic reduction of government subsidies. The Ministry of Finance has since reclassified higher education into a category called "merit 2 goods" that need not be subsidized at the same level as merit goods (Tilak, 2002, p. 12).

21. The bill to provide for the establishment of private universities, introduced in Rajya Sabha (the upper house of Parliament) in August 1995, is still pending (as of

June 2004). While the government is keen on privatization, the private sector is unhappy with some clauses of the bill, such as those concerning the formation of a permanent endowment fund of Rs. 100 million (about U.S.$2 million), the provision of full scholarships to 30 percent of the students, and the government monitoring and regulation of the system (Tilak, 2002, p. 12).

22. In their Report, Mukesh Ambani and Kumaramangalam Birla (2000, pp. 85, 90), two private-sector industrialists who headed the committee appointed by the Prime Minister's Council on Trade and Industry, have recommended the full cost recovery from students of public higher education institutions and immediate privatization of the entire higher education system, except those areas involving "disciplines that have no market orientation."

References

Altbach, P. G., & Chitnis, S. (1993). Introduction. In S. Chitnis & P. G. Altbach (Eds.), *Higher education reform in India: Experience and perspectives* (pp. 11–12). New Delhi: Sage.

Ambani, M., & Birla, K. (2000). *A policy framework for reforms in education*. (Report submitted to the Prime Minister's Council on Trade and Industry. Available at http://www.nic.in/pmcouncil/reports/education.)

Ashby, E., & Anderson, M. (1966). *Universities: British, Indian, and African*. London: Weidenfield & Nicholson.

Association of Indian Universities (AIU). (1997). *Universities handbook* (27th ed.). New Delhi: Association of Indian Universities.

Basu, A. (2002). Indian higher education: Colonialism and beyond. In P. G. Altbach & V. Selvaratnam (Eds.), *From dependence to autonomy: The development of Asian universities* (pp. 167–186). Chestnut Hill, MA: Center for International Higher Education, Boston College.

Bhatt, B. D., & Aggarwal, J. C. (Eds.). (1969). *Educational documents in India*. New Delhi: Arya Book Depot.

Chalam, K. S. (1994). *Performance of academic staff colleges in India*. Visakhapatnam: Andhra University Press and Publications.

Dube, S. C. (1988). Higher education and social change. In A. Singh & G. D. Sharma (Eds.), *Higher education in India: The social context* (pp. 46–53). Delhi: Konark.

Indiresan, J. (1993). Quest for quality: Interventions versus impact. In S. Chitnis & P. G. Altbach (Eds.), *Higher education reform in India: Experience and perspectives* (pp. 309–333). New Delhi: Sage.

Jayaram, N. (1990). *Sociology of education in India*. Jaipur: Rawat.

Jayaram, N. (1991). Higher education in India: State policy and social constraints. *Higher Education Policy, 4*, 36–40.

Jayaram, N. (1992). India. In B. S. Cooper (Ed.), *Labor relations in education: An international perspective* (pp. 157–169). Westport, CT: Greenwood.

Jayaram, N. (1993a). The education-employment mismatch: A sociological appraisal of the Indian experience. In A. Yogev & J. Dronkers (Eds.), *International perspectives on education and society: Vol. 3. Education and social change* (pp. 123–143). Greenwich, CT: Jai.

Jayaram, N. (1993b). The language question in higher education: Trends and issues. In S. Chitnis & P. G. Altbach (Eds.), *Higher education reform in India: Experience and perspectives* (pp. 84–114). New Delhi: Sage.

Jayaram, N. (1997). India. In G. A. Postiglione & G. C. L. Mak (Eds.), *Asian higher education: An international handbook and reference guide* (pp. 75–91). Westport, CT: Greenwood.

Jayaram, N. (1999). Reorientation of higher education in India: A prognostic essay. In S. Aroni & J. Hawkins (Eds.), *Partnerships in development: Technology and social sciences, universities, industry and government.* Proceedings of the Sixth INRUDA International Symposium on the Role of Universities in Developing Areas, Paris, June 8–11, 1999) (pp. 111–118). Paris: Ecole spéciale des travaux publics.

Jayaram, N. (2002). The fall of the guru: The decline of the academic profession in India. In P. G. Altbach (Ed.), *The decline of the guru: The academic profession in developing and middle-income countries* (pp. 207–239). Chestnut Hill, MA: Center for International Higher Education, Boston College.

Kulandaiswamy, V. C. (1993). The open university. In S. Chitnis & P. G. Altbach (Eds.), *Higher education reform in India: Experience and perspectives* (pp. 365–399). New Delhi: Sage.

Kumar, T. R., & Sharma, V. (2003). Downsizing higher education: An emergent crisis. *Economic and Political Weekly, 38*(7), 603–607.

Ministry of Education, Government of India. (1971). *Education and national development. Report of the Education Commission, 1964–1966.* New Delhi: National Council of Educational Research and Training (Reprint Edition).

Ministry of Education, Government of India. (1985). *Challenge of education: A policy perspective.* Delhi: Controller of Publications.

Ministry of Human Resource Development, Government of India. (1986). *Program of action: National policy on education.* New Delhi: Controller of Publications.

Ministry of Human Resource Development, Government of India. (1991). *Towards an enlightened and humane society: Report of the Committee for Review of National Policy on Education 1986.* New Delhi: Controller of Publications.

Ministry of Information and Broadcasting, Government of India. (1999). *India 1999: A reference annual.* New Delhi: Publications Division.

Naik, J. P. (1982). *The Education Commission and after.* New Delhi: Allied.

National Commission of Teachers (NCT). (1985). *Report of the National Commission on Teachers-II, 1983–1985.* New Delhi: Controller of Publications.

Pinto, M. (1984). *Federalism and higher education: The Indian experience.* Bombay: Orient Longman.

Raza, M., et al. (1985). Higher education in India: An assessment. In J. V. Raghavan (Ed.), *Higher education in the eighties* (pp. 95–173). New Delhi: Lancer International.

Reddy, G. R. 1995. *Higher education in India: Conformity, crisis and innovation.* New Delhi: Sterling.

Shariff, A., & Ghosh, P. K. (2000). Indian education scene and the public gap. *Economic and Political Weekly, 35,* 1396–1406.

Singh, A. (1988). Foundation and role of UGC. In A. Singh & G. D. Singh (Eds.), *Higher education in India: The social context* (pp. 234–251). Delhi: Konark.

Singh, A. (1993). Coordinating agencies in higher education. In S. Chitnis & P. G. Altbach (Eds.), *Higher education reform in India: Experience and perspectives* (pp. 207–242). New Delhi: Sage.

Tickoo, C. (1980). *Indian universities*. Madras: Orient Longman.

Tilak, J. B. G. (1993). Financing higher education in India. In S. Chitnis & P. G. Altbach (Eds.), *Higher education reform in India: Experience and perspectives* (pp. 41–83). New Delhi: Sage.

Tilak, J. B. G. (1996). Higher education under structural adjustment. *Journal of Indian School of Political Economy, 8*, 266–293.

Tilak, J. B. G. (1999). Emerging trends in evolving public policies in India. In P. G. Altbach (Ed.), *Private Prometheus: Private higher education and development in the 21st century* (pp. 127–153). Chestnut Hill, MA: Center for International Higher Education, Boston College.

Tilak, J. B. G. (2002). Privatization of higher education in India. *International Higher Education, 29*, 11–13.

Varghese, N. V. (2000). Reforming education financing. *Seminar, 494*, 20–25.

PART III

Economic Prosperity and
Academic Development

5

Japanese Higher Education

Contemporary Reform and

the Influence of Tradition

Motohisa Kaneko

While Japan narrowly escaped colonization, it had to build a modern nation strong enough to survive in a world dominated by Western imperialism. To do so, it had to introduce Western technologies and institutions in every sphere of society. Higher education was one of the critical areas on which the growth of the nation depended.

Initially, the government introduced Western models of higher education through trial and error. These early developments gradually led to growing popular demand for higher education, requiring the government to modify the system and eventually deviate from Western models. After World War II, Japan introduced various aspects of the American model, which later underwent considerable transformation during the years of expansion. The selective introduction of Western models and their adaptation through dynamic interactions between market forces and government policies have been the leitmotif throughout Japanese higher education history. In the twenty-first century, Japanese higher education appears to be entering a new phase—probably with yet another variation of the leitmotif.

Where did those dynamics originate and how did they evolve over time? What are the consequences of such a pattern of development, and what are the future challenges in the twenty-first century? How can Japan respond to those challenges? These questions, which the Japanese are asking themselves, form the focus of this chapter.

HISTORICAL PERSPECTIVES

The history of Japanese higher education spans over 130 years and can roughly be divided into three periods: institutional buildup, system integration, and postwar reform and massification—each covering about forty years. (See Table 5.1.)

Table 5.1 Phases of Development in Japanese Higher Education

1870	Institutional buildup
	Early institutions of higher education
	University of Tokyo (1877)
	Imperial University of Tokyo (1886)
1910	System integration
	1918 higher education law
	Establishment of private universities
	Two-sector, two-tier system
	Expansion of enrollments
1950	Postwar reform and massification
	Postwar education reform
	New universities (1947)
	Rapid expansion of enrollments (1960–1975)
	Stabilization
	Current cost subsidy for private institutions (1976)
1990	Structural reforms

Institutional Buildup

Prior to the Meiji Restoration, the history of higher education in Japan had been long but thin. Institutions of higher learning existed for religious or administrative leaders, but their size and scope of learning were limited. Moreover, Japan did not develop a mandarin class as in China or Korea that would have required some form of advanced learning. In the early nineteenth century, popular demand for education started to rise among lower-class Samurai and the emerging urban merchant and artisan class. In response, various types of schools began proliferating from lower to advanced levels, raising the literacy rate substantially. However, most of the schools were small and lacked systemic links between the lower levels and higher education. Lacking the modern institutions to organize the latent demand into a national education system encompassing basic to advanced levels, Japan would have to wait until the Meiji Restoration.

After the Meiji Restoration of 1868, the new government introduced modern social institutions in Japan. The earliest design of the education system resembled that of France, where "university" signified not only a higher learning institution but also the whole national school system. Thus, the early University of Tokyo was designed not only as a place of higher learning but also as the administrative body for the national education system. The highly structured model of public education must have appealed to the leaders of the fledgling nation. In a development closely resembling the French *grandes écoles*, a number of government departments established their own ministerial schools for advanced and specialized studies: the Ministry of Law, for example, had its own law school, and the Ministry of Industries had its college of engineering.

After ten years of trial and error, however, this model was basically abandoned. The Napoleonic model of public education was too rigid to allow for the gradual implementation of a system of education. In higher education, it proved to be more efficient to consolidate the places of advanced learning into a single institution. The University of Tokyo was reestablished in 1877 as the central institution for advanced learning, and the early ministerial specialized schools were gradually integrated into this newly established university.

How this new university should be managed was not a trivial question. The government naturally tried to control it as an administrative unit of the Ministry of Education. At the university, however, academics started demanding autonomy as a number of them returned from studying in Germany, bringing along the idea of academic autonomy. It should be noted that in the latter half of the nineteenth century the German model strongly influenced higher education reform in France and in the United States. Moreover, it also became evident that the government could not closely control specialized teaching and research. Greater autonomy was gradually given to the university (Terasaki, 1979). In 1886, the University of Tokyo was reorganized into the Imperial University of Tokyo and positioned as the center for learning and research, with a substantial degree of autonomy given to the institution as a whole and to the professors. Nevertheless, this did not completely follow the German model. In contrast to German universities, which consistently resisted the pressure to incorporate practical subjects, the Imperial University had a College of Engineering as one of its original five colleges and soon added a College of Agriculture (Ben-David, 1977). In this respect, Japan adopted forms common to Scottish and American universities (Nakayama, 1989).

Besides the Imperial University—the center of academic research and learning—other types of schools were established for training the midlevel professional workforce. These institutions were focused on providing technical education that could be attained in a relatively short period, and at lower cost, than was possible at the university. Unlike the university, these specialized schools did not require students to have advanced ability in foreign languages, for all the instruction took place in Japanese. These schools constituted one of the significant segments of the prewar higher education system.

Significant numbers of educational institutions were established not by the government but rather by groups of citizens, teachers, or missionaries. Prominent institutions included Keio, founded by a leading social activist and author; Waseda, founded by political leaders and journalists; and Doshisha, founded by a Christian missionary. Some of these private institutions had high academic standards and called themselves universities. However, they were only given the legal status of specialized schools by the Meiji government, whose policy was to dominate institutions of higher learning and research.

System Integration

By the beginning of the twentieth century, after the stage of institutional buildup, Japan had embarked on an initial stage of economic growth. By World War I, the national school system had nearly been established and primary education almost universalized. Enrollment at secondary schools had increased, and the demand for access to higher education started expanding. Meanwhile, the government increased the number of specialized schools as a means of supplying a technical workforce with fewer resources and less time than would be the case through the university. Private bodies also established specialized schools to meet the increasing demands for higher education. By the turn of the century, the entrance and graduation requirements of specialized schools had been standardized.

Against this background, during World War I the government organized a blue-ribbon council to discuss basic reforms in education. Various changes were later put into effect. Most important, from the perspective of higher education, was the 1918 higher education law, which allowed private foundations to establish universities. The private university was thus granted legitimacy as a formal sector of the higher education system.

Through these reforms, higher education in Japan became a two-sector, two-tier system. The two sectors consisted of the national (public) and private sectors. The two tiers consisted of universities, which required three years of preparatory education at "higher schools" after completing secondary school, and specialized schools, which admitted students directly from secondary school. With a few modifications, this structure characterized the pre–World War II higher education system. Amano argues that the two-tier and two-sector system in the prewar period eventually provided the basis for massification in the postwar period (Amano, 1986).

With this framework in place, higher education in Japan kept growing up until World War II. The number of imperial universities increased to seven, and the system included a substantial number of national colleges with university status. There were also a number of private universities. By 1940, the number of universities had increased to 47, with an enrollment of almost 82,000 students. Specialized schools, both public and private, had increased in number to 200 by 1940, enrolling some 141,000 students. Japanese higher education was already on the threshold of the mass stage of higher education.

Postwar Reform and Massification

After Japan's defeat in World War II, the Japanese education system was transformed drastically under U.S. occupation. The prewar school system that was divided into academic and vocational tracks, beyond the primary level, was transformed into a single-track system following a 6-3-3-4 sequence. This change removed a significant institutional barrier to meeting the demand for higher education. As a result of the integration of the two tiers, the universities' preparatory schools (higher schools) and many high-quality specialized schools were transformed into new universities. It was through this process that the number of universities increased substantially, thus creating the basis for expansion from the supply side.

The government faced serious difficulties, however, in securing the necessary financial resources in a devastated economy. The highest policy priority was directed toward consolidating the new national universities. To secure enough resources, financing the national institutions was integrated into the national budget. Financial autonomy given to the prewar imperial universities was curtailed through this process. For their part, meanwhile, private institutions were left without public support.

Toward the end of the 1950s, the economy began showing signs of a steady recovery, eventually accelerating the pace of growth into the 1960s. Rising income levels and expectations for future expansion of employment resulted in an unprecedented increase in popular demand for higher education. On the supply side, government policies concentrated the limited resources available for higher education on qualitative upgrading of the national universities and colleges, rather than on their quantitative increase. The frustrated demand arising from this gap had to be satisfied by expanding enrollments in the private sector of higher education. By the end of the 1960s, the private sector accounted for three-quarters of total enrollments. Total enrollments at four- and two-year institutions increased from 708,000 in 1960 to 2,086,000 in 1975, representing almost a 3-fold growth in just fifteen years. Over the same period, the participation rate increased from 8.2 percent to 27.1 percent. Japan thus jumped from the elite to the mass stage of higher education.

By the mid-1970s, the explosive expansion came to an end, reflecting partly a deceleration in economic growth and partly a shift in higher education policy. At the same time, the government set up "specialized training schools" as a new type of institution in postsecondary education. During the 1980s, many private proprietary schools were converted to this type of school. In the 1990s, participation in four-year institutions increased again primarily due to the shrinking excess demand arising from the decline of eighteen-year-olds.

Today, the level of participation in Japanese higher education ranks among the highest in the world. In 2002, 39 percent of eighteen-year-olds entered four-year institutions of higher education. If enrollments at two-year junior colleges and specialized training schools are included, more than 60 percent of the college age cohort received some kind of education beyond senior secondary school. Private institutions constitute by far the largest segment, accounting for more than 70 percent of undergraduates at four-year institutions and 91 percent at two-year institutions. About one hundred national universities, while enrolling a quarter of undergraduate students, play significant roles in research and graduate education. The remaining 3 percent of undergraduates are enrolled in municipal, or local, public institutions.

THE DYNAMICS OF DEVELOPMENT

The history briefly sketched above is characterized by the dynamic interaction between market forces and the higher education system as a social institution. The dynamics can be analyzed in terms of the interaction between the demand and supply of higher education, the strategy of the government, and the formation of boundary and internal differentiation of the higher education system.

Demand-Supply Interaction

The development of higher education can be interpreted as the product of the dynamic interaction between supply and demand of higher education in the social and economic contexts. In most European countries, the supply and demand for higher education expanded only gradually. In its long history since the Middle Ages, higher education started expanding only in the latter half of the nineteenth century in close relationship with the growth of industries and the power of modern states. At the time the West was experiencing the first wave of modern expansion, Japan introduced its first institutions of higher education.

When it was introduced, higher education was a completely alien institution in Japan—the values of Western knowledge, and the benefit to individuals, were still unclear to most of the population. Higher education was not necessarily an obvious choice among the wealthy urban merchants or landlords. It was rather among the lower-class samurai, who had lost their traditional status and jobs, that aspirations for higher education started to grow.

As modernization progressed, however, higher education rapidly became an attractive alternative for ambitious young persons. Modernization in Japan implied the creation of a small island of the modern sector that promised high wages and good working conditions in the vast ocean of low-productivity agriculture. Given the disparity, competition over employment in the modern sector became increasingly intense. Moreover, Japan as a latecomer to industrialization was able to import modern industrial organization and technology as a complete set, which could be effectively taught in schools. Under these circumstances, recruitment of employees in the modern sector was closely linked to the requisite educational background. The benefits of higher education in Japan thus exceeded those experienced in the West at a corresponding stage of development, creating aspirations, or even a "fever," for higher education. This is what Ronald Dore (1976) called the "late development effect."

As the rising popular demand for higher education gained momentum, political pressure to expand opportunities for higher education mounted. In response, in the 1910s, the government finally ushered in the educational reforms mentioned earlier. Nonetheless, the extent of the demand for higher education was constrained by the small size of the middle class with sufficient resources.

After World War II, postwar reforms and economic development introduced significant changes in Japan. The renewed ideal of democracy, together with the decline of the prewar urban middle class and landlord class due to hyperinflation and land reform, produced a society much more egalitarian in ideology and in actual income distribution. Moreover, the steady growth in family income in the 1960s allowed more families to have sufficient financial capacities to send their children to institutions of higher education. Hence, for a large proportion of the population a middle-class lifestyle, including white-collar occupations and higher education, became something obtainable for the children. It was also expected that the demand for college graduates would grow in subsequent years. These factors combined to induce the phenomenal expansion in popular demand for higher education.

The government, preoccupied with the need for qualitative improvement, was reluctant to allow for the expansion of supply. Popular demand for more places in higher education, however, eventually won the political battle. At the beginning of the 1960s, the then ruling Liberal Democratic Party opted for a less stringent policy on the expansion of private institutions (Pempel, 1978). That induced a tremendous proliferation of private institutions and rising enrollments in the private sector. Private institutions responded to this change quickly. Many existing universities added new faculties and acted to increase their "prescribed size of enrollment," even admitting students beyond the set limit, to gain financial stability. Numerous new institutions were established, and they eventually followed the same pattern as the older ones. The private sector of higher education thus achieved a tremendous quantitative expansion, but that induced sharp qualitative disparities between the public and the private sectors. Against this background, the government implemented a series of policies around 1975, basically reversing the laissez-faire policy of the previous fifteen years. It introduced the "current cost subsidy to private institutions," which allowed the government to subsidize a portion of current costs at private institutions. At the same time, the government moved to restrain the expansion of private institutions. These measures were expected to improve educational conditions at private institutions and to diminish the disparity between national and private institutions.

Since 1975, the participation rate at four-year universities showed a slight decline for males and unchanging numbers for females. These trends were due in part to the stagnating demand for higher education and in part to the government policy of limiting the supply of places in universities. The policy of reducing enrollments at four-year institutions was compensated by the introduction of special training schools, which the government established to provide vocational training for two or three years after high school. The special training schools soon attracted a substantial number of students, enrolling almost 30 percent of high school graduates. In the 1990s, the enrollment rate at four-year institutions started increasing again.

During this period, the changes in the demand for higher education constituted the major driving force. Higher education policies dealt mainly with the problem of how to respond to the demands. The effectiveness of government policies lay in its ability to restrain or allow the private sector to respond to the demands.

The Government and the Market

The developments described above created the basic landscape of Japanese higher education: a large private sector enrolling three-quarters of undergraduate students. This situation, however, created a strain between the government and private institutions.

While the concept of *private* institutions of higher education was evidently influenced by the American system, it was at the same time deeply rooted in the power structure of Meiji Japan. The Meiji regime, as a confederation of old feudal states, won the downfall of the Tokugawa Shogunate militarily to acquire power and tax revenues; it justified its power as the agent for building a modern nation strong enough to compete against the West. Nonetheless, there was a sizable middle class of landowners and urban merchants that were excluded from the social networks dominated by the Meiji government, and this group had considerable wealth, influence, and intellectual capital. Moreover, the ideology of democracy had a significant impact on the society. Despite its

popular image as a powerful monolithic state dominated by the military
and the bureaucracy, the Meiji regime had to be responsive to the demands from various segments of the society.

The national education system was not only the means of introducing
modern culture and technology, but also a way of integrating the whole
nation and consolidating the power of the government. The University
of Tokyo, later the Imperial University, was put at the apex of this system
to attract talented young people who would, with their critical skills and
knowledge for nation building, serve the state and the government. Meanwhile, a few private institutions had a substantial pool of talent and supporters among the urban middle class, landlords, and political dissidents.
Some other private institutions served a large number of students who
wanted more accessible opportunities for higher education. Whereas government policy was to restrict the title of "university" to those established by the government, political support for private institutions remained substantial.

Naturally, the dual structure including both public and private sectors
engendered serious conflicts. The complexity of the relationship between
the government and private institutions can be seen in some of the newspaper articles in the early Meiji period concerning tuition levels at the
national institutions of higher education (Kaneko, 1992). Supporters of
private institutions denounced the unequal treatment of national and
private institutions and demanded subsidies for private institutions as
well as an increase in the tuition at the national institutions. To this, a
person on the government side stated candidly: "if the tuition levels are
raised, the applicants to national institutions will decrease, which implies that the pool from which to choose talented young people will shrink"
(Editorial, 1989). The national institutions and the private ones were
indeed competing not only for government resources but also for talented applicants.

The system integration achieved by the 1918 higher education law
can be seen as a major compromise between these two forces. After the
law was enacted, the government raised the tuition level at national universities, thus allowing the private universities to raise tuition rates and
secure enough revenue. In very subtle ways, the government had sought
a political balance between the national and private sectors.

After World War II, the legal authority of the government over private institutions was curtailed substantially under a new Constitution
that extolled freedom of speech and belief. Even though the education
law stipulated that private schools, as a part of the national education

system, be under the jurisdiction of the Ministry of Education, it was practically impossible for the ministry to regulate any private university. The only avenue left for the ministry was the "establishment permission" process by which each new institution was assigned a prescribed enrollment size based on the "university establishment standards" that specified necessary educational standards concerning teaching staff, facilities, and curriculum. Existing institutions were also required to go through this process whenever they wished to add faculty or increase their prescribed enrollment size. Even though the ministry was deprived of the legal power to penalize institutions that admitted students beyond their prescribed enrollment size, the institutions with excessive enrollment would face difficulties if they were to go through the establishment permission process for expansion. Since private institutions, especially the newer ones, constantly tried to expand their enrollments in order to gain financial stability, this process worked effectively as a way of putting the behavior of private institutions under the control of the Ministry of Education.

In fact, the enormous expansion of the private sector in the 1960s took place after the Ministry of Education, under mounting political pressure, issued an ordinance to the effect that some of the requirements in the establishment permission process could be applied more leniently than before. Following this subtle procedural change, the enormous expansion took place and the ministry lost practical control over the size of enrollments and the quality of education. For the next fifteen years, the private sector kept expanding.

After the rapid economic growth of the 1970s, Japanese society shifted its attention toward social and individual well-being, and government policies headed in the direction of a "welfare society." At the same time, the negative consequences of the demand-led expansion in the 1960s were exposed and, as the campus disputes erupted around 1970, caught the attention of the public and the political parties.

Under these circumstances, government subsidy to private institutions was subsequently formalized in 1975 as the current cost subsidy of private institutions. The current cost subsidy was introduced initially to alleviate strained financial conditions at many private institutions after campus strife, making it possible for private institutions to raise tuition. However, by the end of the 1970s, the subsidy accounted for a quarter of the revenues at private institutions. At the same time, the government initiated the policy of gradually expanding the national universities and colleges in regional areas and beginning to establish "new concept" universities. If these policies had continued, the role of government contributions to higher education finance would have substantially expanded, eventually altering one of the basic characteristics of Japanese higher education. By the end of the 1970s, however, the fiscal conditions had deteriorated due to the accumulating deficit, forcing the government to cut back its expenditures.

The current cost subsidy significantly changed the relationship between the government and the private sector. Even though there was no explicit legal action, introduction of the subsidy led to the understanding that the establishment of new institutions could be constrained on the grounds of fiscal condition. Moreover, the current cost subsidy was based on a formula according to which exceeding the prescribed enrollment size works as a strong negative factor. In extreme cases, the subsidy could be revoked altogether. These procedures created a strong incentive for institutions to reduce excess enrollment.

Moreover, since in practice the regime made it extremely difficult for new institutions to be established, competition among institutions over students became less threatening, allowing the existing institutions to raise their tuition levels. Private institutions, being able to reap benefits from the monopolized higher education market, showed little resistance to restrictions on their freedom. Under this monopolized and protected market, many private institutions increased their tuition levels while slightly reducing enrollments. Through these measures, they could lift their level of selectivity while securing financial stability. Meanwhile, the government succeeded to an extent in improving the educational quality of private institutions. It was ironic, however, that the government subsidy, initially targeted at lessening financial burden on students' families, resulted in tuition increases.

The above analysis indicates that relations between the government and the higher education market have never been stable. This phenomenon has been one of the most critical factors in determining the direction of change and has therefore always been at the center of controversy concerning higher education in Japan.

Segmentation and Differentiation of the System

In the first phase of higher education development, the boundaries of the system were unclear as there were many institutions with various levels of instruction and admissions requirements. As discussed earlier, through system integration around the time of World War I, the higher education system was given a legal definition with respect to the outer boundaries and internal segmentation. The higher education system consisted of two tiers (universities and specialized schools) and two sectors (public, both national and local, and private). The combination produced four segments, and each of them developed its own mission. Through the subsequent years prior to World War II, each of the four segments underwent a significant expansion. In the first segment of national universities, the number of imperial universities, which were centers of excellence in research and education, had increased to seven by World War II. A number of colleges of technology, medicine, and commerce were added to this segment. On the other end, the fourth segment, private specialized schools, was established at the margins of the higher education system, responding to the popular demand for accessible opportunities of higher education. Between the two segments were public specialized schools and private universities. While institutions in these two segments were diverse in prestige and selectivity, many of them had their own niche with respect to field of training, relation to the labor market, or link to the region.

The postwar reform removed the distinction between the university and nonuniversity tiers, while leaving in place the public and private sectors. In subsequent years, this reform left two policy issues unresolved: one was the persistent pressure for revival of a nonuniversity tier, and the other was the development of a hierarchical structure among four-year institutions in terms of selectivity and status.

When higher education institutions were integrated in principle into a single tier of four-year institutions, one exception remained—junior colleges, which provided the associate bachelor's degree after two years. Initially, there was a provision to allow a small number of former specialized colleges to operate before they had met the conditions to become new four-year universities. Some junior colleges, however, found strong market demand especially among young women, who had fewer employment opportunities than did male graduates of four-year institutions. Consequently, the number of private junior colleges increased over time, especially during the period of expansion in the 1960s. In the 1980s, about 24 percent of eighteen-year-old women were enrolled in junior colleges. In the 1990s, however, women began shifting to four-year institutions.

Since the 1950s, industrial leaders had been demanding that specialized schools be revived by creating polytechnic-type institutions. Despite strong resistance from the Ministry of Education, which insisted on maintaining the single-tier principle, "higher specialized schools" were created as a type of secondary school. They admitted fresh graduates from junior high schools and trained them for five years, implying that the last two years corresponded to higher education. The demand for this type of institution, however, failed to expand in subsequent years.

The third case was the creation of special training schools in the mid-1970s. As mentioned above, these schools were created at the time of the shift to a stringent policy on the expansion of four-year universities. Special training schools were expected to absorb some of the unmet demand. In subsequent years, the demand for this type of education expanded rapidly—by the 1980s about one-fifth of eighteen-year-olds, both male and female, were enrolled in the special training schools. Most of these institutions were private, and they quickly responded to skills required by a changing labor market.

Among four-year universities, the most significant development was the sharp differentiation among institutions with respect to selectivity and prestige. To an extent, the hierarchical structure reflected the one that existed in the prewar period. The position of each institution in the hierarchy reflected its history—the old imperial universities tended to be at the top and the old private specialized schools at the bottom. It should also be noted that, unlike their French or German counterparts, Japanese national universities were not required to enroll all the qualified students; each institution had the right to select its students. Moreover, unlike in the United States, a substantial proportion of institutions were concentrated in a few metropolitan areas, which weakened geographical distribution as compared to hierarchical differentiation.

During the postwar expansion the hierarchy developed even further: newly established institutions provided the bottom of the hierarchy, followed by still newer institutions. Meanwhile, traditionally prestigious institutions further enhanced their reputations by limiting admissions to raise their selectivity. Midlevel institutions, once they were financially secure, tried to raise their selectivity by restricting admissions.

The hierarchy in terms of selectivity was reinforced through the link between higher education institutions and business firms. Large business firms with abundant capital were able to invest in newer technology and in human capital, through on-the-job training, thus achieving significantly higher productivity—as well as higher wage and fringe benefits—than smaller firms. Moreover, large firms developed lifetime employment in the postwar period. In this sense, the labor market was segmented also, according to corporate size. It was thus natural for college graduates to seek employment in large firms.[1] The larger firms preferred graduates of selective institutions—if not for their superior education then for the academic competence shown by their success in entrance examinations. Meanwhile, graduates from less selective institutions had to seek employment in smaller firms. It was therefore natural for high school graduates to make every effort to get into the most selective institutions.

Under these circumstances, the selectivity of institutions became one of the most significant signals of desirability. Typically, people tried to get into the most selective of the institutions to which they might be admitted. With every student competing fiercely according to this tactic, the examination system became increasingly accurate in matching academic ability and institutional selectivity. This, in turn, induced employers to favor graduates from prestigious institutions to a greater extent.

Entrance examinations thus had a dual role: first, in selecting those individuals who would earn a college diploma and, second, matching individual applicants with individual institutions. This dual role took on greater significance in the late 1970s and 1980s. Not only did the government take policy steps to control expansion, but many private institutions also reduced the number of entrants in order to raise their status in the hierarchy. Meanwhile, criticisms of excessive competition led to the creation of a standardized examination that can be used as a substitute for, or a complement to, the entrance examinations given by individual institutions. Ironically, however, the standardized examination had an unexpected effect: it provided students with information as to their standing in the national distribution of achievement scores. To this, the education system added information about likely the cut-off level for each individual institution. Thus, students were given more accurate information to identify the most selective institution to which they were likely to be admitted. The position of a college in the hierarchy became an even better predictor of the graduate's academic competence, giving business firms more reasons to recruit students from selective institutions. This self-propelling trend brought about various negative effects that will be discussed later.

ISSUES AND REALITIES

The dynamic developments discussed above had various structural consequences, which have to be rectified before Japan positions itself for the future. At the same time, new factors—demographic structure, the trend toward a knowledge society, globalization, and marketization—pose serious challenges.

Legacies from the Past

In retrospect, the development of higher education in postwar Japan was indeed a significant achievement. Among other things, it provided the opportunity for higher education to a large segment of the population. Enrollment expansion itself worked as a great equalizer of educational opportunities. In the prewar period, when the participation rate at the tertiary level stood well below 10 percent, higher education opportunities were limited to a selected few, mostly from upper- and upper-middle-income families in urban areas and from landowners in rural areas. Access to higher education was beyond the imagination for the vast majority of the population. The postwar expansion of higher education changed this picture drastically. The participation rate at the tertiary level rose to 50 percent by the late 1970s, and to 60 percent by the early 1990s. In the process, the gender gap declined significantly; by the mid-1980s, the female participation rate in postsecondary education actually surpassed the male rate. Higher education is entering a universal stage. The differences among income classes with respect to enrollment had been kept relatively low (Kaneko; 1989; 1997). In addition, the expanded system succeeded in supplying a sufficient number of graduates to the growing economy.[2]

Still, it is evident that the process of expansion entailed serious problems. One of the most serious issues has been the quality of undergraduate instruction. Even though the rapid expansion naturally resulted in the entry of less academically able students, faculty members remained committed to the traditional concept of teaching. According to the Humboldtian idea of freedom of learning and *Bildung,* professors are supposed to influence students by demonstrating the spirit of rigorous academic pursuit; students need to be left in solitude, struggling to capture the truth by themselves. Yet, the academic and mental readiness of the student body changed significantly as more and more students entered colleges. Moreover, the hierarchical structure among institutions created its own problem. Institutions at the lower end of the hierarchy experienced low morale among faculty and students. Even more important, the prestigious institutions had their own problem: since the students knew that they would be recruited by business firms not on the basis of what they learned at the university but rather on the basis of their performance on the entrance examination, their motivation to study was limited. This situation provided good excuses for faculty members not to invest their time and energy in education. The strange combination of the Humboldtian ideal of freedom of learning and a hierarchically segmented labor market created a structural obstacle to any effort toward the qualitative improvement of education. Given that the only element of relevance to society was not education but rather the *selection* of elites, it is no surprise that universities suffered from a serious morale problem.

Another fundamental issue was the relationship between the public and private sectors. Even though national and private institutions served the same purpose of providing higher education and undertaking research, the financial support from the government differed significantly. The levels of current cost subsidy to private institutions had been stagnating since the 1980s due to financial constraints. While the tuition level at national institutions had been steadily rising to lessen the difference from the levels at private institutions, tuition levels at private institutions kept rising. As a result, the tuition at national institutions continued to be only half the tuition charged by most private institutions. Private institutions have criticized the disparity in family contribution as unjustifiable. Moreover, relatively selective private institutions have lost potential students to national universities due the difference in tuition levels. For less selective institutions facing potential financial difficulty, an increase in the amount of government subsidy was an acute necessity. In any case, inevitably, the differential treatment of private and national institutions has become a serious political issue.

Demographic Shift and Universalization

A significant factor affecting the future of higher education is demographic shift. As a result of a decline in the birthrate in the 1980s, the population of eighteen-year-olds will decline dramatically from 2.0 million in 1994 to 1.2 million in 2010. The supply-demand gap is now gradually diminishing, and it will eventually be reversed. There will be redundant capacities at the universities, and any high school graduate will be allowed to enter a university insofar as he or she is willing to pay the cost. In that sense, it appears as if universalization of higher education is going to be realized in an unexpected context.

How the demographic shift will affect the universities depends on a few factors. If the proportion of eighteen-year-olds who enroll in four-year institutions keeps growing to compensate for the decline in the cohort size, then the number of entrants to higher education institutions will remain the same. In fact, as the cohort size of eighteen-year-olds started declining, the participation rate at four-year institutions increased from 30 percent in the late 1980s to 40 percent at the beginning of the twenty-first century. However, the degree of decline is of such magnitude that enrollment rates will have to keep rising even farther to 60 percent if the number of entrants is to remain constant. That increase seems to be unlikely—from 2002 to 2003 the participation rate stagnated at around 40 percent. Meanwhile, signs of insufficient demand have already appeared. Since 2000, a few two-year institutions have been forced to close due to insufficient student numbers. In the spring of 2003, almost one-quarter of private four-year institutions admitted less students than their prescribed enrollment size. It is anticipated that, except for a small group of prestigious institutions, many private institutions will have to reposition themselves to survive in the age of insufficient demands. This is a radical departure from the past, which saw only a few cases of closure of higher education institutions over fifty years.

Equally important, this change will shift the relation between the government and private institutions. As pointed out above, the chronic excess demand has been one of the major factors that defined the development of higher education in Japan. Against this backdrop, the government was able to use establishment permission as an instrument to sustain a minimum level of educational conditions and, presumably, quality of instruction. As excess demand disappears and the prospect of institutional expansion diminishes, the government will lose its leverage over private universities.

Marketization, Globalization, and the Knowledge Society

At the same time as the demand and supply structure undergoes a significant shift, the social and economic contexts of higher education are changing their shape in terms of the future.

One significant factor is the advent of *marketization*. Aside from the financial crisis brought about by exponential increases in social spending, the ideological tide of "neoliberalism" has been acquiring considerable momentum in Japan as elsewhere in the world. Whether or not one accepts the new ideology, it appears to be the case that the increased diversity and complexity of modern society and its needs have made centralized decision making and control less effective. It is thus argued that many social services provided directly by the government should be moved to the realm of the market for the sake of efficiency. This argument can be applied directly to higher education. The basic premise underlying the role of government in higher education has been that government is the best agent to satisfy the various needs of the whole society. This premise, however, appears less plausible when social activities become increasingly diverse and industrial development less predictable. Meanwhile, the financial resources that the government can provide to higher education are shrinking. The government appears to be losing the ideological and fiscal wherewithal to be the sole or primary agent mediating the exchange between society and the university.

A second factor is the coming of what might be called the *knowledge society*. Knowledge has assumed an increasingly central role in society. Fierce competition over technical innovation has caused research and development to become critically important for success in the market. The creation and transmission of knowledge, which has been the central task of the university, is going to assume the central role in the economy. It does not imply, however, that society will become more generous to the present universities. On the contrary, society will more likely criticize universities' ability to respond to the challenges facing them. Since the required knowledge may be very different from traditional academic knowledge, universities will face serious difficulty in responding to those needs. In fact, knowledge is produced and transmitted in various forms and at various locations, often outside the university. Even basic research takes place in business firms that have been developing the capability to produce knowledge and make a profit from that activity. The university no longer enjoys a monopoly in the production of advanced and specialized knowledge.

The third factor is *globalization*. Given the lower barriers to international trade, financial capital and production equipment can now move easily from one country to another, making it possible for many countries to participate in the production of sophisticated goods. The relative strength of a nation's economy, or its competitiveness, rests on the ability to create and accumulate knowledge. At the same time, the direction of economic growth has moved from manufacturing to the service sector and the production of human services based on various kinds of knowledge. For many countries, maintaining a high level of competitiveness in international trade appears to be essential for economic well-being or even for survival; in order to foster competitiveness the knowledge transmitted and created by the university is essential. Moreover, the services rendered by the university are becoming increasingly mobile. Not only do students move across national borders, but the universities are also moving across borders to recruit students. E-learning technology makes it possible for universities to offer courses overseas. In a word, there are growing global markets for higher education.

These arguments can be made anywhere in the world, but they cause a particularly acute sense of crisis in Japan. The marketization argument threatens the delicate balance between the government and private sectors of higher education, as that relationship has been a controversial one ever since the creation of higher education in Japan. If the underlying agenda of the knowledge society lies in the increased involvement of research and education in the market, then the Humboldtian principle of academic freedom and abstract academic pursuit that has constituted the backbone of Japanese research universities will have to be questioned. With the advent of globalization, Japan is threatened on the one hand by China and other low-wage countries in the market for manufactured goods and on the other by the United States and other English-speaking countries in the trade of services, including higher education. In both spheres, the competitiveness of Japan has to be questioned. There is a growing awareness that the former social and economic structure that enabled Japan in the past to succeed in catching up to the West may be losing ground in the face of those new trends. Japanese society has to find a new mechanism for growth, in which higher education must assume a critical role.

TRENDS AND CHALLENGES

The sense of crisis and awareness of the need for reform grew in the 1990s, resulting in various reports from government councils. Some of their recommendations were followed by a series of government policy initiatives in the 1990s and in the early twenty-first century, while others are still awaiting further debates to decide their fate. The reform initiatives are focused in three directions: reconstruction of the linkage between the university and the economy, qualitative assurance and improvement, and a shift away from government involvement.

Linkage with the Economy

Reconstruction of the linkage between higher education and the economy is the goal in both education and research. In education, the policy so far has been directed toward expansion of graduate education as the place for training and retraining highly professional workers. Providing life-long employment, business firms raised skill levels among their workers not only through formal training but also by exposing workers to various tasks in the workplace or by on-the-job training. This has been particularly effective in providing workers with the knowledge and skills relevant to their work (Aoki & Dore, 1994). In recruiting new workers, employers tended to evaluate recruits' basic ability to absorb on-the-job training, rather than their possession of specific knowledge or skills mastered at university. However, it is argued that, with the advent of globalization and rapid technological innovation, this pattern of skill formation will lose its effectiveness. With constant technological innovation and shifts in demands, skill requirements keep changing rapidly, making on-the-job training less effective. At the same time, the demographic shift requires the mobilization of a middle-aged and older labor force. All these factors point to the need for advanced education and training for the young people and adult workers. From this perspective, expansion of graduate programs at universities appears as the logical approach.

In fact, expansion of graduate schools had already been taking place since the 1970s in such fields as engineering and pharmacology. By the end of the 1980s, about one-third of new graduates with bachelor's degrees in engineering went on to graduate programs. In other academic fields, however, graduate programs remained essentially places for training academics. Against this background, in 1988 the University Council, which was established by the Ministry of Education as the central body to outline the basic policies on higher education, released its first report, entitled "Toward a Flexible Graduate Education System," on advanced professional graduate education (Daigaku Shingikai, 1988). To induce greater flexibility and variety in graduate education, the report suggested a few changes in chartering standards, some of which had direct relevance with regard to retraining working college graduates. Following the report, in 1989, the Ministry of Education revised the "chartering standards for graduate education," relaxing requirements concerning class schedules, entrance requirements, and full-time residency.

In 1991 the University Council recommended a two-fold increase in the enrollment in graduate programs by 2000. Following the government initiatives, a number of graduate courses were set up with curricula targeting the training of professionals. Many private institutions established graduate programs in the social sciences and humanities. As it turned out, the goal set by the University Council was achieved at least numerically: enrollment in master's programs increased from 62,000 in 1990 to 143,000 in 2000. Another development was the creation of graduate professional schools. In 2002, the Central Education Council, a government body, proposed creation of professional graduate schools. Meanwhile, the Ministry of Law started reexamining the national examination system for legal professions. More than forty graduate law schools started enrolling students by 2004. There are proposals to assign schools of medicine, currently one of the undergraduate faculties, the status of professional graduate schools.

These developments, however, do not necessarily imply that graduate education has actually become a significant route for retraining adult workers, as the University Council originally intended. Except for the recruitment of engineers, businesses still tend to prefer new undergraduates from selective institutions over those with graduate degrees. This forms a contrast with the situation in Korea, Taiwan, and China, where master's degrees are gaining significance in the labor market. The future development in Japan will be contingent on changes in the labor market.

The university-industry linkage through research has attracted attention since the end of the 1990s. In retrospect, it is ironic that in the 1980s, when the robust performances of the Japanese manufacturing industry alarmed the West, the strong ties of Japanese universities with industry was seen as one of the critical factors supporting its strength. Typical arguments held that Japanese universities were inclined toward applied, rather than basic, research while free-riding on the basic research in American and European universities, and that through close cooperation with universities Japanese manufacturers were able to reap the benefits. In the United States and the United Kingdom, these arguments resulted in a series of policies to fortify the role of higher education institutions in economic development. However, the tide reversed in the 1990s, when the American economy started a steady recovery. The success was attributed to the close collaboration between universities and industry, and the businesses created around universities, as typified by what happened in Silicon Valley.

These stories started making an impact in Japan when the "bubble economy" burst in the 1990s, suddenly undermining Japanese confidence in the economy's competitiveness. Japan had to develop new arenas of industry, and the universities were expected to play critical roles in this respect. From this perspective, however, Japanese universities were found to have critical shortcomings: the cooperation with industry tended to rely on informal and closed relations between a particular laboratory in a university and a particular section of a large manufacturing company. This particular pattern had been created partly because of strong resistance within the university, in the tradition of academic freedom, against university-industry cooperation. Japanese universities thus needed a transparent institutional framework and incentive systems that would induce a creative combination between potential supply of knowledge and the demands of the market.

On these matters, the Ministry of Education issued a series of policies in the 1980s and 1990s—including such measures as financial incentives for joint research programs between universities and industries and the creation of "university-industry cooperation centers" at selected national universities. In 1998, the Diet passed a law aimed at encouraging technology transfer from higher education institutions to industry through the establishment of a "technology licensing organization" for universities. The law also stipulated procedures on the ownership of patents. Since 2000, the government has taken measures to allow faculty members at national universities to serve in private firms on a part-time basis. Meanwhile, the Ministry of Economy, Trade, and Industry (previously the Ministry of International Trade and Industry) has become active in promoting university-industry cooperation. The plan is for there to be one thousand venture business firms established by university faculty members by 2004; the number actually had already reached five hundred by May 2003. Moreover, the reorganization of national universities into more independent bodies is expected to make them more aggressive in pursuing industry-university collaboration. How these measures will work, however, remains to be seen.

Excellence, Evaluation, and Quality Assurance

The second focus of the reforms was to control the quality of higher education and research—promoting excellence and ensuring minimum standards, while developing forms of evaluation.

As "excellence in research and education" became a politically popular catchphrase in the 1990s, a series of government actions were undertaken along these lines. The initiatives included increases in scholarships and other forms of financial support for graduate students and young researchers and in the funding of research projects. In 1997, the government passed a law that allowed universities to employ academic researchers in fixed-term appointments, which had been illegal in the postwar period—when Japanese employees were given strong protection. This measure was aimed at promoting mobility and competition among young researchers. In 2001, the Ministry of Education proposed a "structural reform plan in higher education" that proposed the designation of thirty leading research universities as Japanese centers of excellence by international standards. Faced with the criticism that selection of such institutions would be practically impossible, the ministry revised the plan as the "21st Century Centers of Excellence Plan." Under this plan, the ministry will help set up and finance about two hundred "centers of excellence," in ten fields of research, at national and private universities. The competition for the grant, which started in the summer of 2002, received wide attention not only among universities but also from the media.

Japanese achievement in basic science is in fact improving. According to an international comparison of publication in academic journals in 2003, two Japanese institutions appeared among the top 10 (the University of Tokyo ranked second and the University of Kyoto sixth) and five in the top 20. Japanese scholars won the Nobel Prize for three consecutive years. However, the extent to which these records are attributable to government policy is unclear. Moreover, it is ironic that the Japanese public is now more concerned with the economic value of research.

Significant developments have been made concerning university evaluation. In postwar Japan, there have been two mechanisms for quality assurance: one is the aforementioned establishment permission by the government, and the other is accreditation by the Japan University Accreditation Association. The latter, however, has been criticized for being too lenient on the member institutions and therefore ineffective in assuring quality. Consequently, the establishment permission process remained practically the sole mechanism to maintain the quality of higher education institutions. Over the years, standards for the establishment of universities, on which the permission process is based, became increasingly involved and detailed to accommodate different types of higher education institutions. There were criticisms that the myriad standards tended to thwart any initiatives to experiment with new approaches in undergraduate education. Responding to these criticisms and the trend of deregulation, the Ministry of Education substantially simplified the standards in 1991. At the same time, the revised standards required institutions of higher education to undertake self-evaluation. This logically brings about the need for effective external evaluation and assessment.

In response to this need, as well as to the increasingly strong claims for accountability in cost and performance, the University Council recommended establishment of a government agency for evaluation of the national universities. Subsequently, a National Institute for University Assessment and Academic Degrees was established in 2000. With more than one hundred staff members, it is probably the world's largest evaluation agency. Since 2001 it has been undertaking annual rounds of evaluation—a massive exercise involving several hundred evaluators. The methods and results of evaluation have received mixed reviews from the universities.

A more fundamental issue is quality assurance for the entire higher education system, including private institutions. It was mentioned above that the establishment permission process, together with current cost subsidy, has been the major vehicle of quality control. This approach will inevitably lose its effectiveness, however, due to the inevitable oversupply of places. Moreover, there has been increasing pressure from the United States and other countries through World Trade Organization (WTO) negotiations to open the higher education market for overseas institutions. Japan needs to establish a transparent framework for assuring minimum standards for Japanese institutions to protect the system from domestic and foreign degree mills. In 2002, the school education law was amended to add a clause that stipulated that all universities have to be accredited by at least one of the government-recognized accrediting bodies. The accrediting body can be a private foundation, a government body, or even a private corporation. Through this scheme, the Ministry of Education obtained explicit legal authority, albeit indirect, over the operation of private institutions for the first time in the postwar period.

Deregulation

The third area of reform is deregulation and marketization. After Japan went into a serious economic stagnation in the mid-1990s, the pervasive political ideology moved toward the reduction in the role of government in economic and social activities, either in the form of regulation or by direct involvement. On the agenda of the reforms along this line, higher education assumed a central position for its symbolic value.

Starting in the last decade of the twentieth century there has been steady movement toward deregulation. It was mentioned above that the standards for establishment were considerably simplified. In addition, the regulations and requirements concerning higher education have either been cut back or abolished altogether. For example, the requirement of at least twelve years of schooling before entering institutions of higher education is no longer enforced, allowing some students to "jump" to university before completing high school. It is also possible now to enroll in graduate programs after three years of undergraduate coursework. Requirements concerning university facilities have been substantially reduced. One area of deregulation that remains controversial is the inclusion of for-profit higher education institutions in the national system of education. Under the current school education law, only nonprofit "school juristic persons" can establish legally defined *schools,* including higher education institutions. Many proponents of deregulation are now proposing to remove this requirement. When the Economic Advisory Council under Prime Minister Koizumi proposed its "action plan" in 2002, legalization of for-profit universities was listed among the prioritized issues. While this proposal met staunch opposition from the minister of education, the issue has not yet been resolved.

One reform that has already brought about concrete changes is incorporation of the national universities, which were considered legally as government organizations, even though they had been given substantial autonomy in academic matters. The governance and finance of the national universities have been criticized internally as inflexible and externally as inefficient and unresponsive to the changing needs of the economy and society. Moreover, as mentioned above, there has been a strong sense of resentment among private institutions about the privileged status of national institutions.

In 1996, the government under Prime Minister Hashimoto placed restructuring of government organizations high on the political agenda. The reform was to encompass every part of government, including higher education. "Privatization" of the national universities was frequently mentioned in government committees. Under the subsequent government of Prime Minister Obuchi, the legal status of the national universities was formally changed to that of "independent administrative agencies," serving a public function but organizationally independent from the government. Subsequently, a committee of experts—including representatives from the national universities—issued a report in the summer of 2002 providing the basic outlines of the new body, the National University Corporation (NUC). In 2003, the NUC law was passed in the Diet, and each of the national universities became a National University Corporation in the spring of 2004.

Under this law, the NUC will be an independent entity legally separated from the government, governed by a president and an executive board, in consultation with the academic board and the administrative board. The president will be selected by the selection committee and appointed by the minister of education. The government provides a subsidy to the NUC based on a prescribed formula, and the NUC administers the budget according to an accounting system similar to that of private firms.

The subsidy will be determined in the framework established by the six-year "middle-term goals and plan" approved by the minister.

A variety of criticisms have been raised against this scheme. One of the major concerns is the unusually strong power concentrated in the hands of the university president. The president, together with the executive board members whom he appoints, makes basic decisions, acting as the chief executive. There is no internal organization, such as a board of trustees as in private institutions, to supervise the president and his staff. The Ministry of Education will retain decisive power in approving the midterm goals and plan that would bind the administration legally and fiscally. Meanwhile, the traditional authority given to the faculty body or academic council may be curtailed substantially.

Since many of the internal procedures for decision making are left for individual institutions to design, the actual practice of governance may turn out to be less radically centralized than the law appears to stipulate. At least, it will take some time before the new system of governance and finance takes root. How these changes will affect the organizational behaviors of the national university is unclear, but it is likely that the national universities will become more aggressive in acquiring their own standing in the market and, as a result, become more divergent in their identity and mission. That will inevitably recall the persistent issue of the validity of differences in mission between public and private institutions.

CONCLUSION

Unlike some Asian countries, Japan was not forced by colonization to adopt a single model of higher education from the West; instead, it was able to select, through trial and error, institutional arrangements from various models. Dynamic interaction between demand and supply took place, eventually resulting in transformation of the institutional framework. In this latter process, Japan shares a common pattern with many Asian countries.

Because of the "late development effect," popular demand for higher education expanded at relatively early stages of development, to create chronic excess demand over subsequent periods. Countries have varied widely, however, with respect to the timing and magnitude of the expansion in demand, and the government's power and resources to control the market. In former English colonies, the governments typically resisted market forces. In contrast, in Japan the government allowed, and relied on, the private sector to absorb the excess demand. Similar patterns were observed in such East Asian countries as Korea, Taiwan, and the Philippines.

The Japanese approach made it possible to extend access to higher education to a large segment of the population and to provide the necessary volume of manpower critical for economic development. The negative consequences include a number of issues. Governmental control over the quantity and quality of higher education eventually had to be severely limited. The disparities between the public and private sectors in terms of cost levels to be borne by families created a sense of unfairness. Another problematic consequence was the development of a hierarchy among higher education institutions, which created a mechanism that persistently undermined efforts to improve the quality of instruction.

At the beginning of the twenty-first century, Japan is trying to rectify the problems created as a result of past developments in higher education. At the same time, emerging social and economic trends are causing new challenges. In order to respond to these challenges, Japanese higher education is trying to reshape itself in various ways. That raises a number of critical issues, the most fundamental of which is the role of government in higher education. Thus, Japan has to reexamine the basic premises underlying its higher education system throughout its history.

NOTES

1. For more detailed discussion about in-firm training, see Kaneko, 1992, p. 52.

2. For a detailed discussion and evaluation of the supply and demand of college graduates in the postwar period, see Kaneko, 1992.

REFERENCES

Amano, Ikuo. 1986. Educational crisis in Japan. In William K. Cummings et al. (Eds.), *Educational policies in crisis* (pp. 23–43). New York: Praeger.

Aoki, Masahiko, & Dore, Ronald. (1994). *The Japanese firm: Sources of strength.* Oxford: Oxford University Press.

Ben-David, Joseph. (1977). *Centers of learning.* New York: McGraw-Hill.

Cummings, William K. (1980). *Education and equality in Japan.* Princeton, NJ: Princeton University Press.

Daigaku Shingikai (University Council). (1988). *Daigakuin Seido No Danryakuka Ni Tuite* (Toward a flexible graduate education system). Tokyo: Author.

Dore, Ronald P. (1976). *The diploma disease: Education, qualification, and development.* Berkeley: University of California Press.

Dore, Ronald P., & Sako, Mari. (1989). *How the Japanese learn to work.* London: Routledge.

Editorial. (1989, January 25). *Yomiuri Shimbun,* 2.

Kaneko, Motohisa. (1989). *Financing higher education in Japan.* Hiroshima, Japan: R.I.H.E., Hiroshima University.

Kaneko, Motohisa. (1992). *Higher education and employment in Japan.* Hiroshima, Japan: R.I.H.E., Hiroshima University.

Kaneko, Motohisa. (1997). Efficiency and equity in Japanese higher education. *Higher Education, 34*(2), 165–181.

Nakayama, Shigeru. (1989). Independence and choice: Western impacts on Japanese higher education. In P. G. Altbach & V. Selvaratnam (Eds.), *From dependence to autonomy: The development of Asian universities.* Dordrecht, Netherlands: Kluwer Academic.

Pempel, T. J. (1978). *Patterns of Japanese policy making: Experiences from higher education.* Boulder, CO: Westview.

Terasaki, Akio. (1979). *Nihon ni okeru daigaku jichi seido no seiritu* (Emergence of university autonomy in Japan). Tokyo: Hyouronsha.

6

Korean Higher Education

History and Future Challenges

Sungho H. Lee

The Republic of Korea, a newly industrialized nation, stands out as one of the notable successes in the developing world. In economics and international trade, Korea has received acclaim for its rapid advancement and is recognized as a competent partner. Within a relatively short period, Korean higher education has expanded and created an educational philosophy and academic system that have been recognized as contributing to national development and well-being.

Certain aspects of Korean higher education are rooted in the country's history. During the period of Japanese colonial rule (1910–1945) and that of the U.S. military government in Korea (1945–1948) the Korean higher education system came under foreign influence in terms of structure, curriculum, and administration. Nevertheless, Korean higher education also possesses its own unique character, which has been shaped by both external forces and indigenous circumstances.

However, Korean public confidence in higher education now appears to have been shaken. The system, which should set the standards for other elements of society to emulate, now seems to be suffering from an erosion of institutional integrity. Institutions of higher education are coming under strong pressure to make a commitment to academic nationalism as well as to achieve excellence comparable to that of Western advanced countries. As Korea enters the twenty-first century, with the environment outside of higher education changing rapidly, the Korean higher education system seems ill-prepared to respond to the new challenges.

HISTORICAL PERSPECTIVES

Korean higher education has been shaped by many factors. The present features of Korean higher education evolved from the interaction between the country's historically formed traditions and the universalizing effects of modernization beginning in the mid-nineteenth century—a process that involved what are held to be Western models. However, to ascribe the development of Korean higher education exclusively to Western influence would be a crude oversimplification of modernization, for traditional Korean values and systems have shown an extraordinary resilience and persistence in Korean education.

The Republic of Korea, which occupies a small peninsula in the northeastern part of Asia, takes pride in its history of over 4,300 years. Prior to the late nineteenth century, no well-articulated modern system of education existed in Korea. However, the concepts and practices related to providing people with education were already well developed. In historical accounts, state-run institutions assume a prominent place in Korean higher education (U. Kim, 1985, p. 151). In some measure, this view may be due to the partiality of chroniclers for state-related historical events over the activities of ordinary people. In the premodern period, educational institutions were divided into two categories, state-run and private. Most state-run institutions opened their doors only to selected individuals or to privileged upper-class youths. State-run institutions had their roots in the *taehak* (great schools) in the Koguryo kingdom, as early as in A.D. 372. These institutions were known by various names in later periods—finally as *sungkyunkwan* in the Choson kingdom in the late fourteenth century. The primary goal of state institutions was to educate the students, future members of the bureaucracy, in Confucian philosophy and ethics. The curriculum included the intensive study of Chinese classics, which were intended to maintain the nation's high intellectual and cultural standards. At the time, private institutions existed only at the primary and middle levels of education. Formal education for the general populace was essentially a private matter, while higher education for the ruling class was a public one.

Western Missionaries

At the turn of the nineteenth century, the Western world began to notice Korea. For example, a significant Western missionary effort began on the Korean peninsula in 1832 (Underwood, 1926). Christian missionary work had a great impact on the development of Korean higher education, beginning in the mid-1880s with American Protestant missionaries who later established institutions of higher learning in Korea. At the time, the Choson kingdom was facing difficult internal and external problems, especially when foreign powers threatened the royal government for interfering in their sociopolitical interests. The majority of Confucian bureaucrats showed hostility toward foreigners and their religions. Recognizing that direct evangelical work among Koreans would be difficult or impossible, missionaries turned to education as a central way in which to establish Christianity in Korea (J.-K. Lee, 2002).

In 1885, Drs. H. N. Allen and O. R. Avison opened Kwanghoewon, the first modern hospital to practice and teach Western medicine. The hospital added a medical school, Severance Union Medical College and Hospital, and an affiliated school of nursing (Koo & Suh, 1984). In 1886, Reverend Appenzeller opened Baejae Hakdang, the first college-level normal school for men, and Mrs. Scranton opened Ewha Hakdang, the first girls' school in Korea. Some American missionaries pursued a particular strategy: to establish a secondary school and then elevate it to the level of a higher education institution. For instance, the first college department for girls was opened at Ewha Hakdang in 1910, with 15 students. Between 1885 and 1910, a total of 796 schools, from the elementary to the college level, were established and maintained by Western missionaries, comprising about 35 percent of the total number of formal schools (2,250) in Korea (Sohn, 1987).

The American missionaries' work of establishing institutions of higher learning was very successful, not only in proselytizing on behalf of the Christian faith, but also in introducing the structure and content of Western higher education in Korea. This period influenced the development of higher education in Korea in five major areas: the democratic ideology of education, equal educational opportunity, education for women, curriculum development, and the institutional structure of higher education.

The various Korean responses to the influences of American missionaries from 1876 to 1910 grew out of the many internal and external political conflicts of a period that saw the outbreak of the Russo-Japanese War in 1903 and culminated in 1910 with the assertion of colonial power over Korea by Japan. Some Koreans favored a policy of isolationism and the rejection of any Western or Japanese encroachments upon Korean national sovereignty. Yet, greater numbers of Koreans declared that to survive as an independent entity they would need to adopt contemporary Western practices in science and technology and reform their society, without sacrificing traditional values. This strategy did not, however, represent an argument for Westernization. Rather, it was an effort to deal with domestic ills and foreign threats and to ensure self-preservation through a modernization movement motivated by the human instinct for survival and nationalist aspirations.

The early American missionaries in Korea had to confront a deep-rooted nationalist reform movement due to the fact that they were foreigners and representatives of Western power and influence. The rejection by indigenous groups would later undergo a change: "The Korean people began to have a new interest in Western education and an appreciation of mission education. The Koreans' attitude changed completely" (Choi, 1975 p. 121). The nationalist reform movement and the Western Christian missionaries' advocacy of autonomy and self-determination for Koreans seemed to combine and evolve into a new era of modernization in Korea (Nahm, 1981). Both sides shared a number of beliefs and practices: an emphasis on ensuring the welfare of the people as a whole and helping each individual to attain human dignity and liberation from oppression. Therefore, concerted efforts were made by the missionaries and nationalist leaders to preserve the original goals of education (Nahm, 1981).

Western missionaries made an impact on Korean higher education in a number of other ways. They introduced the concept of Western higher learning into the Korean language, with the word *hangul*, and ended the focus on the Chinese classics (Koo & Suh, 1984; G. L. Paik, 1973). The missionaries were fully accepted into Korean society. The second contribution made by American missionaries was arranging for Koreans to study in the United States. The early group of Koreans who studied in the United States in the period before 1910 included Syngman Rhee, Philip Jaisohn (Chae Pil So), Chi-Ho Yun, and Kil-Jun Yu, who became American-educated nationalist leaders upon returning home from the United States. They launched a movement for national sovereignty in various fields and vigorously opposed Japanese domination. This group contributed to the formation of a pro-American attitude on the part of Koreans.

The Japanese Occupation

In 1910, declaring Korea to be a part of Japan, the Japanese government enacted various regulations and ordinances to control every aspect of the country's political, social, cultural, and economic life. The colonial policy forced Koreans to remain in isolation and to stop developing their own education system. The interaction with the West was intermittent until Korea was liberated in 1945 with the ending of World War II.

The educational policies imposed by the Japanese were extremely oppressive. Seeking to assimilate Koreans by means of education, the Japanese used education to obliterate the Korean nationality in terms of language, family names, religion, and every other aspect of life. The objectives of the Japanese with regard to education in Korea were fourfold: denationalization, vocationalization, deliberalization, and discrimination (Rim, 1952). *Denationalization* meant forcing the Korean people to substitute loyalty to the Japanese emperor for that formerly given to their own rulers. *Vocationalization* implied a concentration on the skills necessary to prepare Koreans to be low-level tradesmen. *Deliberalization* referred to a curriculum for Koreans that ignored both liberal arts subjects and advanced technical programs. *Discrimination* involved the fact that Japanese students were offered better and more advanced educational opportunities than were Koreans. These policies retarded the development of Korean higher education in a number of ways.

Koreans were granted few opportunities for higher education, compared with those given to Japanese living in Korea. In 1939, for example, 143 Japanese students were enrolled in primary schools for every 1,000 Japanese, while there were only 55 Korean primary students for every 1,000 Koreans. Inequalities were even greater at the secondary level— with only 1.3 Korean high school students for every 1,000 Koreans, while there were 32.7 Japanese high school students for every 1,000 Japanese (J. Kim, 1973, p. 21). Under the Education Ordinance of 1911, institutions such as Sungsil Union Christian College and the Ewha School, established by American missionaries to provide higher education, lost their college status. The opportunity for Koreans to obtain higher education was lost.

Immediately following World War I, Korean nationalists initiated a movement to establish their own private university—the People's University. To deflect this movement, in 1924 the Japanese regime opened Keijo Imperial University in Seoul, which became the only university in Korea, and all the other established institutions of higher learning were downgraded to three-year, non-degree-granting institutions. The motives behind the Japanese establishment of a state university can be read in two ways: one was to provide higher education for the Japanese in Korea, and the other was for political expediency (Nam, 1962, pp. 148–157). The political motive consisted of suppressing the growing nationalism among Koreans by preventing the People's University from becoming a reality and by indoctrinating the younger generation of the Korean elite with Japanese nationalism. From a positive perspective, however, the founding of Keijo Imperial University represented the introduction in Korea of the modern four-year university, although the admission of Korean students was restricted to between one-fourth and one-third of the total number of students (Oh, 1964).

For Koreans, admission to Keijo Imperial University was a highly competitive process, which increased the institution's prestige and the preference for state-run institutions over private ones—in keeping with feudalistic concepts of Confucianism. Japanese higher education, through Keijo Imperial University, left Korea with a centralized system of university governance. The Japanese pattern of a rigid centralized bureaucratic structure was observed in many areas of Korean higher education—such as the entrance examinations, the unchallenged authority of professors, and the academic subject-matter-based curriculum.

The Japanese cleverly interfered with the Christian mission schools and institutions of higher education in every conceivable way. One measure prohibited any religious instruction in the mission schools as part of the official curriculum. Another proclaimed Japanese as the medium of instruction. A further demand was for students and teachers to pay homage to Shinto shrines. A number of other complicated requirements were also imposed before the government would approve mission schools. Concerning the reaction of the mission schools to these conditions, James Fisher, in his book *Democracy and Mission Education in Korea*, declared that "it was a case either of conforming to government standards or opting out" (Jayasuriya, 1983, p. 36). The missionaries seemed to choose the approach of complying, at least outwardly, in order to protect their students and institutions. Consequently, in 1925, the missionary institutions of higher education, which had lost their college status under the Education Ordinance of 1911, were reinstated as colleges.

Over the thirty-six years of Japanese occupation, Western missionaries and Korean groups made concerted efforts to resist Japanese educational policies and to preserve the national essence of education. A new and broader sense of unity emerged, and nationalism became one of the principal issues with regard to Korean higher education. Increasingly, Koreans went to the United States for study and returned home to work for Korean independence. Some were active in education and in the vanguard to adopt Western structures and ideas. There was quite a bit of dispute concerning Western influences. Some people were even committed to accepting Western influences that were transmitted by Japan. It has been pointed out "that whatever form of education Korea has had the greatest influence was brought from Japan. Therefore, it is natural to assume that whatever had influenced Japan from the outside would also be brought to education in Korea, in thought and in organization, during the thirty-six years of Japanese occupation" (S.-H. Lee, 1958, pp. 134–137). As an example of indirect Western influence, S.-H. Lee (1958) cited the French origin of Japan's highly centralized system of school supervision and school districts that was later transplanted in Korea.

It can be said that some Koreans chose to accept Western missionaries out of a common anti-Japanese consciousness. As stated, the ideology of freedom and independence promoted by the missionaries was consistent with the Korean goal of independence. Nevertheless, many leading scholars trained in traditional thought and disciplines were reluctant to accept Western influences. What may be called Koreanism and Westernism thus emerged in the academic community and became, in later years, the focal point of ongoing dispute among scholars in institutions of higher education.

Postindependence Developments

After Korea was liberated from Japanese colonial rule in 1945, the next significant Western influence on the development of Korean higher education was the country's close relationship with the United States. The post-1945 U.S. presence in Korea can be divided into two distinct periods. Upon independence the Korean peninsula was placed under a temporary trusteeship, with the United States as the trustee south of the 38th parallel and the Soviet Union as the trustee in the north. Thus, the first U.S. presence in Korea consisted of the trusteeship managed by the U.S. military until 1948, when U.S. military rule ended with the establishment of a new democratic government in the south, the Republic of Korea. However, the new republic then experienced a setback caused by the disastrous consequences of the Korean War between the south and the north, which lasted from 1950 until 1953. The second and more significant period of U.S. influence took place in the decade after the Korean War, during the U.S. participation in the reconstruction of the country.

Impact of the U.S. military government. The primary goal of the U.S. military government in Korea was to help Koreans establish a new democratic nation of their own, as promised at the Cairo Conference in 1943. The educational system was definitely regarded as one of the critical areas that needed to be cleansed of the remnants of Japanese colonialism so that a new democratic system could be instituted. The U.S. military government adopted a strategy for reshaping Korean education. Many prominent Korean educators were appointed as advisers for governmental affairs on education. Another approach was sending Korean educators and students to the United States, with the idea that they would contribute to the rebuilding of the national education system upon their return. By January 1948, a total of 111 Korean students had been sent to study at American colleges and universities (Nam, 1962, pp. 148–157). The so-called new education movement was really initiated and supported by Korean educators who had studied in the United States. Finally, the U.S. military government brought to Korea many American educators and educational specialists to serve as consultants and advisers. Some of these Americans conducted scientific research geared toward immediate and long-range planning for Korean higher education.

The American impact on the development of Korean education has typically been discussed in terms of the primary and secondary levels of education (Nam, 1962, pp. 148–157). In fact, significant progress in the development of Korean higher education can also be traced to the U.S. military government. The first development concerned the introduction of four-year undergraduate education. Most of the nineteen institutions in existence before liberation were not four-year institutions and did not offer American-type bachelor's degrees. The military government, with the help of educators in the private sector, sought to reorganize the Korean higher education system on the basis of the American model. As a consequence, the establishment of new institutions of higher education and the reorganization of established institutions accelerated. As of November 1947, the number of colleges and universities had reached twenty-nine, with more than twenty thousand students (Nam, 1962, pp. 148–157).

The second development facilitated by military government officials was the organization in 1947, by thepresidents and deans of institutions of higher education, of the Korean Association of Colleges and Universities. The association was created to set up standards for institutions of higher education and to serve as the accrediting organization, following the American model, to control the quality of institutions of higher learning (Nam, 1962, pp. 148–157). To a certain extent, the association did help to improve qualitative and quantitative standards for Korean higher education, but the total effectiveness of the association was questionable.

The third development promoted by the U.S. military government involved changes in the curriculum. As in primary and secondary education, democratic principles were encouraged when defining educational objectives in higher education. The curriculum, including course titles and programs themselves, was modeled after the American system. The process of reorganizing the education system under the U.S. military government was relatively successful and rapid, compared to the country's political and economic development—the reason being that while political and economic progress was largely dependent upon the results of negotiations between the United States and Russia, educational work was relatively unaffected by external circumstances.

The U.S. military government's policy on education in Korea has been criticized as motivated by U.S. imperialism, which has pursued the expansion of American influence all over the world since World War II. Critics cite as evidence of the Americans' true agenda the fact that policies were implemented without adequate preparation and in ignorance of traditional Korean modes of thought and behavior. In hindsight, however, some other interpretations of events have gained credibility. Contemporary documents dealing with educational policy make it clear that the U.S. military government intended to "Koreanize" the education system—a policy that seemed to be welcomed by the Korean people. The main goal of Koreans after liberation was to rid their country of Japanese influences. At the time, however, Koreans seemed unable to come up with alternatives or their own unique ideas and were therefore obliged to accept the ideas and practices of American educators. American policies on Korean higher education were thus, in a sense, self-imposed by Koreans, with American encouragement and friendly assistance.

An inevitable conflict began to arise in the academic community and among national leaders. On one side were those groups that favored American educational ideas. In particular, they strongly advocated the American philosophy of expanded access to higher education—a sort of universalism at the tertiary level of education. On the other side were Japanese-trained Korean scholars who were committed to the Japanese philosophy of higher education for the select few. Accordingly, when looked at from the traditional elitist viewpoint, the U.S. military government's policies were seen as having failed and having increased the chaos in higher education.

U.S. educational aid. In 1952, the U.S. educational aid program to Korea in the post–Korean War period began when the United Nations formed an education mission under the joint sponsorship of the United Nations Educational and Cultural Organization (UNESCO) and the United Nations Korean Reconstruction Agency (UNKRA). The UNESCO/UNKRA education mission prepared a report, "Rebuilding Education in the Republic of Korea," which included 108 recommendations for the overall improvement of Korean education (Adams, 1956, p. 202). In response, the United States organized three education missions to Korea between 1952 and 1955. These missions provided consulting services and in-service teacher training workshops. In particular, the third mission, led by Harold Benjamin, made a great contribution to the movement to improve teacher education in Korea (Yoo, 1983).

The United States carried out a large number of aid programs in Korea, investing over $19 million from 1953 to 1967 (Dodge, 1971, pp. 199–201). All programs were based on institutional contracts; three programs in particular deserve further discussion. The first and largest, in terms of amount of investment, was the contract sponsored by the U.S. Foreign Operations Administration between the University of Minnesota and Seoul National University, with the objective "to upgrade the faculty members to the point where the programs there would compare favorably to those of high-ranking universities anywhere in the world" through a faculty exchange program (McGinn et al., 1980, p. 91). The program began in 1954, and the total funding until its termination in June 1962 amounted to about $6.5 million (Dodge, 1971, pp. 199–201). The second U.S. technical aid program for Korean higher education was the contract with George Peabody College for Teachers that lasted from 1956 to 1962. This contract aimed at improving teacher training programs, and U.S. financial assistance for this program amounted to $3.8 million (Yoo, 1983). The third program was the contract between Washington University and two leading private universities, Yonsei and Korea, in the field of business administration. As a result of the program, the curriculum and instruction in business administration at both universities were improved and strengthened.

Through increased emphasis on higher education, these U.S. aid programs reshaped existing colleges and universities. Many new colleges and universities were established and enrollments increased rapidly (Mason et al., 1980). It was hoped that by investing in Korean higher education the phenomenon of brain drain could be countered—that the "availability of advanced high-quality centers would reduce the outflow of talented students seeking training in foreign universities . . . and also draw back to Korea outstanding scholars who had settled abroad" (Dodge, 1971, p. 281). The U.S. aid authorities failed, however, to assess accurately Korea's high-level manpower needs for national development. Critics charged that the aid programs' overemphasis on higher education resulted in an overproduction of college and university graduates and, in turn, rising unemployment among graduates. In fact, critics went on to say, the provision of centers of excellence for high-level training may have exacerbated the brain drain problem. Koreans highly trained in technologies that are abundant in more advanced countries but not yet established in Korea were more likely to emigrate, especially given the changes in U.S. immigration laws (McGinn et al., 1980).

It has been reported that through the various U.S. projects aiding Korea's development from 1954 to 1967, a total of 2,883 Koreans received advanced training in the United States and other Western countries (Dodge, 1971, pp. 199–201). By 1956, the third largest group of foreign students in the United States was from Korea, behind those from Canada and Taiwan. The leadership role played by U.S.-trained scholars at Korean colleges and universities extended into every corner of university administration, governance, financing, and curriculum development.

ISSUES AND REALITIES

Since the mid-1960s, Korea has made significant progress and is regarded as one of the few developing countries to have achieved such rapid economic and social development. As one of the newly industrializing countries in Asia, Korea is making a great effort to maintain its economic prosperity and to restructure its economy around knowledge- and technology-based industries. The effort to shift the national economy away from a reliance on labor-intensive industries highlights the importance of higher education because universities play such a central role in producing highly skilled human resources. In a country like Korea, with few natural resources, a well-educated workforce becomes the engine for socioeconomic development. The rapid expansion of higher education in Korea was a key element in the country's drive to restructure its economy (S.-J. Paik, 1999). Higher education in Korea deserves to be recognized for its contribution to such levels of national development. The Korean higher education system is the product of indigenous modernization in conjunction with accumulated Western influences (S. H. Lee, 1989a; 1989b; J.-K. Lee, 2000).

Expanded Higher Education Opportunity

Since the mid-1960s, along with the country's economic development, opportunity for higher education has expanded rapidly. The wave of growth is now cresting, as depicted in Table 6.1. The number of schools of all types increased 16-fold, from 85 in 1960 to 1,321 in 2002. The number of students enrolled in higher education increased more than 35-fold, from 101,041 in 1960 to 3,577,447 in 2002. The Korean example of massive growth in higher education may not be observed in many other countries.

A number of factors contributed to this rapid expansion of higher education, including the continued rise in the birthrate in the decades after the Korean War and the social and national demand for a more equal distribution of educational opportunity by region, gender, and discipline. The demand for equal opportunity arose in part from the reality that the prestigious universities were concentrated in the major cities—particularly in the capital city, Seoul—which made it difficult for students in peripheral areas to obtain a good undergraduate education. Furthermore, some academic disciplines were better supported than others because of the value or status attached to them. In addition, the emergence of new fields of study and of promising job opportunities stimulated the expansion of higher education. However, the most salient factor was the traditional attitudes of Koreans, who view a four-year undergraduate education as essential for upward mobility. That was the key reason why academe was widely regarded as a growth industry in Korea and why private institutions mushroomed.

While some of Korea's colleges and universities had earlier origins, most modern institutions of higher education were established after World War II. When Korea was liberated from Japanese colonial rule in 1945 there were only 19 institutions of higher education, with 7,819 students and 753 faculty members. By 1960, however, the number of institutions and students had increased by 450 and 1,300 percent, respectively. Since then, the high growth rate has continued up until today.

Table 6.1 Quantitative Growth of Higher Education, 1945–2002

	1945	1960	1970	1980	1990	2000	2002
Institutions[a]							
Numbers	19	85	232	357	556	1,184	1,321
Post-1945 increase	100%	450%	1,220%	1,879%	2,926%	6,232%	6,953%
Post-1960 increase	—	100%	273%	420%	654%	1,392%	1,554%
Students							
Numbers	7,819	101,041	201,436	615,452	1,490,809	3,363,549	3,577,447
Post-1945 increase	100%	1,290%	2,586%	7,871%	19,066%	43,018%	45,753%
Post-1960 increase	—	100%	199%	306%	740%	3,329%	3,541%

Sources: Korean Educational Development Institute (2002, pp. 584–585); Ministry of Education and Human Resources Development (2001, p. 19).

[a]The total number of institutions includes graduate schools that are either attached to four-year universities or are separate institutions without undergraduate programs.

As shown in Table 6.2, by 2002 Korea had a total of 376 institutions of higher education: 159 two- or three-year junior vocational colleges; 194 four-year colleges and universities; 18 graduate schools that have no undergraduate programs; and 5 miscellaneous postsecondary schools. Including the 927 graduate schools established in affiliation to four-year universities brings the number of all types of institutions to 1,321. Enrollments at these institutions of higher education amounted to 3.58 million, which accounted for about 7.61 percent of the entire population.

Higher education in Korea has expanded so rapidly that the country has already achieved mass higher education with universal access. Korean higher education has passed the threshold of an elite system, in terms of enrollment of the relevant age group. According to the OECD education statistics (OECD, 2001), net enrollment rates for tertiary education in Korea at various ages are very high.

Table 6.2   Higher Education Institutions, Students, and Faculty Members, 2002

Type of Institution	Institutions	Students	Full-time faculty
Two- or three-year vocational colleges			
Public	16	38,845	717
Private	143	924,284	11,439
Total	159	963,129	12,156
Four-year			
Colleges and universities			
Public	26	387,299	11,632
Private	137	1,384,439	32,545
Total	163	1,771,738	44,177
Industrial universities[a]			
Public	8	85,956	1,296
Private	11	101,084	1,247
Total	19	187,040	2,543
Teacher training universities			
Public	11	23,259	721
Private	0	0	0
Total	11	23,259	721
Air and correspondence universities			
Public	1	367,305	112
Private	0	0	0
Total	1	367,305	112
Miscellaneous two- to four-year institutions[b]			
Public	0	0	0
Private	5	2,109	41
Total	5	2,109	41
Graduate schools			
Public	0 (164)	80,585	0
Private	18 (781)	182,282	179
Total	18 (945)[c]	262,867	179[d]
All types			
Public	62 (226)	983,249	14,487
Private	314 (1,095)	2,594,198	45,451
Total	376 (1,321)[c]	3,577,447	59,929

(continued)

Sources: Korean Educational Development Institute (2002, pp. 584–585); Ministry of Education (2000).

*a*Industrial universities were established in order to serve industry's needs for skilled manpower.

*b*These are institutions that were established for various unique purposes at the postsecondary level, not as regular universities.

*c*The number of graduate schools in parentheses (945) includes graduate schools that are either attached to four-year universities or separate institutions without undergraduate programs.

*d*The number of faculty members in graduate schools is for 2000 and includes only those members in the eighteen separate graduate schools without undergraduate programs.

The Korean net enrollment rate at age 18 is 44 percent, compared to the average rate of 16 percent in other OECD countries. At age 19, the rate in Korea is 59 percent, compared to the average rate of 26 percent in other OECD countries. At age 20, the rate in Korea is 53 percent, but the average in other OECD countries is 29 percent. Of course, institutions in Korea vary widely in size, ranging from less than 100 students to more than 35,000 students.

This trend toward a mass higher education system was observed a decade ago. Total enrollments in higher education institutions had reached 1.6 million in 1992, which amounted to about 3.6 percent of the entire population. Enrollments at higher education institutions per 1,000 people in Korea numbered about 45.4 in 1992. Furthermore, enrollments at all types of higher education institutions, excluding graduate schools, exceeded 62 percent of the total Korean population aged 18 to 21 in 1996, while about 44 percent of this age group was enrolled at four-year institutions of higher education. The quantitative growth in institutions and enrollments has been prodigious.

Private institutions of higher learning greatly outnumber public institutions, with the former enrolling about three-quarters of all students. The preponderance of private institutions dates back to before the 1960s, but since then their number has multiplied rapidly. Private institutions have made a considerable contribution to the development of high-level human resources. In Korea, many entrepreneurs, leaders of private organizations, and foundations have invested their limited resources in establishing four-year colleges and universities. In spite of their considerable contribution to the development of higher education, it is also true that many private institutions were established primarily for the purpose of making profits from student tuition. Yet many private institutions today are faced with grave problems concerning educational quality and financial constraints. Private institutions rely on student tuition to cover more than 70 percent of their expenses, while about 54 percent of the budget at public institutions is covered by student tuition.

Curriculum and Administration

Teaching and learning in Korea's Confucian society had traditionally embraced only literature, in keeping with the deep-rooted reverence for the *culturati*. Then, in 1962, Korea launched the first Five-Year Economic Development Plan. Since then, the government has gradually increased enrollment quotas in the natural sciences and engineering each year, while limiting the increases in the humanities and the social sciences. In 1993, science and engineering accounted for 54 percent of the freshman enrollment quotas for four-year institutions of higher education.

The curriculum in many departments at Korean universities and colleges is based on the American model. Although certain conditions in Korea have affected curriculum development, the content and organization of the curriculum have largely been shaped by American-educated faculty members. At the graduate level, the procedure for conferring degrees is quite similar to that at American graduate schools. For example, course requirements, qualifying examinations, foreign-language requirements, thesis writing, and oral defenses are all standard practice in Korean higher education. At the undergraduate level, the baccalaureate degree requires at least 140 credit hours, of which about 32 percent are devoted to general education. In addition to the semester system, the major-minor and double-major systems were introduced through a pilot program in 1973. An advanced placement program for top students in some subject areas was also introduced. In 1984, summer sessions were set up at every four-year institution of higher education.

Despite remarkable developments in the curriculum area, while the goals of general education have been formulated the actual objectives are not clearly defined. In theory, general education is recognized as an important element of college education, but in practice it is treated as peripheral and is poorly designed and organized. For example, a major may simply be a collection of courses in a certain specialty area, lacking balance or cohesion with regard to depth and breadth. The undergraduate curriculum is departmentally fragmented and overspecialized, shaped by the dominant faculty specializations. At the undergraduate level in 1990, there were 558 distinct designated majors and 4,315 departments, but only 26 different undergraduate degrees. Given the fact that the curriculum at Korean universities was largely patterned on the American model, it is not surprising that the problems and issues facing Korean colleges and institutions are also confronting American institutions.

Overcentralization

The government has strictly controlled enrollments for the purpose of coordinating the supply and demand of human resources in Korean society, as well as regulating the quality of education in the colleges and universities. Strong government control has been exercised despite the significant role of the private sector in higher education.

For a long time, a salient feature of Korean higher education has been direct government involvement in the administration of higher education. In an attempt at enforcing quality control, the government has directly participated in the accrediting of institutions, faculty, and programs. Gradually, however, support rose for a new development strategy to rejuvenate institutions of higher education by mobilizing academic expertise, culminating in 1982 with the creation of a nongovernmental, collective body of four-year institutions of higher education, the Korean Council for University Education. The council is an association of presidents, reminiscent of a similar organization that existed under the U.S. military government. Its primary function is to ensure a basic level of quality and a significant amount of autonomy through the professional evaluation of higher education institutions and programs. The primary mode of evaluation is the same as that of the accrediting system prevalent in the United States. Since its establishment, the council has conducted annual institutional and programmatic evaluations. While the council has played a part in increasing the degree of academic autonomy in Korean higher education, the government's direct control system is still valid in various aspects.

Graduate Education

Until the mid-1960s, graduate education remained relatively undeveloped. It was modeled after the Japanese system, which in turn was originally based on the German system. Graduate education following the U.S. model began to develop when Yonsei University, a comprehensive research-oriented university, opened a new U.S.-style doctoral degree program in 1961, conferring the doctoral degree upon three medical graduate students in 1965.

The following years saw enormous advances in the size, structure, and function of Korean graduate education. The number of graduate institutions rose from 37 in 1965, to 335 in 1992, to 945 in 2002, while the number of students approached 97,000 in 1992 and more than 260,000 in 2002. Today, Korea's graduate schools are divided into three types: academic graduate schools, which are research-oriented and offer master's and doctoral degree programs; special graduate schools, which provide evening classes for practitioners and award master's degrees; and professional graduate schools, which emphasize professional knowledge and award master's and professional doctoral degrees. This last type of graduate school is still in its formative period, as it was introduced in the 1990s (S. H. Lee, 1996).

TRENDS AND CHALLENGES

Korean higher education has achieved impressive progress in the past century. After the long struggle to establish a higher education system, Korea became one of the leading countries in terms of providing access to higher education by creating a system of mass higher education. It is generally recognized that Korean higher education has greatly contributed to the nation's socioeconomic development, even though an ongoing debate exists on the role of higher education in national development. The perspective offered in this chapter is that Korea was able to utilize Western influences in ways that benefited the country's higher education system. Nevertheless, many problems and issues remain that could pose serious obstacles in upgrading Korean higher education in the future.

At the beginning of a millennium of global competition among institutions of higher education, Korean higher education faces a formidable challenge. It must continually cross and recross the boundaries between intellectualism and careerism, between the ivory tower and the world of work, providing academics with a sense of self-actualization in bringing competitive new ideas and products to the institution and society. Higher education must also excite young people about academic inquiry, tackle growing social problems, and ensure that coming generations of Koreans are capable of living and working in a multicultural global society.

Institutional Diversity

Diversity in higher education is critically important not only because it allows the system to meet institutional and societal needs but also because differentiation among component units leads to stability that protects the system itself. It is widely believed that diversity is an essential and primary factor in the birth and death of an institution of higher education. In reality, the only distinction among institutions in Korea lies in the average student scores on the college entrance examination (the Korean SAT). It is quite difficult to find differences in curriculum, organization, governance, funding, or even in expressed goals.

Uniformity among colleges and universities has been a major problem in Korean higher education and extends to academic and professional orientation. In the case of four-year colleges and universities, institutions with large enrollments are uniformly structured as research universities. They usually have all the popular departments and majors. Consequently, the level of teaching and research in these fragmented departments and majors is often inferior. The situation is not all that different in the case of small colleges and universities (S.-J. Paik et al., 1998).

A strong drive for institutional diversification among colleges and universities was part of the educational reform of 1996. *Institutional diversification* and *institutional specialization* have been catch phrases since 1990 in the campaign to help Korean higher education achieve institutional competitiveness and academic excellence in a changing environment. In addition to diversifying the profiles and academic focus of institutions of higher education, the strategy also calls for each college or university to specialize in certain areas. The number of institutions pursuing the status of research university needs to be reduced. Both the government and academics drove the movement to create research universities. However, the degree of success in introducing diversity has been restricted due to the long tradition of uniformity in the system. At the present time, institutional diversification and specialization remain important objectives of higher education reform and are being pursued at both national and institutional levels.

Significant changes lie ahead for Korea's higher education system as the competition over increasingly scarce resources intensifies, leading to institutional crisis of existence. Therefore, the maintenance and enhancement of diversity and specialization are critical to the future stability and relevance of Korean higher education. Each college or university will need to address a variety of issues as they devise their strategies: the curriculum development needs of students; higher education's political, social, and economic functions; their stated educational mission; and measures to ensure institutional stability in a changing environment.

Calls for institutional differentiation arise not only from the declining size of the college-age population and the increasing preference of students for studying in the Seoul metropolitan area but also from the shift in educational goals from intellectualism to careerism. Higher education needs to serve the diverse requirements of students who think of a college education as the path to professional career development. Many four-year colleges and universities have begun to respond to the current climate by providing vocationally oriented majors, diverse programs, resources recruited from the professional world, flexible time schedules, residential alternatives, and opportunities for experiential learning. Moreover, these innovations are being developed not simply by a few off-beat specialized institutions but by institutions ranging from the established and elite to the marginal and unsophisticated. In contrast to the conformity of the twentieth century, a plethora of models exists in Korean higher education.

Academic Nationalism

As discussed earlier, the Western, especially the American, influence on Korean higher education was facilitated by American-educated faculty members at Korean universities and colleges. Their influence included classroom teaching methods, curricular content, university administration and governance, as well as concepts relating to teaching and research. The overall impact of American-educated faculty members on Korean higher education has been positively evaluated: "At an early stage, Korean professors imported American learning almost indiscriminately, but this was an inevitable process of development. Despite this weakness, they made a considerable contribution to the development of learning in Korea" (Koo & Suh, 1984, p. 277).

However, during the 1970s, a number of conflicts began to appear in higher education. First of all, there was conflict between the American-educated younger faculty and the older faculty who had no doctoral degrees. This tension shifted to the divide between Korean-educated doctoral degree-holders and American-educated degree-holders. A kind of neonationalism arose in the academic community. This nationalist consciousness in academia obtained government support in the form of the Academy of Korean Studies, which was established for the purpose of encouraging instruction and research in traditional Korean culture, philosophy, history, and literature. The movement to foster the self-identity of the Korean people has spread throughout all fields in higher education.

Now, dependence on Western theories and practices is being overcome not only by Korean-educated scholars but also by American-educated scholars. Scholars are attempting to Koreanize their teaching and research in universities and colleges. Modernization is no longer considered synonymous with Westernization or Americanization. Modernization can take the form of a true Koreanization, a policy of seeking Korea's own potentialities and building on its own unique resources. Accordingly, there is a growing preference for Korean research articles over foreign ones and for faculty members with Korean degrees over those with foreign degrees in some academic specialties such as the humanities. There is, however, a continuing reliance on Western developments in the social and natural sciences and in engineering fields. Yet, it is unclear whether such dependence is a threat to Koreanization or what separates subtle from overt acceptance of Western theories and practices.

The Academic Labor Market

The academic labor market consists of the demand of institutions for persons to fill faculty positions and the supply of educated persons, particularly doctoral degree-holders, who seek academic jobs at colleges and universities. During the current (and, possibly, future) depressed period in Korean higher education, the number of young persons who are specifically preparing for the academic profession far exceeds in size the demand for members of the professoriate. At present, more than 13,000 young scholars who hold Ph.D.s but have not found employment in academe flood the market as poorly paid, part-time lecturers. According to a 2002 Ministry of Education report, between 2002 and 2006 more than forty thousand people with doctorates will join the labor market, and many of them will inevitably be engaged in part-time college teaching or research, with temporary appointments. In the past, colleges and universities in Korea have employed local professionals—such as practicing lawyers, doctors, researchers, or accountants—on a part-time basis. Frequently, institutions employed new doctorate-holders on a probationary basis. However, this is now changing. As the financial position of higher education institutions becomes more precarious, part-timers may be hired in larger numbers as an economy measure, which will weaken the job market for potential faculty. The growing dependence of academe on part-time faculty is now widely regarded as a serious problem, because of the declining quality of instruction and the waste of highly capable talent.

One may ask why the production of Ph.D.s continued at such a high rate despite the worsening academic market. One reason is the economic depression of the nation in the 1990s. Many talented young college graduates could not find jobs and thus just continued their studies. Another reason is that government policy increased the number of young people studying abroad, opening a door that had been closed for a long time. Still another factor is that the women's movement encouraged and emboldened many young women to seek Ph.D.s. Women were entering the academic labor market in unprecedented numbers. The growing pool of highly educated people seeking to enter the academic profession would create stiff competition for both new Ph.D.s and established members of the professoriate.

Government Control

The government in Korea has long assumed responsibility for the provision of higher education. As a result, not only public but also private institutions have become the recipients of government administrative input. The Korean higher education system has moved beyond the principle that public national universities were to serve the needs of the state while private institutions catered to the aspirations of individuals. This explicit dualism assumed that the government had total responsibility for national institutions but not for private ones, particularly in terms of their finances. In reality, government subsidies for private institutions, which educate about 75 percent of the country's students, have been nominal in the past but are now increasing to some degree.

From the beginning, both private and public institutions have been under strict government control. For example, in Korea, the government quota on enrollments in higher education applies not only to public but also to private institutions. Under the quota policy, designed to maintain standards by limiting total enrollments in the nation, the government sets the maximum number of students allowed for each institution on the basis of educational conditions at each institution, market demand, and other factors. Consequently, most institutions have always devoted their energies to winning larger quotas in the annual assessments. Private institutions, which are without other sources for financial support and depend on revenue from student tuition fees, often seek to expand their operations by adding buildings, departments, and faculty, which will allow an increase in enrollments and thus more income from tuition fees.

Declining Enrollments

As of 2000, it was widely recognized that higher education in Korea had entered an uncertain period because of the downturn in the number of high school graduates. To make matters worse, four-year colleges and universities, which were traditionally preferred over two- or three-year junior vocational colleges, are being challenged by the flourishing careerism in higher education. Many high school graduates now want to obtain practical vocational training in two- or three-year junior colleges and thus join the world of work as early as possible. It has already been reported that many private four-year colleges and universities are suffering from low enrollments. In 2000, 33 percent of private four-year institutions had enrollments more than 20 percent below their government quotas (Ministry of Education, 2001b). The institutions' financial situation and faculty expectations of the academic work environment are correspondingly bleak.

About 29 percent of four-year colleges and universities are located in the Seoul metropolitan area, accommodating the same percentage of total enrollments. The concentration of jobs, the attractions of city life, and the pull of a few top-ranked institutions have increased the flow of college and university students to the Seoul metropolitan area. Often students at local colleges or universities withdraw from their institutions and try to gain admission to institutions in the Seoul metropolitan area as transfer students or by retaking the entrance examinations and reapplying. The movement of the student population into the Seoul metropolitan area, in addition to the downturn in the number of high school graduates, is exacerbating the decline in enrollments and the financial crisis at local private colleges and universities. It is now feared that many local private colleges and universities may go into bankruptcy.

In Korea, the time has passed when colleges and universities need only open their doors and select their students from among the surging crowds of high school graduates. With the exception of a few top-ranked elite institutions, faculty and staff are now expected to go out and recruit students to their institutions—a task that adds a fourth function to professors' three traditional functions of teaching, research, and provision of social services. To attract more students, institutions in local areas as well as in Seoul are working quickly to reform their educational programs and student services. The emphasis has been on differentiation of the curriculum, academic management, student services, and scholarship programs. Private colleges and universities are implementing many ideas to renew their identities, develop their unique strengths, and restructure their organizations in a cost-effective way.

Private Institutions and Public Support

The government has direct and indirect financial assistance programs for higher education institutions and their students. In 2000, such programs accounted for only 9.9 percent of the entire government education budget. Government financial support for private four-year colleges and universities rose to 3.79 percent of the institutions' total expenditures in 2000 from 1.39 percent in 1990. Government support per student at private institutions is now equal to about 5 or 6 percent of support per student at public institutions. Of course, more government support for higher education institutions, particularly in the private sector, will be necessary in the future. The immediate question, however, is not whether more assistance will be needed and given, but how it will be given and in what amounts. It is easy to distribute government funding equally, as it has been, to private institutions in proportion to their student numbers. However, it is not so easy to ensure the best use of the limited government funding by each recipient institution. For this reason, the government introduced a new policy of government financial support to higher education institutions beginning in 1999.

The new policy was named "Brain Korea 21" because it was designed to elevate the quality level of Korean higher education in the twenty-first century to world-class standards, particularly in selected graduate schools and selected fields in the natural sciences. The total amount of the subsidy, 1.4 trillion won (U.S.$1.1 billion) over seven years (1999–2005), is quite enormous in scale, compared to the previous subsidies provided by the government. The assistance is directed at selected public and private four-year colleges and universities and includes full financial aid to graduate students; grants for specific programs; and specific education reforms such as the restructuring of a department-based organization into a division-based one. The effect of this new policy is that the relative amounts of subsidy to private institutions vary enormously from institution to institution, from major field to major field, and from student to student. This policy has stimulated change at some elite public and private institutions, where admissions tend to be more competitive than before. It is not surprising that students have clearly been affected by such targeted subsidy programs. Faculty have also been greatly affected because they have to conform fully to government reform guidelines. Thus, this new policy may pose another threat to academic freedom and institutional autonomy and may put heavy pressures on academic ethics.

Faculty Governance and Student Government

The growing role of faculty governance and the shrinking role of student government raise complex issues that Korean higher education will have to resolve. Student activism at Korean colleges and universities has historically been strong and politically assertive. Students became involved in national economic affairs, the issue of registering for military service, and expressing their views to political leaders as early as 1948, but the event that initiated a period of unprecedented student activism was the 1960 April Revolution against the dictatorial Rhee government. For the next three decades, national attention was focused on the students' flaunting their control on campus and the violent tactics they employed that in some cases resulted in closing down a university. More significantly, in retrospect, for activists the student movement represented a channel to a career in politics. The most powerful student activist organization was the General Association of Korean College and University Students. However, with the democratization of Korean politics in the early 1990s, student involvement in political protest has declined. In a gradual process, after many years of struggle, students at most institutions have gained increasing control over academic core issues—such as tuition, curriculum, space allocation, and other internal governance matters.

On the other hand, the faculty traditionally had become marginalized in academic affairs at colleges and universities. Student governments, in contrast, have had an official status. They are recognized and approved by the governing boards; specific powers are often delegated to them; and they always have an official budget, made up in part of the compulsory student fees collected by the administration. However, faculty governance is not yet well established at Korean colleges and universities. From the late 1980s, some leading faculty began to urge their colleagues to organize faculty councils, composed of all faculty members, and faculty senates, composed of representatives of the faculty members at each institution. Supporters called for direct elections for the president of the institution and for recognition of the faculty council or senate as a legitimate organization. Faculty councils and faculty senates in the Korean academic workplace are now more than ever vital channels of communication among academic workers.

Despite government efforts to circumvent union activity, some radical faculty proponents of faculty governance have found new ways to protect the rights of their colleagues. The new approach includes nationwide unionization of faculty and the creation of a strong association representing all college and university professors. As of 2003, the majority of faculty members seemed indifferent to a movement to unionize and hesitant to take an active part in the movement. However, when the unionization of faculty becomes a reality on campuses, it is likely that the faculty and the administrator-trustees will be firmly polarized in adversarial positions. And as members of bargaining units, faculty members may lose their individuality, flexibility, seniority, and the emotional relationships between individual faculty members and administrators.

Faculty Evaluation

At present, most faculty at four-year colleges and universities are disgusted with the faculty evaluations that have been instituted in recent years. Some faculty members confess to a sense of malaise and apprehension, while others override and ignore the practice of evaluation. For a long time in Korea, faculty were completely free from being evaluated by others. Once a faculty member was first appointed, he or she was promoted and granted tenure based on the passage of time. That was the very reason why the profession of college or university professor has always been given the highest status.

However, in the early 1990s, the situation began to change. Many institutions of higher education began to advocate faculty evaluation and to develop effective procedures for it. Now, all faculty agree upon the need for faculty performance evaluation, but no agreement has been reached on which practices work effectively and which do not. The core of the debate over faculty evaluation is its intended purpose, which determines the kinds of information used, sources of data, depth of data analysis, and dissemination of findings. Two main purposes for faculty evaluation have now been identified: one is to promote and improve faculty performance in research, teaching, and service. The other is to provide the rationale for administrative decisions on promotions in rank and tenure, on academic rewards (including sabbatical leave), on provision of research funds, on salary level, and so on. Each institution now is developing its own measures for judging faculty performance, which it applies through a variety of evaluations. However, differences in perception and interpretation of the measures among administrators, faculty members, and even students have created multiple conflicts on campus. It is clear that the work environment of faculty in Korea will undergo many changes, not only in the theoretical framework but also in the practical execution. Acquiring consensus and stability among faculty members in this regard and achieving academic excellence in Korean higher education will depend on the academic community's response to these challenges.

CONCLUSION

In an era of international interdependence, all countries borrow some features for their systems from those of other countries. The development of Korean higher education during the last century is no exception. The arrival of Western missionaries in Korea, the Japanese occupation, the independence movement, the management of independence under a trusteeship, the Korean War, and the division of the country into South and North Korea—all these experiences have forced Koreans to come to terms with Western influences in every aspect of their lives. Higher education in Korea has developed in the context of such Western influences. At the same time, however, Korean higher education has developed its own unique character, shaped by both external forces and indigenous circumstances.

If development means exploration and creation, not pale imitation or blind conformity, what developments can Korean higher education really claim? Is it possible to reinterpret the development of Korean higher education as an unfolding or revelation of indigenous thought and philosophy? Is the best defense against acculturation to return to more traditional forms or to experiment with idiosyncratic Korean forms, without referring to Western developments? These questions cannot be answered in a few words but are complex and require an integrated analysis. A useful approach for dealing with these questions might be to view Western developments as one of the sources challenging endogenous change, while also treating it as a potentially influential force. One mistake Korea may have made in the course of developing its higher education system was in treating the American system as a compelling example, rather than as a source of data. To achieve success in the future, Korean higher education institutions must not fall victim to narrow-minded attitudes of self-preservation but rather must move to establish a full psychologically interdependent membership with their counterparts in the academic community worldwide.

In this context, Korean higher education needs to confront current and upcoming challenges effectively. Some of the issues that have recently emerged are rooted in past traditions and the historical development of higher education with regard to government control, academic nationalism, and the lack of diversity. Consequently, dealing with these problems will not be easy. Furthermore, the Korean educational environment of the twenty-first century is quite different from that of the past century. One of the most critical changes as of 2003 is the fact that colleges and universities are no longer in the position of being able to select the students they want and instead must attract students to their institutions. Recruiting students will become an essential task to ensure an institution's survival, given the declining population. The pressure to achieve standards of excellence comparable to that of advanced Western countries is also increasing in comparison to earlier periods. In conclusion, different roles will have to be assumed by the government, individual institutions, faculty members, and even students. Not only effective communication but also consensus and integrated action in the academic community will be required of all the different entities and sectors. The future shape of higher education in Korea will depend largely on whether Korean academe meets current and upcoming challenges with collective wisdom.

REFERENCES

Adams, Donald K. (1956). *Education in Korea, 1945–1955.* Unpublished doctoral dissertation, University of Connecticut.

Choi, Sungchan. (1975). *Korean Christian higher education in transition: The impact of Western philosophies.* Unpublished doctoral dissertation, University of California, Berkeley.

Dodge, Herbert W. (1971). *A history of U.S. assistance to Korean education, 1953–1966.* Unpublished doctoral dissertation, George Washington University.

Jayasuriya, J. E. (1983). *Education in Korea: A third world success story.* Seoul: Korean National Commission for UNESCO.

Kim, Jin-Eun. (1973). *An analysis of the national planning process for educational development in the Republic of Korea, 1945–1970.* Unpublished doctoral dissertation, University of Pittsburgh.

Kim, Uchang. (1985). The autonomous development of the university in Korea. In Committee of International Conference (Ed.), *The university in the future world* (pp. 149–170). Seoul: Yonsei University Press.

Korean Educational Development Institute. (2002). *Statistical yearbook of education 2002.* Seoul: Author.

Koo, Youngnok, & Suh, Dae-Sook (Eds.). (1984). *Korea and the United States: A century of cooperation.* Honolulu: University of Hawaii Press.

Lee, Jeong-Kyu. (2000). *Historic factors influencing Korean higher education.* Seoul: Jimoondang Publishing.

Lee, Jeong-Kyu. (2002). Christianity and Korean education in the late Choson period. *Christian Higher Education, 1,* 85–99.

Lee, Sung-Hwa. (1958). *The social and political factors affecting Korean education, 1885–1950.* Unpublished doctoral dissertation, University of Pittsburgh.

Lee, Sungho H. (1989a). The emergence of the modern university in Korea. In P. G.

Altbach & V. Selvaratnam (Eds.), *From dependence to autonomy* (pp. 227–256). Dordrecht: Kluwer Academic.

Lee, Sungho H. (1989b). Higher education and research environments in Korea. In P. G. Altbach et al. (Eds.), *Scientific development and higher education* (pp. 31–81). New York: Praeger.

Lee, Sungho H. (1996). The academic profession in Korea. In P. G. Altbach (Ed.), *The international academic profession* (pp. 97–148). San Francisco: Jossey Bass.

Mason, Edward S., et al. (1980). *Studies in the modernization of the Republic of Korea, 1945–1975: The economic and social modernization of the Republic of Korea* (chap. 10). Cambridge, MA: Harvard University Press.

McGinn, Noel F., et al. (1980). *Education and development in Korea.* Cambridge, MA: Harvard University Press.

Ministry of Education. (2000). *Ministry of Education survey of independent graduate schools.* Seoul: Author.

Ministry of Education. (2001a). *Education in Korea: 2001–2002.* Seoul: Author.

Ministry of Education. (2001b). *Ministry of Education 2000 institution survey.* Seoul: Author.

Nahm, Andrew C. (1981). Modernization process in Korea: A historical perspective. In C. S. Lee (Ed.), *Modernization of Korea and the impact of the West* (pp. 25–68). Los Angeles: East Asian Studies Center, University of Southern California.

Nam, Byung-Hun. (1962). *Educational reorganization in South Korea under the United States Army Military Government, 1945–1948.* Unpublished doctoral dissertation, University of Pittsburgh.

OECD, Centre for Educational Research and Innovation Indicators of Education Systems. (2001). *Education at a glance: OECD indicators.* Seoul: Author

Oh, Chon-Suk. (1964). *Hankook Shinkyoyooksa* (History of Korean education). Seoul: Hyundae Kyoyook Chongsu.

Paik, George L. (1973). *Hankook Kaeshinkyosa* (The history of Protestant missions in Korea, 1832–1910). Seoul: Yonsei University Press.

Paik, Sung-Joon. (1999). Educational policy and economic development. In Korean Educational Development Institute (Ed.), *Economic development and educational policies in Korea* (pp. 13–40). Seoul: Author.

Paik, Sung-Joon, et al. (1998). *Educational development in Korea: An analysis of investment and development strategies.* Seoul: Korean Educational Development Institute.

Rim, Han-Young. (1952). *Development of higher education in Korea during the Japanese occupation, 1910–1945.* Unpublished doctoral dissertation, Teachers College, Columbia University.

Sohn, Insoo. (1987). *Hankook Kyoyooksa* (History of Korean education), Vol. 2. Seoul: Muneumsa.

Underwood, H. H. (1926). *Modern education in Korea.* New York: International Press.

Yoo, Hyung-Jin. (1983, February). Korean-American educational interchange. *Korea Journal, 23,* 4–18.

7

Singapore

Small Nation, Big Plans

Jason Tan

Two important features of Singapore higher education are the overriding importance of economic relevance and the dominant state presence in decision making and planning. By the early 1980s Singapore had entered the ranks of the newly industrialized countries. The government launched its second industrial revolution in 1979, which involved restructuring the economy to focus on high-technology, skill-intensive manufacturing, and service sector activities. Higher education enrollments were increased to meet the anticipated new manpower demands. Several government economic reports published since the mid-1980s have stressed the role of higher education institutions in maintaining Singapore's international competitiveness in the global economy in the face of increasingly acute competition from other countries.

Sustained economic growth over the past four decades has also meant increasing social demand for access to higher education. During the 1960s and 1970s the government consistently adopted a cautious attitude toward expanding higher education enrollments, citing among other reasons the negative social consequences of graduate unemployment and the devaluation of university degrees. However, from the mid-1980s on the government has had to provide increased opportunities in response to the growing social demand, as well as to the needs of economic growth. The latest enrollment figures are 21 percent and 40 percent for universities and polytechnics, respectively, with a target of 25 percent to be achieved by the year 2010.

OVERVIEW AND HISTORICAL PERSPECTIVES

Universities and Polytechnics

In 1823 Sir Stamford Raffles, who had earlier succeeded in securing Singapore as a British trading post, proposed the establishment of a native college. Raffles intended that the college should offer instruction in Chinese, Siamese, Malay, and other local languages and subjects such as history for the sons of neighboring rulers and merchants. He also envisaged that the college would provide facilities for research into the history, societies, and economies of neighboring countries (Chelliah, 1947). Unfortunately, Raffles' enthusiasm was not shared by other colonial administrators, and the idea failed to materialize.

It was not until 1905 that the colonial government opened a medical college in response to a petition from local community leaders. In 1920, the college, which served Singapore and Malaya, was named the King Edward VII College of Medicine. Further pressure from the local Straits Chinese British Association, as well as the threat of an American-sponsored tertiary college, spurred the government into making plans to open a college of higher education (Turnbull, 1989). Raffles College, which began admitting students in 1928, awarded diplomas, and most of its graduates went into secondary school teaching or into junior civil service posts.

The immediate post–World War II years were marked by the acceleration of civil service localization, as well as initial moves toward self-government. As a result of the Carr-Saunders Commission's recommendations, the King Edward VII Medical College and Raffles College merged to form the degree-granting University of Malaya in 1949. The university served the needs of Singapore, Malaya, and the Borneo Territories for the next ten years. Two autonomous divisions of the university, one in Singapore and the other in Kuala Lumpur, were established in 1959. Subsequently, two separate national universities were formed, and the University of Singapore came into being in 1962.

A key factor in all the above developments in higher education was that they catered only to students from English-language schools. The British colonial authorities displayed a lack of interest in Chinese-language education, and there was a history of antagonism between the government and the Chinese community regarding education, dating back to the early decades of the twentieth century (Wilson, 1978). In response to declining standards and enrollments in Chinese-language schools, prominent local Chinese merchants proposed establishing a community-funded Chinese-language university as early as 1950. Nanyang University was originally registered as a company in 1953 and was officially opened in 1956 with the help of substantial donations from the Chinese community. It had three colleges—a College of Arts, a College of Science, and a College of Commerce. The university faced many difficulties from its inception, including left-wing student agitation, problems in recruiting quality academic staff, and low academic standards (Wilson, 1978). The government granted Nanyang University statutory status in 1959 but did not formally recognize Nanyang degrees until 1968.

By the early 1970s, Nanyang University's future was under threat, not only because of falling standards and difficulties with staff recruitment and retention, but also due to the shrinking pool of Chinese-language secondary school students. The situation was aggravated by the increasing numbers of students who had opted for the English-language University of Singapore or for foreign universities from 1960 on (Lee, 1978). In 1980 the Nanyang University Council unanimously accepted the prime minister's proposal to merge the two universities to form the English-language National University of Singapore (NUS). The prime minister's proposal was in turn based on the recommendations of a British academic, Sir Frederick Dainton, in favor of developing a single, strong comprehensive university. The NUS now has undergraduate and postgraduate courses in seven faculties (arts and social sciences, business administration, dentistry, engineering, law, medicine, and science) and two schools (computing, and design and environment). The closing down of the Nanyang University effectively signaled the death knell to Chinese-language higher education in Singapore and established the supremacy of English-language education.

After the formation of the NUS, in 1981 the English-language Nanyang Technological Institute (NTI) was set up on the Nanyang University campus. The government intended to develop this institute into a technological university in 1992. The NTI initially offered engineering degree courses and its graduates received NUS degrees. In 1991 the government decided on the basis of yet another Dainton report to convert the NTI into a second comprehensive university, the Nanyang Technological University (NTU). With the benefit of hindsight, it was now clear that the earlier Dainton report in 1979 had seriously underestimated the social and economic demand for higher education. Besides engineering courses, the NTU now offers degrees in accountancy, business, and communications studies. The Institute of Education (with its origins in the Teachers' Training

College established in 1950) and the College of Physical Education (established in 1984), both teacher training institutions, were also merged to form the National Institute of Education, an autonomous division of the NTU, in 1991. This new institute is the main teacher training institution in Singapore and offers diploma, undergraduate, and postgraduate programs.

The Singapore Management University (SMU) was officially incorporated as a private company by an Act of Parliament in early 2000. Its establishment marked an interesting development in Singapore higher education because it was officially private, while at the same time receiving substantial government funding. It was modeled after the Wharton School at the University of Pennsylvania with both its presidents up to that point having come on attachment from Wharton. This dependence on Wharton was aimed at establishing quality benchmarks for the university to enable it to compete effectively with the two older universities. It currently offers English-language degree programs in business management, accounting, and economics and is considered one of three mainstream universities alongside the NUS and the NTU. Right from its inception it marked itself apart from the other two universities by instituting additional admissions criteria in the form of the SAT I reasoning test and personal interviews.

Soon after the establishment of the SMU, the government announced in late 2000 that it was considering the establishment of a fourth state-funded university to cater to the demand for university degrees on the part of polytechnic graduates. The idea received support in early 2001 from a government-commissioned international panel of experts who recommended the setting up of a technologically focused university. More than a year later, the plans for a fourth university appeared to have been abandoned. Instead, the NUS announced its intention to set up two more campuses, one offering undergraduate engineering courses and the other postgraduate medical courses.

There are currently five polytechnics—the Singapore Polytechnic, the Ngee Ann Polytechnic, the Temasek Polytechnic, the Nanyang Polytechnic, and the Republic Polytechnic—that form the lower tier in the binary system of higher education in Singapore. They offer diplomas in a variety of fields such as engineering, information technology, health sciences, and business studies to students who have completed high school.

Up until the late 1980s, enrollment rates in higher education were relatively low by the standards of industrialized nations. For instance, in 1980 only 5 percent of each birth cohort was enrolled in local university undergraduate programs, while an additional 8 percent were enrolled in full-time polytechnic diploma courses. Since then, as a result of rapid government expansion of enrollments and the creation of new institutions, these figures have grown dramatically. In the early 1990s, the government announced its targets for the year 2000 of 20 percent and 40 percent of each birth cohort to be enrolled in university and polytechnic courses, respectively. Having met these targets successfully, it announced in 2000 that it planned to further increase the percentage of each birth cohort enrolled in local universities to 25 percent by the year 2010.

Other Higher Education Institutions

A number of privately funded institutions exist outside the mainstream, and cater to the ever-increasing social demand for higher education qualifications. This demand is largely driven by the continuing strong links between educational attainment and work income (Leow, 2001b, pp. 99–100). The largest among these is the Singapore Institute of Management (SIM), which was established in 1964 by a group of senior management executives from various fields in the private and public sectors to provide management training. It offers doctoral, master's, and bachelor's degree programs in finance, management, information technology, mass communications, accountancy, early childhood studies, education and training, and health sciences, as well as diploma and certificate courses in management and preschool teaching. The degree courses are run in conjunction with various universities in Britain, Australia, and the United States.

As part of government moves to make higher education more accessible to working adults, an Open University started functioning in January 1994. The SIM administers the part-time bachelor's degree programs in English and literature, humanities, mathematics, economics, business, psychology, and information technology. The Open University of the United Kingdom awards these degrees.

There are two fine arts colleges, the Nanyang Academy of Fine Arts and the La Salle-Singapore Airlines College of the Arts, both of which offer diploma courses as well as bachelor's degree programs conducted jointly with foreign universities in Britain and Australia. In 1999, as a result of a government-commissioned study that was published the previous year, these two colleges were granted government funding on a par with local polytechnics, while continuing to exist as private institutions.

Lastly, there are numerous external diploma, undergraduate, and postgraduate diploma programs being run by statutory boards, professional groups, and private for-profit commercial schools. These courses are predominantly in business, administration, and information technology, with most of the awarding institutions being in Britain, Australia, and the United States. The government estimates that enrollment figures in diploma and degree programs were 33,200 and 36,700, respectively, in 2001 ("Educational Upgrading," 2002, p. 18). A large part of the demand for these programs stems from the fact that admission to the local universities is still heavily weighted in favor of those who have passed the national General Certificate of Education Advanced Level examinations.

ISSUES AND REALITIES

Government Control of Higher Education

The NUS, the NTU, and the four polytechnics are under the direct charge of the Ministry of Education, which in 1992 established a University Grants Commission to advise the minister on the allocation of funds and resources for the universities. The main control mechanisms are finance and the appointment of senior academic and administrative staff. In addition, all the constitutions of the various institutions, including the SMU, are prescribed by parliamentary acts. For instance, when introducing the second reading of the SMU Bill in Parliament, the education minister said:

> SMU will be structured as a private company . . . This gives SMU as much operational autonomy as possible to innovate and to pursue excellence. At the higher level, SMU's activities will be governed by the SMU Bill. This is necessary because of the wider national role played by SMU, and the fact that SMU will receive significant public funding. The SMU Bill will therefore provide the necessary mechanisms for the Government to guide SMU's strategic development in the public interest, and safeguard the use of public funds. (C. H. Teo, 2000, p. 10)

The government clearly plays a dominant interventionist role in controlling and directing major policy decisions concerning the higher education institutions. Its role is consistent with its preference for state-directed economic and social development (Cheung, 2002). Part of this influence comes in the form of heavy financial subsidies for recurrent expenditure and 100 percent of development expenditure, and the bulk of research funding. The high state subsidies mean that students' tuition fees account for less than 30 percent of overall recurrent expenditure. Given the pivotal role the higher education institutions play in human resources development, which has in turn been identified as the cornerstone of national economic survival, it is perhaps understandable to some extent that the government is unwilling to completely divest itself of any influence over these institutions. A recent Ministry of Education committee recommended that the NUS and the NTU be given greater operational autonomy within key government-determined policy parameters (Ministry of Education, 2000).

There is a British legacy in the management pattern in the universities. Both universities have the president of Singapore as their chancellor, along with pro-chancellors who are appointed by the chancellor to act on behalf of the chancellor whenever necessary. The NUS vice-chancellor and the NTU president, both of whom are appointed by the respective councils, are the chief academic and administrative officers in their institutions, and both of them are assisted by deputies. The councils, which are the executive bodies, comprise the vice-chancellor or president, several professors, and a mixture of people appointed by the government, the council, and the chancellor. Academic matters are governed by the respective senates, which provide for faculty representation. The SMU is overseen by a board of trustees with the president of the university as chief executive officer and the provost as chief academic officer. Apart from the president and the provost, the board comprises individuals from the business world and senior civil servants. In practice, the government exerts heavy control over the general policy parameters within which individual university heads may have a certain degree of decision-making flexibility and autonomy.

All four polytechnics have similar administrative structures, with boards of governors forming the chief governing bodies. With the exception of the principals, all board members are appointed by the minister of education. The respective senates or boards of studies take charge of academic matters and provide for faculty representation.

With regard to diplomas and degrees offered by private commercial schools, the Ministry of Education has so far not been in favor of taking on an accrediting role. Its current role is limited to requiring these schools to fulfill minimal registration requirements in terms of space, facilities, teacher qualifications, and proof that the diplomas and degrees are granted by bona fide overseas universities. It prefers instead to let such programs be subject to market forces (*Parliamentary Debates*, vol. 74, May 21, 2002, col. 1965).

Higher Education and Economic Development

The first phase of Singapore's industrialization program, which was launched in 1960, involved the policy of import substitution. After independence in 1965, this policy was replaced by one based on export-oriented and labor-intensive industrialization. A major restructuring program was launched in 1979, involving an emphasis on skill- and technology-intensive industries, with a focus on research and development (R&D). The economic recession of 1985–1986 led the government to form an Economic Committee to chart new directions for future economic growth. The committee's report outlined various strategies to attain its goal of Singapore becoming a developed nation by the 1990s. Among these was the need to upgrade the education level of the population. The committee also recommended that universities and polytechnics increase their annual intake, at both the undergraduate and postgraduate levels in the former case. In addition, heavy emphasis was placed on the development of competence in selected technologies: information technology, biotechnology, robotics and artificial intelligence, microelectronics, laser technology and optics, and communications technology (Ministry of Trade and Industry, 1986).

In the early 1990s, more economic reports were launched, including *The National Technology Plan 1991* and *The Strategic Economic Plan* (Ministry of Trade and Industry, 1991; National Science and Technology Board, 1991). The former plan was drawn up by the newly established National Science and Technology Board (NSTB, now known as A*STAR, or the Agency for Science, Technology and Research), which was formed to enhance Singapore's international competitiveness in science and technology. The NSTB stressed the need to improve R&D capability to match that of the other newly industrialized countries, the United States, and Europe. The list of selected technologies identified in the 1986 Economic Committee report was expanded to include food and agrotechnology, manufacturing technology, materials technology, and medical sciences. The NSTB also stressed the role of the universities in expanding the pool of R&D personnel. The *Strategic Economic Plan* outlined the government's goal for Singapore to have the same per capita GNP as the United States by the year 2030. Several recurrent themes were stressed: the need to upgrade the education levels of the population and to nurture a pool of skilled personnel in key technologies, along with the importance of developing innovative and creative skills.

As part of the drive to promote R&D, the NUS and the NTU have established over ten specialized research institutes, which are funded by A*STAR. These include the Bioinformatics Institute, the Genome Institute of Singapore, the Institute of High Performance Computing, the Institute of Microelectronics, the Singapore Institute of Manufacturing Technology, and the Institute of Molecular and Cell Biology. Both the NUS and the NTU have strengthened their links with industry by establishing industrial liaison networks to promote technology transfer, offer consultancy and training services, and embark on joint commercial projects.

Toward the end of the twentieth century, the government's concern with ensuring Singapore's continued economic relevance continued unabated. In 1999 it announced reforms to the undergraduate admissions system (Shih, 1999). From the year 2003 on, the NUS and the NTU will consider not only applicants' performance in the national General Certificate of Education Advanced Level examinations, but also their performance in the SAT I reasoning test and participation in co-curricular activities. Male applicants who perform well in national service may also obtain bonus points. From the year 2005 on, students' performance in interdisciplinary project work will also be included as an admissions criterion. These reforms are aimed at better preparing students for what the government perceives as the needs of an emergent knowledge-based economy. In addition, they are supposed to dovetail with the "Thinking Schools, Learning Nation" policy initiative that was launched nationwide in 1997 in a bid to promote critical and creative thinking in primary schools, secondary schools, and junior colleges. Being a privately run university, the SMU instituted admissions criteria right from its inception in the year 2000 that included not only examination performance but also SAT I scores, a personal essay, and an individual admission interview.

Even before the new criteria came into force, a review committee formed by the Education Ministry recommended in 2002 that the Advanced Level examinations be revamped to include greater emphasis on reasoning skills and to incorporate greater breadth of subject coverage. It recommended too that local universities revise their admissions criteria in line with these changes. Another recommendation was that different universities might wish to devise their own distinctive admissions systems (Ministry of Education, 2002).

Yet another Economic Review Committee report was released in 2002. This report highlighted the potential of developing Singapore into an international education hub (a theme raised earlier by the prime minister in 1996) to contribute to the national gross domestic product (GDP). It suggested having three tiers of universities. The first of these would consist of world-class universities operating branch campuses in Singapore, offering primarily postgraduate degrees, and carrying out R&D. The second would consist of the NUS, the NTU, and the SMU. The third would consist of private universities, either local or foreign in origin. The setting up of this third category of universities would help attract the bulk of foreign full-fee-paying students (Ministry of Trade and Industry, 2002).

A major theme that has emerged so far is the single-minded gearing of higher education, under firm government direction, toward economic development goals and targets. For instance, the government has stated unequivocally on various occasions that university education cannot be divorced from economic needs (*Parliamentary Debates*, vol. 50, March 21, 1988, col. 1114). The universities and polytechnics have been assigned clearly demarcated roles. The universities are to serve four main objectives: to provide top-level professionals, managers, planners, and researchers; to raise the intellectual tone of society; to act as a benchmark in maintaining high standards in Singapore; and to create wealth for Singapore (*Parliamentary Debates*, vol. 55, March 28, 1990, col. 986; vol. 74, May 21, 2002, col. 1933). The polytechnics serve to provide midlevel technologists, supervisors, and managers (*Parliamentary Debates*, vol. 55, March 28, 1990, col. 986). The government has also not been in favor of following the examples of the United Kingdom, Australia, and Hong Kong in upgrading the polytechnics and allowing them to become degree-granting institutions.

The concern with economic relevance extends beyond monitoring enrollments and course offerings to regulating access to certain fields of study. For instance, from 1979 on a quota was placed on the percentage of top-scoring university entrants who could be admitted to medicine and dentistry courses in the NUS, on the grounds that a more even spread of talent was needed in the various disciplines (*Parliamentary Debates*, vol. 38, March 16, 1979, cols. 763–766). Replying to criticism that this quota denied some students the right to freely pursue their career ambitions, a government spokesman said: "The Government subsidizes the cost of training in the universities not to satisfy personal ambitions but to meet the nation's economic and social needs" (*Straits Times*, May 21, 1991). Another method used to influence the choice of courses is the offering of both local and overseas scholarships in fields identified as priority areas in national economic and social policy.

TRENDS AND CHALLENGES

Internationalization of Higher Education

A major prong of the national economic development strategy outlined in the *Strategic Economic Plan* is a policy of internationalization, to use "global resources, global technology and global talent" (p. 59). As part of this plan, Singapore is to develop into an international center of learning. At the macrolevel, international panels of prominent academics from prestigious Japanese, U.S., and European universities have been invited several times during the 1990s and the first decade of the twenty-first century to advise the Ministry of Education on higher education curriculum and development policy and strategy. In addition, various local review committees have visited overseas institutions as part of their fact-finding missions before publishing their policy recommendations.

At the institutional level, the universities and polytechnics have steadily increased their research and staff and student exchange links with overseas institutions of higher learning. Although the universities and polytechnics were originally modeled on British institutions, there has been growing influence from the North American academic model. Both the NUS and the NTU have introduced a modular system for undergraduate courses, and have abandoned the British nomenclature system for academic job titles in favor of the North American nomenclature. All the polytechnics have adopted a modular academic system. In 1996 the prime minister announced the government's intention to turn Singapore into the "Boston of the East," with Harvard University and the Massachusetts Institute of Technology serving as role models for the NUS and the NTU to develop into world-class institutions (C. T. Goh, 1996). These role models appear to have been replaced subsequently by the University of California. Further inroads were made by the North American model of higher education when the SMU was established along the lines of the Wharton Business School.

After the prime minister's announcement about turning Singapore into the Boston of the East, the state-run Economic Development Board was put in charge of attracting ten prestigious foreign universities to set up branch campuses in Singapore by the year 2008 so as to turn Singapore into an international education center. The board has announced that it aims to surpass this target (Nirmala, 2001). The universities that have already established campuses or will be doing so include Johns Hopkins University, the University of Chicago, INSEAD, the Georgia Institute of Technology, the Technische Universiteit Eindhoven, and the Shanghai Jiao Tong University.

Staff flows. Besides increasing institutional linkages, the flow of teaching and research personnel into and out of Singapore has grown tremendously, in particular since the 1990s. Many local teaching staff have been sponsored for postgraduate studies at overseas universities, especially in North America, while others are involved in academic staff exchange programs. At the same time, large numbers of foreign-born teachers and researchers from all over the world have been recruited for local higher education institutions. Two important sources of teachers and researchers that have emerged over the past decade are India and the People's Republic of China. Many of these individuals have obtained their doctoral degrees at North American universities. The use of the English language as the medium of instruction at all higher education institutions, along with relatively higher salaries and generous government support for research funding, has provided Singapore with a distinct advantage in staff recruitment compared to many countries in East Asia.

The government has recognized that it is not possible to completely localize staff recruitment because of a shortage of qualified individuals, due in part to the absence of an indigenous R&D tradition and the relative lack of interest among many local undergraduates in an R&D career (C. B. Goh, 1998a; 1998b). The increase in foreign-born staff at higher education institutions has been part of a similar trend with other professional jobs in the rest of the economy. Although the government has claimed on numerous occasions that these individuals, referred to as "foreign talent," are indispensable for Singapore's economic growth, there has been persistent criticism of this policy of aggressive recruitment on several grounds (Low, 2002). One concern is that they take jobs away from qualified Singaporeans. Furthermore, such foreign-born individuals are readily granted permanent residence status, leading to the perception that they are receiving the economic and social benefits enjoyed by Singapore citizens without having to fulfill national service obligations.

Student flows. Two-way student flows represent another form of growing regionalization and internationalization. The official target for foreign undergraduate enrollments in local universities is 20 percent. A major recruitment target source of these students is the People's Republic of China. Not only are Singapore government scholarships being awarded at the undergraduate level to students from this country, recruitment teams from prestigious Singapore secondary schools are visiting large urban centers in China to entice students to study at their schools on full scholarships. The hope is that these students will grow to like Singapore and will eventually continue their studies at the undergraduate level.

As with recruitment of foreign staff, concerns have been raised among parliamentarians and members of the public that foreign students may be depriving Singaporeans of university places, and that taxpayers have to subsidize their fees. The government has stated that local students will be awarded first priority for admission. In addition, foreign students have to satisfy more stringent entry requirements than local students (*Parliamentary Debates,* vol. 45, March 26, 1985, cols. 1444–1446; vol. 58, May 7, 1991, cols. 46, 63).

Its rationale for admitting foreign students is characteristically pragmatic. First, all foreign students have to sign a bond to live and work in Singapore for at least three years upon graduation, thus adding to the limited local talent pool. Admitting these students thus represents a prime investment, since Singapore is able to tap into their talent without having had to pay for their prior education. In addition, Singapore needs to compete aggressively to capture a bigger slice of the estimated U.S.$2.2 trillion world education market (Ministry of Trade and Industry, 2002). Next, local students have the opportunity to interact with students from other societies and learn more about these societies. This interaction will not only contribute toward a better-rounded university education, but will also help local students in their future job-related contacts with foreigners. Lastly, when foreigners return to their home countries, there will eventually be a network of such students, especially in neighboring countries, occupying key positions in the public and private sectors (*Parliamentary Debates,* vol. 45, March 26, 1985, col. 1447; vol. 50, March 21, 1988, cols. 1103–1104; vol. 58, May 7, 1991, cols. 63–64).

In addition to the inflow of foreign students, the number of Singaporean students studying at foreign higher education institutions has steadily increased in the past few decades. The most popular destinations for Singapore students heading overseas are the United States, Australia, the United Kingdom, and Canada. No authoritative figures are available on how many Singaporeans are studying outside of the country. A key point to note is that the government annually sends top-scoring school leavers to prestigious foreign universities, largely in Europe and the United States, for undergraduate programs. These students will assume key administrative positions in the civil service on their return. The former prime minister has explained in characteristically pragmatic terms the advantages of top students studying in a top university in the United States or the United Kingdom: "You have the opportunity to network, to build up friendships and lifelong relationships with their best, their future political and corporate leaders" (*Straits Times Weekly Edition*, August 20, 1994). Another form of local student flows out of Singapore has been the sending of local undergraduates overseas on short work stints and study exchange programs.

Access and Equity Issues

Access to higher education was relatively restricted and selective until the mid-1980s (see Table 7.1). This policy of restricted access existed even while social demand for higher education, especially at the university level, was steadily increasing. Many students have had to turn to overseas institutions. The growing number of external degree programs conducted by various institutions and commercial schools is testimony to the scale of this demand. This demand continues unabated even as the government has significantly democratized access and expanded enrollments in local universities over the past fifteen years. Much of the demand for external degrees and overseas study is attributable to the fact that local universities give priority in admissions to students who have General Certificate of Education Advanced Level qualifications over polytechnic graduates. Thus, while the government has assured school leavers that polytechnic diplomas afford them a viable route to university entry, the transition rate to local universities for advanced level students far surpasses those of polytechnic graduates.

There are several reasons for the high social demand for higher education qualifications, especially university degrees. First, continued economic growth in the postindependence period (except during the 1985–1986 economic recession and the current economic downturn) has meant a steady demand for university and polytechnic graduates in the workforce. Another key reason, mentioned earlier in this chapter, is the strong link between higher education qualifications and high-income employment and socioeconomic mobility. A third reason is the rapid expansion of primary and secondary enrollments, as well as increased pass rates in national primary and secondary school examinations, which have resulted in an increased pool of candidates meeting the minimum entry qualifications for higher education.

Table 7.1 Higher Education Enrollments, 1960-2000

Year	Universities	Polytechnics	Teacher Education	Total
1960	3,502	2,342	2,327	8,171
	(23.0)	(2.3)	(51.7)	(25.2)
1965	4,996	3,208	5,603	13,807
	(28.1)	(9.9)	(58.0)	(36.0)
1970	6,990	4,692	2,001	13,683
	(34.8)	(8.1)	(69.5)	(30.7)
1975	8,540	9,276	685	18,501
	(44.1)	(18.8)	(79.4)	(32.7)
1980	9,078	11,105	2,328	22,511
	(44.2)	(22.5)	(84.9)	(37.7)
1985	17,071	21,610	1,232	39,913
	(46.6)	(27.4)	(78.2)	(37.2)
1990	24,341	29,550	1,781	55,672
	(46.7)	(34.8)	(75.7)	(41.3)
1995	28,529	41,002	1,341	70,872
	(48.8)	(44.3)	(74.3)	(46.7)
2000	35,816	52,033	3,072	90,921
	(49.6)	(46.6)	(73.1)	(48.7)

Sources: Department of Statistics, 1983, p. 238; Department of Statistics, 1993, pp. 301–302; Ministry of Education, 2002, p. 43.

Notes: Figures in parentheses denote the percentage of females. University enrollments refer to undergraduate students.

Gender. Female participation rates at all higher education institutions have increased over the past four decades (see Table 7.1). The increase in female enrollments has been so great that females now predominate over-whelmingly in certain faculties and courses, such as the arts and social sciences faculty in the NUS, the teacher education courses in the National Institute of Education, and the accountancy, business studies, design, and health sciences courses in the polytechnics. However, females still remain underrepresented in other courses, such as medicine and engineering.

Gender imbalances in certain fields have been the subject of government concern. In the case of the NUS medical faculty, the proportion of female students has been kept at about one-third since 1979 as a result of a deliberate government policy. The health minister justified the decision on the grounds that not only was the attrition rate for women doctors very high; they were also very choosy about hospital postings and were "clock-watchers" (*Parliamentary Debates,* vol. 38, March 16, 1979, cols.

766–767). He described the high attrition rate as "a considerable loss in investment," clear evidence yet again of the constant use of economic language in discussions of higher education.

The validity of these claims was repeatedly challenged for over two decades. Only recently did the Health Ministry indicate that it would revisit the quota, the main impetus being an overall review of medical services by an Economic Review Committee. The committee recommended that Singapore increase the number of medical researchers to become a regional biomedical center. The implication is that this kind of work will afford women more opportunities to work regular hours and that the quota may therefore be unnecessary (Liang, 2002). The chairman of the government parliamentary Committee for Community Development and Sports pointed out that the quota was contrary to the United Nations Convention on the Elimination of All Forms of Discrimination Against Women, which Singapore ratified in 1995. Furthermore, the policy was incongruent with the government's claim that Singapore society is meritocratic (G. Teo, 2002). The discriminatory quota was finally lifted in 2003.

Another issue that has aroused official concern is the rapid feminization of the teaching profession since the 1960s. Two official reasons cited for the concern are that women are less ambitious and therefore less willing to apply for senior positions, and that boys need male role models. However, repeated government advertising campaigns to recruit more male teachers have had little success to date.

Ethnicity. Both government and community leaders have expressed increasing concern since the 1980s over the problem of minority educational achievement, with most of the focus being on the two numerically largest communities, the Malays and Indians, who form 14 percent and 8 percent, respectively, of the total population of 3.4 million. The 2000 population census showed evidence of minority underrepresentation in higher education enrollments. The ethnic breakdown of local students in local universities was as follows: 92.4 percent Chinese, 2.7 percent Malay, and 4.3 percent Indian. These figures represented a deterioration in minority representation compared to the 1990 population census figures (Lau, 1993, pp. 168–169). In 2000, Chinese students comprised 84.0 percent of the local students in the polytechnics, Malays 10.0 percent, and Indians 5.2 percent (Leow, 2001a, pp. 34–36). These figures show an improvement in minority representation over the corresponding 1990 figures (Lau, 1993, pp. 168–169).

Malay university and polytechnic graduates continue to be grossly underrepresented in all fields of study, constituting 2.1 percent in 2000 (1.8 percent in 1990) of all university graduates and 5.9 percent (3.3 percent in 1990) of all polytechnic diploma-holders in the 2000 population census. It is noticeable that Malays' proportional representation at the polytechnics has improved much more rapidly over the past decade than at the universities. The advances made by female Malays have also outstripped those of Malay males, with the result that Malay female holders of university degrees now outnumber their male counterparts. Indian representation in the population of polytechnic graduates is still small (3.6 percent). The corresponding figure for university graduates (10.1 percent) is much better than that of the Malays, due to the inclusion of Indian nationals who hold professional degrees and who have adopted Singapore permanent residence. They have consequently been included in the population census figures in the same category as Singapore citizens (Leow, 2001a, pp. 66, 70).

The government has explicitly rejected the use of affirmative action initiatives and admissions quotas along the lines of those in neighboring Malaysia as a means of redressing these long-standing ethnic disparities in educational attainment. Instead, since the early 1980s it has encouraged the formation of, with financial and infrastructural assistance, several ethnically based organizations. These groups have the specific mission of improving socioeconomic conditions and educational achievement. The bulk of their efforts involve tuition classes for primary and secondary school students, the provision of financial aid, family counseling and referral services, and parent outreach programs. These various initiatives over the past two decades have been slow to bear fruit in terms of improved representation, especially at the university level. It is likely that the problems of minority underrepresentation are deeply rooted in various structural and socioeconomic factors and will take much longer to address.

CONCLUSION

Higher education in Singapore has undergone rapid expansion and structural reorganization in the past four decades. Throughout this period a prime concern has been the relentless gearing of higher education toward meeting economic needs. This has been manifested in several areas such as curricular changes, enrollment policies, and research priorities. Even the move in 1999 to upgrade the two fine arts colleges to polytechnic status was motivated by the desire to let Singapore "compete in the next century as a creative nation with additional sets of skills and capabilities" (*Creative Singapore,* 1998, p. 38). The most recent trend in this respect involves marketing Singapore as a regional higher education center.

Another inescapable feature of Singapore higher education is the dominant interventionist government role in directing a frenetically orchestrated flurry of higher education policy initiatives toward prescribed social and economic goals. It is perhaps understandable that in a newly independent nation lacking in natural resources, the government has been loath to leave higher education entirely in the hands of private enterprise. The Singapore case illustrates that a heavy state presence in higher education need not necessarily impede the successful functioning of higher education. It has led to swift responses to perceived changes in national and wider international economic circumstances.

After a period of relatively selective access to higher education, there are now plans to enroll 25 percent of each birth cohort in local universities and an additional 40 percent in local polytechnics by the year 2010. These plans have been formulated in response to economic needs as well as increasing social demand for higher education qualifications, especially university degrees. In addition, greater opportunities are now available for mature students to obtain these qualifications.

The Singapore higher education system holds several key lessons for other countries within and outside of Asia that are concerned with problems of quality and quantity in higher education. The government has been quick to identify potential niches for Singapore within the wider global economy and then to marshal resources within the higher education system toward the filling of these niches. Next, the higher education system continues to be generously funded and resourced, at a time when many higher education institutions worldwide have suffered years of financial stringency. This point is testimony to the resolute belief that the money thus spent represents a prime national investment. Another useful lesson concerns the active encouragement of staff and student flows into and out of Singapore. The government has prudently recognized the value of fostering international links to keep Singapore up-to-date with the latest developments in teaching, research, and technology. At the same time, the almost exclusive use of the English language has facilitated the fostering of such links.

What are the trends and challenges that await Singapore higher education at the beginning of the twenty-first century? In some respects, the prospects are extremely bright. The entire system is internationally well regarded in terms of academic standards and overall efficiency. The major funding problems plaguing many other systems are noticeably absent, and plans for further expansion have been announced. A few major trends and challenges can be highlighted.

It is clear that the perennial, almost obsessive, concern with economic relevance will continue. Course curricula, enrollment patterns, and R&D will be monitored closely to ensure that they are consonant with government-perceived social and economic needs. There appears no end in sight to the regular pace of reviews and reports urging reform. However, it appears increasingly difficult for these reviews and reports to keep track of, and accurately predict, areas of need amid the rapidly changing nature of the global economy. For example, in the early 1990s, the government claimed that there were too many doctors in Singapore and announced limits on local medical undergraduate enrollments and on the number of foreign medical degrees that it recognizes. Less than a decade later, it backtracked on both these decisions in the wake of doctor shortages in public-sector hospitals. Another example is seen in the promotion of computing courses in the late 1990s in the wake of the dot.com boom and the subsequent unemployment of numerous computing graduates after the dot.com crash.

Another policy trend that appears likely to persist is that of internationalization. However, the Singapore higher education system will face increasing competition from other countries keen to cash in on the growing international demand for higher education. Policymakers will be hard pressed to position Singapore universities competitively vis-‡-vis more established universities in the West. Perhaps one advantage that can be capitalized upon is relative living and tuition costs. Another might be the lure of top-name degrees awarded by the Singapore branch campuses of prestigious foreign universities.

Despite official ambitions and heavy funding of higher education, the quest for world-class stature and a creative, innovative university culture will not be easily attained. The reforms currently underway in the primary schools, secondary schools, and junior colleges to foster creativity and innovation are more than five years old and have yet to result in demonstrable changes in well-entrenched modes of teaching and learning. Teachers, students, and parents have become too comfortable with the proven success of repetitive drills, even involving so-called "higher-order thinking" questions, in attaining examination success for change to come easily and readily. This last point is manifested in the recent NUS proposal to establish its own mathematics and science specialist secondary school in a few years' time. Its deputy president was quoted in the press as saying, "Why don't we try . . . and see if we can produce a different breed of students who don't expect to be spoon-fed with notes but, with the right guidance from teachers, go and discover and explore things on their own?" ("NUS Plans," 2002). The importation of foreign-born professors and researchers can only be a partial solution to this problem because of the attendant social tensions that might arise with an increase in immigration.

In the same vein, it is unrealistic to expect local universities to attain the same degree of worldwide renown and stature of an institution such as Harvard University. Some academics have suggested instead that the NUS model itself after the University of California at Berkeley. It has also been suggested that Singapore consider the California university model, with two parallel university systems offering a diversity of programs for different groups of students. It is rather doubtful to what extent Singapore will ever be in a position to attract enough world-class faculty on anything like the scale at more prestigious institutions. The fact remains that in several senses, the advances in information technology notwithstanding, Singapore still remains on the periphery of the international academic world. It is therefore unlikely that a substantial number of top-notch researchers would contemplate giving up their posts in North America and Europe for long-term careers in Singapore.

At the same time as the government attempts to make higher education internationally competitive, there is a need to meet increasing social demands for higher education qualifications. The government has committed itself, as part of its efforts to foster a lifelong learning society, to providing greater opportunities for working adults to acquire such qualifications. The burgeoning demand raises questions of quality and competition (Anonymous, 2002). Right now there is no central accreditation agency to guide prospective students and help them assess the claims and promises of international recruitment agents and sales staff in private commercial schools. There will inevitably come a time when concerns over quality of educational provision come into increasing tension with the official insistence on a hands-off approach to the courses offered by the private sector. After an Economic Review Committee recommended in 2002 that a quality assurance mechanism be put in place (Ministry of Trade and Industry, 2002), the Economic Development Board announced a quality assurance system that would dispense awards to privately run commercial schools offering external programs.

More worrying is the prospect that it will be some time before the Malay and Indian ethnic minorities overcome their long-standing problems in educational attainment. Twenty years of government assistance to ethnically based self-help groups have yet to yield results in terms of proportional ethnic representation in higher education institutions. The government is ever mindful of the potential impact of ethnic disparities on wider social integration.

What will be interesting to watch is the tension between the government's desire to be in overall charge of higher education development and planning, on the one hand, and trends that militate against the effectiveness of government controls, on the other. One such trend is the increasing tendency among a growing middle class to demand a say in official policy instead of being passive recipients of policy determined by a few individuals. Another trend is the growing affluence that allows individuals to bypass government enrollment quotas and suggestions on career choices. Already there is a small percentage of government scholarship awardees who have chosen to repay their scholarship liabilities and pursue their preferred study or work choices instead of returning to Singapore to serve in the civil service. Official labeling of these individuals as "lacking a sense of moral obligation" and public "naming and shaming" of these individuals have so far proved futile.

It is ultimately questionable to what extent heavy government intervention is consistent with its concurrent quest for greater creativity and innovation. For instance, the president of the Singapore Management University has said that "we can provide an environment that will help people develop their capability, but the ability to use that capability depends not just on them but on those that are in the older generation being willing to free up the society" (A. Teo, 2003, p. 3). One wonders how the Singapore government will be able to attract a critical mass of members of the "creative class" (Florida, 2002) necessary for Singapore universities and polytechnics to make that crucial breakthrough into the ranks of world-class institutions.

References

Anonymous. (2002). Singapore stings: Tales of international malfeasance in higher education. *International Higher Education, 29,* 5–7.

Chelliah, D. D. (1947). *A short history of the educational policy of the Straits Settlements.* Kuala Lumpur: Acting Government Printer.

Cheung, A. B. L. (2002). Public service reform in Singapore: Reinventing Singapore in a global age. In A. B. L. Cheung & I. Scott (Eds.), *Governance and public sector reform in Asia: Paradigm shifts or business as usual?* (pp. 138–162). London: RoutledgeCurzon.

Creative Singapore: A renaissance nation in the knowledge age. (1998). Singapore: Committee to Upgrade LASALLE and NAFA.

Department of Statistics. (1983). *Economic and social statistics Singapore 1960–1982.* Singapore: Author.

Department of Statistics. (1993). *Yearbook of statistics Singapore 1992.* Singapore: Author.

Educational upgrading through private diploma and degree programs. (2002, September). *Statistics Singapore Newsletter,* 18–20.

Florida, R. (2002). *The rise of the creative class: And how it's transforming work, leisure, community and everyday life.* New York: Basic Books.

Goh, C. B. (1998a). Science and technology in Singapore: The mindset of the engineering undergraduate. *Asia Pacific Journal of Education, 18*(1), 7–24.

Goh, C. B. (1998b). Imported technology: Its idea and development. *Journal of the Malaysian Branch of the Royal Asiatic Society, 71,* 41-54.

Goh, C. T. (1996). NUS and NTU must aim to become world-class universities. *Speeches, 20*(5), 14–18.

Lau, K. E. (1993). *Singapore census of population 1990, statistical release 3: Literacy, languages spoken and education.* Singapore: Department of Statistics.

Lee, K. Y. (1978). Bilingualism and higher education in Singapore. *Speeches, 1*(7), 7–37.

Leow, B. G. (2001a). *Census of population 2000—statistical release 2: Education, language and religion.* Singapore: Department of Statistics.

Leow, B. G. (2001b). *Census of population 2000—statistical release 3: Economic characteristics.* Singapore: Department of Statistics.

Liang, H. T. (2002, January 30). Female medical students exceed quota. *Straits Times,* 3.

Low, L. (2002). Globalisation and the political economy of Singapore's policy on foreign talent and high skills. *Journal of Education and Work, 15,* 409–425.

Ministry of Education. (2000). *Fostering autonomy and accountability in universities: A review of public university governance and funding in Singapore.* Singapore: Author.

Ministry of Education. (2002). *Report of the junior college/upper secondary education review committee.* Singapore: Author.

Ministry of Trade and Industry. (1986). *The Singapore economy: New directions.* Singapore: Author.

Ministry of Trade and Industry. (1991). *The strategic economic plan: Towards a developed nation.* Singapore: Author.

Ministry of Trade and Industry. (2002). *Developing Singapore's education industry.* Retrieved September 16, 2002, from www.mti.gov.sg/public/ERC.

National Science and Technology Board. (1991). *National Technology Plan 1991.* Singapore: Author.

Nirmala, M. (2001, May 26). 9 world-class universities here by December. *Straits Times,* 4.

NUS plans to set up its own secondary school. (2002, October 24). *Straits Times,* 3.

Parliamentary Debates Singapore: Official report, vol. 38.

Parliamentary Debates Singapore: Official report, vol. 45.

Parliamentary Debates Singapore: Official report, vol. 50.

Parliamentary Debates Singapore: Official report, vol. 58.

Parliamentary Debates Singapore: Official report, vol. 74.

Shih, C. F. (1999). *Preparing graduates for a knowledge economy: A new university admission system for Singapore* (Report of the Committee on University Admission System). Singapore: Ministry of Education.

Teo, A. (2003, March 15–16). Well schooled. *Weekend Business Times,* 3.

Teo, C. H. (2000). *The second reading of the Singapore Management University Bill.* Retrieved February 22, 2000, from wysiwyg://12/http://straitstimes.asia1.com. sg/parl/parl_0222.html.

Teo, G. (2002, September 9). GPC backs call to end gender inequalities. *Straits Times,* H4.

Turnbull, C. M. (1989). *A history of Singapore 1819–1988* (2nd ed.). Singapore: Oxford University Press.

Wilson, H. E. (1978). *Social engineering in Singapore: Educational policies and social change 1819–1972.* Singapore: Singapore University Press.

PART IV

Middle-Income Countries and Higher Education Investment

8

Thai Universities

Past, Present, and Future

Paitoon Sinlarat

"Tradition without revolution is empty; but revolution without tradition is blind" (Rubinoff, 1971, p. 13, quoted in Ross, 1976).[1] What this statement means is that any traditions that have not undergone revolutionary change will not be of use in the present, and at the same time any revolution that does not look to the past will lack a connection to the country's roots and be of little benefit to society.

This chapter uses this concept as a framework to examine how Thai universities have developed and changed over time; the influences underlying those changes, both past and present; the ways in which the current situation of Thai universities reflects Thai history and traditions; and the lessons that can be drawn from the past as Thai higher education confronts present realities and future trends.

OVERVIEW

If defined broadly as postsecondary education, Thai higher education constitutes an enormous sector that encompasses so many people and resources that it can be described as a huge educational industry. In 2002, there were 736 higher education institutions in Thailand providing higher education ranging from postsecondary schools at the prebachelor's level, to bachelor's programs, master's programs, and doctoral programs (National Education Commission, 2003). The Ministry of University Affairs is mainly in charge of education at the university level while the Ministry of Education takes care of specialized education and two-year vocational colleges. Other ministries also provide specialized education that is at a level equivalent to bachelor's degree programs or lower. As set forth in the 1999 national education act, in July 2003 the Ministry of University Affairs merged with the Ministry of Education into one ministry in charge of the education of the nation, with an Office of the Higher Education Commission to be established in the new ministry.

In 2002, there were 1,976,234 students in Thai higher education in programs leading to the associate degree, the bachelor's degree, the master's degree, the doctoral degree, or the diploma. While this is quite a large number of students, when compared with the total population (7,590,000), it constitutes only 26.04 percent of the eighteen- to twenty-four-year-old age group. This figure is regarded as small in comparison with the percentage of this age cohort in developed countries.

The Thai university system consists of the seventy-eight higher education institutions under the supervision of the Ministry of University Affairs. Twenty-four are public universities (including 2 open admission universities), and 54 are private universities and colleges. In 2002, the total number of students was 1,273,096; 1,022,354 attend public universities (including the open admission universities), and 250,742 attend private universities. The proportion of students at private universities is not as high as that of students at public universities. However, if the open universities are excluded, the private universities can be seen as having a considerable role. This profile reveals the extent to which the Thai university system relies on open admission universities and private universities to expand access to higher education. (See Table 8.1.)

An overview of faculty members at the university level shows a certain imbalance: 52.28 percent are lecturers, 26.12 percent are assistant professors, 20.10 percent are associate professors, and only 1.50 percent are professors. Faculty qualifications show a similar trend: 55.66 percent have master's degrees, 14.86 percent have bachelor's degrees, and only 29.45 percent have doctoral degrees (Ministry of University Affairs, 2001). These figures clearly reflect the quality and the performance of faculty at Thai universities. It would be quite difficult for Thai higher education to put an emphasis on producing knowledge-based research. The large proportion of lecturers means that more than half the faculty do not have sufficient academic or research qualifications and cannot be promoted to higher academic positions.

Table 8.1 Enrollments and Graduates, 2001 and 2002ᵃ

Type of Institution	New Enrollments	Total Enrollments	No. of Graduates
Total	400,787	1,273,096	179,071
Public Institutions	308,841	1,022,354	131,154
Limited admission universities	102,420	317,821	72,706
Open universities	198,891	684,138	54,522
Autonomous universities	7,530	20,395	3,926
Private institutions	91,946	250,742	47,917
Public-to-private ratio	77:23	80:20	74:26

Source: Ministry of University Affairs, 2002.
ᵃThe figures for enrollments are for 2002, those for graduates are for 2001.

HISTORICAL PERSPECTIVES

The First University

Before universities in their present configuration were established, higher learning in Thailand took place in the palace, at temples, and in traditional professional communities. The education in the palace stressed political science and the liberal arts for future leaders of the country who would require high levels of knowledge, understanding, and skills. The education that was provided at temples consisted of what could be considered the essence of higher learning in Asia, to the extent that it involved study, training, and ordination for the purpose of enlightenment and the preparation of teachers. Higher education in traditional professional communities included the training of practitioners of traditional Thai medicine and of architects for the building of houses and the designing of Buddhist temples and assembly halls (Saisaeng, 1982). These forms of higher learning corresponded to the social conditions of that period and did not require any foreign technology or ways of thinking. Based on the nature and needs of the local society, early Thai higher learning had independence and sufficient resources and did not put much emphasis on change (Sinlarat, 1989).

Dating from the Ayuthaya period, foreign countries, especially those in Europe, began to have some influence on Thailand. This influence steadily increased, and during the reign of King Rama V in the Rattanakosin period (1868–1910) there were extensive changes in attitudes, way of life, and the direction of society, which in turn led to the emergence of modern higher education in Thailand.

Visiting the British colonies in Asia and seeing the advances in Europe caused King Rama V to realize the need for Thailand to develop and thus keep up with global changes during that period. The king accelerated the improvement and the development of the country in every aspect (Wyatt, 1969), beginning with the economy, which expanded into a capitalist economic and trading system. Development of the country's infrastructure (e.g., roads, steamboats, and communications) occurred parallel to that of the financial and banking system. King Rama V also promoted advances in medicine, public health, and the education system. A significant step was the establishment of modern government ministries and departments to implement the transformation of the country and to keep abreast of developments in the world (Mulsilp, 1996).

In 1910 King Rama VI transformed the Royal Page School into the Civil Servants School, which taught government officials in the fields of law, public administration, foreign affairs, agriculture, engineering, medicine, education, and commerce. Then in 1916 a royal decree was issued to elevate the status of the Civil Servants School to Chulalongkorn University:

> Now, His Majesty the King has decided that the education in this school should be widely expanded. It is not exclusively for persons studying to be civil servants; anyone who wishes to study high-leveled subjects can enter this school. Thus, it should be established at the *university* level in order to meet the demands of this age. Consequently, royal permission was granted to establish the Civil Servants School of King Rama V as a university and name it Chulalongkorn University as a mark of honor to King Rama V. This university is under the Ministry of Education, and the minister, whose duty is to oversee general education, will be responsible for it. The council of the Civil Servants School is appointed by the King as the Advisory Council of Chulalongkorn University. (Ministry of University Affairs, 1992, p. 22)

At the beginning, Chulalongkorn University had four faculties—the Faculty of Medicine, the Faculty of Public Administration, the Faculty of Engineering, and the Faculty of Arts and Science. It offered only the high diploma degree, the first one of which was awarded in 1930. Classes were mainly taught by foreign teachers. In most fields the curriculum was patterned after English models, and the standard teaching method was based on lectures (Sinlarat, 1973).

During its initial period of existence, Chulalongkorn University's main purpose was clearly viewed as the production of government officials

who were more the recipients of vocational education than "the graduates" that other universities produced worldwide. Furthermore, the university was also particularly oriented toward teaching rather than knowledge production, which is currently defined as research.

Thai universities were first established out of the need for well-trained
personnel in some areas of the civil service. In later periods, the institutions would become comprehensive universities. These developments drew
upon foreign concepts that were compatible with Thai realities and needs.
For a chronology of the establishment of universities in Thailand, see
Table 8.2

Table 8.2 Chronology of the First Universities in Thailand

Dates	Main events
1868	Founding of first modern school in the Royal Palace
1871–1872	Founding of language school at the Royal Palace
1878	Founding of Boys' School at Nantha-utthayan Palace
1882	Founding of Geodesy School
1884	Expansion of education to ordinary people
	Founding of first public school at Mahanpharam Temple
1886	Founding of thirty public schools at temples all over the country
1887–1892	Establishment of Department of Education and the Ministry of Education
1889–1899	Founding of higher professional schools such as the Royal School of
	Medicine, the Teacher Training School, the Public Administration School,
	the School of Law, and the Civil Servant Training Academy (later the Royal
	Page School)
1910	Upgrading of Royal Page School to the Civil Servant School
1916	Upgrading of Civil Servants School to Chulalongkorn University
1917	Establishment of Department of Universities in the Ministry of Education

Source: Ministry of University Affairs, 1992.

Specialized Universities

That Chulalongkorn University was intended principally to produce
graduates to serve in state agencies can be seen from its curriculum, which
focused on preparing graduates to work in the civil service. Those who
finished their studies in the Faculty of Medicine went on to work in the
Ministry of Public Health; those from the Faculty of Public Administration worked in the Ministry of the Interior; and those from the Faculty of

Engineering would work in the Ministry of Transportation. Even the Faculty of Science and the Faculty of Arts, which taught the basic courses for other faculties, had Teacher Training Departments to produce teachers for the Ministry of Education. While some graduates were employed in non–civil service jobs, their number was not so large.

The concept of the university as the institution responsible for training specialized personnel for state agencies was reflected in the founding of four other universities: Thammasat University (1934), the University of Medicine (1943), Kasetsart University (1943), and Silpakorn University (1943). Thammasat University was established for the purpose of upgrading the legal profession commensurate with the country's need for it. Another goal of the university involved enhancing politics and promoting democracy by educating a critical mass of people who had knowledge and understanding of law and politics.

The University of Medicine, Kasetsart University, and Silpakorn University were also designed to enhance the respective professions. Prior to the founding of the University of Medicine, the Faculty of Medicine and Nursing, the Faculty of Dentistry, and the Faculty of Agriculture and Veterinary Science were transferred from Chulalongkorn University and placed under the newly established Ministry of Public Health in 1942. In the following year the University of Medicine was established.

Kasetsart University started out, in 1917, as the Agricultural Primary Teacher Training School, within the Department of Teacher Education of Chulalongkorn University. It then expanded to the provinces—to Nakhon Ratchasima (1933), Kho Hong in Hat Yai (1934), and Mae Jo in the north. These schools later developed into secondary schools. In 1938, the Agricultural Primary Teacher Training School was dissolved, and the work of the four secondary schools was placed under the Ministry of Agriculture. The school at Mae Jo was called the Agricultural College.

Silpakorn University evolved from the Pranit Silpakam School, which was established in 1934 under the Fine Arts Department of the Ministry of Education, and became the Silpakorn School. In 1943, the government upgraded it to a university in order to promote the nation's art and culture.

The universities that were established in Thailand during this period placed greater emphasis on teaching than on research. The curriculum and the teaching were oriented toward the professions rather than toward scholarly inquiry. These universities were in essence upgraded to professional schools. Teaching, learning, and grading continued to emphasize memorization, and grading was based on percentages as in Europe. University administration was structured under the civil service system, in addition to some special agencies (Sinlarat, 1973).

The history and the operation of Chulalongkorn University, Thammasat University, the University of Medicine, Kasetsart University, and Silpakorn University illustrate the Thai model of higher education, which was designed to meet the demand for high-level personnel. The aim of universities consisted of creating educated people rather than academic knowledge—thus policies focused on upgrading former professional schools into universities instead of creating new universities.

The new universities arose in response to the needs of government agencies for personnel in specific fields. The institutions were located primarily in Bangkok, and the subjects were specialized in structure. In keeping with its civil service structure, university administrators had the principal role and power in operations while the teachers had little involvement. The students themselves basically concentrated on studying.

Comprehensive Universities

After World War II, the United States expanded its influence in Southeast Asia by offering support to those countries that did not fall under the influence of the Soviet Union, developing liberal industrial economies with an emphasis on the private sector. America spread this concept and gave extensive assistance to countries in this part of the world, particularly Thailand (Sinlarat, 1996).

Such assistance consisted not only of military and economic aid but also of educational programs, especially granting scholarships for Thai government officials to continue their studies abroad and sending U.S. experts to help in Thailand. American forms of educational management were explored and widely implemented, particularly those found in U.S. comprehensive universities (Altbach, 1985).

This period saw the establishment of three new universities: Chiang Mai University in the northern region (1964), Khon Kaen University in the northeastern region (965), and Prince of Songkla University in the southern region (1968). These three new universities represented a break with the older concept of upgrading existing institutions to university status. These newly opened universities had the characteristics of U.S. comprehensive universities.

The five already existing universities also developed into comprehensive universities, opening new programs in more disciplines. The University of Medicine became Mahidol University. As comprehensive universities, these institutions have to focus on conducting research and providing academic services, in addition to teaching. Comprehensive universities need to go beyond producing civil servants to produce graduates whose studies prepare them for the private sector by imparting an understanding of the economic system, society, and the culture and work of the business world.

General education was introduced into the curriculum in the hopes of providing students with a broader knowledge and better understanding of the world and society. These goals were addressed in a 1972 speech by the president of Thammasat University:

> The ideal of this is that we will mould Thammasat graduates to be gentlemen and gentlewomen who have the knowledge of a general education that will make them decent people who have a broad way of thinking and not only the knowledge needed for earning their living. (Sinlarat, 1996, p. 68)

The general education curriculum was introduced first at Chulalongkorn University in 1957 and subsequently at Thammasat University, spreading to other universities in 1974 once the Ministry of University Affairs had set the curricular criteria for universities throughout the country requiring at least 30 credits of general education.

The provision of a general education curriculum was accompanied by the introduction of the course-credit system. This system enabled students to take courses in any subject without enrolling in year-long programs as in the former system. If they failed any course, they could retake that course. Marking by percentages was changed to grades, constituting a significant change in the Thai education system. Teaching at the graduate level was also introduced.

The changes in the system were also clearly reflected in a student activism that had never existed in the past. The comprehensive study of society and its problems in the general education curriculum and the participation in more socially relevant activities led to more protests against the state and the social system. Students wanted to play a more influential role in society and believed that society should move in the proper direction, toward greater democracy (this, in a period when the country was ruled by a military dictatorship) (Bunnag & Buranareak, 1979). These changes led to the student protests of 1973. The rise in students' awareness was accompanied by the teachers' increasing awareness of issues concerning the university administration.

Before World War II, the university council was composed of administrators. The affiliated minister, the president, and the deans were the ex officio members; the external members consisted mostly of government officials from the relevant ministries, bureaus, and departments. From World War II on, the chairman of the council was appointed by the king for a specified term. The membership became more diverse, and more teachers were appointed to the council. At many universities, faculty councils were created and became the representatives of the teachers (Sinlarat, 1996).

University reforms during this period responded to the demands of society for economic development and industrialization according to U.S. guidelines. A system of producing new knowledge was implemented. The American approach that emphasized participation, comprehensive knowledge, and liberalism was also put into practice. The traditional Thai way of thinking that stressed the professions, government supervision, and the teaching of ethics and values began to decline in influence.

Although in theory the concept of transforming universities into comprehensive universities was widely promoted, in practice institutions continued to stress producing professionals rather than academics. Research constitutes only part of student theses. Faculty do not produce new knowledge. What is taught and learned still is derived to a great extent from foreign academic knowledge.

The Path toward Mass Education

Although more than eight universities had been established, the number of students who wanted to study at universities still exceeded the available places. The traditional universities operated according to a closed system, with students required to take entrance examinations before being admitted because the seats available were limited. Consequently, it was decided to create a university that provided open admission, meaning that students could enter the university without any restrictions. In 1971, Ramkhamhaeng University was established as an open-enrollment institution (Ramkamhaeng University, 1996). Any student who finishes high school can now enroll and study—either by attending the university, by reading textbooks on their own, or by listening to the radio and watching television. Ramkhamhaeng University also provides lectures in the provinces. It operates through a combination of lectures (as in traditional universities), independent study, and distance-education technology.

Another model for the open admission approach was the British Open

University. A committee was formed to study and implement the open university project, and in 1978 Sukhothai Thammathirat Open University was established (Sukhothai Thammathirat University, 1990).

The development of the comprehensive university and the open university to increase access to higher education was widely implemented. At the same time, educational institutions that opened at the higher education level but did not have full university status tried to upgrade themselves—as was the case with Srinakharinwirot University, which was upgraded from Prasanmitr College of Education; the three campuses of King Mongkut's Institute of Technology, which were originally part of the Institute of Technology of the Ministry of Education; and the Mae Jo Agricultural Institute, formerly Chiang Mai Agricultural College (Ministry of University Affairs, 1992).

The expansion of higher education access would clearly involve attending to the legal status and regulation of the private sector. In 1955, an act was proposed, although not approved, in Parliament to establish private higher education institutions. Extensive arguments and discussions ensued about this matter in the National University Commission and in the press. In 1965, the National Education Commission put forth an important resolution, stating that "the opportunity is given to the private sector to establish higher education institutions and universities and to provide teaching at a level not beyond the first three years of public universities" (Ministry of University Affairs, 1992, p. 95). Three months later, the cabinet agreed, in principle, to allow some private universities to offer programs at the diploma level, under the supervision of the Ministry of Education.

After broad discussions, the Private College Act was issued in 1969. In 1971, it was announced that private higher education institutions could offer programs leading to the associate's degree (Ministry of University Affairs, 1992). Thereafter, private higher education grew rapidly, but the status of the colleges remained the same until 1979, when the Private Higher Education Institution Act allowed the private sector to offer university-level programs. Then the number of private higher education institutions increased steadily. In 1993 there were twenty-nine private higher education institutions, eleven of them universities, most of which offered programs in law and business administration.

The growth of universities during this period was primarily in accordance with the demands emanating from Thai society. The demands reflected a society that was more open, with greater freedom and democracy, and rising pressure for civil rights and equality. Higher education then developed in response to these conditions. In spite of the application of foreign concepts such as the Open University of England or the idea of private higher education in America, the overall picture of Thai higher education does not reveal an image of complete success. As will be discussed later, one of the persistent problems that emerged concerned the issue of quality.

The broad expansion and restructuring of Thai higher education had a great impact on economic and social growth. At the same time, however, the country was facing many issues concerning urban life, the environment, crime, and the institution of the family. In addition, the rise of internationalization that was driven by technology led to globalization, which meant that Thai higher education had to adapt and put in place a long-term plan to ensure that Thai universities would achieve the necessary level of modernization.

Overall, it can be said that the history of Thai universities has been shaped by changes in Thai society. Thai universities have in turn always functioned as the "tool" for development. To expand the higher education system, Thai society slowly considered various foreign perspectives and methods. The development of Thai universities was in line with the Thai approach, which favors the middle path and one not marked by extreme changes.

ISSUES AND REALITIES

Graduates' Qualifications

The problem of the qualifications of university graduates still exists. When universities were first established, it was clearly recognized that they would produce graduates with the characteristics required of government officials. The qualifications were related principally to the jobs graduates would assume. After World War II, the country focused mainly on the growth of the economy and on promoting businesses and industries in the private sector, while the civil service wanted the personnel to work in the new government projects. The qualifications of graduates had to change; yet, the goal and the direction of the changes were not clear. In the age of greater access and equality, a large number of people went on to higher education. However, graduates often had problems finding work in a labor market with limited job opportunities. The question is unresolved as to what kinds of academic backgrounds graduates need to qualify for a wide variety of jobs, especially during a period of globalization requiring rapid advances in information and knowledge. In Thai higher education these issues are still under debate (C. Suwanwela, 1998). The requisite qualifications of graduates in general, as well as of those able to work at international competency levels, have become issues that must be addressed before the future concepts and direction of Thai higher education can be decided.

Apart from the immediate problem of meeting national and international competency levels, the other challenge for Thai universities is to produce graduates who are able to think, create new things, and provide good leadership. The challenge of producing Thai graduates with the right qualifications was outlined by a former president of Chulalongkorn University as follows (D. Suwanwela, 2002):

- to have knowledge vs. to have wisdom
- to have wisdom vs. to have ethics
- to accumulate knowledge vs. to use knowledge
- to know how to think vs. to know how to do things
- to be all-knowing vs. to be well informed
- to have sufficient knowledge vs. to seek knowledge
- to depend on others vs. to be independent
- to be a good follower vs. to be a good leader

The obvious trend is that in the production of graduates Thai higher education will emphasize a more progressive direction.

Knowledge Dependence

In Thailand, the production of knowledge was not deeply rooted in higher education. Although, on paper, more importance began to be attached to knowledge creation in the post–World War II period, this approach was not put into practice and did not become part of the culture. Therefore, a large proportion of teachers at Thai universities hold the rank of lecturer or assistant professor because the main condition for promotion to associate professor or full professor is to do research and to publish.

At the same time, the current sources of knowledge in the form of books, journals, and electronic media originated mainly in Western countries (Altbach, 1987). Since the production of knowledge or research does not occur at Thai universities, the result is that the instructors have to depend on knowledge produced in Western countries, particularly in America, Europe, and Australia. The phenomenon of knowledge dependency that has long existed in the Thai university system will continue if no serious university reform takes place.

Evaluation and Quality Standards

The problem of quality at Thai universities has been commented on since the establishment of the institutions. When Chulalongkorn University was founded, a member of the university's board of trustees said, "If Oxford and Cambridge are held as the standard, we are not ready to establish a university and would have to invest a lot. . . . But if we reduce our standard to that of the modern universities that are mushrooming in the West and East, we will be able to make it" (Ministry of University Affairs, 1992, p. 27). Even though Thai universities do award degrees, they have never undertaken basic research or set their own goals for the types of graduates they would produce. Furthermore, all Thai universities have the characteristics of public universities. Quality evaluations of institutions or academic staff are usually undertaken initially, but with little follow-up, and everything proceeds according to civil service guidelines. The system does not entail any accreditation or evaluation after an institution's establishment. However, universities should have ongoing assessment for the purpose of quality assurance, which would involve inspections and evaluations. A recognition of the value of evaluation and quality standards is growing in Thai society as it is in the rest of the world, but while Thai universities are at the initial stages of acculturation a lack of clarity in terms of policy is visible everywhere.

An Office of Educational Standards and Evaluation has now been established by the new 1999 education act. Evaluations of educational institutions will take place every five years. However, extensive debate exists as to whether or to what extent this office will promote real quality because agreement has not yet been reached on the criteria. The evaluators do not yet have adequate training, and the real purpose of evaluation still needs to be defined. A system will have to be instituted to provide support, assistance, promotion, or punishment following evaluations. The principal problem is that the Thai university system is not yet characterized by a culture based on quality. These issues are still being widely debated at present within the Thai university system.

TRENDS AND CHALLENGES

Key Roles

The economic downturn, known as the "Tom Yam Kung Crisis" of 1997, led to questions being raised in Thai society about Thai universities. How could the crisis occur in Thailand when it has so many leading universities that offer courses in business administration and international business and faculties of business administration that offer master of business administration courses (Sinlarat, 1999)? Universities are being called upon to play a progressive role in the development of society. The universities are being asked to provide guidance with regard to the principal issues facing society. While universities were developed in response to society's needs in the past, they still have a unique asset in the form of accumulated academic wisdom. If these resources are properly used, they will help society to move in the proper direction and thus make progress in the necessary areas.

Thai academicians have long recognized the duty of universities to provide leadership to society. However, this duty was only carried out once in a while, even though society would have benefited from guidance from the university community. Greater clarity is needed concerning the ways in which universities might work concretely with the society in the joint development of institutions and policies.

Globalization and Universities

Although internationalization is an inherent characteristic of the university, borders do exist and time is also a factor. The exchange of knowledge may require a trip to a certain country and may take a long time. The new wave of internationalization involves information technology and is driven by the global business sector. In this new environment, Thai universities will have to make drastic adjustments. Almost all Thai universities rapidly upgraded their information technology (IT) systems. The number of computers became the major indicator of university reform. Academic exchange programs together with cooperation in the form of joint course offerings with foreign universities were introduced. Both within the country and abroad new forms of teaching and learning through distance learning or e-learning are emerging. Business-oriented management is playing a role in universities with the application of concepts such as privatization, corporatization, and autonomy.

Nevertheless, the globalization of Thai universities is viewed as a one-way process. It is a passive globalization, with Thailand on the receiving end. Thai universities take in knowledge, ideas, personnel, equipment, and technology from abroad more rapidly and extensively than during previous waves of internationalization. Thus, the issue of knowledge dependence continues to exist in Thai universities.

Competitive Ability

The changes to the economic system and the growth of globalization have made education a commodity that can be bought and sold at the national and international levels as stipulated by the World Trade Organization (WTO). Thai higher education must now confront more competition at the regional and the international levels. Thai universities emerged primarily from Thai society, and competition did not play a large role. As competition at the international level rose over the last decade, Thai universities have been at a disadvantage because they did not participate in many comparative studies, benchmarking, or collaboration at the international level (Srisa-an, 1999). Furthermore, the findings of many national and international studies have indicated that Thailand's level of competitiveness in the international arena is still not high.

Apart from the pressure of international competition, national competition became more intense with the introduction of institutional rankings. The competition among institutions resulted in competition among faculty members. Obviously, the lifestyle and sense of community among Thai university faculty will give way to a competitive business culture.

CONCLUSION

Looking into the future requires looking in two directions. The first approach relates to the past, for without change or reform, the past will determine what Thai universities will be like in the future. The second approach involves looking in a new direction, which should be the choice for Thai universities.

If universities continue along their traditional path without change, their mission will continue to emphasize producing graduates with the same qualifications as in the past. Graduates of Thai universities will remain consumers or followers of the concepts and roles that have their origins in foreign countries.

Indeed, the whole Thai system of higher education is characterized by consumerism. Teaching essentially still stresses making students fully receptive to foreign knowledge. The teaching-learning process is still conceived of as the spoon-feeding of children. The administration of universities continues to have the characteristics of the civil service. These elements have made Thai universities dependent on foreign concepts, methods, and values. For more than a hundred years, when Thais have wanted to develop any new things or set any new guidelines, they invited foreigners to accomplish these goals. The production of knowledge and the discovery and introduction of new options occur very rarely in Thailand. Recognizing or acknowledging social problems is also seldom observed. Thai higher education has always been criticized for being alienated from society and for failing to ensure that universities serve society. Today, universities are market-driven and blindly focused on the needs of the business sector. If the universities intend to continue to move in this direction, they will not need to implement much in the way of change or reform. However, such an approach ensures that Thai universities will become a problem for the country.

In order to benefit the people, the society, and the world, Thai universities need to adjust their mission to become producers of innovations in the academic world. The first thing that Thai universities should do is recognize the importance of the production of new knowledge for the country. Unless Thai universities are able to create knowledge, they will lose the chance to determine if the country will remain dependent on the academic knowledge, procedures, and techniques from abroad.

The development of knowledge in Thailand would not mean the country's detachment from the international academic world. On the contrary, collaboration with foreign countries will be more important because if Thailand is going to create new knowledge, it must keep informed about the latest scientific and scholarly advances in the rest of the world.

The production of knowledge would also enhance the research conducted in Thailand. Once this research is disseminated in Thai research books, journals, and other publications, it will become an academic resource within the country that can be studied along with the material originating in foreign countries (Higher Education Reform Committee, 1999).

Establishing the link between research and teaching is another necessary step to enable research to become part of the culture of Thai universities. Teachers should engage in their own research. Once teachers have learned how to create new knowledge, they can teach others to do the same. The process of promoting research-based instruction must occur at universities. Research funding needs to be enhanced, and research assistantships at different levels need to be created.

Thailand's investment in higher education is high, consuming almost half of the money spent on education. If higher education does not contribute significantly to society, it will be difficult to defend the investment in it. The history of Thai higher education points to the fact that education was expected to be of use for daily life and for society, whether in a temple, palace, or community. In the present, higher education still needs to be relevant—that is, upon completing their studies, students should be able to use their knowledge and skills right away.

A process that seems to be well established in other countries but needs to be introduced in Thailand is the evaluation of the real outcomes of the Thai university system. The system needs to look at the qualifications of graduates, the teachers' research, and the real effects of the system on society. Therefore, an evaluation system needs to be put in place and kept functioning all the time.

There needs to be a close relationship between higher education and society. This has always been the weak point regarding Thai universities and universities in developing countries generally. The idea of the university and the process of education are "imports," and thus were alienated from Thai society from the beginning. Ordinary people thought that the first building constructed at Chulalongkorn University was a temple (the architecture was similar to that of a Thai temple) and that university graduates and ordinary people belonged to different social classes. Graduates (and universities) have always been regarded as enjoying high status.

Diversity and differentiation need to be promoted in the universities. After their establishment, Chulalongkorn University and Thammasat University became the standard institutional models. New universities were based on the concept of the comprehensive university, with a lot of land, high-rise buildings, and other common components.

Yet, in reality, the essence of a university is to create spirit, soul, and knowledge. However, these elements require diversity in the system, which in turn will lead to creative thinking and innovation in the university—attributes that are of the utmost importance for the future of Thai higher education.

One of the main features of Thai universities is that each institution works and exists independently. While there is much autonomy in Thai universities, in reality universities always have contacts and relationships with other groups and institutions. Moreover, they are educational institutions that came into existence through internationalization. Because knowledge is universal and progress occurs in every corner of the world, Thai universities need to build a networking system that will promote joint work at the personal, institutional, and international levels (Wei & Ma, 1998).

In the future, Thai universities will need to attach greater importance to management. However, there is no guarantee that the management of the universities will improve. A number of university administrators lack the necessary vision or skills. Faculty members are focused exclusively on their own work and devote little attention to the future of universities. A system needs to be designed to create an understanding of university management. An effective form of management would enable university administrations to encourage and guide universities to accomplish the task of creating the knowledge and the educated citizenry that society needs.

Higher education studies and research must be systematically developed. The development of the universities and the higher education system needs to be based on an understanding of the field of higher education. Higher education studies must thus be promoted within the university system. To promote higher education studies, it is essential to establish higher education as a field of study in the curriculum. Studies should also be undertaken by other, nonuniversity, groups, focusing on a variety of issues. The results must have systematic dissemination so that the concepts and methods will be implemented correctly and effectively.

REFERENCES

Altbach, P. G. (1985). The American academic model in comparative perspective. In P. G. Altbach (Ed.), *An ASEAN-American dialogue: The relevance of American higher education* (pp. 15–36). Singapore: RIHED.

Altbach, P. G. (1987). The knowledge context. Albany: State University of New York Press.

Bunnag, P., & Buranareak, C. (1979). *Botbat khong karnsuksa radap udomsuksa tor karn patana tang karnmuang knong pratetthai (2475–2518)* (Roles of higher education in Thailand's political development (1932–1973). Bangkok: Chulalongkorn University.

Higher Education Reform Committee. (1999). *Naew thang karn patirub karn udomsuksa thai* (Framework for higher education reform). Bangkok: National Education Committee.

Long-term Planning Committee. (1990). *Udomsuksa thai: Su anakottee tatai* (Thai higher education: Toward a challenging future). Bangkok: Ministry of University Affairs.

Ministry of Education. (1964). *Pravat kasoung suksathikarn 2535–2507* (History of the Ministry of Education, 1892–1964). Bangkok: Kurusapa.

Ministry of University Affairs. (1992). *Song thosawat thaboung mahavithyalai* (Two decades of the Ministry of University Affairs). Bangkok: Chulalongkorn University Printing House.

Ministry of University Affairs. (2001). *Higher education data information.* Bangkok: Ministry of University Affairs.

Ministry of University Affairs. (2002). *Higher education data information.* Bangkok: Author.

Mulsilp, V. (1996). *Nayobai karn chad karnsuksa knong thai nai rachasamai prabat somdej pra chulajomkhua chao yu hua* (Policy on educational management in the reign of King Chulalongkorn). Bangkok: Srinakarinthvirot University.

National Education Commission. (2003). *Kohmul karnsuksa khang pra thet thai pee karn suksa 2545* (Thai education data, academic year 2002). Bangkok: Office of the National Education Commission.

Ramkhamhaeng University. (1996). *Yisib ha pee ramkhamhaeng* (Twenty-five years of Ramkhamhaeng University). Bangkok: Ramkhamheang Printing House.

Ross, M. G. (1976). *The university: The anatomy of academe.* New York: McGraw Hill.

Rubinoff, L. (Ed.). (1971). *Tradition and revolution.* Toronto: Macmillan.

Saisaeng, P. (1982). *Karn udom suksa samai sukothai* (Higher education in the Sukothai period). Phisanuloke: Srinakarinvirot University.

Sinlarat, P. (1973). *Patanakarn khong mahavithayalai nai pra thet thai* (Development of universities in Thailand). Bangkok: Faculty of Education, Chulalongkorn University.

Sinlarat, P. (1996). *Karn prub pean su sungkom samai mai knong thai: suksa koranee mahavithyalai lung songkram loke klung tee song* (The transformation to a modern Thai society: The case of universities after World War II). Bangkok: Chulalongkorn University.

Sinlarat, P. (1999, October 18). "Education policy under the social and economic crisis in Thailand." Paper presented at the International Symposium on Educational Policy under the Social Change and Economic Crisis in Asian Countries, Kyshu University, Japan.

Srisa-an, W. (1999). Karn patiroob karn udomsuksa thai: sumret rue lomlue (Thai higher education reform: Success or failure). *Varasarn Karusart* (Journal of the Faculty of Education), 28(2), 33–49.

Sukhothai Thammathirat University. (1990) *Pravat mahavithayalai* (History of Sukhothai Thammathirat Open University). Bangkok: Sukhothai Thammathirat Printing House.

Suwanwela, C. (1998). *Vikrit udomsuksa thai* (Thai higher education crisis). Bangkok: Department of Higher Education, Chulalongkorn University.

Suwanwela, D. (2002). Udom suka thai (Thai higher education). Bangkok: Chulalongkorn University Press.

Wei Xin, & Ma Wanhua. (1998). *The university of the 21st century.* Peking: Peking University Press.

Wyatt, D. (1969). *The politics of reform in Thailand: Education in the reign of King Chulalongkorn.* New Haven: Yale University Press.

9

Malaysian Universities

Toward Equality, Accessibility, and Quality

Molly N. N. Lee

Universities play an important role in national development in terms of economic growth, political development, and sociocultural transformation. But the link between universities and national development is not a one-way relationship, for while the university can shape society, it, in turn, is shaped by society. The contribution of universities to national development may take different forms in different countries, depending on the historical context of the countries. Conversely, universities seldom rise above their socioeconomic and political setting, and the current and future trends in university education are related to past developments. In the era of globalization, the development of universities is also influenced by global challenges and how nations respond to these challenges. The global economy is changing as knowledge supplants physical capital as the source of present and future wealth. As knowledge becomes more important, so do universities. The quality of knowledge generated by universities is becoming increasingly critical to national competitiveness. While the benefits of universities are continuing to rise, the costs of higher education are also increasing rapidly. Financing higher education continues to be a challenge because, in a globalized knowledge society, higher education is no longer a luxury but rather essential to national, social, and economic development.

Malaysia is one of the smaller countries in Asia, with a total area of 329,750 square kilometers and, in 2000, a population of 23.27 million. It is a multiethnic society with an ethnic composition of 66.1 percent Bumiputera,[1] 25.3 percent Chinese, 7.4 percent Indian, and 1.2 percent

others (*Eighth Malaysia Plan*, 2001). In a multicultural society, education is a contested terrain, with different ethnic groups struggling to protect and advance their own interests. In the context of higher education,
issues such as who gets access to higher education and the determination
of the language of instruction continue to be politicized in Malaysia. The
development of Malaysian higher education has always been shaped by
ethnic relations and politics, with issues of equality of educational opportunities, social mobility, and national unity dominating the public
discourse on education.

OVERVIEW

As in many other Asian countries, higher education in Malaysia has undergone massive expansion and restructuring brought about by the increasing social demand for higher education and financial constraints. In
2002, the system included 11 public universities, 5 university colleges, 6
polytechnics, and 27 teacher training colleges, and there are plans to
build a community college in each of the 193 parliamentary constituencies. In the past, the state was the main provider of higher education.
However, over the last decade the massification of higher education has
resulted in a tremendous expansion of private higher education. The number of private higher education institutions increased from 156 in 1992
to 706 in 2001. Of these 706 private institutions, 15 are private universities and 1 is a private university college; the rest are private colleges (Ministry of Education, 2001b).

The total number of students enrolled at the tertiary level, in both the
public and private sectors, nearly doubled from about 300,000 in 1995
to 550,000 in 2000. The participation rate in tertiary education of those
in the 17-to-23-year age cohort is expected to increase from 25 percent
in 2000 to 30 percent in 2005 (*Eighth Malaysia Plan*, 2001). The rapid
expansion has been fueled by strong demand for higher education, facilitated by the universalization of secondary education and the growing
economic affluence of Malaysian society. University education has always been viewed as the main avenue for social mobility and social justice, and the government has used access to universities as a means to
restructure Malaysian society with the aim of uplifting the Bumiputera
community.

The government allocates around 18 to 20 percent of its annual budget to education, and this public expenditure is about 6 percent of its
gross national product (GNP). Under the Eighth Malaysia Plan (2001–

2005), the allocation to education and training comes up to a total sum of U.S.$6 billion, and 40 percent of this amount is allocated to tertiary education. This allocation is relatively high when compared to other Asian countries like China, India, and the Republic of Korea, where the percentage of public expenditure allocated to the tertiary level was 15.6, 13.7, and 8.0 percent, respectively (UNESCO, 2000).

Malaysian universities do not have a long history; many of them are less than ten years old. It is argued that university education in Malaysia may have originated from the British model, but over time Malaysian higher education has become a hybrid model with American features as well as indigenous characteristics. Although the impact of the colonial past can be seen in some of the older universities, the newer universities have been shaped by the changing socioeconomic and political demands of the nation and by the contemporary global trends in the restructuring of higher education.

During the colonial period and the early postindependence years, university education in Malaysia was elitist. There was only a single university, and most of the students were non-Bumiputeras—that is, Chinese and Indians. To redress this ethnic imbalance more universities were established after the 1969 ethnic riots, and a positive discrimination policy was implemented that favored the Bumiputeras. This policy brought about the ethnic quota system under which student admissions to public universities was based on the ethnic composition of the Malaysian population. The implementation of the quota system served to extend access to higher education to greater numbers of Bumiputera students, who were economically disadvantaged. One of the most significant developments has been this opening up of the system to render it more inclusive and thus address the issue of equity. However, as the education system expanded and the move toward universal secondary education occurred in the 1980s and 1990s, public universities were unable to cope with the strong demand. Because of the ethnic quota system, many of the qualified non-Bumiputera students were denied admission into the public universities, thus causing a bottleneck. To meet the excess demand, the Malaysian government encouraged the private sector to play an active role in providing higher education. This deregulatory move by the government brought about the mushrooming of private higher education institutions that saw sixteen private universities established since the mid-1990s. More universities may have increased access to higher education, but the quality of education is an issue among the providers, consumers, and regulators of the education system. Therefore, equality, accessibility, and quality are the key current issues in the development of Malaysian universities.

HISTORICAL PERSPECTIVES

The historical origins and growth of Malaysian universities can be grouped into three distinctive waves of expansion. The first wave featured the struggle to establish the first independent university in the Federation of Malaya during the British colonial period. The second wave occurred in the 1970s and 1980s, when there was an urgent need to establish more public universities to rectify the existing imbalances in educational opportunities among the different ethnic groups. The third wave took place in the 1990s, with the establishment of private universities aimed at meeting excess demand and seeking profits through the commercialization of higher education.

The historical origins of higher education in Malaysia date back to 1905, when King Edward VII College of Medicine was first established in Singapore. In 1929, the British colonial government set up a second tertiary institution, called Raffles College. The main function of these two colleges was to provide a small elite group, in both Malaya and Singapore, with higher education, using English as the medium of instruction and based on the British model (Selvaratnam, 1989). In 1949, these colleges were merged into the University of Malaya in Singapore with degree-granting status. In 1959 the university started an autonomous division in Kuala Lumpur that became a separate entity in 1962.

When Malaysia was formed in 1963, the University of Malaya (UM) was the sole multidisciplinary university in the country. The university had faculties of arts, science, engineering, and agriculture. Basically, it was an implantation of a British model for much of the curriculum. Reading and reference materials were mainly British in content, and the administrative structure and examination system were British in character (Selvaratnam, 1986). Although the UM grew quite rapidly in student numbers, staff, and facilities, it was not able to meet the unprecedented increase in demand for university education that followed new government policies pertaining to access to higher education after the 1969 racial riots in the country.

The 1969 riots were a watershed in Malaysian history, with implications for all aspects of life—including higher education. The government blamed the bloody riots on the socioeconomic disparities between the Bumiputera and non-Bumiputera ethnic groups and faulted, among other things, the British-model university for contributing to ethnic economic imbalances and the lack of national unity (Lim, 1995). Immediately after the riots, the government implemented the ethnic admissions quota for public higher education institutions. This ethnic quota coincided with the rapid increase in the number of universities to meet the sharp rise in demand for university places.

Four additional universities sprang up between 1969 and 1972, conceived as truly "national" universities with comprehensive changes in university administration. The major change was the shift from a relatively autonomous system prior to 1969 to a state-controlled system. The Ministry of Education assumed full control over all the universities in the country in terms of financing, staff recruitment and promotion, curriculum, medium of instruction, and student enrollments (Lim, 1995). The four additional universities established during this period were the University of Science (Universiti Sains Malaysia) in 1969, the National University (Universiti Kebangsaan Malaysia) in 1970, the Agricultural University (later renamed as Universiti Putra Malaysia) in 1971, and the Technology University (Universiti Teknologi Malaysia) in 1975 (Ministry of Education, 2001a).

In the 1980s, two more universities were added to meet the increasing demand for higher education. The International Islamic University Malaysia was established in 1983, with both Arabic and English as the medium of instruction. The institution's main purpose is to train manpower based on Islamic principles. The country's seventh university, Northern University (Universiti Utara Malaysia, UUM) was established in 1984 and focused on management science and information technology. This second wave of expansion saw the Ministry of Education playing a dominant role in the development of university programs, to avoid the unnecessary duplication of courses of study in universities. Therefore, each of the newly established universities had an area of specialization.

The third wave of expansion saw the establishment of four new public universities, five university colleges, nine private universities, and five branch campuses of foreign universities. Due to strong political pressure, a new university was established in each of the states in East Malaysia: Sarawak University (Universiti Sarawak Malaysia) in 1992 and Sabah University (Universiti Sabah Malaysia) in 1994. In the late 1990s, another two colleges were upgraded to universities. One of them was a teacher training college in Tanjong Malim, Perak, which became Sultan Idris Education University (Universiti Pendidikan Sultan Idris) in 1997—the only single-discipline university in the country that deals specifically with education. The other is the MARA Institute of Technology, which was established in 1967 to train Bumiputeras in middle-level management and technical positions. This institute was upgraded to become the MARA Technology University (Universiti Institut Teknologi Malaysia) in 1999.

Besides this group of new universities, the Malaysian government has recently embarked on setting up a string of college universities in various parts of the country. The aim of these college universities is to offer practical programs that provide students with hands-on experience in specific fields of study. Nearly all of these college universities were purposely sited outside the Klang Valley to reach out to the wider population in the other states besides Selangor.

With the deregulation of higher education in the mid-1990s, there was a rapid proliferation of new private universities. In 1995, not a single private university existed in the country, but by 2002 there were a total of fifteen new private universities and one private university college. Three were set up by state-owned enterprises (public utility companies that were privatized in the early 1990s): Multimedia University, owned by the Malaysian Telecommunications Company; Petronas Technology University, owned by the National Petroleum Company; and National Energy University, owned by the National Electricity Company. Two of them are distance-education universities: University of Tun Abdul Razak and the Open University of Malaysia. A political party (the Malaysian Chinese Association) owns the newest private university, University of Tunku Abdul Rahman. Four foreign universities from Australia and the United Kingdom also set up branch campuses in Malaysia.

The expansion of Malaysian universities saw the diversification of higher education, the emergence of private higher education, the presence of corporate and foreign players in the education market, dispersal of university locations, and the tightening of state control. All these developments were aimed at meeting the demand for higher education, widening educational opportunities, and expanding the role of the state with respect to higher education.

ISSUES AND REALITIES

Equity Issues

The above discussion on the expansion of universities shows that it was not until 1969, twelve years after political independence, that a second university was established in Malaysia. For the most part in the early years after independence, the country relied on a single university to train manpower for the "Malayanization" policy—that is, the replacement of expatriates with Malaysians—and for the rapid development and expansion of public and private sectors (Selvaratnam, 1985). During this period, the university was elitist and admission to a university was based on academic merit. But following the tragic events of the 1969 ethnic riots, Malaysian universities became focused on expanding access to economically disadvantaged groups.

The inequitable distribution of income, which was closely linked to the inequality of educational opportunities, became a prominent political issue among the different ethnic groups in Malaysia. The Malay ruling class realized that the ethnic economic imbalances between the Bumiputeras and non-Bumiputeras, if uncorrected, would lead to intense political and social conflicts. Thus, the Malay-led government took concrete steps to restructure Malaysian society by providing educational opportunities to the Bumiputeras so as to create a Bumiputera middle class in income, occupational status, and wealth. In 1970, the New Economic Policy was implemented, and it was aimed at redistributing the country's wealth among the various ethnic groups by increasing the Bumiputeras' share of corporate equity from 2.5 percent in 1970 to 30 percent in 1990 (Second Malaysia Plan, 1971).

With the New Economic Policy, the role of education, especially university education, became highly politicized. To stimulate and facilitate Bumiputera demand for access to higher education, the Malaysian government instituted the ethnic quota system for admission to public universities that set a ratio of 55:45 for Bumiputera-to-non-Bumiputera students. In order to effectively coordinate the implementation of this policy, the Ministry of Education established a Central Processing Unit for Universities that controls the selection of students for admission to all public higher education institutions. As observed by Selvaratnam (1988),

> The implementation of this tightly controlled process of selection and admission into the country's universities eroded one of the deep-rooted and jealously guarded academic traditions of university autonomy, that is, the practice of allowing each university to determine its own admissions policy and criteria. (p. 184)

The government's justification for this policy was to widen access to university education in keeping with the needs, aspirations, and expectations of the people and, more important, to the Bumiputera community, on whose support the ruling regime relies. This ethnic quota policy has been in place since 1970. In 1985, enrollments in degree programs were distributed by ethnic group as follows: Bumiputera (63.0 percent), Chinese (29.7 percent), and Indian (6.5 percent) (*Fifth Malaysia Plan*, 1986), as compared to the corresponding figures in 1969[2]—35.6 percent, 52.9 percent, and 11.5 percent, respectively (Singh, 1989). The proportion of Bumiputera students at public universities has increased significantly.

To ensure sufficient numbers of Bumiputera candidates qualified to be admitted to the universities, the government set up special secondary schools—such as fully residential schools and the MARA science colleges for Bumiputera students. In addition, nearly all public universities provide matriculation programs specifically for Bumiputera students. The matriculation program is a preuniversity program designed to admit Bumiputera students into scientific and technical fields in the universities. These matriculation programs are the equivalent of form six or A-level programs. The existence of a matriculation program at a public university that targets a specific ethnic group is quite unique and may not exist in other countries.

Besides setting up special schools and programs for Bumiputeras, the Malaysian government also provides scholarships and loans to Bumiputera students. The MARA Institute of Technology was established in 1967 specifically to increase the participation of Bumiputera students in diploma and degree courses. In fact, before the proliferation of private colleges in the 1990s, access to middle-level management and semiprofessional programs was reserved mostly for Bumiputeras. When the Mara Institute was upgraded to a university in 1999, it became the largest university—with a student population of 79,274 in 2001 (Ministry of Education, 2002).

After the early years of independence, the development of Malaysian universities was shaped by social and political forces aimed at making university education more accessible to the Bumiputera community. The affirmative action policy implemented by the Malay-led government had managed to change the ethnic mix of the student population. The government's direct intervention in the administration of admissions policies has increased the Bumiputera participation in tertiary education.

Enrollment Trends

The ethnic quota system may have provided the mechanism for shifting the balance of enrollments, but it has also resulted in an oversubscription in arts and humanities programs. In numbers and percentages, Bumiputera students have predominated in humanities and social science programs. The ratio of enrollments in first-degree programs in the arts and applied arts to programs in science and technical fields was about 60:40 in 1995 (*Eighth Malaysia Plan*, 2001). However, with the increasing importance of science and technology in economic development, the Malaysian government has taken steps to increase enrollments in scientific and technical fields. It is projected in the Eighth Malaysia Plan that the ratio of enrollments in arts and applied arts to those in science and technical fields will be reversed to 40:60 by 2005 (*Eighth Malaysia Plan*, 2001).

A recent disturbing trend is the gender imbalance at public universities. In the 1999–2000 academic year, the ratio of male to female students at public higher education institutions was 41.7:58.3 (More Females, 2000). The main reason for this gender imbalance is that female students perform better than male students in the university entrance examinations. This trend has evoked a growing concern among the authorities about marital compatibility of male and female graduates in the future.

With the increasing social demand for higher education, enrollments in Malaysian public universities increased from 33,969 in 1980 to 96,590 in 1990 and to 234,106 in 2000 (see Table 9.1). It is interesting to note that the number of students enrolled in degree programs far exceeded those in diploma and certificate programs. This is probably due to the fact that there are great discrepancies in the wage levels between graduates with first- and second-tier qualifications, thus leading to more demand for degree than for diploma or certificate qualifications. Table 9.1 also shows that the number of postgraduate students increased about six-fold, from 4,868 in 1990 to 30,477 in 2000.

In general, the cost of tertiary education is high. Tertiary education at public universities is heavily subsidized by the government. The tuition fees are in the range of U.S.$200 to U.S.$300 per annum. The Malaysian government offers scholarships and loans to students who need financial assistance. To increase the accessibility to higher education, the government, under the Eighth Malaysian Plan (2001–2005), allocated U.S.$684.2 million to the National Higher Education Fund, which provides financial assistance to students (*Eighth Malaysia Plan*, 2001).

Table 9.1   Enrollments at Public Universities, 1980-2000

	1980	1985	1990	1995	2000
Certificate	122	283	2,550	2,932	4,145
Matriculation	2,014[a]	5,280[c]	8,170	12,453	25,480
Prediploma			384	2,509	3,240
Diploma	11,641	23,596	30,491	40,329	71,787
First degree	20,192[b]	35,692[b]	50,127	75,709	170,794
Postgraduate			4,868	8,895	30,477
Total	33,969	64,851	96,590	142,827	234,106

Source: Ministry of Education, 2001a; Fifth Malaysia Plan, 1986
[a] Includes prediploma enrollments.
[b] Includes postgraduate enrollments.
[c] Includes prediploma enrollments and students enrolled in A-level and language courses.

Until recently, the Malaysian government has been the sole provider of higher education, and therefore large amounts of public funding have been channeled toward driving the second and third waves of higher education expansion. The Sixth Malaysia Plan (1991–1995) contained U.S.$815.7 million and the Seventh Malaysia Plan (1996–2000), U.S.$1.4 billion (*Seventh Malaysia Plan*, 1996). Nevertheless, the Ministry of Education has always been faced with tight budgetary constraints in meeting the ever-increasing demand for tertiary education. While the number of places in public universities has increased tremendously over the years, there is still a great unmet demand. Starting in the early 1990s, the more established universities began to increase their student intakes, and by the year 2000, most of them had enrollments that exceeded 20,000. The problem of meeting the strong demand for higher education is further exacerbated by the ethnic quota system, under which many qualified non-Bumiputera students were unable to gain admission to public universities. Initially, many of these non-Bumiputera students went overseas to further their studies, but with the sharp increase of overseas tuition fees in the late 1980s and the devaluation of the Malaysian ringgit during the Asian financial crisis, many Malaysians could not afford to study overseas. To overcome this problem, the government has been forced to seek alternative means of financing higher education by allowing the private sector to establish higher education institutions. The private sector responded overwhelmingly and, by 2000, of the total tertiary-level enrollments of 548,199, 232,069 (about 42.3 percent) were registered in private higher education institutions. However, the number of students enrolled in private universities is comparatively low—only about 22,480 in 2001—because most of the students are registered in nonuniversity private institutions (Ministry of Education, 2001b).

Studying at a private university costs much more than studying at a public university. The tuition fees charged by private universities range from as little as U.S.$2,000 per annum (for distance-learning programs) to as much as U.S.$25,800 per annum (for medical programs). Despite the high tuition fees, students do seek admission at private universities either because they could not gain admission to public universities or were not offered the programs of their choice. Students who prefer to obtain a tertiary education in English are attracted to private universities, at nearly all of which English is the medium of instruction. The use of English as the medium of instruction at private higher education institutions is part of the state's liberalization of education policy.

The Strong Interventionist State

The relationship between the state and universities centers around the issue of autonomy and accountability. Universities and the state are constantly redefining their mutual relationship, with the former usually insisting on more autonomy and the latter demanding more accountability (Albornoz, 1991). As discussed in the previous section, all public universities in Malaysia are funded by the government. Thus, not only does the government exert its authority over broad policies through legislation, but it also presides over the detailed operations of the universities. As for private universities, the Malaysian government has also passed legislation to monitor and regulate private higher education.

After the 1969 ethnic riots, the Malaysian government began to take full control over the country's universities. The Universities and University Colleges Act of 1971 (UUCA) set a legislative framework for all Malaysian universities (*Universities and University Colleges*, 1971). Under the UUCA, the minister of education assumed responsibility for the general policy direction of higher education. The act stipulated that no new faculty or course could be added without prior consultation with and approval from the minister of education. The appointment of vice-chancellors and deputy vice-chancellors, which was previously the prerogative of the university council, is in the hands of the government and the minister of education in particular. Deans and heads of departments, who had formerly been elected, are appointed by the vice-chancellors of the respective universities. Under this act, the government has full authority over enrollments, staff appointments, curriculum, and financing at all the public universities. Furthermore, this act does not allow students or faculty to be involved in any political activities or to be affiliated with any political party or trade union. This new act and the philosophy behind the New Economic Policy brought the universities under close government surveillance.

The government's control of public universities was further strengthened by the Constitution (amendment) Bill of 1971, which required universities to implement the ethnic quota admissions policy and to convert their medium of instruction in stages from English to Bahasa Malaysia by 1983. By converting the medium of instruction to the national language, it was hoped that Malaysian universities would acquire a national identity as well as develop an indigenous knowledge culture. As noted by Altbach and Gopinathan (1982),

> the university is inevitably involved in broader issues of political, public policy and cultural contestation. The choice of the language of instruction is then a matter of great sensitivity and also of immense consequence to the university. (p. 33)

Until recently, all public universities used the Malay language as the medium of instruction. Much effort has been put into developing the Malay language for academic and scientific purposes, and many resources have been invested in the translation of foreign textbooks into Bahasa Malaysia. Although progress has been slow, costly, and problematic, public universities have been using the indigenous language for instruction at the undergraduate level (Lee, 1997).

The state intervened directly in order to effect drastic changes in the administration and organization of Malaysian universities so as to enable the universities to serve the national interests, in particular, the interest and aspiration of the ruling elites. However, as the higher education system expanded, the Malaysian state is no longer the sole provider of higher education. With the explosive growth of private higher education, the state has taken on the additional role of regulating and monitoring the quality of higher education in both the public and private sectors. Beginning in the 1990s, the Malaysian state also embarked on the restructuring of higher education by corporatizing public universities and privatizing higher education on a large scale.

Restructuring Higher Education

The restructuring of higher education is a worldwide phenomenon, and it is possible to identify some of the global trends in Malaysia. Studies on the restructuring of higher education in different countries reveal a convergence of higher education policy ideas on how to allocate resources, generate new revenue, adapt to new demands, and reorganize so as to lower costs, increase efficiency, raise productivity, and improve teaching quality (Gumport & Pusser, 1999). However, the steps taken vary in different settings because policy ideas are often received and interpreted differently given political contexts, national infrastructures, and national ideologies (Ball, 1998). The restructuring of higher education in Malaysia is an interaction between global influences and local responses.

With the expansion and diversification of the higher education system, the Malaysian state expanded its role from main provider to regulator and protector of higher education. The state plays these additional roles through legislative interventions. In 1996, the National Council on Higher Education Act was passed, which put into place a single governing body to steer the direction of higher education development in the country. Since the establishment of this council, there has been a gradual shift from state control toward state supervision in the relationship between the Malaysian government and universities. With the privatization of higher education, the trend has also been toward market-based policies that aim at increasing the range of choices for students and addressing the needs of an increasingly complex social order. However, the state still maintains a central steering role to ensure equity of access, consumer advocacy, and national identity, which are broader social and cultural goals that transcend the market.

In 1995, the UUCA was amended to lay the groundwork for all public universities to be corporatized. Corporatized universities are empowered to engage in market-related activities—such as entering into business ventures, building endowments, and setting up companies. The Malaysian government continues to own most of the public universities' assets and to provide development funds for new programs and expensive capital goods. But the corporatized universities are expected to shoulder the burden of raising a portion of their operating costs because the government funding for recurrent expenditure was expected to be reduced gradually. However, as it turned out, the Malaysian government has deferred its plan to reduce funding to the public universities. Therefore, the public universities were "corporatized by governance" only and not financially.

Although the corporatized universities are required to raise revenues from market-related activities, they are not allowed to raise tuition fees at their own discretion, particularly at the undergraduate level. Any increase in tuition fees has to be approved by the National Council on Higher Education. Some of the strategic plans that corporatized universities use to seek revenues include research grants and consultancy, franchise educational programs, the renting out of university facilities, and recruitment of full-fee-paying foreign students.

In 1996, the Private Higher Educational Institutions Act was passed, which defines the government's regulatory control over all private higher education institutions, including private universities. Under this act, approval must be obtained from the minister of education before a private institution can be set up or before any programs can be offered at a particular institution. Private universities can only be established at the invitation of the minister. Foreign universities are allowed to set up branch campuses in the country, but they can only do so at the invitation of the minister. Furthermore, all courses must be conducted in the national language, but with the approval of the minister some courses may be taught in English or Arabic. This act enables the government to exercise tight control over the types of private universities that can be established and the kinds of educational programs that can be offered by these universities. To maintain this control, the Ministry of Education has set up a Private Education Department to regulate all the private universities, as well as a Higher Education Department to oversee all public universities.

The restructuring of higher education in Malaysia has led to the deregulation of the higher education sector and in turn to the marketization of higher education, which is very much influenced by a neoliberal economic ideology. Neoliberalism argues for a reduction of the welfare state and an increase in economic efficiency through the privatization of public-sector agencies. However, in the case of Malaysia, public funding of higher education has not been reduced. Besides financing higher education, the Malaysian state continues to play an interventionist role vis-à-vis universities, implementing national policies that have a direct effect, in particular on the governance and quality assurance in both public and private universities.

University Governance

The governance of all Malaysian universities comes under a common legislative framework of the 1971 UUCA. Private universities come under the Private Higher Educational Institutions Act of 1996 as well. Before 1971, the administrative and academic structure of Malaysian universities was based on the British model, with some American influences among the newer ones. As in Britain, the authorities of the university include the court, the council, the senate, the faculties, the institutions, the boards of studies, the boards of selection, the board of student welfare, the guild of graduates, and other such bodies (Selvaratnam, 1989). The vice-chancellor was appointed by the university council as the principal academic and executive officer of the university. The council was the governing body of the university, and it was the principal authority in that it determined the broad policies of the whole university. The senate was in charge of academic matters, and it was made up solely of academics. However, with the passing of the UUCA in 1971 the vice-chancellors were no longer appointed by the university council but rather by the minister of education. The newer universities established between 1969 and 1975 were broadly based on British models but with some changes in the direction of departmental structure.

Over the years, the trend has been toward adopting many aspects of American higher education. The academic year at public universities is divided into two semesters instead of three terms. The "unit/credit" system, continual assessment throughout the course, and the use of "grade performance aggregate" or "grade-point average" in assessment have been implemented at most universities. Some public universities have schools instead of faculties, and many have established graduate schools. Many of the programs are multidisciplinary in approach, and at the postgraduate level some master's programs are based on coursework. It can be said that Malaysian universities are hybrids of British and American models (Lee, 1997).

However, when the 1971 UUCA was amended in 1995, the governance of public universities changed drastically. This amendment created the framework for the corporatization of public universities. Corporatization frees public universities from the shackles of government bureaucratic provision and allows them to be run like business corporations. Within this new framework, the university court is abolished, the university council replaced by a board of directors, and the size of the senate reduced from about three hundred to about forty (*Universitites and University Colleges*, 1995). The reduction in the size of the senate may be viewed as an erosion of academics' power in the governance of the university. A trimmer senate could mean less consultation with and feedback from academics on university policies. In the governance of a corporatized university, much of the power lies in the hands of the vice-chancellor, who functions like a chief executive officer, and a central management team.

Private universities are often governed by boards of governors or directors, usually comprised of representatives of the stakeholders. Although some universities separate the governance body from the management team, at others the board and the management team consist of the same group of people. Usually, the type of ownership determines the form of corporate governance. Some private universities are governed by public corporations, and consortia of private companies govern others. Some of the local private universities started offering degree programs with the help of foreign universities because they lacked the academic expertise to design their own curricula. These foreign linkages enabled Malaysian universities to acquire and deliver new educational programs at minimal cost. Besides foreign linkages, some private universities also form different kinds of partnership with philanthropic foundations, private entities, as well as public agencies to meet capital needs for their establishment or expansion.

This discussion on university governance shows that much of the earlier development of Malaysian universities followed the models of British and American universities. But with the passage of time, Malaysian universities have developed some distinctive indigenous characteristics like the strong presence of the state in the governance of public universities, innovative partnerships in the governance of private universities, and various institutional linkages with foreign universities among private universities.

Quality Assurance

With the increasing enrollments at public universities and the explosive growth of private universities within a short period of time, the quality of university education in Malaysia became a great concern among the stakeholders in higher education. In recent years, the government has instituted different quality assurance mechanisms for both the public and private university systems. At the institutional level, Malaysian universities are beginning to pay more attention to quality management, quality assessment, and quality improvement.

After an initial period of unregulated expansion, in the mid-1990s, the Malaysian government took steps to regulate and consolidate the development of private higher education. In 1996, another important act was passed, which led to the establishment of the National Accreditation Board, often referred to as LAN,[3] to monitor and control the standard and quality of all the educational programs offered by private higher education institutions. LAN has two primary functions: (1) to ensure that all programs offered by private institutions meet the minimum standards as determined by the board, and (2) to award certificates of accreditation for the certificates, diplomas, and degrees conferred by private institutions, including the private universities. The criteria for meeting the standards for minimum requirements and for accreditation are based on the courses of study, teaching staff, syllabi in all subjects, facilities, management systems, and rationale for the curriculum. With the introduction of accreditation, it is hoped that the quality of educational programs offered by private universities will be assured and guaranteed.

In December 2001, the Quality Assurance Division was set up by the Ministry of Education to manage and supervise the quality assurance system for public universities (Kementerian Pendidikan Malaysia, 2002). Its primary function is to organize academic audits of public universities so as to gain and maintain public confidence in the quality of higher education provided by these institutions. One of the new division's initial tasks is to develop a quality assurance system that involves setting up subject benchmark standards and a qualification framework for different programs in the various fields of study at the universities. However, these standards are nonprescriptive and take into account the dynamic development of each program. These standards do not specify the exact quality of the products but set forth the criteria and guidelines for the structure and process of higher education (Kementerian Pendidikan Malaysia, 2002). Once the list of benchmark standards has been established for each subject, the Ministry of Education would encourage each public university to carry out an internal assessment of all its academic programs so as to identify its strengths and weaknesses and to initiate improvements. This internal quality assessment would be done at the faculty level but was usually initiated by the university's central management.

The LAN and Quality Assurance Division are external mechanisms set up at the national level by the Malaysian government to monitor and supervise the quality of education at Malaysian universities. However, with the corporatization of public universities, each university has also taken steps to improve its institutional management. Following global trends, many Malaysian universities have adopted a whole range of symbolic trappings of "corporate culture" in their attempts to improve accountability, efficiency, and productivity (Currie, 1998). Management techniques from the private sector such as mission statements, strategic planning, total quality management, International Standards Organization certification, right sizing, and benchmarking have been institutionalized among corporatized public universities and private universities. All these changes in management practices can be seen as granting a more powerful role for the university's central authorities in resource management and in orienting and controlling departmental activities. These new management practices have impinged on the academic profession, resulting in academics having less say in the governance and management of their universities.

The Changing Academic Profession

The number of academics in Malaysia is small when compared with the profession in other Asian countries. In 1999, there were 10,920 academics at public universities, out of which 5.6 percent were professors, 18 percent associate professors, and the rest lecturers (Lee, 2003). The number of female academics varies from institution to institution and from department to department, but on the whole their proportion is much lower than that of male academics. Although there is no salary differential between male and female academics, there seems to be a "glass ceiling" impediment to women's career advancement in the universities. The underrepresentation of women in the higher ranks of the academic profession can be attributed to sociocultural factors as well as organizational and structural factors (Luke, 1998).

As universities expand, the direct power of academics over the structures of governance has been limited by a new layer of professional bureaucrats who have significant power in the day-to-day administration of the university (Altbach, 1991). The emphasis on accountability has forced academics to submit to more fiscal control, pressure to increase productivity, and compliance with rules and regulations as well as rigorous assessment procedures. As a consequence, academic culture loses its collegiality and becomes more bureaucratic and hierarchical with a concentration of power at the top (Lee, 2003). The penetration of the corporate culture into public universities has required academics to behave like entrepreneurs and to market their expertise, services, and research findings. The emergence of a corporate culture in the universities is beginning to cause a cleavage between academics in the natural and applied sciences, who are constantly subjected to the pressure of engaging in entrepreneurial activities, and those in the social sciences and humanities, who perceive the social value of their research being undermined by the university authorities. The corporatization of public universities may have brought about increased institutional autonomy, but it has also raised the demand for accountability on the part of academics. The corporate culture in universities emphasizes performance. Academic staff at all public universities have to work out "personal performance contracts" with their respective heads, and annual salary increments are based on performance.

Academic freedom in Malaysia is limited when compared to that in other countries. Restrictions cover what can be researched and what the academic community can express to the public. Topics related to ethnic conflict, local corruption, and other politically sensitive issues have been banned from academic research. There have been cases of censorship of research findings, which are deemed to be politically sensitive by the powers that be. A ruling exists that requires academics to seek permission from the vice-chancellor before expressing their views publicly. The Malaysian government has used legislation to gag both the dons and students from participation in shaping public discourse and national debate (Lee, 2003). Academics teaching at private universities have even less academic freedom because many of them are teaching in educational programs that are not designed by them. In most of the foreign-linked programs, the curriculum is developed and set by overseas partner institutions.

The system is experiencing an acute shortage of well-qualified academics at both private and public universities. In 2000, out of a total of 13,033 academics in public universities only 21.6 percent had Ph.D.s, 72.1 percent had master's degrees, and the rest had first degrees. The situation in the private sector is even less encouraging. Out of a total of 8,928 academics at all private higher education institutions (universities and colleges), only 4 percent had Ph.D.s, 25.6 percent had master's degrees, 58.3 percent had bachelor's degrees, and 11.9 percent did not have a first degree (Ministry of Education, 2001b). There is very little institutional mobility among academics in public universities—except after retirement, when quite a number of them take up appointments in the newer universities. To overcome the shortage of academics, private universities hire a substantial number of part-time lecturers, either from industry or from more established universities. The recent forces of change in higher education have affected the academic profession in Malaysia. The shift from elite to mass higher education, from higher education as a public service to higher education as a commodity, and from the role of the state as a provider to that of regulator—all have vast implications for the academic profession. The strong intervention of the state and the influence of market ideology have resulted in a hybrid bureaucratic and corporate academic culture in Malaysia (Lee, 2003).

As in other countries, Malaysian universities expect their academic staff to teach and be involved in research. However, in the 1970s and 1980s, the Malaysian universities had a relatively low rate of research productivity (Singh, 1989). A study on research productivity among the Universiti Pertanian Malaysia academic staff shows that they spent about 30 percent of their time on research, with active researchers producing an average of only one article per annum (Haris, 1985). Most of the academic staff ranked research as a second priority behind teaching. Many reasons were given for this poor performance, including lack of time, finance, training, equipment, research assistants, motivation, and leadership from senior academics. This is especially true among the newer universities, which are still in the developmental stage in terms of research personnel and facilities. Research activities are given a low priority at private universities, where most of the academic staff is bogged down with teaching. However, the situation improved in the 1990s. With the corporatization of public universities, more resources are allocated to research and development with the aim of developing indigenous knowledge and technology for commercialization. The Malaysian government has designated three older universities as research universities: the Universiti Malaya, Universiti Kebangsaan Malaysia, and Universiti Sains Malaysia.

Teaching and training are important functions of the university. The emphasis on teaching tends to be greater among the newer universities, in particular the new private universities, where expanding enrollments and shortage of academic staff have hindered research. The pedagogical inputs at many Malaysian universities leave much to be desired. Because of the sharp increase in enrollments, many lecturers have to carry heavy teaching loads. Over the years, the ratio of staff to students has deteriorated from 1:20 to as high as 1:40, and the average number of teaching hours per week for each lecturer has increased from ten to sixteen hours per week (Lee, 2003). Of course, these figures vary from department to department. Some of the more established public universities are bursting at the seams because the development of physical infrastructure has not kept up with the increase in student intakes.

TRENDS AND CHALLENGES

Malaysian universities face many challenges in their future development. It is inevitable that future developments in Malaysian universities would be closely linked to past and present developments as well as influences from global trends. The higher education system in Malaysia will continue to expand, in the process becoming more diversified and stratified. As higher education becomes massified, it is important that there be different types of higher education institutions to meet the needs of a diverse student population. At the apex, there will be a small number of research universities, followed by a larger number of teaching universities together with some university colleges and polytechnics in the middle, and many colleges, training institutes, and community colleges at the base. The private sector will continue to play an active role, especially in absorbing excess demand for higher education. The number of private universities will increase as a number of the more established private colleges are poised to be upgraded to university status if given the opportunity. Private universities will continue to seek alternative delivery systems to make their educational programs accessible and affordable to their clients. In this respect, distance education will be featured more prominently and will expand with the development of advanced information communications technologies. As the Malaysian educational market is limited, virtual universities in Malaysia will be competing in the global arena for a share of the market in the Asia-Pacific region.

As for the public sector, many of the corporatized universities will expand their operations in income-generating activities. Currently, an increasing number of public universities are franchising their educational programs to private colleges, particularly matriculation and diploma programs. Through these franchises, universities increase their revenues and, at the same time, deploy more academic staff to teach higher degree programs. This is only one of the many public-private strategic partnerships that can create a win-win situation among the key players in the educational market. Other public-private partnerships include establishing university-industry links in research and development activities. Quite a number of public universities are beginning to set up technology incubators with high-tech companies located in the vicinity of the campuses. The hope is that a union of private and public money will produce the necessary mix of talent, facilities, and funding to stimulate high-quality research that will eventually lead to economic returns.

The global trend toward "the enterprise university" indicates that there is a steady pressure for greater accountability and cost-efficiency from a variety of sources, notably from the state (Marginson & Considine, 2000). These external pressures have led to the restructuring of universities in terms of governance and institutional and financial management. It should be noted that the restructuring of higher education in Malaysia did not take place in the presence of a shrinking welfare state, as in many Western countries, but rather through the initiative of a strong interventionist state. The state may not be the sole provider of higher education, but it has full control of the governance of public universities and acts as a strong regulator of the quality of both public and private higher education. Instead of cutting back on educational expenditure, the state continues to invest heavily in education and human resource development so that Malaysia can become a fully developed nation by the year 2020.

In response to external pressures, the Malaysian universities will continue to adopt corporate practices that call for the clarification of institutional mission and objectives as a basis for systematizing managerial action to improve accountability, efficiency, and productivity. Many of the universities are currently seeking ISO certification, applying total quality management, and managing an information system on the basis of various performance indicators for strategic planning purposes. The universities will also carry out internal academic audits and research assessment exercises more frequently in preparation for external quality assessment by LAN and the Quality Assurance Division, which will likely merge to form a single national body of quality assurance for all the universities in the future.

The state will continue to use higher education as a means to restructure Malaysian society, and the affirmative action policies will remain in place to reduce the interethnic differences in educational attainment. However, the ethnic quota policy for admission into public universities may be reviewed and replaced by a "merit system." Access to universities will always remain a contentious issue in Malaysian politics. In 2002, a "merit system" was hastily introduced whereby 32,752 students were offered places at public universities; the overall ratio of Bumiputera, Chinese, and Indian students was 69:26:5. This has become a controversial issue because the percentage of Bumiputera admissions has risen from the stated quota of 55 percent to 69 percent. The move from a quota system to a merit system becomes problematic when selection is not based on one common university entrance examination but instead on two different examinations—that is, the Sijil Tinggi Pelajaran Malaysia (STPM)[4] and matriculation examinations, which are not characterized by comparable standards.

To make university education more accessible to all those who are qualified and wish to continue their studies, the Malaysian government has set up the National Higher Education Fund, which provides loans to students who are in need of financial aid. In so doing, the government has followed the global trend of subsidizing the consumers of higher education—that is students. Besides subsidizing consumers, the government also subsidizes some private universities. The accessibility of university education will be further broadened if and when Malaysia signs the General Agreement on Trade in Services (GATS). Signing the GATS provisions for education guarantees that institutions can set up branches anywhere, export degree programs, and award certificates with minimal restrictions. It will also encourage investment by foreign institutions, allow mobility for academic staff, and promote training programs through distance modes. When this happens, a range of policies in Malaysia could be affected, including recognition of foreign qualifications, employment of foreign academics, government monopolies, quota systems, and subsidies. If Malaysia wants to become an educational hub in the region, then it has to review many of its educational policies, and one of them is its language policy.

The globalization of higher education has resulted in a U-turn in language policy at Malaysian universities. All private universities are using English as the medium of instruction, and public universities are taking steps to increase English usage in many of their programs. Starting in 2003, science and mathematics are now taught in English. The reemphasis on the importance of English will breathe life into the country's fledgling academic system, which has turned inward-looking since the implementation of the national-language policy.

If Malaysia wishes to remain competitive in the global economy, it has to develop its universities so that they can produce a highly skilled workforce as well as high technology and technoscience to yield new products and processes with relevance for the global market. Therefore, universities should be innovative and responsive to the needs of the rapidly changing globalized knowledge-based economy. It is essential that Malaysian universities be international in their outreach, generate new knowledge, customize their curricula, offer more choices to their clients, diversify enrollments, and produce graduates employable in the global market. These are some of the big challenges faced by Malaysian universities.

CONCLUSION

This chapter analyzes the contemporary issues facing Malaysian universities and the way these issues relate to the historical development of higher education in the country. It also examines how the development of Malaysian universities has been greatly shaped by the colonial past and the socioeconomic and political context in the country. It argues that the contemporary realities of higher education are closely linked to the past and the impact of global trends such as the democratization, privatization, and decentralization of higher education systems. However, the analysis of the Malaysian higher education system shows that there are distinctive national responses to these global trends.

This chapter shows that there has been rapid expansion of both public and private universities to meet the increasing social demand for higher education. The broadening of access to universities has been accompanied by the redistribution of educational opportunities in terms of ethnicity, gender, and region. The Malaysian state plays a dominant role in funding, governing, and developing public universities. It also monitors and regulates the quality of university education through various laws and quality assurance mechanisms. Malaysian universities face many challenges in trying to achieve the broad goals of equality, accessibility, and quality. The biggest challenge of all is how to develop world-class universities and to make Malaysia the educational hub in the region.

NOTES

1. *Bumiputera* is the term used for the Malays and other indigenous people, such as the Orang Asli, Kadazandusuns, Dayaks, Ibans, and others.

2. These are the proportions of the total student populations at public universities and not just degree programs.

3. LAN stands for Lembaga Akreditasi Nasional.

4. The STPM is equivalent to the A-level examination taken at the end of form six.

REFERENCES

Albornoz, O. (1991). Autonomy and accountability in higher education. *Prospects,* 21(2), 204–213.

Altbach, P. G. (1991). The academic profession. In P. G. Altbach (Ed.), *International higher education: An encyclopaedia* (pp. 23–45). New York: Garland.

Altbach, P. G., & Gopinathan, S. (1982). The dilemma of success: Higher education in advanced developing countries. In P. G. Altbach (Ed.), *Higher education in the third world: Themes and variations* (pp. 25–44). Singapore: Maruzen Asia.

Ball, S. J. (1998). Big policies/small world: An introduction to international perspectives on education policy. *Comparative Education, 34*(2), 119–130.

Currie, J. (1998). Globalization practices and the professoriate in Anglo-Pacific and North American universities. *Comparative Education Review, 42*(1), 15–29.

Eighth Malaysia Plan 2001–2005. (2001). Kuala Lumpur, Malaysia: Percetakan Nasional Malaysia.

Fifth Malaysia Plan 1986–1990. (1986). Kuala Lumpur, Malaysia: Percetakan Nasional Malaysia.

Gumport, P. J., & Pusser, B. (1999). University restructuring: The role of economic and political contexts. In J. C. Smart & W. G. Tierney (Eds.), *Higher education: Handbook of theory and research* (pp. 146–200). New York: Agathon.

Haris, G. T. (1985). Constraints on research in Malaysian universities. *Southeast Asian Journal of Social Science, 13*(2), 80–92.

Kementerian Pendidikan Malaysia. (2002). *Kod Amalan Jaminan Kualiti IPTA di Malaysia* (Quality assurance codes of practice for public higher education institutions in Malaysia). Kuala Lumpur, Malaysia: Author.

Lee, M. N. N. (1997). Malaysia. In G. A. Postiglione & G. C. L. Mak (Eds.), *Asian higher education* (pp. 173–197). Westport, CT: Greenwood.

Lee, M. N. N. (2003). The academic profession in Malaysia and Singapore: Between bureaucratic and corporate culture. In P. G. Altbach (Ed.), *The decline of the guru: The academic profession in developing and middle-income countries* (pp. 135–165). New York: Palgrave.

Lim, T. G. (1995). Malaysian and Singaporean higher education: Common roots but differing directions. In A. H. Yee (Ed.), *East Asian higher education* (pp. 69–83). Oxford: Pergamon.

Luke, C. (1998). Cultural politics and women in Singapore higher education management. *Gender and Education, 10*(3), 245–263.

Marginson, S., & Considine, M. (2000). *The enterprise university.* Cambridge: Cambridge University Press.

Ministry of Education. (2001a). *Education in Malaysia: A journey to excellence.* Kuala Lumpur, Malaysia: Author.

Ministry of Education. (2001b). *Maklumat Pendidikan Swasta 2001* (Private education information). Kuala Lumpur, Malaysia: Jabatan Pendidikan Swasta, Kementerian Pendidikan Malaysia.

Ministry of Education. (2002). *Annual Report 2001.* Kuala Lumpur, Malaysia: Author.

More females in local universities. (2000, December 31). *Sunday Star,* 12. *Second Malaysia Plan 1971–1975.* (1971). Kuala Lumpur, Malaysia: Government Printer.

Selvaratnam, V. (1985). The higher education system in Malaysia: Metropolitan, cross-national, peripheral or national? *Higher Education, 14,* 477–496.

Selvaratnam, V. (1986). Dependency, change and continuity in a Western university model: The Malaysian case. *Southeast Asian Journal of Social Sciences, 14*(2), 29–51.

Selvaratnam, V. (1988). Ethnicity, inequality, and higher education in Malaysia. *Comparative Education Review, 32*(2), 173–196.

Selvaratnam, V. (1989). Change amidst continuity: University development in Malaysia. In P. G. Altbach & V. Selvaratnam (Eds.), *From dependence to autonomy: The development of Asian universities* (pp. 187–205). Dordrecht, Netherlands: Kluwer Academic.

Seventh Malaysia Plan 1996–2000. (1996). Kuala Lumpur, Malaysia: Percetakan Nasional Malaysia.

Singh, J. S. (1989). Scientific personnel, research environment, and higher education in Malaysia. In P. G. Altbach (Ed.), *Scientific development and higher education: The case of newly industrializing nations* (pp. 83–136). New York: Praeger.

UNESCO. (2000). *World education report 2000.* Paris: Author.

Universities and University Colleges Act, 1971. (1971). Kuala Lumpur, Malaysia: Government Printer.

Universities and University Colleges (Amendment) Act, 1995. (1995). Kuala Lumpur, Malaysia: Government Printer.

PART V

Development in the
Context of Massification

10

The Evolution of Higher Education
in Indonesia

Mochtar Buchori & Abdul Malik

Higher education in Indonesia has evolved in many ways during its long history, which started before the Dutch came to the archipelago in the early seventeenth century. The history of higher education in Indonesia can be roughly divided into four stages: the precolonial era, the Dutch colonial period, the Japanese occupation, and the postindependence era. This chapter will discuss the evolution of the system, including the interaction with the rest of the society and the role of higher education in politics and nation building.

OVERVIEW

There are five types of institutions within the Indonesian higher education system: universities, institutes, polytechnics, advanced schools, and academies. The 1961 higher education law stipulates that universities consist of at least four different faculties that provide training and research in various fields of study. Institutes consist of a number of faculties providing training and research in related fields. Advanced schools (*sekolah tinggi*) offer training in a single cluster of disciplines, such as economics or theology. Academies provide professional training at the associate degree level in a single field—such as public health or secretarial education, among others. Universities, institutes, and some advanced schools offer a full range of degrees from bachelor's, master's, and doctoral degree programs, as well as nondegree programs. Academies and polytechnics, on the other hand, offer only two-, three-, or four-year nondegree programs.

The system currently encompasses more than 1,900 schools, of which less than 100 are publicly funded and more than 1,800 are privately operated. In 2001 approximately 3.4 million students were enrolled in all types of schools in the higher education system. More than 1.5 million of them, or 46 percent, were female. With regard to the 18- to 24-year age cohort, which numbered about 26 million in 2001, the national enrollment rate was 13 percent. While this is certainly a low enrollment rate in comparison with those of more advanced countries in the region, from a historical point of view it represents a very high rate of expansion, especially in the last 35 years. The system produced more than 680,000 graduates of varying degrees and levels in 2001.

In 2001, private institutions—private universities, institutes, advanced schools, and academies—enrolled almost 1.9 million, or about 60 percent of all students. The large majority of students, almost 74 percent, were enrolled in schools located on Java island, which has just over 60 percent of the country's population. Regarding the distribution of students by field, a disproportionately large number were enrolled in the social sciences and humanities (59 percent), compared with the number in engineering fields (17 percent). Islamic tertiary education institutions—such as Islamic institutes of higher learning (both public and private) and Islamic advanced schools (both public and private)—comprised almost 15 percent of total national enrollments.

Academic staff are one of the areas of concern in the higher education system. Staff numbers and qualifications have not kept up with the expansion in enrollments and the demand for quality improvement. Indeed, this is the area with the greatest impact on the quality of higher education. In 1997, of the approximately 50,000 academic staff at public institutions, less than 4,200 (8.6 percent) were doctoral degree-holders and less than 14,000 (29.2 percent) were master's degree-holders—for a combined total of only 37.8 percent. The remaining academic staff were college graduates, and only a few, mainly those in medical schools, had received some professional training. These numbers involve public universities; the situation with private universities is even worse.

Public schools are funded through government budget appropriations, student tuition fees, support from donors and charities, and proceeds from collaboration with other parties—especially in the private sector. Tuition fees have formed a relatively small part of public higher education revenues, but they have been steadily increasing over the last three decades. In the 1970s, tuition fees accounted for less than 10 percent of revenues in public institutions; they now account for some 20 percent of the total. The increasing proportion of student and parental contribution is important from a public finance and equity point of view, in light of the fact that enrollment in the higher education system is heavily dominated by the upper segments of society. A survey conducted in 1995 showed that more than 80 percent of students are from families belonging to the top quintile of socioeconomic status.

Private schools are funded largely through student tuition fees. Other sources of revenue, including charitable donations and proceeds from collaboration with other parties, are in most cases small and insignificant. Private schools receive government subsidies, mostly in kind—in the form of employment of academic staff paid for by the government and access to common facilities, including laboratories, set up by the government through a private university coordinating body (*kopertis*) to serve private universities in each region. Currently, some 10 percent of private school academic staff are paid by the government.

HISTORICAL PERSPECTIVES

Each stage in the development of Indonesian higher education has its own characteristics, historical context, and environment. One common theme throughout all stages of development is the role played by educational institutions and students in political movements involved in the country's nation building. Even the colonial higher education system, which was professionally oriented, produced unintended results—such as the building of nationhood and the flourishing of the nationwide movement against the Dutch. Student movements in the 1950s influenced government policy in every aspect of the nation's life, including the nationalization of higher education institutions, the repatriation of Dutch academics, and the adoption of the national language as the medium of instruction.

The other theme in this chapter concerns the role of Islam at every stage of the nation's development. Islam and Islamic education have shaped Indonesia's higher education system. Indeed, Islamic education predated secular higher education, even though it was only in unstructured formats. There is substantial evidence to suggest that Islam, especially cultural Islam, has had a pronounced influence on the higher education system—while, conversely, academic thinking has also influenced the development of Islam in Indonesia.

The Precolonial Period

The early period of higher education was characterized by Islamic, nonformal, and less structured education.[1] Higher education, as well as lower levels of education, was provided mainly by *pesantren*, located across the country, mostly in Java, and led by Muslim clerics (*kiyai* and *ulama*).[2] Islamic education during precolonial times—the period before 1831—did not classify schools into levels equivalent to those of Western systems. The *pesantren* learning system was centered on the *kiyai* or *ulama* as the central figure. Levels of education were distinguished by the way the teaching and learning process was conducted. *Pesantren* education was not structured as is the secular education of today. The schools varied from one *pesantren* to another and were highly autonomous with respect to curriculum and institutional development (Wahid, 2001).

Initially, students studied the Qur'an, usually in mosques, to learn to read Arabic. The goal was to read fluently and accurately, starting with the last chapter (*juz*) of the Qur'an, known as Juz Amma, consisting of the shorter *surah* and *ayat* (verses), and then continuing on to read the entire thirty chapters of the holy book. Completion of Juz Amma and the thirty chapters was marked by graduation ceremonies. The next stage after the reading lessons was to learn the Arabic language. Instruction in Arabic was considered important, as it would open the door to further studies, since virtually all books in Indonesia at the time were written in Arabic. In addition to learning the language, students at this stage also started to learn *syariah* (rules and regulations) pertaining to *ibadah* (worshiping Almighty God), as well as being introduced to theology and other basic knowledge.

Upon mastering the basics, students went on to study advanced-level books, including discussions of certain branches of Islamic knowledge. For example, in the area of *fiqh* (law), students studied several schools of thought and the debates on certain issues. At this level, the highest level of education at *pesantren,* students studied advanced religious subjects under individual tuition, known locally as *ngaji sorogan*, directly from the *kiyai*. The character and relative strength of *pesantren* varied, depending on the field of expertise of the *kiyai*. This advanced level was considered higher education because the graduates were expected to establish *pesantren* of their own. Furthermore, when graduates of this level decided to pursue further learning in the Middle East, such as at al-Azhar University in Cairo, they were admitted directly to the postgraduate level.[3]

The Colonial Period (1831–1942) and the Japanese Occupation (1942–1945)

Secular higher education began in the late nineteenth century, during the colonial era, with the establishment by the Dutch of a medical school for indigenous doctors that in 1902 became School Tot Opleiding Van Indische Artsen (SLOVIA) and later Geneeskundige Hooge School (GHS) in Batavia (Jakarta).[4] The engineering school Technische Hooge School (THS) was later founded in Bandung (1920), followed by the agricultural school Landbouwkundige Hooge School (LHS) in Bogor and the law school Rechts Hooge School (RHS) in Jakarta (1924). Higher education in the then Nederland Indie (Dutch Indies) was mainly focused on professional training and less on research-oriented academic studies. It was intended mainly to address the need for professional manpower to support the colonial administration, due to a shortage of engineers and other professionals from the Netherlands, caused by World War I.

The student body reflected the strict social stratification introduced by the Dutch, with the Europeans at the top, the native aristocracy and prominent Eurasians next, Chinese businessmen a step lower, and various layers of the indigenous people as the broad base. Dutch was the exclusive language of instruction and effectively served as an instrument of selection to admit students from among the small numbers of high school graduates. Enrollments of indigenous people as late as 1930 amounted to a mere 106 students.

Despite the colonial higher education system's focus on professional training rather than academic and research-oriented schooling, it succeeded in producing a generation of leaders who went on to build the nation and state. Indeed, the founding fathers, the leaders who introduced and cultivated a sense of nationhood at the beginning of the twentieth century, were the graduates of the colonial higher education system—either in Indonesia or in the Netherlands. The rise of political leaders was an unintended result of the high-quality education. One explanation for this phenomenon would be that although the institutions were professional schools, their students were high school graduates with strong backgrounds in the liberal arts and humanities. In addition, mastery of foreign languages (Dutch being the primary one) and access to books of the liberal genre made the students aware of the country's political situation. Professional careers were regarded as a symbol of modernity. Entering a new profession meant entering modern life. Thus, the students became aware of the moral and political consequences of becoming modern professionals.

When the Japanese took over the archipelago from the Dutch in 1942,
they soon overhauled the education system. The stratified school system
at the lower levels was eliminated, and Dutch was replaced by Malay-
Indonesian as the medium of instruction. The school system in a sense
became more democratic and egalitarian. However, the overall condition
of the education system deteriorated greatly in comparison to the previous years under Dutch administration. The number of primary schools
declined by more than one-third, and almost all secondary schools were
closed. Accordingly, enrollments at the primary and secondary levels
dropped by approximately 30 percent and 90 percent, respectively. The
number of primary school teachers decreased by 35 percent, while only 5
percent of secondary school teachers remained on active duty. Many higher
education institution ceased operation, leaving quite a few schools barely
surviving.

There are several reasons why the education system underwent such a
drastic decline. First, banning Dutch books effectively destroyed the
sources of modern knowledge. Second, putting teachers and intellectuals
under strict political surveillance took away freedom of thought and communication. Third, the deterioration in the welfare of teachers degraded
their dignity. And finally, inclusion in the curriculum of basic military
training and public service programs (*kinrohoshi*) curtailed time allocated for intellectual exercises.

The Reconstruction Phase, 1945–1950

The short five-year period following the nation's independence was marked
by two important developments. The strong belief in education on the
part of national leaders who themselves were mostly highly educated,
combined with the deterioration the education system suffered during
the Japanese occupation, prompted the country to move quickly to re-
construct higher education. Schools that previously had ceased operation were reopened, and new schools were established. The dynamic of
the period reflected both the high spirit of the people following independence and the clear vision of the nation's founding fathers concerning the
role of education in shaping society and national unity.

This period also marked the beginning of competing agendas of education between the two most prominent elements of the national struggle
for independence, the nationalist wing and the Islamic wing (covered in
the section on "Islam and Higher Education").

Immediately following the proclamation of independence on August

17, 1945, an institution named Balai Perguruan Tinggi Repoeblik Indonesia (Center for Higher Learning of the Republic of Indonesia) was established. The center, chaired by Sarwono Prawirohardjo, offered courses in medicine, law, and literature. One of the tasks of the center was to take steps to ameliorate the damage inflicted on medical training during the Japanese occupation. When the Dutch colonial forces returned to Indonesia in December 1945 and reoccupied Jakarta, the center moved to Yogyakarta, together with the new Indonesian government. In early 1946 the center changed its name to the Balai Perguruan Tinggi Gajahmada (Gajahmada Center for Higher Learning). The institution benefited from strong support from Sultan Hamengkubuwono IX, the ruler of Yogyakarta, and opened its Faculty of Law and Faculty of Letters. On December 19, 1949, President Sukarno inaugurated the center as Universitet Negeri Gajahmada (Gajahmada State University).

In the meantime, as part of the Netherlands' propaganda to reclaim Indonesia as a colony, in 1947 the Dutch reopened the schools that had operated prior to the outbreak of World War II and grouped them into the Universitet van Indonesie. The university consisted of schools and faculties located in five cities: Jakarta (medicine, law, literature, and philosophy), Bogor (veterinary medicine and agriculture), Bandung (the sciences and engineering), Surabaya (medicine), and Makassar (economics). The vast majority of the academic staff (professors and lecturers) were Dutch nationals, and instruction was conducted in Dutch. Therefore, at the time there were two main state universities—Gajahmada State University, based in Yogyakarta, and the Universitet van Indonesie, based in Jakarta.

On December 27, 1949, less than two weeks after the inauguration of Gajahmada State University, the Dutch recognized the sovereignty of the Federal Republic of Indonesia, with Jakarta as its capital city. A debate then ensued over whether Gajahmada State University should remain in Yogyakarta or follow the state administration to Jakarta and merge with the Universitet van Indonesie. Those in favor of transferring the university to Jakarta argued that the limited facilities and low number of academic staff nationwide necessitated the amalgamation of available resources to create a stronger national university. Those in favor of the new university remaining in Yogyakarta argued that due to the critical shortage of educated manpower in the fledgling republic, it would be much better to have two universities, one in Jakarta and one in Yogyakarta. The government accepted the latter argument and decided that Gajahmada State University would remain in Yogyakarta.[5]

Along with the reconstruction of the higher education system, the re-opening of existing schools, and the establishment of new ones, popular demand for higher education soared. Between 1945 and 1950, enrollments nationwide increased more than three-fold, from 1,600 students to 5,200 students. It is also important to note that at such an early stage of nation building the private sector had also taken part in the provision of higher education. Two private universities, the Indonesian Islamic University in Yogyakarta and the National University in Jakarta, were established in 1946 and 1949, respectively.

The Nationalization and Expansion Phase, 1950–1965

Developments in the 1950s touched on substantial issues in higher education—such as objectives, missions, and the structure and organization of the system. Many conceptual changes took place, or were at least initiated, during this period. Changes in the medium of instruction were introduced, and the system made the transition from the European free study approach to a more structured system resembling the Anglo-American model. The education system's quality and relevance to the nation's needs also began to be addressed in the same period.

Following the recognition of sovereignty in 1950, the nationalist spirit was at a high point, as was the desire for education. The higher education system continued to make dramatic advances. One by one, schools outside Jakarta that used to be part of the Universitet van Indonesie became separate universities or institutes. These included Airlangga University in Surabaya (1954), Hassanuddin University in Makassar (1956), Bandung Institute of Technology (1959), and Bogor Agricultural University (1963). Three teacher training colleges (*IKIPs*) were also established. The rising demand for higher education continued and within a relatively short period manifested itself in the establishment of at least one university in each province. As a result, enrollments reached more than 108,000 by 1961, an almost twenty-fold increase over ten years.

Despite all this, however, the 1950s marked a decline in the quality of the higher education system. There are at least three reasons for this. First, the system might have expanded too quickly amid limited infrastructure, equipment, and quality academic staff. Second, the rapid expansion consequently lowered the standards of selectivity for new entrants, giving students with weaker precollege education access to higher education, who soon constituted the majority of the student community. At the same time, economic hardship and political turbulence constrained productive learning.

The third reason for the decline in quality during this period was the rapid nationalization of the system. In a large part of the system, the Universitet van Indonesie, Dutch nationals comprised much of the academic staff, the language of instruction was Dutch, and virtually all literature was in Dutch. The wave of nationalist sentiment and the fierce confrontation with the former colonial power in the late 1940s resulted in the swift nationalization of the previously Dutch-operated institutions, particularly the former components of the Universitet van Indonesie. The nationalization of the university consisted not merely in the taking over of its ownership and management, but more substantially in the banning of Dutch as the language of instruction and its replacement with Bahasa Indonesia. These steps were followed by the mass exodus of Dutch professors and lecturers who had previously constituted the main body of the academic staff.

One of early important developments in building the newly independent nation was the formulation of the function of higher education, better known as the Tri Dharma Perguruan Tinggi (three pillars of service of higher education), which defined the three missions of higher education institutions as education, research, and community service. Another development, and perhaps the culmination of efforts since the early 1950s, was the 1961 law on higher education, which is still in effect today.

The law was the first to include Tri Dharma Perguruan Tinggi as the mission of national higher education. It also spells out the principles concerning the roles, function, responsibility, and character of the higher education. The law stipulates that the development of science should be accompanied by character development, to benefit Indonesian society. To ensure their effectiveness, higher education institutions should not remain as ivory towers but rather must be closely connected to contemporary realities and the community they serve. In a closely related point, the law states that science and research should not be pursued merely for the sake of their own development but rather to enhance the well-being of the community. Higher education institutions are open to all citizens with necessary talents, perseverance, and character. Higher education institutions are supposed to recognize academic freedom but not to house subversive activities. Finally, higher education institutions are called on to produce graduates with intellectual maturity, critical thinking capacity, creativity, and problem-solving ability, as well as ethical and emotional maturity.

The enactment of the 1961 law provided the basis for various changes and laid the groundwork for later stages of higher education development. Universities have since become more structured, with a more standardized division of faculties. Requirements for establishing a university, college, academy, and other variants of higher education institutions, as well as procedures for setting up faculties, were clearly stipulated. The law sets the standard for every university's organizational structure, which was comprised of a university president and a university senate, which would interact with one another on a consultative basis. The law also set the requirements for the various stages and degrees for the different levels of higher education, as well as the criteria for instructors and their classification.

It should be noted, however, that despite the fundamental changes brought about by the law, its contents were colored by the political climate of the time, during which Sukarno introduced his "Guided Democracy" concept. There were requirements for professors and instructors concerning their political views and ideology. In addition to meeting academic and professional requirements, lecturers also had to adhere to Sukarno's socialist political manifesto to become legitimate instructors and professors.

A further important development during this period was the beginning of international cooperation to develop higher education in the form of assistance from Western agencies—such as the U.S. Agency for International Development (USAID) and the Ford Foundation—to modernize colleges by supporting advanced training for faculty members and providing books and equipment. University-to-university cooperation, funded by USAID, accelerated the growth in the number of Indonesian faculty members with advanced degrees from leading U.S. universities. This development, which put American-educated faculty members in a dominant position, led to changes in Indonesia's system of higher education based on aspects of the U.S. system.

ISSUES AND REALITIES

The System of Teaching and Learning

The growing number of American-educated faculty members brought about important consequences beyond just fulfilling the growing need for quality academic staff. Interaction with the academic world in the West, especially the United States, had raised awareness among these faculty about the value of productivity and efficiency in the education process. The concept of the economics of education and a better understanding of the social investment of education had prompted more serious steps toward improving the teaching and learning process. These trends in turn led to a reevaluation of the European-style system of higher education that was associated with an unstructured, lengthy period of study and low productivity.

In a long process beginning in the 1950s, the European model was gradually replaced by a more structured Anglo-American-style system. The evolution began with the introduction of a more structured teaching and learning process, one that enabled students to pursue their studies with better planning. The new system required students to attend lectures and complete class assignments. Work loads for both students and faculty members were part of academic planning. Examinations and other means of evaluation were established, and a well-structured educational administration was instituted.

The application of clear rules and regulations was expected to help improve the quality of higher education. The new system facilitated the application of more institutionalized objective standards regarding student competency. In the early 1970s, some leading universities introduced the credit-hour system, which is now standard practice at practically all universities. The new system gave students more flexibility in organizing their study plans and strategies. Bogor Agricultural University was one of the institutions that succeeded in significantly reducing the duration of degree programs. At this university a four-year time-to-degree was already the rule, rather than the exception. Structural changes in the system must be accompanied by improvement in the quality of faculty members, infrastructure, and equipment.

While statistical documentation for the improved productivity and efficiency of the system is lacking for 1960s and 1970s, a recent study conducted by the Directorate General of Higher Education (2003), in cooperation with the Japan Bank for International Cooperation, shows that while none of the leading public universities had achieved 20 percent internal efficiency in 1980, a number of leading universities had achieved almost 25 percent internal efficiency by 2000.[6]

Enrollment and Access

Enrollment grew sluggishly in the 1960s compared to the previous decade, with the number of students nationwide increasing by only around 50 percent between 1961 and 1968—from 108,000 to 156,000 students

(Malik, 1994). The situation began to change in the late 1960s and early 1970s following the establishment of the New Order government, which brought on a more favorable climate for education. Even though it was clearly dominated by the military, the new government relegated economic management to civilians, mostly academicians, and thus created an image of a technocratic government.

The shifting of the national agenda away from politics to economics had a spillover effect in the education sector. Rapid expansion of capacity at all levels of education began to take place. New schools were built or had their capacity expanded. In the last three decades, higher education enrollments have been increasing rapidly by international standards, with the highest growth rate recorded in the 1970s and 1980s. Currently, enrollments exceed 3.4 million students, which means a more than twenty-fold increase in thirty-five years.

The growing enrollment rate has obviously broadened the socioeconomic spectrum of student family backgrounds. In the early periods following independence, the student body consisted of the children of elite and wealthy families; this is no longer the case. However, the equity issue has not gone away, and this is particularly important in view of the structure of the higher education system and the role of private schools. At the macro level, enrollment is distributed in a very skewed way across the socioeconomic spectrum. More than 80 percent of students come from the top quintile of the population in terms of socioeconomic status.

Unlike private schools in other countries that have become centers of excellence, many private schools in Indonesia grew rapidly in response to demand, without sufficient support to provide quality education. While in other countries many students chose to enroll in private schools out of consideration for the quality of the education, in Indonesia students often ended up in private schools after failing to gain access to public schools. Unfortunately, many students who ended up at low-quality, affordable private schools came from lower socioeconomic backgrounds. Publicly funded higher education institutions are naturally more accessible for students from families of higher socioeconomic status—a potential perpetuation of inequality.

It is also interesting to look at the distribution of access by gender. A recent study reveals that throughout the public university sector, males still dominate, with 60 percent of enrollments (Asian Development Bank, 1998). The largest gender disparity in enrollments was found in engineering fields, where more than 80 percent of students were male. Despite this aggregate picture, it is interesting that at the public university on the Sumatera island, female enrollments constituted 51 percent of the total student body.

The Quality of Education

Higher education's rapid expansion in capacity and access has had some problematic consequences. First, the quality of education has been slow to improve or has perhaps even remained stagnant. Although some young faculty have received advanced training in the West, their numbers are overwhelmed by the growth in enrollments nationwide, leaving higher education institutions staffed with minimally trained lecturers.

As outlined earlier, the low proportion of faculty members at public universities with advanced degrees has long been a concern for Indonesia's higher education system. Another concern relates to the low commitment to teaching and research activities. The poor remuneration at public universities has driven academic staff to seek higher-paying, nonacademic, off-campus activities. Many faculty members devote more of their time to consulting work for government offices and private business than to teaching and research. Many others are involved in management and teaching at private universities. As a result, faculty members often come to campus to teach their classes and leave immediately afterward, which deprives students of sufficient interaction with their instructors outside of class. In the absence of formal office hours, students are unable to consult with faculty when they experience difficulty in understanding the material.

The situation at most private schools—private universities, institutes, advanced schools, and academies—is even worse. Not only do these schools suffer from the low proportion of academic staff with advanced degrees, they even lack full-time academic staff. A substantial number of academic staff at private schools work on a part-time basis only. Many of them are permanent academic staff at public universities who teach at private schools as side jobs. Others are permanent employees at public and private nonacademic institutions who may teach at more than one private university in addition to their main jobs.[7]

Insufficient infrastructure and equipment also constitute a long-standing problem for higher education, as mentioned earlier. The lack of classrooms, laboratory space, and facilities is an issue common to both public and private schools, even though the situation at private schools is generally worse. Since the 1970s, construction of facilities has substantially improved the public schools' infrastructure. At the systemwide level, sufficient classroom and laboratory space is available, although some schools or departments have excess classroom and laboratory space, while others lack both facilities. Private schools often have limited space and are located in crowded areas unsuitable for academic activities.

Insufficient funding is another constraint facing the higher education system in general. A disproportionately large share of the recurrent budget for public universities goes to salaries of academic and supporting staff, leaving only 22 percent for academic and research activities.[8] A study on education finance commissioned by the Asian Development Bank (Bray & Thomas, 1998) illustrates the magnitude of the problem facing higher education in Indonesia. A marine science program at a public university had no funds to operate or maintain its newly acquired research vessels; an agricultural faculty had to restrict student training on a farm tractor to 6 meters of actual driving for the duration of the degree program, because there was insufficient money to buy fuel.

The Relevance of Education

Beginning in the early 1980s, concern rose over the imbalance in enrollments across fields of study, notably the low proportion of students in engineering and the sciences compared to those in the social sciences and humanities. The distribution of enrollments had become a serious concern to policymakers and was perceived to be inconsistent with the policy on economic development—particularly industrialization—which required more engineers and scientists than the system could supply. At the same time, the rapid growth in the number of graduates in the social sciences and humanities raised concerns over the possibility of rising educated unemployment rates, given that the supply of graduates in these fields would soon far exceed the demand in the labor market.

Enrollment shifts in the various fields of study have followed a somewhat natural and market-driven path, accompanied by the rapid expansion of the private sector in the higher education system. When public universities were unable to keep up with the fast-growing demand for higher education beginning in the 1970s, the private sector responded by establishing schools in the social sciences and humanities, given their lower start-up costs and greater affordability to consumers. It would indeed be difficult to imagine a high-quality, self-supporting engineering school. Many private schools provide engineering education without sufficient equipment to support the curriculum and end up compromising the quality of their graduates. A few leading private universities manage to provide a fair quality of engineering education on a cross-subsidy basis—enlarging their enrollments in the social sciences to support enrollments in their engineering departments.

For the last fifteen years, the government has invested more in the fields of science and engineering. Expansion of capacity, improvement of infrastructure, and procurement of equipment, as well as provision of advanced training for academic staff, have been concentrated more in these fields.[9] Despite stronger policy focus, it is difficult to expand enrollments in these priority fields. As stated earlier, only about 17 percent of students are enrolled in engineering fields.

As part of the effort to expand engineering education capacity, beginning in the early 1970s the government introduced the more practically oriented polytechnic education. In the early 1970s, the first polytechnic, the Swiss-ITB Polytechnic for Mechanics, was established in Bandung. The school was oriented toward practical skills training, compared to the more theoretical courses offered by engineering faculties at universities and academies. The successful implementation of the Swiss-ITB Polytechnic for Mechanics led to a full-scale program to develop polytechnics across the country. About twenty-seven polytechnics (in fields such as engineering, agriculture, and commerce) were established, most of them attached to existing universities.

Polytechnic education enjoyed much support, at least on conceptual grounds and from the point of view of labor economics. Theoretically, there were compelling arguments for expanding the polytechnic subsystem. A 1995 joint study by the Ministry of Manpower and the National Development Planning Agency, in cooperation with the Japan International Cooperation Agency, confirmed the need for engineering manpower with the skill levels of polytechnic graduates. The study not only confirmed the need for diploma-level education, especially in engineering fields, but also went further to warn of an ongoing lack of development of engineering skills within the nation's workforce. The findings suggested that the expansion of low-skilled vocational education at the high school level and the effort to increase enrollments in engineering fields at universities had created a hollow center in the skills' pyramid of the nation's workforce.

Concern over the weak relevance of higher education has also been articulated in a policy to promote academic and research programs closely related to the needs of the university's local community. This policy, along with the need to put the nation's limited education resources to their best use led each university to focus its academic and scientific activities in a certain area, which then became the university's *pola ilmiah pokok* (PIP—

literally translated: primary scientific pattern). The PIP of a university would influence the nature of teaching and learning at the university. The Medical School of Gajahmada University, given the university's PIP in rural and community development, would emphasize medical and health services to the rural community compared to the Medical School at the University of Indonesia. Another manifestation of PIP would be the emphasis on development in the fields directly related to the institution's PIP. For example, much of the resources at Mulawarman University were employed to develop capacities in disciplines related to the forestry sciences.

Accreditation System

Accreditation as a means of ensuring quality control in the higher education system has evolved over time. In the past, the legitimacy and inherent quality of public universities were taken for granted. Accreditation was considered relevant only for private universities and was generally carried out at the faculty or departmental level.[10] Public universities, which themselves varied in quality, were used as benchmarks to which private universities were compared. The earlier system recognized three levels of accreditation. The highest level, *disamakan* (equalized), was awarded to faculties considered good enough to provide education equivalent in quality to that in a public university. Private university faculties with this level of accreditation are allowed to conduct their own final graduation examinations.

The next level of accreditation was *diakui* (recognized), and the lowest level of accreditation was *terdaftar* (registered). At private schools with accreditation levels of *diakui* and *terdaftar* students would have to go through final examinations organized by the *kopertis*, the private higher education coordinating body, and conducted at a designated public university. The process was intended as a quality control mechanism for private schools, and only after successfully completing it could the private university confer the degree.

The increasing concern over the need for overall quality improvement has led to the overhaul of the accreditation system. Recent developments show that the implicit assumption of across-the-board inferiority of private schools relative to public schools is no longer valid. Further, and more important, to assume high-quality education at all public schools is no longer reasonable. The new accreditation system requires every program at both public and private schools to be subject to accreditation.

The National Accreditation Board (Badan Akreditasi Nasional or BAN), established in 1996, is mandated to carry out the accreditation process.

Roles of the Private Sector

The private sector has been instrumental in the development of higher education, specifically in terms of expansion. Much of the growth in enrollments was due to the private sector. Figures over the last fifteen years consistently show that more than 60 percent of the total numbers of tertiary education students are in private schools. The private school sector has demonstrated an extremely rapid response to the fast-growing demand for higher education. Private schools are on average much smaller than public schools. In terms of the number of schools, the private sector consists of more than 1,800 schools, compared to less than a hundred public schools.

The rapid increase in the number of private schools contributed to the national effort to expand human resources, although there were also some ramifications. The smaller size of private schools means they generally operated less efficiently. Many private schools lacked sufficient funding and therefore relied on fees and parental contributions to cover virtually all operational costs. Private schools are usually established and operated by foundations. However, in contrast to the practice in most countries, where foundations work as money-making machines to fund a sizeable part of universities' expenditures, in Indonesia they merely manage the resources and revenue originating from student tuition fees and other parental contributions.

As was mentioned earlier, given the low purchasing power of parents, there was a strong tendency for private schools to provide education services in fields that required the least investment, mainly the social sciences and humanities. This situation was a contributing factor in the low proportion of students in engineering fields, which now stands at approximately 17 percent, mostly concentrated at public schools. The large proportion of students, and therefore graduates, in social sciences and humanities fields, and the low proportion in science and engineering fields, contributed to the mismatch in the labor market. The effectiveness of investments in the higher education sector declined due in part to lower external efficiency in terms of producing the necessary human resources.

Low investment and spending per student in private schools also explain the low education quality, given the vast number of students enrolled in private schools. The lack of supporting facilities and quality academic staff not only lowered the quality of graduates but also lengthened the duration of studies, therefore lowering internal efficiency.

Islam and Higher Education

Modern Islamic higher education institutions contribute about 15 percent of total higher education enrollments nationwide. It is therefore useful to shed light on how these institutions have developed alongside their secular counterparts. The most important Islamic higher education institution, the Institute of Islamic Higher Learning (Institut Agama Islam), is the highest level of one branch of the dualistic national education system. It is also the highest level of the educational sequence beginning with *pesantren* and *madrasah*, which we can regard as a subculture.[11]

A pioneering development in modern Islamic education took place on July 8, 1946, with the establishment of Sekolah Tinggi Islam (STI, Islamic College) under the leadership of Abdul Kahar Mudzakir. The school was a realization of the work by the Badan Pengurus Sekolah Tinggi Islam (Islamic Higher Education Board), led by Mohammad Hatta, then vice-president of the Republic of Indonesia, as chairman and Mohammad Natsir as secretary.[12] The initial designation of Yogyakarta as the national capital brought with it the Islamic College (STI), which formally commenced operations in April 1947. In November 1947, a committee was established to strengthen the STI, which later decided to establish the Universitas Islam Indonesia (UII, Indonesian Islamic University) in Yogyakarta. The university opened in March 1948 with four faculties: religious study, law, economics, and education. In the next stage of development, the Faculty of Religious Study was upgraded to become the Islamic Higher Learning Center (Perguruan Tinggi Agama Islam, PTAIN) through a government decree.

The establishment of the Islamic Higher Learning Center in the infancy of the republic, in the then capital city of Yogyakarta, was an acknowledgment of the influence and significance of Islam, particularly its role in the development of the nation. The policy, nominally, was positive and accommodated the interests and aspirations of Islamic groups in the country. However, reading between the lines, this policy indeed sowed the seeds of dualism in the Indonesian education system, with general (secular) education on the one side and religious education on the other.[13] It also marked the beginning of competition between Muslims and nationalists in the development of the national education system.[14]

The work to strengthen the institutional basis of Islamic education continued in the following years. Within this framework the government established an Academy of Religious Sciences (Akademi Dinas Ilmu Agama, ADIA) in Jakarta in 1950. Later, in an attempt to integrate, to combine resources, and to strengthen Islamic higher education, the government amalgamated PTAIN and ADIA into the Institute of Islamic Higher Learning (IAIN) in 1960. The newly established IAIN's educational structure, durations of studies, and stages of learning resembled those of secular higher education institutions. IAIN graduates were, and indeed still are, considered to have the equivalent status of graduates of secular higher education institutions.

IAIN developed rapidly, following a rising demand for IAIN education in the provinces. The situation resulted in a policy allowing the establishment of new IAIN institutes in every province. Based on historic and human resources considerations, Jakarta was awarded the first mandate to establish a new IAIN, the IAIN Syarief Hidayatullah, in December 1963.[15] The New Order government that came to power following the abortive coup attempt of 1965 made no significant policy changes, and indeed facilitated demand for the establishment of new IAINs.

IAINs have since played an important role in the development of Islamic studies through higher education and therefore serve as a barometer for the development of Islamic studies.[16] Islamic learning became increasingly more open, modern, empirical, historical, sociological, and even anthropological in the era of the new generation of IAIN intellectuals, represented by Mukti Ali, Harun Nasution, Nurcholish Madjid, and others, who effectively became the locomotive for the modernization of Islamic thinking at IAIN institutes. The convergence between the richness of the classical Islamic tradition and the modern methodology of religious studies in the West progressed in a productive manner. The IAINs benefited from cooperation with a variety of prominent universities, such as the University of Chicago, Columbia University, and Ohio University (United States); McGill University (Canada); Australian National University, Melbourne University, and Monash University (Australia); Leiden University (the Netherlands); and many others.

Recent developments have led IAINs in a new direction, toward becoming higher learning institutions founded on research strength. To support research activities, some IAINs, notably those in Yogyakarta and Jakarta, have established a variety of research institutions and promoted publication of periodicals. This new orientation toward research is clearly visible, not merely reflected in the building of IAINs institutionally, but also in the strengthening of education and research among IAIN intellectuals. The research agenda within the IAIN community is growing increasingly diverse, encompassing issues and subjects traditionally beyond the reach of Islamic higher education institutions. Many IAIN and Western academics are now working on research on similar subjects. Research topics such as gender equality, civil society, civic education, and good governance, to mention a few, that until recently were the research domain of Western intellectuals have now become areas of interest among IAIN academicians.

The current hot issue concerning IAINs is the plan to transform them into Islamic universities. The plan is still being heatedly debated. Those advocating transformation argue that it is an important means to further develop Islamic higher education, by boosting their research strength and ability to adapt to the rapid changes in the environment. Besides that, the diversity created by the transformation and the new and more fruitful intellectual tradition it potentially could create would elevate Islamic studies to higher ground in terms of higher education quality.

The argument against the idea of transforming IAINs into Islamic universities is well rooted in one of the reasons for establishing IAINs, which was to ensure that Islamic education would serve the needs of the government and community in accordance with the Jakarta Charter of June 22, 1945, which was initially intended to be an inseparable part of the 1945 Constitution.[17] In other words, there was a religious mission underlying the establishment of this higher learning institution. IAINs are expected to produce quality human resources to staff the public religious bureaucracy and to serve as preachers. Consequently, as the argument goes, it would be more natural for IAINs to develop into institutes of Islamic studies, rather than into universities.

The debate on this is expected to continue on, at least into the near future, and will definitely enrich the dialectics in the area of higher education, particularly in its interaction with Islam. This dynamics serves to underline the historical facts that Islam, especially cultural Islam, has a pronounced influence on the development of the higher education system and, conversely, that academic thinking has had an important impact on the development of Islam in Indonesia. The growing number of intellectuals from families with a traditional and cultural Islamic background could potentially strengthen the productive interaction between the two branches of higher education in the coming years.

Higher Education and Politics

The student movement in Indonesia has a long history. It started well before the nation's independence in 1945; indeed, the student movement was one of the most important elements in the overall struggle for independence. Virtually all preindependence leaders started their political activities during their school years. Sukarno and Muhammad Hatta, the founding fathers, began their political organization and political movement when they were students. Sukarno had been deeply involved in serious political discussion back in his high school years when he stayed at the home of a prominent Islamic leader, H. O. S. Tjokroaminoto in Surabaya. In 1926, in his final year in school at the Technische Hoogeschule in Bandung, he was elected secretary of the Algemene Studieclub, an organization that conducted a wide range of discussions in the area of politics. Hatta had been actively leading the Perhimpunan Indonesia (Indonesia Association), a prominent student movement in the Netherlands, where he studied economics.

The student movement intensified in the 1920s, and many student activists became involved in the establishment of political parties. The decade also marked the birth of the nation, signified by the Sumpah Pemuda (Oath of the Youth) to declare the One Land, One Nation, and One Language: Indonesia. The movement continued into the 1930s, and by then a broader education community had become part of the resistance movement against the colonial power. The 1930s also saw an increasing nationalistic stance adopted by the various national school systems and by individual teachers in confronting the existing social, political, and economic conditions—as part of a national movement for political independence. During the Japanese occupation period, student political activism took a slightly different form. Many students and educators were involved in a variety of military groups, some created by the Japanese. Indonesians took this step with the purpose of preparing themselves for a bigger political role in securing political independence (Buchori, 2001a).

The tradition of student involvement in politics during the colonial era and during the Japanese occupation continued in the postindependence era. From time to time, campus political activities have effectively shaped the dynamics of national politics. The government and politicians have also at times involved universities and students in political struggles. One such instance was a decree issued by the Provisional People's Consultative Assembly, stating that one of the functions of education is to organize the people's power. Based on this decree, the government imposed the state ideology, *pancasila* (the Five Principles),[18] and Sukarno's socialist political manifesto, Manipol USDEK,[19] as the basic principles of the national education system. The primary objective of national education was defined as producing citizens of a socialist Indonesia, with a moral responsibility to develop Indonesia into a just and prosperous society while spiritually upholding the values of *pancasila*. The politicization of education at the time effectively curtailed academic freedom, constrained academic staff in terms of acceptable teaching methods, and therefore negatively affected the overall quality of education.

The dynamics of the national political struggle of the early 1960s saw students become intensely involved in political maneuvers. The climax of the student movement was its active role in the toppling of Sukarno and his Old Order government in 1965–1966. The students, once again, demonstrated their social control function and played an instrumental role in the fall of the Sukarno government, following the abortive coup attempt in 1965. The students successfully articulated the people's demand for change in a mismanaged country mired in deep economic hardship and messy political conflict among the Communists, the religious parties, the nationalists, and the military. The years following the 1965 upheaval could be considered the zenith of student politics in Indonesia. Students were involved in practical politics; they had representatives in the Parliament. It was also a period when the quality of higher education was in decline, as the high intensity of political activities overshadowed academic activities.[20]

Since 1966, student movements have at times aspired to act as a force of social control on the government. Several uprisings took place in the ensuing years, such as in 1974 and 1978, protesting various government policies, as well as social injustice and poor law enforcement. The 1978 student movement lacked public support and was therefore unsuccessful. The failure also marked the beginning of a decline in student politics that lasted for nearly twenty years. The authorities strictly controlled campus activities during this time, effectively suppressing student politics.

Despite the ups and downs in the political arena, Indonesian students have never been completely divorced from the political scene. Almost two decades later, following some unsuccessful movements in the 1970s and 1980s, students returned to the forefront in the late 1990s. The student movement was revived and again played a significant role in the nation's development, this time leading to calls for reform in 1998. Amid severe political and financial turmoil, fueled by the crippling regional economic crisis, students from various campuses across the country launched a massive movement that led to the toppling of President Suharto and his New Order government.

TRENDS AND CHALLENGES

Among the various unresolved issues lingering in the higher education system in Indonesia, there are two outstanding ones. First, the higher education system needs to improve its quality and relevance in order to fulfill its role in the national agenda of succeeding in an increasingly competitive world. Second, the higher education system needs structural adjustment, which is necessary to achieve better quality and relevance.

Countries all over the world are undergoing social, economic, and political shifts, perhaps most notably the dynamics of changes in the world economy, that have an enormous impact on higher education. Globalization and its association with freer international trade confront higher education with new challenges and rising levels of competition. International benchmarking of quality has now become imperative, which implies the need for improvement in every aspect—including human resources, infrastructure, and institutions. It is now increasingly realized that the higher education system needs to improve its ability to adjust quickly in response to the dynamics in the environment locally, nationally, as well as globally.

The national development strategy and recent dynamics in the country largely dictate higher education policies. Influential and strategic economic sectors in the economy along with the necessary labor force skill structure would determine academic programs, enrollments, and research agendas. Development of natural-resources-based industry, especially marine-based industry, and transportation and communications would need support from the higher education system to supply high-quality manpower and research. On the social sciences and humanities side, the sociopolitical dynamics in the last couple of years has prompted a more aggressive development of the academic and research agenda. Besides that, quality improvement in the social sciences and humanities needs more attention in the coming years, given their relative neglect in the last few years in contrast to the high-demand fields in engineering and the hard sciences.

Improvement in the ability to respond to changes in the environment necessitates a new institutional setting, involving a more responsive organizational structure and appropriate regulatory instruments. Approaches on management of the overall system and individual schools need appropriate adjustment, primarily with respect to human resource management and funding mechanisms. Currently, public higher education institutions—public universities, institutes, advanced schools, and academies—are essentially still part of the bureaucracy in the sense that they receive most of their funding from the government, with little autonomy in financial management. Besides that, faculty members are government employees, subject to the same law governing public servants in general, leaving practically no flexibility to adjust academic manpower to suit the needs of individual schools.

In view of the above, higher education institutions in Indonesia need structural adjustment to allow greater autonomy to move toward a more effective management and a more accountable system. The bureaucracy needs to cease its involvement in the more technical aspects of public university management and start to relegate more financial and human resources management to the individual schools. To implement this, however, the higher education system must devise instruments to measure performance to ensure that the public funds entrusted to the universities are spent properly in line with the agreed-upon outcomes.

Reforms in the public schools are an important aspect of the overall improvement of quality in the national higher education system, even though the public sector only enrolls about one-third of the total number of students. Public investment in a variety of forms has been quite substantial in the public sector. Public higher education is equipped with comparatively better human resources, infrastructure, and equipment and is therefore better positioned to improve performance once appropriate changes in management and regulatory framework are in place. In other words public higher education is the potentially most productive sector in which to implement changes toward quality improvement.

Private schools are facing a lack of resources and some bureaucratic inflexibility. These schools rely on financial resources in the form of tuition and in some cases insignificant amounts from other sources. The *yayasan* (foundation) that established a school tends to get involved in the management of resources generated by the school rather than in generating funds for the school operation. A *yayasan* therefore unnecessarily adds to bureaucratic constraints on the school management, while contributing little, in most cases, to the generation of school resources. Given the dominant scope of enrollments in the private sector, it is necessary to support extensive reforms in private school management; provide a regulatory framework for private schools to manage themselves more flexibly, rationally, efficiently, and effectively; and enable them to progress and compete on an equal footing with the rest of the system.

CONCLUSION

Looking into the future, three issues need to be addressed seriously concerning the Indonesian higher education system: qualitative improvement, the academic basis of professional training, and academic culture.

On the issue of quality improvement, graduates need to have the ability to think analytically, have good mastery in language in a broad sense, communicate effectively in a multidisciplinary setting, and contribute positively to cultural changes. Improvement in the quality of scholarship should constitute the focus of the first two years of undergraduate training. The rest of undergraduate training should focus on improving professional technical knowledge and skills in the field of concentration. With sufficient skills in the technical knowledge of the profession, graduates can be expected to solve questions of *what* to do rather than merely those of a *how to* nature.

Strengthening the academic basis of professional training relates to qualitative improvement. The increasingly rapid changes in technology and the environment require high adaptability, which will therefore put those with a weak academic background for the necessary retraining in a disadvantageous position. This is the reason why a strong academic basis is important, for it serves as the foundation for ongoing professional development. A strong academic basis is also needed for advanced professional training at the graduate level. Besides that, a stronger intellectual basis will also enable graduates to lead more diverse and meaningful lives. Preparing students for employment without giving them the necessary basic academic background will cost graduates in the long run.

The essence of an academic culture is threefold: a continuous search for truth, an ongoing acquisition of new knowledge, and a defense of knowledge against falsification. Indonesia's higher education system, thus far, has only achieved academic freedom. It has yet to develop an academic culture, without which the academic freedom it has will be meaningless. Only with the synergistic combination of the two can the system deliver what the society expects from it. In the past, a number of factors, including primarily the political situation, have constrained the cultivation of an academic culture.

On the issue of the need for nurturing an academic culture, therefore, we must look beyond the university world. We must start by understanding the significance of university graduates in Indonesia's overall development. The small proportion of university graduates within the workforce means that future leaders can be expected to come from this community. Only those with strong commitments to ethics and institutional development can provide leadership in the various areas of national development. Such characteristics are best cultivated within a strong academic culture, coupled with academic freedom.

The long history of higher education in Indonesia has always involved a considerable degree of student political activism. Even during the colonial era, when it was intended merely to supply quality manpower for the benefit of the colonizers, higher education unintentionally produced the nascent nation's future leaders. Students have also displayed leadership and played pivotal roles in the many changes the country has undergone since independence: in 1965–1966 with the downfall of Sukarno, and more recently the 1998 downfall of Suharto. In view of the record so far, should Indonesian universities continue to participate in the movement to improve Indonesia's political life? If handled properly, universities could indeed potentially provide the foundations for more civilized political conduct in the future. They are the places where the future generations of politicians are being trained. However, if the pragmatism of current political practices infiltrates and contaminates students' lives and behavior during their period of development, this could endanger both the future education system and political culture.

A brief note should be added in connection with the role of university graduates in political reform. Within the context of the current political culture, the most effective role for intellectuals in promoting change would be to position themselves as a critical element but one acceptable to the mainstream.

NOTES

1. Influences from Hinduism and Buddhism predate Islamic influences in Indonesia. However, it is difficult to substantiate whether the existence of higher education in that era was comparable to standards in the rest of the world.

2. For the discussion of Islamic education and the roles of Islam in higher education in Indonesia, the authors are indebted to Jamhari Makruf, who was originally intended to coauthor this chapter but was unable to do so for personal reasons.

3. A wave of Indonesian students pursuing advanced education in the Middle East in the nineteenth century resulted in a substantial number of *ulemas* (Islamic scholars) who produced great scholarly works of international reputation. Wahid (2001, pp. 157–169) discusses the origin of the scientific tradition in the *pesantren*.

4. The evolution of the medical school GHS began with STOVIA in Batavia. After

that, the Dutch established the Nederlands-Indische Artsen School (NIAS) in Surabaya, which then evolved into the Medische Hooge School (MHS) in Batavia. The latter subsequently changed its name to Geneeskundige Hooge School (GHS).

5. There were many arguments for Gajahmada University to remain in Yogyakarta, in addition to the need to produce more graduates. The founders of the university had been actively involved in the revolution and the war for independence. Therefore, it was argued, it would be wise to leave the university in Yogyakarta in memory of the struggle. Besides, Yogyakarta was located just 60 kilometers from Surakarta, and the two cities formed important cultural centers of the republic and were perceived as conducive to university learning. In later years, the university built its prestige by characterizing itself as being part of the development of grassroots rural society. It is also important to note that since its foundation, the university used Bahasa Indonesia as the medium of instruction. This choice initially caused a lot of difficulties. Besides the fact that the "young" language lacked terms needed in the higher levels of learning, most academic materials were available only in Dutch and a few other foreign languages (Cummings & Kasenda, 2002).

6. Internal efficiency was defined as the ratio between the number of graduates per year and the total number of students.

7. Moonlighting at private universities is clearly due to both supply and demand factors. Low remuneration in public offices, in particular, has driven employees to seek second and third jobs to obtain adequate incomes. Most private universities, which operate on the limited amount of tuition revenue, could not afford to recruit full-time quality academic staff.

8. The amount of research funding within the university recurrent budget is very limited, if not negligible. Some research funding comes from the government, mostly awarded on a competitive basis. A more important source of research funding in the university consists of the competitive funds administered by the Ministry for Research and Technology. The total sum of all the funding that goes to research in the university, however, is still very small—even though it consumed most of the national research budget. The national research budget currently amounts to less than 0.18 percent of the country's GDP.

9. Indeed, the concentration of public resources in the hard sciences and engineering thus far has raised concern among many because of the worrisome neglect of the social sciences and humanities. The level of education quality in the social sciences and humanities is no less alarming and therefore needs more attention and resources.

10. *Faculty* is a term commonly used for a group of departments and is roughly equivalent to the term *school* in many U.S. universities. For example, the Faculty of Industrial Engineering at the Bandung Institute of Technology consists of the Department of Mechanical Engineering, the Department of Electrical Engineering, the Department of Industrial Engineering, the Department of Chemical Engineering, and the Department of Engineering Physics. The term, however, is not uniformly used across all universities; in some private universities a faculty consists of one single field, such as the Faculty of Mechanical Engineering.

11. *Madrasah* literally means school. Its structure is similar to its secular version, beginning with *madrasah ibtidaiyah* (primary school), *madrasah tsanawiyah* (junior high), and *madrasah aliyah* (senior high). *Pesantren*, as described previously, has levels, although less structured, from the equivalent to elementary up until the equivalent

of higher education. The Institute of Islamic Higher Learning admits graduates of secular high schools and *madrasah aliyah*, as well as of *pesantren*.

12. In one memorandum, Muhammad Hatta stated very clearly that religion was one of the pillars of the nation's culture. Since Muslims comprised the great majority of the population, Islamic education became essential for individual members of society. This context explains the urgency of the establishment of the Sekolah Tinggi Islam (Islamic College). See Makruf (2002).

13. The former has been managed under the supervision of the Ministry of National Education, the latter under the auspices of the Ministry of Religious Affairs.

14. The competition was superficially suppressed in the later period, especially during the New Order era, but now seems to be resurfacing as a result of the openness unleashed by democratization.

15. The establishment of IAIN Syarief Hidayatullah in Jakarta was soon followed by IAIN Ar-Raniry in Banda Aceh (1964), IAIN Raden Patah in Palembang (1964), IAIN Antasari in Banjarmasin (1964), IAIN Sunan Ampel in Surabaya (1965), IAIN Alaudin in Makassar (1965), IAIN Imam Bonjol in Padang (1966), and IAIN Sultan Taha Saefuddin in Jambi (1967).

16. For elaboration, see Azra (2000).

17. The Jakarta Charter stated that the nation was founded on five principles, the first of which was "the belief in One Almighty God, with the obligation to practice the Islamic law for its adherents." This was dropped from the preamble of the 1945 Constitution at the last minute following objections from nationalists and non-Muslim parties.

18. *Pancasila*, the state ideology, comprises the nation's five basic founding principles: (1) belief in one supreme God; (2) just and civilized humanitarianism; (3) Indonesian unity; (4) popular sovereignty through deliberation and consensus among representatives; and (5) social justice for all.

19. Manipol USDEK, introduced in 1960, was the political manifesto set forth in Sukarno's August 17, 1959, Independence Day speech. USDEK was an acronym encompassing the 1945 Constitution, Indonesian socialism, guided democracy, guided economy, and Indonesian identity.

20. The period with most deterioration in the quality of higher education was perhaps that between 1959 and 1965, when political interests successfully penetrated the educational system and fragmented students, teachers, and lecturers into factions—notably into those for and those against the leftist political agenda.

REFERENCES

Asian Development Bank. (1998). *Draft interim report for the technological and professional skills development project.* Jakarta: Author.

Azra, A. (2000, November 23–24). "The Making of Islamic Studies in Indonesia." Paper presented at the Islam in Indonesia: Intellectualization and Social Transformation conference, Jakarta.

Bray, M., & Thomas, R. M. (1998). *Financing of education in Indonesia.* Manila: Asian Development Bank.

Brodjonegoro, S. S. (2001). Implementasi Paradigma Baru di Perguruan Tinggi (Implementation of the new paradigm in higher education institutions). In F. Jalal & D. Supriadi (Eds.), *Reformasi Pendidikan Dalam Konteks Otonomi Daerah* (Education reform in the context of regional autonomy) (pp. 361–387). Yogyakarta: Adicitra.

Buchori, M. (2001a). *Notes on education in Indonesia*. Jakarta: Jakarta Post and Asia Foundation.

Buchori, M. (2001b). Peranan Pendidikan Dalam Pembentukan Budaya Politik Di Indonesia (Roles of education in political culture formation in Indonesia). In Sindhunata (Ed.), *Menggagas Paradigma Baru Pendidikan: Demokratisasi, Otonomi, Civil Society, Globalisasi* (Conceptualizing the new education paradigm: Democratization, autonomy, civil society, and globalization) (pp. 17–34). Yogyakarta: Penerbit Kanisius.

Cummings, W., & Kasenda, S. (2002). The origin of modern Indonesian higher education. In P. G. Altbach & V. Selvaratnam (Eds.), *From independence to autonomy: The development of Asian universities* (pp. 143–166). Chestnut Hill, MA: Boston College, Center for International Higher Education.

Directorate General of Higher Education. (2003). *Higher education sector study*. Jakarta: Ministry of National Education.

Makruf, J. (2002). *IAIN Jakarta: Konteks Sejarah, Masa Kini, dan Prospek Ke Depan* (State Institute for Islamic Studies Jakarta: Historical context, current situation, and prospects for the future). Unpublished manuscript.

Malik, A. (1994). "Education, employment, wages, and earning: A case study of Indonesia." Unpublished Ph.D. Diss., University of Michigan, Ann Arbor.

Wahid, A. (2001). *Menggerakkan Tradisi: Esai-esai Pesantren* (Mobilizing tradition: Essays on Islamic boarding schools). Yogyakarta: LkiS.

11

The Philippines

Past, Present, and Future Dimensions

of Higher Education

Andrew Gonzalez, FSC

The higher education system of the Philippines is characterized by a large number of institutions (colleges and universities), for the most part privately funded and established to meet the social demand for higher education but largely dysfunctional because of the poor quality of instruction and inadequate training with regard to research, resulting in a mismatch between the country's needs and educational output. To understand how the present situation has developed, one has to delve into the past and the evolution of the system. The realistic prospects for reform and amelioration must then be considered, based not on wishful thinking but on current trends and realistic prospects.

The system of higher education has succeeded in meeting the social demand resulting from an expanding population of 78 million in 2002 and a continuing 2.3 percent rate of population increase. The response has been to establish private higher education institutions and to pass legislation allowing the addition of new state universities and colleges (which increased from seven in 1946 to 112 in 2003). While the Commission on Higher Education has attempted to discourage further additions to the state system and continues to impose quality controls on private institutions, the existing laws of the country are such that ultimately the additions can only be delayed, not stopped.

While the response to quantitative needs has been effective in the sense of making access available to all high school graduates (their choice limited only by the admissions standards of individual institutions), the response has been ineffective from the point of view of meeting the needs of the new century since the competencies of the graduates are inadequate by international and national standards. There continues to be a mismatch between the output of universities and the country's needs. The best and the brightest seek employment abroad while those who stay have inadequate skills and qualify only for clerical jobs. Technical and higher technology jobs continue to lack takers; on the other hand, the Philippines has a 10.2 percent unemployment rate and 15.3 percent underemployment rate.

This chapter traces the development of higher education in the Philippines over time from the Spanish period (1565–1898), through the American period (1898–1946), to the Independence period (post-1946) as a prelude to discussing likely future scenarios, based on past trends. The historical account will reveal the dysfunctionality of the present system, the likely future trends in the absence of interventions, the kinds of interventions that are needed, and the feasibility of these interventions.

HISTORICAL PERSPECTIVES

The Spanish Period (1565–1898)

The Philippines was governed by a succession of governors general appointed by the Crown in Madrid. There was no system of basic education sponsored by the central government but rather a number of small schools that taught reading, writing, some arithmetic, and much religion in the Spanish language. School activities consisted mostly of reading and the memorization of prayers and answers to the catechism in Spanish. The literacy (not necessarily comprehension) achieved in Spanish was pursued among the elite through private tutors or maestros. In the meantime, the Spanish friars were more practical, quickly learning local languages, writing and eventually publishing grammars (*artes*) and bilingual wordlists *(vocabularios)*. Their prayer books were published and handed down from one religious member to another in the same religious order—to be revised, edited, and improved upon by later religious members. Reform-minded prime ministers under the monarchy during the second half of the nineteenth century oversaw the passing of the 1863 Moret Decree reforming education in the colonies and educational reform in the Philippines. The goal was to establish a system of schools in each parish—essentially primary schools teaching literacy, arithmetic, and religion in Spanish. The Escuela Normal Superior, run by the Jesuits, was established for male teachers, and the Colegio de Santa Isabel, a normal school run by the Daughters of Charity in Naga, was established for females. By the end of the Spanish regime in 1898 there were some 2,167 primary schools (Bazaco, 1989).

Postsecondary, post-*bachillerato*, higher education was represented by the royal and pontifical university of Santo Tomas, which was the only chartered university during the whole Spanish period. Established in 1611 as a postsecondary seminary for future priests, it was granted a pontifical title in 1645 and a royal charter by King Charles III in 1785. Initially, it offered degrees in theology, philosophy, and the arts—and later in canon and civil law and, in 1871, medicine and surgery. The final licensure needed to be granted by the Universidad Central de Madrid, until 1859, when the Philippine Universidad was given powers to award the licentiate to practice medicine. Other tertiary-level institutions established during the Spanish period included the Academy of Drawing and Painting, the Nautical Academy at Manila, and a military school (Bazaco, 1989).

After almost 350 years under Spanish rule, only the Universidad de Santo Tomas granted degrees in philosophy, theology, canon and civil law, and medicine and surgery. Some special institutions offered teaching in specific skills in the fine arts and in nautical studies. A few universities predated the University of Santo Tomas—such as the Colegio de San Ignacio, which was founded in 1595 but closed when Rome, upon the urging of the Spanish Crown, terminated the Jesuits from 1768 to 1859. Another early institution was the higher seminary at San Carlos in Cebu, which was founded as a theological or tertiary-level institution in 1783 but underwent a series of changes that caused it to lose its status as a university. In 1948, it was finally granted a university charter under the existing policies of the newly independent country.

The Spanish tradition held that knowledge was a treasure from the past to be conserved. It was, like faith, something to be handed down intact and included the wisdom of religious tradition, philosophic learning, literary classics, the law of the Church and of Roman and Renaissance traditions, and the laws of the Spanish Crown. In the field of medicine and surgery, the body of knowledge included the analysis of nature by Aristotle, Galen the Physician's teachings, the writings of Hippocrates, and pharmacology for different kinds of ailments, with the addition of surgery in the late nineteenth century.

Research was oriented not toward the future but rather toward the past and relied upon traditional wisdom and the use of precedents, not experiments. The branches of knowledge had not really been defined and were for the most part historical and literary—the social sciences had not yet been established, and the natural sciences were quite inchoate. Much of learning consisted of memorization and recitation, authoritarian rather than participatory teaching, and demonstration rather than discovery.

Higher Education in the American Tradition (1896–1946)

The American colonial government initiated a democratic form of government with the 1935 Constitution, which was preceded by the establishment of a National Assembly in 1907, a bicameral Senate and House of Representatives in 1916, the organization of the courts in 1899 and the appointment of a Filipino supreme court justice (Cayetano Arellano) in 1901, and the Filipinization of the bureaucracy under Governor General Francis Burton Harrison (1913–1921). The American colonial government's most lasting legacy, however, was the establishment of a public school system. The American colonial government rightly considered education to be of the highest priority in its avowed mission of bringing the blessings of democracy and civilization to the islands. It began with a system of public elementary schools in every municipality, secondary schools in every city and province, and different types of tertiary institutions in the capital city—to meet the demands of the bureaucracy and of government at the national level. Although the secretary of the Department of Public Instruction throughout the American period was the vice governor general—until 1935, when Vice-President Sergio Osmeña of the Commonwealth government became secretary of education—the Filipinization of public instruction began almost immediately at the start of the Burton administration in 1913. The initial group of American educators were called "Thomasites" because the first batch of six hundred American teachers arrived aboard the U.S.S. Thomas (Gonzalez, 1996; 2001a; Sacerdoti, 2002). Between 1901 and 1920, a total of two thousand Thomasites arrived, and teaching in the first public elementary school system began almost immediately with the help of Filipino teachers who had learned some English.

At the secondary level, the American colonial government instituted a four-year secondary (high) school (after seven years of elementary schooling) in each province (Alzona, 1932), special arts and trade schools, and agricultural schools. At the tertiary level, the first schools to be established included a teacher training institution in 1901, called the Philippine Normal School; a School of Medicine in 1908; a School of Agriculture at Los Baños in 1909; a special school for the "distributive arts" (commerce), known as the Manila Business School (which later became Philippine College of Commerce) in 1904; and a school for the practical arts, known as the Philippine School of Arts and Trades in 1901.

In 1908, the medical college, the agricultural college, and the basic liberal arts program at the teacher training college constituted the earliest components of the University of the Philippines. The College of Law was not established at the University of the Philippines until 1911, but the Faculty of Derecho Patrio, established in 1835, continued to train students in law (in Spanish).

A master's degree could be earned at the University of the Philippines beginning in 1922 (University of the Philippines, 1922), but throughout the American period, the University of the Philippines did not grant a doctoral degree outside of medicine. During this period, only the University of Santo Tomas granted doctoral degrees in theology, philosophy and the arts, canon law and civil law, and from 1871, licentiates in medicine and pharmacy.

At the tertiary level, the Spanish University of Santo Tomas resumed its institutional activities after the arrival of the Americans but did not introduce English as the medium of instruction until 1926 (Gonzalez, 1996). Beginning in 1921, the Ateneo Municipal, a Jesuit institution, used English. The new private schools organized during the American period all began using English—with the University of the Philippines (1908) and De La Salle College (1911) setting the new trend.

Under the American government, research was carried out under the Bureau of Science, the Bureau of Plant Industry, the Bureau of Animal Industry, the Bureau of Public Health, the Bureau of Forestry, and the Bureau of Water. The National Research Council of the Philippines was established in 1933, and the *Philippine Journal of Science,* founded in 1906, gained recognition abroad. The researchers, for the most part scientists at the University of the Philippines in Los Baños, were Ph.D.s trained in the United States and Europe. However, research under university auspices was not institutionalized as a tradition except at the University of the Philippines in Los Baños and the University of the Philippines in Manila.

Professors at the University of the Philippines and elsewhere who saw the hunger among Filipinos for higher education became educational entrepreneurs, establishing private tertiary educational institutions offering a bachelor's degree, with government permission—first at colleges and subsequently at universities. The religiously oriented schools also began offering degrees: De La Salle College in business (1930) and Ateneo de Manila in the liberal arts (1948) and law (1936). Charters granting university status to private institutions were instituted as early as 1921.

By 1939, when the last census under the U.S. colonial administration was undertaken, the total population of the Philippines had risen to 16 million (*Census*, 1939). In 1939, enrollments had reached 1,915,296 in elementary schools, 154,168 in secondary schools, and 39,790 in tertiary education (Aldana, 1949). There were 10,829 elementary schools, 467 high schools, and 101 colleges and universities; 44,018 elementary school teachers and 2,751 secondary school teachers. The public colleges and universities were staffed by 148 college instructors. No data are available on the number of tertiary teachers in the private schools (FAPE, 1991).

Thus, the American colonial government left a legacy of an integrated school system, separated from Church influence but allowing private institutions at all levels. At the beginning of the period of independence, the tertiary level encompassed 12 state colleges and universities and 77 private colleges and universities, with an enrollment of 1,861 in the state institutions and 44,878 in the private institutions.

A specific contribution of the American regime, an improvement on conditions during the Spanish period, was a fully developed system of free elementary schooling of seven years, subsidized secondary schooling of four years, and a subsidized tertiary system—not only in the liberal arts and sciences and the traditional professions but also in the newer professions in vocational education, engineering, accountancy, commercial sciences, teacher training (normal schools), dentistry, nursing, and above all, agriculture. By 1948, the literacy rate was estimated at 59.8 percent. Research was organized under different bureaus, and was beginning to be centered in the graduate schools of the University of the Philippines in Manila and in Los Baños.

During this period, what the Philippines inherited from the American tradition of higher education was the concept of the land grant college (after which the University of the Philippines, especially in Los Baños, was patterned). The university was expected not only to hand down past wisdom but also to provide training at the highest level for community service and for productive employment. As part of the process, research is required to be of service to the community. Professional schools were raised to the level of full colleges in the university—including schools in the fine arts, music, vocational education, engineering, architecture, veterinary medicine, the agricultural sciences, forestry, education, business, and accountancy.

A university system and what would now be considered polytechnics were in place, with a preparatory system of basic education (seven years elementary, four years secondary), a teacher training institute, and a society for research in different fields. The system of credit units was introduced, and graduate programs were taught by part-time and full-time faculty and students (the latter especially in evening colleges, now called continuing education). Neither fully developed nor marketed—unlike the British tradition in India—were pure (nonapplied) programs in mathematics and the natural life sciences or basic research.

ISSUES AND REALITIES

For Filipinos who lived though the experience of World War II and the Japanese occupation of the archipelago from early 1942 to mid-1945, the war was the "Great Divide" that changed the character of Philippine life. The achievement of independence was secondary to the impression, perhaps somewhat romanticized, that life had been so much more pleasant and less difficult during peacetime than after the war.

One of the most significant factors has been the growth in the population: the prewar population totaled about 16 million in 1939, when the last census under the American colonial government was completed, and in the year 2000, 54 years after independence, 76.5 million. In terms of basic and higher education, this meant almost a 5-fold increase in the burden of providing public education at the elementary level, exacerbated by a generous but unrealistic new Constitution in 1987 that guaranteed free secondary education for all. Over the next 15 years, the proportion of secondary school students paying tuition in private high schools declined from 60 percent to 24 percent, with the number of secondary school students rising as a result of better retention rates. Table 11.1 summarizes the changes between 1940–1941 and 2001–2002 in terms of enrollments, numbers of institutions, numbers of teachers, the balance between public and private education, and other factors.

The American forms of higher education are intact. The mission statement of the university still encompasses teaching, research, and service. However, the reality is that the substance of higher education has changed as a result of the expansion in numbers. In spite of World War II and the loss of almost a million Filipino lives, the population of the country grew at a per annum rate of over 3 percent in the 1950s and 1970s, declining to 2.3 percent in the 1980s and to as low as 2.2 percent in the 1990s but rising again to 2.3 percent in 2000. After independence, the Philippine government expended its scarce resources in expanding elementary education, maintaining only provincial and national secondary schools and charging a moderate tuition. The government nationalized the budget for all high schools beginning in 1987 (many of which had previously been funded by local governments) and, as mentioned earlier, making secondary education universal. At the tertiary level, the share of public education has remained more or less stable at 20 percent in spite of the proliferation of state colleges and universities. The country currently has 112 state colleges and universities, an increase of 15 to 20 percent within the past five years.

Table 11.1 Developments in Philippine Higher Education

	1940–1941	2001–2002
Enrollments	16,000,303	78,000,000
Colleges and universities		
Public	7	170
Private	92	1,294
Students		
Undergraduate		
Public	4,232	760,416
Private	na	1,670,426
Graduate		
Public	na	60,878
Private	na	71,833
College instructors		
Public	148	31,995
Private	na	61,889
Entering Freshmen	2,478	636,137
Graduates (undergraduates)	na	440,206

Sources: CHED, 2002a; FAPE, 1991.

A laissez-faire attitude was taken by the Department of Education and its Bureau of Higher Education with regard to private colleges and universities. Private institutions proliferated based on the growing demand for tertiary-level education, but tended to offer cheaper lecture-based studies in the liberal arts, commerce, accountancy, education, and law, with little emphasis (because of low demand) on pure science and graduate education. The science programs, with little in the way of laboratory facilities and equipment, were concentrated in fields with lucrative employment opportunities such as medicine, nursing, and engineering—the first of which are significant in the foreign markets. By the 1960s, development economists and students of social and economic development had noted a mismatch between the country's needs (for science teachers, vocational and technical specializations, advanced science, and engineering) and university output (an overproduction of graduates in the liberal arts, commerce, law, and education).

The loss of so many medical doctors (at one time as many as 75 percent of the graduates eventually ended up working abroad, mostly in the United States) and Ph.D.s who never returned after graduate studies abroad began to take its toll in terms of the ability of the system to perpetuate itself with properly trained faculty for university teaching and research. Moreover, while a moderate number of vocational and technical graduates finished their studies each year, when the market for foreign workers, especially in the Middle East, opened up in the 1970s, most of the competent vocational and technical workers ended up overseas. As a result, the quality of workers who remained in the country was less than adequate.

Perhaps the clearest and most regrettable feature of the tertiary system is linked to the fact that many colleges started out as part-time evening programs using the same facilities as those of the secondary schools. Thus, the notion of having full-time faculty with enough time to teach, prepare their classes, do research, and take academic control of programs never really took hold except in state institutions modeled after the University of the Philippines. The University of the Philippines trained many of the faculty at state institutions, at least during the early decades of independence. Some of the more enlightened private universities in the 1960s decided to imitate the University of Philippines system, paying full-time faculty by the month rather than by the hour and limiting teaching loads (12 units on average, instead of the usual 24 units) to allow the faculty to prepare their classes and to pursue graduate studies.

Given the pressing need for faculty, college instructors with only a bachelor's degree, some graduate units, and practical experience were recruited to teach. Thus the university system was staffed by faculty who had not even completed a master's degree. Even in 2003, 58 years after independence, at the 1,428 colleges and universities in the country (CHED, 2002a), of the total number of (93,884) part-time and full-time faculty, only 32 percent have at least a master's degree, and among the 32 percent, only 7 percent have doctorates. Except at the state colleges and universities and the more enlightened private institutions, faculty still carry a teaching load of 24 units (or even more, under the guise of "consultancy"), and have little time to prepare classes or even to study for higher degrees, thus contributing to the reality that much of tertiary-level schooling in the Philippines is not very productive in terms of learning. The learning process consists of repetition of subject matter already learned, handing down knowledge that is out of date especially in the social and natural sciences, and, generally, demanding little from the college student other than rote memorization of notes.

There is little or no quality control in fields of specialization that do not require final evaluation through board examinations administered by professionals working under the umbrella of the Professional Regulation Commission. Hence, except for screening at the company level or recruiting from the top colleges and universities in the area, it is difficult to be assured of the competence of graduates. In fields that do not demand board examinations, the quality of graduates ranges from near zero competence in the specialization to an international level of competence (depending on the kind of college program that they enrolled in and the institution from which they graduated).

In the Philippines, therefore, to provide a form of necessary quality control, board examinations administered by the associations of the different professions are mandatory and cannot be waived. In fact, in spite of the reluctance of the IT professions to prescribe board examinations, it will be imperative to do so in the future to make sure that the graduates being released into the system by the large number of IT institutions have minimum competencies. For the Philippines, board examinations are essential to quality control especially in fields such as medicine, dentistry, nursing, physical therapy, law, teaching, accountancy, and engineering—for which certification by a group of professionals is demanded.

However, because board examinations are so important for quality control, they dominate the current state of institutional and program evaluations. Almost total reliance is placed on the record of institutions in the board examinations, some of which are outdated because the examiners are themselves not up to date in their knowledge and unaware of current developments in the field. The work of private accreditation agencies at different levels is encouraged by the Commission on Higher Education, which grants financial and administrative deregulatory rewards to institutions that attain a certain level of accreditation. Nevertheless, what spells quality in the minds of the Filipino public is success in board examinations and not any other criterion. Little attention is paid to research (except among an emerging group of research-conscious academics), community service, or publications (which at the highest levels are better gauges of an institution's excellence than merely a good track record in board examinations).

American influence on the higher education system in the Philippines, besides the basic structure, was the concept of tertiary education as a means of achieving social mobility and not merely a way of maintaining the status quo and the privileged position of the elitist or land-owning class.

However, the spirit of free enterprise and laissez faire on the establishment of private institutions of higher learning has let loose a plethora of institutions in which quality control is a rare occurrence. Although private higher education was allowed during the American period, the number of institutions that appeared was small and quality was maintained as a result of guidelines set by the Department of Education, which were easy to impose because of the small numbers involved. At least for the first decades after the war, the influence of the United States was described as a continuation of cultural imperialism. The legacy of English was likewise maintained and continues intact at the tertiary level. Some subjects may now be taught in the national language, based on Tagalog—called Wikang Pambansa, Pilipino, and (since 1987) Filipino.

However, the very strengths of the system from its American legacy and postindependence policy of free enterprise in private education have become sources of weakness and dysfunctionality in the face of uncontrolled population growth. Moreover, the laissez-faire attitude taken by the Department of Education (since 1984, the Department of Education, Culture, and Sports) and the lack of proper staffing at the Bureau of Higher Education resulted in inadequate planning at the national level. State colleges and universities were established by Congress at the initiative of congressional representatives who wanted a tertiary-level institution in their districts even in the absence of resources or rationalization as to need. Useless duplication of courses has occurred, with institutions offering basically the same areas of specialization and competing for scarce state resources. The mismatch between national and regional needs and tertiary-level outputs has worsened. The excess number of graduates have found employment only by going overseas or by taking jobs in fields unrelated to their major subjects, resulting in a downgrading of qualifications. At the same time, there is a dearth of manpower in areas needed by the economy.

What the Philippine experience has thus far shown is that private education has an essential role to play in developing economies. If nothing else, private higher education serves as an interim arrangement until national income in the country permits a sufficient level of rational investment in higher education that will enable the society to compete in the worldwide knowledge-based economy. For a long time, private proprietary universities were viewed with disdain by respectable educators in the country because of the profit motive on the part of the school founders. However, the opening of similar private institutions in the ASEAN region (first in Thailand and Indonesia and now in Vietnam, Singapore, and Malaysia) and before that, in the North Asian region (in Japan, South Korea, and more recently China) has made this option credible, realistic, even desirable. In an age of globalization, even nonprofit world-class universities in the developed world (for example, the United States, the United Kingdom, and Australia) are now establishing for-profit units in Asia. What the Philippine case demonstrates is that good-quality teaching—although probably not research except for financially productive research of an applied nature—is possible to achieve while still ensuring a reasonable return on investment for the school founders. In the Philippines profits range from 10 to 12 percent per annum. For a short time during the 1980s, a law was passed declaring that all new private institutions had to be nonstick and nonprofit. This stipulation discouraged the creation of new schools and resulted in a shortage of tertiary-level places, since government schools were unable to meet the demand. The stipulation has since been dropped.

The ideal of research and teaching tied together remains intact, with one mutually reinforcing the other. However, based on the old French model and now on the experience in the Philippines, it is possible to separate teaching from research, consign research to institutes separately funded by subsidies, and make teaching self-paying and even income-generating. To carry out teaching effectively and efficiently, the system must not only provide modern information and communications technology facilities but, more important, must retool the teaching faculty systematically to make sure they are current and up-to-date in their knowledge. This does not mean that all university faculty need to be researchers, nor that they all need the research doctorate.

TRENDS AND CHALLENGES

The problems of higher education in the Philippines have been the subject of analysis and program formulation since 1969. In 1970, the Presidential Commission to Survey Philippine Education issued its findings. Initially, the approach was to focus on the Bureau of Higher Education, one of the key bureaus within the Department of Education. Subsequently, as a result of another survey, this time commissioned by both houses of the legislature, Congress came up with the proposal to separate higher education from basic education by creating a cabinet-level Commission on Higher Education (enacted as law in 1994 and known as Republic Act No. 7722).

The Commission on Higher Education (CHED), headed by a chair and four other commissioners acting together, has taken over the helm of private education and exercises some control over the 112 separately chartered state colleges and universities. The private sector consists of 1,470 institutions, which enroll 75 percent of the students in higher education. At these state colleges and universities, the CHED chair or one of the commissioners as his representative serves as ex officio chair of the board of trustees or board of regents—this system applies to the University of the Philippines as well.

In 2002, CHED administered a fund consisting of contributions of more than Php200 million (U.S.$3,773,585) from state agencies (CHED, 2002b)—the Higher Education Fund—which is used for the improvement of all colleges and universities through grants for excellence (including institutional support, facilities' upgrading, faculty development, and research). In addition, CHED arranges for technical grants and soft loans from world financial agencies such as the World Bank, the Asian Development Bank, and the Japan Bank for International Cooperation to assist higher education.

CHED has organized "technical panels" of professional scholars and researchers from different public and private institutions to help it draw up policies on criteria for university status, support for different accreditation agencies in the country, recognition of new programs of study (majors leading to a bachelor's degree or a graduate degree), and certification of various kinds. In addition, the panels draw up national policies on standards and formulate a higher education plan to meet the needs of the country.

The problems of higher education are extensive because of the large numbers involved. The burden of higher education is shared with the Technical Skills Development Authority (TESDA), another cabinet-level agency that is in charge of all nondegree technical education, especially short-term six-month courses (leading to a certificate) and one- to two-year technician courses (leading to a diploma). There is a coordinating council of all educational bodies, the National Coordinating Council for Education—consisting of the Department of Education, the Commission on Higher Education—that was established by an executive order following a recommendation of the Presidential Commission on Educational Reform during the Estrada administration.

Accreditation at various levels is granted by member associations of the Federation of Accrediting Associations of the Philippines, which CHED supports. CHED likewise gives both financial grants and administrative deregulation privileges to institutions that merit certain levels of accreditation. Finally, because CHED cannot stop Congress from enacting laws creating additional colleges and universities, it is now demanding that funds for these institutions be raised by local government with the involvement of congressional representatives to supplement the meager funding that CHED is able to grant these state college and universities through its own annual budget. In effect, CHED is exerting its influence to make decentralization and control by local government a reality through the power of the purse. In the meantime, deserving institutions that have established a record of excellence over time have now been deregulated and rendered semiautonomous, like chartered state colleges and universities, and given incentives through actual program development grants. There are likewise many scholarship programs in place to provide access to higher education to less affluent students for both public and private universities. In turn, private universities, especially the more affluent ones, have significant programs of student aid for deserving students.

Thus, the laws, policies, plans, implementation schemes, and agencies are in place for genuine reform. Given the relatively poor performance of the system since 1969, when some of these new policies of reform began to be formulated, it is unclear whether the political will can be found to implement such reforms by prioritizing higher education against competing demands from other social sectors, including infrastructure demands. Moreover, the executive branch itself has to show that it means what it says rhetorically about making education and higher education a priority by releasing funds. In spite of approved budgets and programmed funds, the pace and the order of release are subject to the control of the executive branch, which in the past has directed funds to other priorities.

To scan the future of the higher education system, one must thus go beyond what one would like to see happen. It is not even sufficient to look at existing or pending legislation (since what is legislated is not necessarily going to be implemented) or current structures, as well as stated policies. The most effective approach is to look at trends and see where they are leading. However, these trends are not ineluctable or inevitable since there may be intervening factors that could change the direction substantially. Thus, no studies of the system have as yet attempted a multifaceted trends analysis, although there have been many informal SWOT (strengths, weaknesses, opportunities, threats) analyses and some informal force field analyses to which the system has been subjected in seminars and workshops.

More certain are the population forecasts by demographers. The population of the Philippines was 6 million at the beginning of the twentieth century (Philippine Commission, 1905). Based on the last census under the American colonial government, the population was 16 million in 1939. In 2000, the most recent national census year, it was up to 75.6 million, and it was estimated in 2003 to be 79.99 million. By conservative estimates, the population will rise to 96.3 million in 2015 and to 108.5 million in 2025, at which time it is expected to stabilize (*United Nations World Population*, 2002). In this decade, two-thirds of the population is recorded as being under 25 years of age. Presently there are about 760,500 entering the formal tertiary system as students each year and about 450,000 graduates of the system each year (CHED, 2002a).

The proportion of Filipinos ages 16 to 21, the college age cohort, is expected to increase in proportion to the increasing population. Moreover, as survival rates improve, one expects larger numbers at the various levels. Currently, for every 100 students who begin grade 1, 69 finish grade 6. Of these 69, 49 finish high school. About 26 enter college, and of these 26, 16 finally graduate. One expects the number of entering freshmen in the tertiary system to go beyond the 26 out of 49 rate as the survival rate in high school improves.

Correspondingly, there will be more institutions established and expanded enrollments at existing ones, resulting in the need for more faculty members. Based on the last count (CHED, 2002a), there were 1,470 higher education institutions, 85 percent of them private, and 93,884 college teachers. A rise of 25 percent is predicted among entering freshmen, the number of faculty, and the number of classrooms over the next 10 years (Gonzalez, 2000).

Unfortunately, unless there is a significant increase in funding for state colleges and universities, a rise in quality cannot be expected given the competing demands for public funds. There are funding shortages in the system of education nationally, with a growing consensus that any increases in appropriations should benefit basic education rather than higher education. While all members of Congress are expected to enact legislation to create a state college in their bailiwicks or to elevate an existing state college into a university, CHED itself has attempted to limit the numbers without success since the legislature can create institutions even without the approval of the commission. As noted earlier, the policy introduced by the commission is to demand that every state college or university raise its own funds by increasing tuition rates (at present tuition revenues cover only 5 percent to 10 percent of the total per capita cost of collegiate schooling) or by asking local government to support the schools. The overall aim, thus far not implemented, is that the 91 percent subsidy of state universities for every student will drop to 60 percent and then to 50 percent, with the balance supplied by other sources. Unless these sources are forthcoming, the quality of state higher education will continue to decline rather than improve.

To meet the social demand for higher education, private institutions will need to expand. This expansion is likely to occur because of increased freedom and reduced regulation, but the prospects for quality are not high since tuition is the main source of revenue and tuition will support only what demand dictates. If these private institutions do improve, it will be as teaching institutions but not research institutions, since research is not possible on the basis of tuition alone.

There are really only about ten research-oriented universities in the country—that is, institutions that consciously encourage research carried out by faculty through allocating a specific proportion of operational and endowment income to research each year, with a planned annual increase (Gonzalez 2001b; 2002; 2003). There are about one hundred moderately effective teaching institutions that produce the bulk of graduates in the professions who are sought after by foreign markets as overseas Filipino workers; the rest of the institutions produce substandard graduates.

Even by the most optimistic estimates, the number of research-oriented institutions in the country over the next quarter century may go up to sixteen (one center of excellence for every region), probably increasing by fifty the number of competent teaching institutions (dictated by the demands of the market), and the rest will continue to multiply and will be substandard.

Thus, the function of higher education in the Philippines will be to continue to supply the research needs of the country to a minimal extent and to train a moderate number of competent professionals for local and international markets. The rest of the system will consist of academic custodianship—that is to say, the institutions will meet the demand of families for tertiary schooling at the parents' expense, with little benefit to the individual since the training and knowledge provided are in many instances equivalent to that of a secondary school in the developed countries. These colleges are really only producing qualified graduates for clerical and low-level routine jobs in offices and factories.

More challenging than meeting the growing demand for higher education are the attempts being made by many good high schools to channel enrollments in response to job opportunities instead of adding to the number of unemployed (10.2 percent) and underemployed (15.3 percent). The educational market is surprisingly sensitive to job opportunities and attracts students to programs where the prospects of employability are better. Thus with the reopening of the international market for nurses in the late 1990s there has been large numbers of applicants for nursing programs. Nursing schools, have experienced a revival, after enrollment numbers took a dramatic downturn. In fact, some medical school graduates in the Philippines are even going to nursing schools so that they can be employed abroad. Computer schools of all sorts are proliferating from the very poor to the very good, and the numbers of enrollees in these programs will continue to be substantial because of the need for IT workers in the West and because of the outsourcing by foreign companies of their need for IT workers. There will likewise be a resurgence of interest in education programs because of the need for teachers in the United States and a demand for graduates with advanced language skills from telephone service companies that are now hiring workers located in developing countries.

However, while there is an overenrollment in these programs with market value (especially in the West), a shortage continues to exist for students in mathematics and science to meet the needs for pure science education of Philippine society. Inadequate numbers of students choose vocational and technical programs because of a traditional disdain in the Philippine value system for blue-collar work. One foresees a local shortage in areas such as education, IT, medicine, and nursing—not because of a lack of students but because the best and the brightest graduates leave for foreign employment. Thus, the mismatch continues between the programs now in high demand and those providing the knowledge and skills urgently needed in Philippine society. The state is helpless to do much to counter this trend since most college students choose the programs they want, paying tuition with family funds.

The rising numbers have forced many Philippine educational policymakers to meet the need for education through various forms of distance education, at all levels, even as early as elementary school. However, these alternative modes of delivery of basic and higher education are all at the conceptual and pilot stage. Few programs have been successful thus far, with the exception of graduate programs for teachers being offered by the Open University at the University of the Philippines.

Accreditation as a course of action to improve quality is an idea whose time has finally come in the Philippines. Credible private institutions are now voluntarily undergoing accreditation. CHED has made accreditation one of its strategies for improvement and has added incentives (deregulation, public recognition, small grants for institutions designated as centers of excellence in particular fields of study). Moreover, private enterprises are now more prepared to fund fellowships and scholarships and to enter into cooperative programs with universities to provide sites for applied research undertaken by graduate students working on their theses and dissertations.

The basic constraint on quality improvement is the lack of faculty graduate qualifications. Little progress has been made in this area in the past thirty or more years. In 1972–1973, when the Fund for Assistance to Private Education (FAPE, 1975) made its first study of nationwide qualifications, 28 percent of faculty had master's and doctoral degrees, and of these only about 4.6 percent had doctoral degrees. More than thirty years later, while the number of college teachers has increased as a result of the increase in the number of students, the proportion of qualified college teachers with requisite degrees has not improved significantly. By 2000, the percentage of faculty with graduate degrees had only gone from 28 percent to 32 percent, and within the 32 percent the proportion of college faculty with Ph.D.s had only increased from 4.6 to 7 percent. The other positive development is that a consensus now exists that the surest and quickest way to improve tertiary education in the country is to put the bulk of the resources into faculty development by sending more faculty members on sabbatical for full-time study to finish their theses or dissertations (many have completed the coursework) or to give them the opportunity to update themselves, and by sending younger faculty to undertake full-time graduate study at full subsidy. In CHED programs, faculty development now constitutes the main focus of future activities.

CONCLUSION

The higher education system of the Philippines can be characterized as one that meets the social demand for higher education at minimal cost to the public. In the process, however, the neglect of research and the mismatch between public needs and the system's output continue although the configuration of needs and outputs has changed over time. Quality remains a gigantic problem, with solutions possible only for specific fields in selected institutions designated as "centers of excellence."

Emerging from the Philippine experience is the pivotal role private schooling can play in a country's higher education strategy, an approach that has been taken by many developing countries. Still to be addressed is how to maintain and upgrade the qualifications of faculty short of providing full-time graduate study for the majority (which would not be affordable for the system). The Philippine system supplies this professional development through continuing education and distance-education programs, as well as through short-term fellowships and a few full-time graduate fellowships. Still to be discovered and institutionalized are the accreditation and other evaluation instruments that will bring about substantive improvement in the quality of instruction and training so that the discourse at the university level will meet the demands of a knowledge-based economy in the twenty-first century.

To get institutions to work together instead of competing and to take initiatives and to maximize resources; to ensure that the system makes effective use of the funds for the improvement of facilities, especially laboratories; and to support research at a few centers of excellence and pursue institutionalized linkages with industry for research will be the challenges that the Philippine higher education system will have to tackle in the coming century. Given the fact that many developing countries confront similar challenges, the Philippine situation and the country's attempt may have a broader relevance.

REFERENCES

Aldana, B. (1949). The educational system of the Philippines. Manila: University Publishing Company.

Alzona, E. (1932). A history of education in the Philippines 1565–1930. Manila: University of the Philippines Press.

Bazaco, E. (1989). History of education in the Philippines 1565–1989. Manila: University of Santo Tomas.

Census of the Philippines. (1939). Manila: Bureau of Printing.

Commission on Higher Education (CHED). (2002a) Distribution of higher education *institutions by region, sector and type of institution.* Pasig City, Philippines: Author.

Commission on Higher Education (CHED). (2002b) Schedule of fund contributions from PTA, PCSO, PRC per year. Pasig City, Philippines: Author.

Department of Education. (2002). *Fact sheet (October 1).* Pasig City, Philippines: Office of Planning Service, Research and Statistics Division, Department of Education.

Fund for Assistance to Private Education (FAPE). (1991). Philippine educational indicators. Vol. 1. Makati, Philippines: Author.

Fund for Assistance to Private Education (FAPE). (1975). *The Philippine atlas.* Vols. 1–2. Manila: Author.

Gonzalez, A., FSC. (1996, July 3). "The role and contribution of the Thomasites and the Filipino pensionados." Paper presented at the Symposium on Independence and Fifty Years of Philippine-American Friendship, Ateneo de Manila University.

Gonzalez, A., FSC. (2000). Our increasing school population: Educational cross currents. *Philippine Journal of Education, 79(2),* 76.

Gonzalez, A., FSC. (2001a, August 24). "The role and contribution of the Thomasites to language education." Paper presented to the American Studies Association of the Philippines Annual Assembly and Conference, Ateneo de Manila University.

Gonzalez, A., FSC. (2001b, October 18). "Research and academic excellence." Paper presented at the research faculty session, Lyceum of the Philippines, Manila, Philippines.

Gonzalez, A., FSC. (2002, February 28). "Some notes on Philippine higher education." Paper presented at the Rotary Club of Manila executive meeting, Manila, Philippines.

Gonzalez, A., FSC. (2003, February 12). "The context of the rationalization of the public higher education system." Paper presented at the Workshop on the Rationalization of the Public Higher Education System, SEAMEO INNOTECH, Quezon City, Philippines.

Philippine Commission. (1905). *Census of the Philippine Islands 1903.* III. Washington, DC: U.S. Bureau of the Census.

Sacerdoti, G. (2002). *Spanning the decades 1902–2002.* Makati, Philippines: American Chamber of Commerce of the Philippines.

United Nations world population prospects. (2002). New York: United Nations Population Division, Department of Economics and Social Affairs.

University of the Philippines. (1922, September 2). *55th university council meeting.* Manila: Author.

PART VI

Building Universities in
Low Per Capita Income Countries

12

Universities in Vietnam

Legacies, Challenges, and Prospects

Pham Lan Huong & Gerald W. Fry

Unlike many developing nations, Vietnam has a long history of higher education. Many important influences, particularly Chinese, French, and Soviet, have shaped the evolution of Vietnam's university system. This chapter examines challenges Vietnam has faced while attempting to create an indigenous system of higher education despite such powerful external influences. A critical review of the contemporary realities of Vietnamese higher education reveals a number of strengths and weaknesses. Central to the discussion is the impact on higher education of the introduction of *doi moi* (economic renovation) in 1986. *Doi moi* and the shift from a state-planned to a free-market economy have led to a dramatic expansion of the higher education system, facilitated by the introduction of a private higher education sector. As suggested by the book title, *A Phoenix Rising* (Schramm-Evans, 1996), Vietnam is a country with great but unrealized potential. The country's success in realizing its economic and intellectual potential will depend on improving both the quality and efficiency of its university system.

HISTORICAL PERSPECTIVES

When analyzing contemporary economic and educational issues, people often ignore the historical and political context. Such historical myopia and amnesia can lead to tragedy, as was the case with the U.S. war in Vietnam. Within the historical and political context of Vietnam, five themes are important: (1) the continual struggle of the Vietnamese to free themselves from external domination; (2) the struggle against natural disasters, such as floods and typhoons; (3) *nam tien* (expansion to the South); (4) Chinese cultural and intellectual influences, particularly in the cities; and (5) the importance of village life as the heart of Vietnamese culture.

Fondness for learning and respect for morality in education have been important traditional Vietnamese values. Since respect for learning and teachers has been an enduring trait in Vietnam throughout its history, these values have contributed to the shaping of Vietnamese culture and society. Traditionally, careers in education have held an extremely significant position in Vietnamese society. Intellectuals usually taught, and teaching was thought of as an elevated career. Teachers were highly valued, and it was believed that "without a teacher, you can do nothing."

Vietnam has a long tradition of higher education. In fact, Vietnam has the oldest known institution of higher education (founded in 1076) in Southeast Asia, which significantly predates both the colleges at Angkor Wat in the Khmer empire and the University of Santo Thomas in the Philippines. Vietnam, along with China, Japan, Korea, and Singapore, is part of the Confucian world. However, the Vietnamese have adapted and modified the values from that world, resulting in the Vietnamization of Confucianism. At the Temple of Literature, the statue of Confucius shows him wearing a teacher's hat, instead of the crown that is usually seen on Chinese statues—a symbol of the value placed on learning and the reverence bestowed by the Vietnamese on teachers, scholars, and mentors.

The Feudal Period

After over a thousand years of being dominated by Chinese imperial regimes, Vietnam became an independent country in 938, and education developed during subsequent feudal dynasties. In 1076, the Royal College was founded at the Temple of Literature during the Ly dynasty to provide moral education and training to the sons of dignitaries (Sloper & Le, 1995, p. 43). Later, in 1243, the Institute for Children of the Nation was also established at the Temple of Literature. During the feudal period, the Vietnamese system of higher education resembled China's, with important Confucian, Taoist, and Buddhist influences. Special examinations were held to select persons with the talent to become mandarins. Only a limited number of members of the educated elite could participate in state governance. Between 1442 and 1779, the Temple of Literature produced 1,307 graduates, including eighty-two who received doctorates.

It is also significant to note that Vietnam has an advanced written language system dating back several thousand years. Due to an earlier period of Chinese rule, Vietnam used Chinese characters for seventeen centuries. However, in the thirteenth century it developed its own unique system of Vietnamese characters called *Chu Nom*. Then, in the seventeenth century, with the assistance of Portuguese, Spanish, Italian, and French scholars—in particular, Alexandre de Rhodes, a French missionary and scholar—the Vietnamese developed a romanized script known as *Quoc Ngu*. Starting in 1919, *Quoc Ngu* became widely used, particularly in primary schools. After 1945, *Quoc Ngu* was used at all levels of education. Eleven of Vietnam's fifty-four ethnic nationalities also have their own scripts (Do, 1998).

During this period, examinations from the Interprovincial (*thi huong*) to the Pre-Court (*thi hoi*) were competitive in nature. The highest level was the Court examination (*thi dinh*), granting the title of bachelor (*tu tai*) and licentiate (*cu nhan*). In 1375, the title of doctor (*tien sy*) was added, and after 1829 those holding this title had to pass four competitive exams. The curriculum included literature, history, and feudal administration. The examination system was reformed in 1400 by Ho Quy Ly, and mathematics became a subject on the national exam. However, in 1406, Ho Quy Ly was killed and the national exam reverted to its original form (Phan & Truong, 1996).

The Period of French Colonial Rule

In 1847, the French navy attacked Danang. From that time on, French colonizers looked for many ways to dominate the Vietnamese, and the West became known as the "white devil" to many Vietnamese. French military dominance dismayed the imperial Nguyen court. The court became deeply resentful of the French and their "civilizing mission," which encouraged the development of opium and liquor trades to generate revenues to support their colonial empire and the export of rubber, rice, and coal to gain profits from their colony (T. B. Lam, 1967).

During this time, Vietnamese education remained backward, with a system of traditional competitive examinations based on old-fashioned and narrow-minded scholarly values of the old China. Students studied history, morality, and ancient Chinese classics. In November 1867, an intellectual "missionary," Nguyen Truong To, who had great enthusiasm for his homeland, wrote an innovative report calling for an important change in pedagogy and methodology. He urged a shift to "practical learning" that would include some Western curricular content. This was a progressive report for its time. However, the suggestions in the report were not implemented because of the weak character of Emperor Tu Duc and the old-fashioned mandarins of the time. In 1867, the French repressed the movements of the patriots, and many leaders, including a number of scholars, were exiled. In 1887, the French proclaimed Indochina to be a colony, which included what is now Vietnam, Cambodia, and Laos. However, resistance activities persisted.

This feudal education system continued until 1919, when the French abolished the Confucian system. The radical thinking that existed in China at the time spread into Vietnam and inspired a similar resistance. Phan Chau Trinh and Huynh Thuc Khang led a movement known as the Duy Tan (1902–1908) (V. X. Nguyen, 1995). The group advocated a model of education that opposed the old methods of learning and allowed for theoretical and practical learning. It also started the first schools that provided equality for men and women. While these changes were occurring within the country, there were also important developments abroad. Phan Boi Chau organized a program for hundreds of students to study in Japan. The French colonial regime's policy was to keep the Vietnamese ignorant so as to be able to control them. However, local activism eventually forced the French to start changing their policies and led to the establishment of the colony's first college, on January 8, 1902: the Ecole de Plein Exercice de Medecine et de Pharmacie de l'Indochine (D. H. Nguyen, 1948, p. 5). Under the leadership of Governor-General Beau, the College of Indo-China at Hanoi was created in 1904 but was soon closed in 1908 by Governor-General Klobukowski, because of fears stemming from native uprisings (D. H. Nguyen, 1948, p. 7).

After 1917, the education system was entirely transformed into a French one (Nguyen & Phan, 2000). Consequently, elementary schools were established in villages. In some large cities, such as Hanoi and Saigon, "higher elementary education" schools were created that provided four additional years of education. Schools of upper-secondary education existed only in Hanoi, Hue, and Saigon (M. H. Pham, 1998, p. 47). The French established the following colleges: Teacher Training College (1917), the College of Law and Administration (1918), the College of Agriculture and Forestry (1918), the College of Civil Engineering (1918), and the College of Fine Arts and Architecture (1924). In addition, they established some technical schools, such as the School of Practical Industry and the School of Fine Arts. In Hanoi, several schools and training programs (in medicine, law, science, and agronomy) were merged in 1940 into the University of Indo-Chine (IU), which also served students from the Khmer and Lao parts of the French colony.

In the 1939–1940 school year, total enrollments at IU (the only university in the colony) numbered only 582, which reflected the highly elitist nature of the system (M. H. Pham, 1998, p. 4). In 1945, 95 percent of the Vietnamese people were illiterate. In their struggle against the French colonial system of higher education, the Vietnamese called for instruction in the indigenous Vietnamese language and for curricula that included Vietnamese history, geography, and culture. They also expressed bitterness toward French racism, which viewed the Vietnamese as backward and unable to manage their own affairs, even at the lowest levels (Grey, 1982, p. 9). Nguyen Ai Quoc (an earlier name of Ho Chi Minh) bitterly criticized the French educational system:

> education only disrupted the character of the learner by teaching him to develop a wrong sense of loyalty, to be subservient to superior force, and to love a fatherland which was not his, a country which had oppressed his people. The young man turned back to despise his own race, his own origin and become more idiotic. What could help train the student to think and analyze were never taught in schools. (Duong, 1978, p. 181)

During the period of French colonial rule, total school enrollments amounted to only 2.6 percent of the population. The training of manpower existed mainly for the purpose of maintaining colonial rule. There were very few students in higher education—only 2,051 from 1935 to 1938. In 1941, 68 percent of IU students were Vietnamese, 28 percent French, 1.5 percent Khmer, and 1 percent Lao (Duong, 1978, p. 210). In 1943–1944, the IU had 1,575 students, accounting for 77 percent of the total number of students. It was similar to a French provincial university (Altbach, 2002, p. 8). Also, some Vietnamese were able to pursue higher education in France, which often had a radicalizing impact on them (McConnell, 1989). In Vietnam, some fields were totally neglected, such as Vietnamese history, politics, and culture (Q. T. Nguyen, 1993). The highest-quality education was provided at the IU's Medical and Law Schools, and their degrees were recognized as comparable to those provided by institutions in Europe. In terms of pedagogy at the time, a former student at the Law School describes his experiences as follows:

> The lectures were delivered in the big amphitheater, wherein a class of some three hundred first year students were jammed together. They had to be at the door at

6 a.m. if they wanted a good seat near the professor's desk. The late comers had to go to the balcony. At 7 o'clock the bell rang and the instructor walked in from the back stage, with cap and gown. The students stood up; he took his cap off and remained standing for a moment then sat down and read out of his manuscript for an hour. Then he stood up and walked out of the room while the students applauded. (D. H. Nguyen, 1948, p. 12)

Though the French education system in Vietnam was intended to subject the Vietnamese to French rule, it did lay a foundation for the development of Vietnamese higher education. In addition, the elitist French educational system established high academic standards, focused on theory, and taught essential basic sciences such as mathematics. The colonial enterprise also produced considerable research (in French) about the countries and cultures of Indochina, reflected in the numerous publications of l'Ecole française d'Extrème-Orient.

The 1945–1954 Period

The August Revolution of 1945 transformed colonial Vietnam into the Democratic Republic of Vietnam, which celebrated its national independence on September 2, 1945. At the inception of the newly formed government, its revolutionary leader, Ho Chi Minh, made the following declaration on September 3, 1945: "An ignorant nation is a weak one. Therefore, I propose that a campaign against illiteracy be launched." Also, on the same day in a special letter written to Vietnamese students, he stated:

Whether the Vietnamese mountains and rivers will attain glory and whether the Vietnamese land will gloriously stand on an equal footing with the powers in the five continents, this depends to a great extent on your studies. (M. H. Pham, 1998, p. 13)

However, after a short time, the French returned and colonialism continued until 1954. During this time, Vietnam was divided into the French-controlled area and the liberated areas of the Vietminh. In the French-controlled area, the education system was based on French programs and content. At the university, students studied in French and lecturers were both Vietnamese and French. In the liberated areas, three higher education centers were established that focused on teacher training, medicine and pharmacy, and the sciences. Both the academic language and the lecturers were Vietnamese. The curricula were translated from French materials and adapted to the local situation.

The 1954–1975 Period

After the Vietminh victory at Dien Bien Phu in May 1954, Vietnam was divided into two parts, the Democratic Republic of Vietnam in the north and the Republic of Vietnam, protected by U.S military forces, in the south. In the north, the language of instruction for higher education was Vietnamese. In the south, before 1966, the language of instruction was French. Thereafter the medium of instruction was French, Vietnamese, and English.

In 1956, after two years of economic rehabilitation, Vietnam established a number of educational institutions at the university level in the north. Among these institutions were the University of Hanoi, the Teacher Training College of Hanoi, the Hanoi Polytechnic University, the Hanoi College of Medicine, the Hanoi College of Agriculture, the College of Economics, and the College of Fine Arts. The majority of the universities' curriculum and programs were modeled after institutions in the Soviet Union and Eastern Europe, with the exception of the University of Medicine, which was modeled after French institutions. Most of the lecturers were trained in the USSR. As a result, the Soviet education system strongly influenced Vietnamese higher education, resulting in narrowly defined subjects and a curriculum that emphasized in-depth specialized knowledge. During this first stage, educational institutions helped to build and develop Vietnamese industry. However, Vietnam had a much smaller industrial sector than the Soviet Union, and as a result, the narrowly defined curriculum did not match the work that was available to students after they graduated. At the time, people ignored this inconsistency because every student was provided a job by the state.

In the 1974–1975 academic year, there were thirty institutions of higher education in North Vietnam, serving 56,000 students of whom 40 percent were women (M. H. Pham, 1998, p. 152). During the war, some of the larger universities were divided into smaller colleges. For instance, Hanoi Polytechnic was divided into the College of Mining and Geology, the College of Construction, and the College of Engineering. Students received scholarships under subsidies from the state.

During this period, there were eighteen institutions of higher education in South Vietnam. They included four public universities: the University of Saigon, the University of Hue, the University of Can Tho, and the Polytechnic University of Thu Duc; three public community colleges in My Tho, Nha Trang, and Danang; and eleven private institutions of higher education, mostly run by religious groups, such as the University of Dalat (Catholic), Van Hanh University (Buddhist), the Hoa Hao University, and the Cao Dai College. Hoa Hao and Cao Dai were important religious sects in the south. Three of these universities—the University of Saigon, established by the French during the colonial period; the University of Hue in central Vietnam, established in 1957; and the University of Can Tho in the southern Mekong Delta region, established in 1967— were considered major national universities. Unlike most universities in the north, these institutions were multidisciplinary (Sauvageau, 1996, p. 110).

Unfortunately, there was little coordination among the various institutions of higher education. Another major problem involved the widespread unemployment of graduates (Sauvageau, 1996, p. 111). Staffing at these universities was facilitated by U.S. economic assistance. For example, between 1954 and 1960, 729 South Vietnamese were sent for training in the United States (Sauvageau, 1996, p. 124). During the war period, numerous U.S. universities developed relationships with Vietnamese institutions of higher education. Among the prominent U.S. schools and institutions involved in Vietnam were the University of Southern Illinois, the University of Wisconsin, Michigan State University, Stanford Research Institute, Harvard University, and the North Dakota Institute of Linguistics (Sauvageau, 1996, pp. 122–124). Both people in the north of Vietnam and radicals in the United States were critical of these relationships, arguing that they were fostering Americanization, dependency, and supporting the training of police and military related to the counterinsurgency goals of the U.S.-backed government in the south.

Under U.S. influence the system of higher education in the south became less elitist, with greater emphasis on training related to the economic needs of the country. In 1971, a decree was issued establishing community colleges (Sauvageau, 1996, p. 113).

During the period of U.S. influence, enrollments at universities and colleges in the south grew dramatically, from an enrollment of 4,985 in 1957–1958 to 87,608 in 1972–1973 (Green, 1973, p. 13). Eventually, the institutions in the south served a total of 166,000 students (M. H. Pham, 1998, p. 152). Before 1970, the curriculum and programs of these institutions continued to be modeled after those of French universities that had moved in 1954 from Hanoi to the south. However, over time the Vietnamese language became the more commonly used medium of instruction in these institutions. After 1969–1970, the United States strongly advocated the use of the Vietnamese language at the country's educational institutions. University programs began to become more like university programs in the United States. Also, some academic pedagogy was changed, and the U.S. system of credits began to replace certificates. Graduate students could study in Vietnamese, French, and English, and some professors came from countries other than France, such as the United States.

The Post-1975 Period

Following the reunification of the country, the education system was rebuilt under the leadership of the Ministry of Education and Training. The curriculum of universities was divided into two stages: the first two years consisted of basic courses, followed by two or three years, during which students were expected to take more specialized courses. Universities were organized into six groups—according to their specialties, which included teacher training, industry and technology, agriculture, economics, medicine, and the arts.

Vietnam's higher education system has continued to be strongly influenced by the Soviet system. The second language at universities was either Russian or Chinese. An encouraging sign about the quality of Vietnamese education apparently is the recent success in math and science of Vietnamese students in the Scientific Olympics. This success over students from many other countries with more advanced economies and educational systems demonstrates the potential of Vietnamese higher education and also shows how both the Chinese and Soviet academic legacies have had certain beneficial aspects. It is important to keep in mind that prior to 1990, 4,500 Vietnamese had received doctorates from Eastern bloc countries (3,500 from the former Soviet Union) (M. H. Pham, 1998, p. 163). While Soviet training in the modern social sciences was certainly weak, educational levels in math and science were generally quite high, which augurs well for Vietnam's future potential in research and development and information technologies.

When the demands of the market changed due to government reform policies, the curriculum at each university also changed. Following the collapse of the socialist systems of the Soviet Union and Eastern Europe, documents and curricular materials from the West were introduced into Vietnamese universities. Western European nations and the United States were among the countries that influenced institutions of higher education, and the second language at these institutions shifted suddenly to English. This Western influence was most evident in the curriculum and the methods of teaching and learning. However, on the negative side, there is concern that the introduction of the free-market economy has adversely impacted the morals of students, weakening their commitment to important social values associated with Confucian and socialist traditions.

The Legacy of Ho Chi Minh

Father Ho (Uncle Ho) is a dominant figure in modern Vietnamese history. He is viewed as the father of the nation and represents the country's independence from foreign domination. In addition to his significant political role, Ho also represents an important role model for Vietnam's students. He was a lifelong learner who mastered an amazing number of European and Asian languages. When he was young, he traveled to diverse parts of the world and became familiar with a wide range of ideas and perspectives. Father Ho displayed many qualities of a protean individual, while also maintaining a modest personal style that was exemplary in an age of increasing materialism (Duiker, 2000).

ISSUES AND REALITIES

With a population of 79.9 million (July 2001), Vietnam is one of the most densely populated countries in the world and the thirteenth largest country in the world. Its population is approximately one-third that of the United States, but its land area is only 3.5 percent of that of the United States, and much of the land is mountainous and forested and not available for settlement or cultivation. This special demographic status gives Vietnam both special advantages and disadvantages. On the positive side, it allows for valuable economies of scale related to the development of physical and human infrastructure. It also forces the Vietnamese to be highly innovative and efficient in using a scarce amount of space. The impressive development of intensive agriculture has made Vietnam the world's third largest rice exporter. The negative side of Vietnam's demographics is the tremendous pressure placed on the economy to provide meaningful employment and educational opportunities for its large population. This is especially true for the younger generation. With respect to Vietnam's special demographics, important Confucian traditions, and recovery from the war experience, the country mirrors Japan in some remarkable respects. Vietnam, as Japan and Thailand earlier, has experienced a rapid decline in fertility, which is now nearing replacement levels (Gubry, 2000; 2001). This means that the Vietnamese will be able to invest more in developing the human capital of each child.

The Impact of Socioeconomic Changes

Since 1986, a profound socioeconomic policy change has taken place in Vietnam, with the introduction of what the Vietnamese term *doi moi*—that is, economic renovation through the shift from a centrally planned to a more privatized market economy (Boothroyd & Pham, 2000; RonnÂs & Ramamurthy, 2001). Thus, Vietnam's economy has now become one of the many that are classified as transitional economies. From 1991 to 2000, the average gross domestic product (GDP) per year in Vietnam increased by 7.4 percent, despite the Asian economic crisis. The Asian Development Bank projected Vietnam's annual GDP growth to be 6.3, 6.7, and 7.0 percent for 2002, 2003, and 2004, respectively.

During the past fifteen years, Vietnam's system of higher education has undergone major reforms stemming from the challenges presented by the transition from a state-planned to a free-market economy (Q. T. Tran, 2000; Q. T. Lam, 1998; Sinlarat, 1997). Key elements of the reform include the introduction of tuition fees, encouragement of links with business through contracting research services, consolidating state research institutes with universities, development of large national multidisciplinary universities through the amalgamation of institutions, and expansion of the community college system to respond to local needs (Sauvageau, 1996, p. ix).

In recent years, there has been a dramatic expansion in Vietnamese higher education. This expansion reflects both the rapid economic development in the 1990s and the related growth in social demand for higher education to prepare young people for jobs in the modern sector. Between 1995 and 1996, the number of students in higher education increased by 16.4 percent, and between 1996 and 1997 that number increased by 38.3 percent (Education Management Information System Center, 2001). In 1999–2000, the gross enrollment rate in higher education was 8.1 percent for females and 11.2 percent for males. This success relates directly to the earlier significant expansion of secondary education and the dramatic closing of the gender gap at that level. (See Table 12.1.)

Among the public universities, there are two national universities: Vietnam National University, Hanoi (formerly the University of Hanoi) and Vietnam National University, Ho Chi Minh City. Thai Nguyen, Hue, and Danang are the three regional universities. Other universities and colleges belong to different ministries or provinces.

Table 12.1   Institutions and Students in Vietnamese Higher Education, 2001

Type of Institution	Number of Institutions	Number of Students
Public universities	74	630,000
Open universities	2	35,621
Public colleges	103	183,963
Private universities	17	82,902
Private colleges	197	936,286

Source: Education Management Information System Center, 2001.

With increased access made possible by private institutions of higher education, Vietnam now has almost one million college students, who are being served by about 32,000 teaching faculty. Of these faculty, only 14.8 percent hold a doctoral degree, 14.9 percent a master's degree, and the large majority, 68.3 percent, only hold a bachelor's degree (Education Management Information System Center, 2001). That the majority of Vietnamese faculty have only a bachelor's degree is an indication of the major quality problems facing Vietnamese universities. There are two ways to address this issue. The first is to expand graduate education in Vietnam itself and the second, to provide more opportunities for Vietnamese to do graduate work overseas. Vietnam is utilizing both strategies, but serious financial constraints limit the second option.

Of the total number of employees in Vietnamese higher education, 65.4 percent are performing teaching functions. Women represent 36.2 percent of the faculty (Tran & Le, 2000, p. 154). Only 1.2 percent are full professors and 4.9 percent are associate professors (Education Management Information System Center, 2001).

Management and Organization

The Ministry of Education and Training implements the state management of education. The major responsibilities of the Ministry of Higher Education include formulating regulations for enrollments; monitoring students inside the country and overseas; establishing regulations for assessing institutions; establishing quality criteria; standardizing the number of teachers; and establishing, amalgamating, or dissolving universities.

Several major features characterize the structure of Vietnam's system of higher education. Higher education must serve multiple constituencies. Under Vietnam's special model of socialism, higher education has been diversified into public universities, semipublic universities, private universities, joint ventures with overseas universities, and international universities.

With respect to the legal framework and basic policies on higher education, the 1992 Constitution of the Socialist Republic of Vietnam states: "Education and training is the nation's foremost priority." The higher education system was institutionalized by a decree in November 1993 establishing the structure of the national education system and qualifications during the renovation period. The Education Law, which was passed in December 1998, sets forth basic stipulations for the higher education system (*Education Law*, 1999).

Financing and Infrastructure

The financing of higher education is a complex process. In the late 1990s, the government gave priority to investing in the development of education. Government support for education increased from 10 percent of the national budget in 1996 to 15 percent of the national budget in 2000, of which 80 to 85 percent went for personnel (including salaries, allowances, and scholarships) and only 15 to 20 percent for educational facilities and infrastructure. Funding for higher education constitutes 18.14 percent of the budget for education (Education Management Information System Center, 2001).

From 1996 to 2000, higher education institutions grew dramatically, and the size of the higher education system increased 20 percent each year. This rate of growth is noticeably greater than in many other countries. Funds allocated for education in Vietnam have risen and now amount to 4.5 percent of GDP. While the Vietnamese government has supported education, it has been constrained by the limited national budget. There are also concerns related to the efficiency with which funds invested in higher education are used (Sauvageau, 1996, p. 11). The emergence of private higher education, discussed later in this chapter, has significantly increased the funds available for the expansion of higher education. The financial resources of universities now include budgeted funds from the state, tuition fees paid by students, contributions of shareholders (for the private universities), revenues from research and service activities, and international grants and loans.

For public universities, the government contributes 47 percent of the budget, with the rest coming from other sources. For private universities, the majority of the budget comes from tuition fees. For one academic year, attending a public university costs about U.S.$100 to U.S.$200 per student and U.S.$200 to U.S.$300 for private universities. This differential is much less than in many other countries. The primary reason is that private universities in Vietnam employ many guest lecturers at low hourly rates.

Students can receive scholarships from institutions or the state. There are two different types of scholarships—one designed for high-achieving students and the other for poor students. Approximately 15 percent of students at public universities receive scholarships from the state. Approximately 3 to 8 percent of students at private universities receive scholarships. The availability of such support depends on the financial capability of the particular private institution.

Another important finance issue is the higher education infrastructure. It is critical for the renovation of higher education to have adequate and modern facilities. However, financial constraints make this difficult in Vietnam—often resulting in inadequate space and teaching environment in classrooms. Moreover, universities lack equipment, especially cutting-edge technology.

The financial management of universities is complicated by the lack of administrative uniformity. Control is exercised by different administrative units. Some universities are managed directly by the Ministry of Education and Training; some are managed by other ministries—such as the Ministry of Health, Ministry of Arts, or Ministry of Transportation and Communications; some colleges are managed by provincial governments; and two national universities have considerable autonomy, while receiving state funds. Private universities are managed by boards of directors but must conform to certain Ministry of Education and Training rules and regulations, and open universities are managed by both the ministry and boards of directors.

The national budget is expected to increase 18 percent by 2005 and 22 percent by 2010. Thus, the financial situation of universities should gradually improve. However, universities need to have greater autonomy in using generated income and in allocating their financial resources in accord with their special needs.

Examinations, Curriculum, and Teaching Methods

Universities use entrance examinations to select students with the highest abilities. During the past ten years, the examination system has undergone several important changes. Initially, there was one standard centralized examination. Subsequently, the system was modified to allow several different entrance examinations at different times, depending on the curriculum of the institution in question. This flexible system reflected the fact that many Vietnamese universities were highly specialized—a legacy of the Soviet period. The examination system has now been reunified into a national system. The examination is used for both public and private universities, and universities no longer have their own local entrance examinations. The Ministry of Education and Training also dictates the number of entering students.

The higher education curriculum in Vietnam has been developed by professors who have been trained in many different countries. As a result, programs and curricula have excessive theory content and often follow external models without appropriate adaptations to the special context of Vietnam. Unfortunately, the curriculum still does not correspond to the practical needs of Vietnamese society. As part of the *doi moi* reform process described above, the old Soviet system of specialization that was introduced to the south after national unification in 1975 has now been rejected throughout Vietnam. The Soviet system clearly was not compatible with the new economy that emphasizes free-market mechanisms.

Teaching methods currently used in Vietnam are often obsolete (Q. T. Lam, 1998). In recent years, the Ministry of Education and Training, as well as many universities, have expressed concern about this problem. Typically, students are not being taught according to innovative progressive pedagogy. In class, students still passively take in the lecturer's knowledge and are required to write down and follow every instruction from the lecturer. Accordingly, students often do not have the opportunity to research documents on their own or engage in practice-based learning. Consequently, it is difficult for universities to produce high-quality students.

The quality of Vietnamese higher education is, thus, still considered to be problematic both with regard to official evaluation and public opinion (*Education in Vietnam*, 1996, pp. 47–48). Currently, there are no fixed standards to evaluate students' educational competence, making accountability difficult.

Faculty and Research

The shortage of university teaching staff in Vietnam will become a serious problem in the near future. The number of lecturers has been increasing but not at a fast enough pace to keep up with the recent explosion in the number of students enrolled in universities. Between the 1993–1994 academic year and 2000, the number of students rose 3.96 times, from 225,274 to 893,754. However, the number of lecturers only rose 1.47 times, from 20,648 to 30,309. The Vietnamese lecturer-to-student ratio of 1:29 is one of the highest in the world (Education Management Information System Center, 2001).

The already high lecturer-to-student ratio is further compounded by the fact that many top professors are approaching retirement age. Among 927 full professors, none are less than 50 years old (Education Management Information System Center, 2001). Reaching the rank of full professor is extremely difficult, given the high research standards and heavy teaching loads. Young lecturers receive extremely low salaries and are attracted to the higher earnings that they can receive in the private sector. Given such low salaries, many faculty teach at multiple institutions to enhance their incomes. For example, at public universities, 10 to 15 percent of faculty are part-time instructors. The emergence of the private higher education sector has dramatically increased the opportunities for such extra teaching jobs, since 70 to 75 percent of the faculty at such institutions are part-time instructors.

Scientific research is one of the main tasks of Vietnamese universities. The goal of scientific research is to strengthen education, broaden the knowledge of lecturers and students, and apply theoretical concepts to practical situations and needs. To ensure the high quality of lecturers, universities should require that lecturers teach and do scientific research. Currently, it is difficult for lecturers to do research because they lack the facilities and laboratories. Also there are no close links among universities, institutes, and companies. With severe constraints on state funds, public universities receive only 3.6 percent of the national budget. In this context, universities are unable to respond to society's needs for scientific and applied research.

Internationalization

The forces of globalization are creating an international educational market. Universities now need to have training programs, facilities, and teaching staff that meet international standards. Higher education is becoming a highly competitive sector throughout the world. Considerable support of higher education has been provided by international donor agencies and governments that sympathize with the challenges that Vietnam faces. In recent years, Hung Yen Pedagogy College; the Agriculture Department of Can Tho University; the polytechnic universities of Hanoi, Danang, and Ho Chi Minh City; the Environment Center of Van Lang University; and the Mechanics Center of Ho Chi Minh City Technical-Pedagogy University have received a total of U.S.$47.5 million in grants and loans from Germany, Japan, Austria, and the Netherlands.

Between 1987 and 2000, 17,000 students were sent abroad—53 percent to Russia and Eastern Europe, 30 percent to Northwestern Europe, 7 percent to Australia and New Zealand, 7 percent to Asia, and 1 percent to the United States and Canada. Foreign study is made possible through Vietnamese state funds and international support. Studying overseas is highly regarded among Vietnamese students and their parents. There are three different types of overseas study: self-funded overseas study, local "overseas study" (programs with an overseas curriculum but primarily in a local setting), and overseas study with financial support.

Some nations such as Australia and Canada attract Vietnamese students by providing access and scholarships, but in other nations such as the United States, scholarships are extremely limited and access is difficult. Students face various financial constraints and obstacles. For example, the Vietnamese currency, the *dong*, is a soft currency, with no value outside Vietnam. Currently, some banks in Vietnam provide services for borrowing hard currency to facilitate overseas study. Teekens (2002) provides a fascinating account of a brilliant Vietnamese female student "Thi" from a remote part of the Mekong Delta who goes on to become a top international graduate student in mathematics in the Netherlands (Altbach, 1998, p. 155; Poras, 2002). Teekens expects "Thi" to return to Vietnam and mentions that Vietnam has not faced a serious brain drain problem. Usually, after some initial difficulties, overseas graduates readjust to life in Vietnam. The strength and richness of Vietnamese culture and traditions along with a strong family system are influential factors. Some problems of brain drain do exist, given the difficult economic conditions in Vietnam, and this is a challenge Vietnam is likely to face in the future, if regulations and mechanisms are not put in place to encourage students to return upon graduation.

Postgraduate Education

Prior to 1990, the most highly educated Vietnamese (with master's or doctoral degrees) were trained with assistance from the former USSR and countries of the Eastern European bloc. Annually, three hundred to five hundred staff were sent to participate in formal programs leading to doctoral degrees at overseas universities. Others were sent abroad to study on a short-term basis. Since 1976, Vietnam had followed the Soviet model of higher education that is based on programs leading to *pho tien si*, which is equivalent to a doctor of philosophy (Ph.D.). Starting in 1991, the government initiated training in Vietnam at the master's degree level. As of 2002, 4,279 Ph.D.s, 38 doctors of science, and nearly 10,000 masters have been trained.

Postgraduate training is divided into two levels—master's and doctoral. Master's level programs are now based on a modern credit system. After a policy of openness was instituted, Vietnamese professors had many opportunities to interact with Western professors and learn about their curricula and graduate programs (L. H. Pham, 2001). As a result, training at the Ph.D. level has been restructured and changed from the prior Soviet model. The new system provides for two options: one more European, with an emphasis on the research for the dissertation, and the other involving considerable coursework, as in the U.S. system. Both are based on the modern credit system.

Since 1986, postgraduate training has increased considerably. In 1995, the number of newly enrolled students was four times higher than it was in 1986 and the number of graduates increased ten-fold during this period. The rapid expansion of postgraduate training at the doctoral level reflects the increasing need for highly qualified professionals. The policy of standardized qualifications for state officials, including the education and training of staff, has expanded the need for master's degree programs.

The weak infrastructure and facilities in higher education mentioned earlier are a serious obstacle to developing high-quality graduate education. The lack of quality libraries and laboratories is a particularly serious problem. The number of volumes in many libraries is limited, and much of the material is old and in the Russian language, which most contemporary graduate students are no longer able to use. There is a dramatic need for increasing the acquisition of current journals and books in English and other major international languages—a necessary step for developing international partnerships to enhance the quality of graduate studies. Also, Internet access to the world of information is limited by inadequate infrastructure and bandwidth problems, curtailing the use of electronic information and knowledge sources.

In addition to postgraduate training at universities and institutes in Vietnam, other countries assist Vietnam by providing about two hundred to three hundred scholarships every year. The countries and agencies awarding scholarships frequently and regularly to Vietnam are Australia, Russia, Canada, the Netherlands, Austria, Japan, the United States, South Korea, China, India, Sweden, Switzerland, Belgium, the Asian Institute of Technology, and the Southeast Asian Ministers of Education Organization. At the same time, self-funded postgraduate candidates overseas have also gradually increased. Interestingly, Vietnam offers a significant number of postgraduate scholarships for Lao nationals to receive training in Vietnam.

To encourage the exchange of scholars, the Vietnamese government signed an agreement in April 2000 that provides funding for sending teachers to other countries to study and do research.

Private Higher Education

Since national funds for education and training are limited, it is not enough simply to develop public universities while failing to meet the country's need for new institutions, particularly in the private sector. In line with the global trend toward greater privatization of higher education (Altbach, 1999), the government has introduced a flexible policy of mobilizing diverse sources of investment for education that has allowed for the emergence of a rapidly growing private higher education sector. Currently there are seventeen private universities and colleges serving 104,255 students—11.4 percent of the total enrollments in higher education (Pham & Fry, 2002; Glewwe & Patrinos, 1999). Such a policy is responsive to both socialist ideals (with its emphasis on equity and social justice) and *doi moi* (and its focus on efficiency and incentive systems). Without a mixed system of public and private institutions of higher education, many needs would go unmet, which would adversely affect both equity and efficiency. Further, integration into the international economy requires openness in terms of privatization. In Japan, the private sector played a major role in the expansion of higher education from 1960 to 1990, during which Japan experienced remarkable growth in economic productivity.

In 1988, Hoang Xuan Sinh, concerned about the backwardness of higher education in Vietnam, chose to experiment with a new form of higher education in Vietnam to provide an education of quality in accord with international standards. The experiment began with the establishment of Thang Long University. Hoang and Sloper (1995) provide a detailed history of this first private university in socialist Vietnam.

Thereafter, a number of other private universities and colleges were established. Among such institutions were Dongdo University, Phuong Dong University, the Management & Business University, Van Lang University (VLU), the University of Technology (HUTECH), Hong Bang University, and the University of Foreign Language and Information (HUFLIT). Some private universities and colleges were also established in the provinces.

In these initial phases, most private universities offered such programs as business administration, foreign languages, and accounting. These programs did not require laboratories or special facilities. Programs in information technology (IT) have now become particularly "fashionable." Given the growing demands of the market for graduates with IT skills, every university and college opened programs in this popular field of study. The curricula of the private universities are highly pragmatic and fail to provide a strong grounding in the liberal arts (Task Force on Higher Education and Society, 2000, pp. 83–90).

Van Lang University is the largest of the new private institutions. In its first year, 4,700 students enrolled. The Ministry of Education and Training later decided to limit enrollment to between 800 and 1,500 students per year for each private university, even though the number of people wanting to matriculate quickly reached 20,000 at Van Lang University. In contrast, at Lac Hong University, the number of students seeking to matriculate is less than the number of students that are needed. Such discrepancies reflect the competition resulting from market mechanisms that have been mandated by the *doi moi* policy.

Teachers at public universities, scientific research institutes, and private companies are invited to lecture at the new private universities. Only 10 to 30 percent of faculty at private universities have full-time positions. Campuses of private institutions are often rented from public institutions, and curricula follow the program guidelines of the Ministry of Education and Training. Some universities and colleges were provided with land or campuses by local authorities.

The social policy of the government to diversify higher education has been a most timely approach. The opening of private universities has helped the government to provide access to more than 104,255 students out of a total of 918,228 students nationwide. As mentioned, the number of private students is 11.4 percent of the total number of students, and over 20 percent of the total number of students in the southern region of Vietnam attend private institutions. Funds for all the activities of private universities are from nongovernmental sources. This is a remarkable achievement that demonstrates the timely and judicious policy of the Vietnamese government.

The principal source of income for private universities is tuition fees, which now range from U.S.$200 to U.S. $300 per year. In the initial phase of privatization, the private sector provided reasonably good equipment, facilities, and infrastructure. After only five years of operation, some universities stopped renting classrooms and purchased and renovated their own buildings. With international assistance such universities have also added important new laboratories to facilitate study in fields such as electronics and information technology.

While some people still have a negative impression about the quality of students entering private universities, in the last several years this point of view has started to change. Competition over gaining admission to the better-quality private universities, such as Van Lang, has increased significantly. The issue of quality of private universities (as well as of public ones) persists, however, as a major concern in Vietnam (L. H. Pham, 2000).

One approach to assessing quality is to look at the job success of graduates of these new private institutions. Among the private universities, only a few universities have graduated students—such as Van Lang University, HUTECH, and HUFLIT. At Van Lang University, approximately 75 percent of students graduating have found jobs. Given the serious unemployment and underemployment problems in Vietnam, this is not a small accomplishment. A number of graduates of Van Lang University's Faculty of Tourism have found excellent jobs in the rapidly growing tourist sector of the Vietnamese economy.

Since the Ministry of Education and Training regulates and approves private universities in Vietnam, their degrees are recognized ones. However, as yet no formal accreditation system has been put in place. Also, in terms of public image and social charter, degrees from highly selective elite public universities such as Vietnam National University, Hanoi; Vietnam National University, Ho Chi Minh City; Hanoi Polytechnic University; and the National Economics University of Vietnam have greater social prestige and recognition. For capable students who cannot gain acceptance at one of the elite public universities and who may be seeking a more dynamic, modern curriculum, private universities offer a new and valuable alternative. The future prestige of degrees from approved private universities will depend largely on the quality of their teaching facilities and the success of their graduates.

Some private universities have established innovative programs in fields such as tourism studies (at Van Lang University), nutrition and fashion (HUTECH), Vietnamcology (Hong Bang), and labor protection (Ton Duc Thang). These are subjects that have never before been offered at public universities.

With respect to the civic engagement of private universities, many have contributed funds for the Heroine Vietnamese Mother organization, donations of blood, and scholarships. Most students participate in movements, such as the Youth Union, and related campaigns, such as "Culture Light" and "Green Summer." During vacation, many students go to the countryside in remote areas to teach reading to Vietnamese and to provide new knowledge to farmers and workers. This reflects the socialist ideal that asserts that universities should be established to serve the people. In this sense Vietnam may differ from many other developing nations in which private universities demonstrate little sense of social responsibility (Altbach, 1999, p. 11).

The private university system in Vietnam is a recent development, and thus, both the government and university administrations are still learning from their experiences in this new arena. In recent years, the government and the Ministry of Education and Training have issued many guidelines for private university operations under the regulations of the law on private universities. This is the first basic law to help private universities function easily and effectively. However, this basic statute is only general legislation and does not deal with many specific situations.

In general, the majority of people are in agreement that educational organizations should be nonprofit. However, beginning with the name itself, private or people-founded university, the new form of higher education has led to intense debates. The owners of the universities are not clearly defined. According to a governmental regulation, a private university's assets belong to capital contributors, lecturers, and staff. Because investments are considered charity, capital contributors cannot expect financial returns from their investments, which does not encourage such activity.

There are a number of important faculty issues at private universities. Currently, at private universities, lecturers can be divided into two main groups. Most lecturers in the first group are recruited from public universities. Due to the "high" compensation (VND 50,000–80,000 [U.S.$3.25–U.S.$5.19] per period taught), private universities are able to attract many good lecturers from state universities and some lecturers from research institutions or managers of businesses. The reliance on professors from public universities has both positive and adverse effects. The positive effects are enhanced remuneration for underpaid academics and access to some outstanding lecturers. The adverse effect is that it makes it difficult for such lecturers to engage in research work because of heavy teaching commitments.

The remaining group of lecturers consists of the permanent staff of the university and they are relatively few in number. At Hung Vuong University they represent only 17 percent of the lecturers, while they represent 20 percent at the Technology University and 25 percent at Van Lang University. These lecturers are young and often have just graduated from the university (most with a master's degree). The rest tend to be engineers or outstanding bachelor's degree recipients of public universities. According to the Ministry of Education and Training requirement, 20 percent of lecturers should be university staff in the first year and 50 percent in the next five years.

Another important issue is research and the impact and role of private universities. Private universities, which are newly established, do not receive any government subsidies. Many universities have established science research funds for lecturers and students. Van Lang University, for example, sets aside 3 percent of its budget for such purposes; the Technology Private University allocates 2 percent of its budget.

Although the private university system is a relatively new phenomenon in Vietnam, it has already contributed significantly to educational and economic development. The system has faced many complex and difficult challenges. Already, important improvements have been made based on the efforts of the universities and the macropolicies of the state.

Relying only on state funds for the expansion of higher education places an excessive burden on the public sector. Thus, the decision of the government of Vietnam to diversify higher education by allowing for a private parallel system was most timely. Having a dual system enhances both efficiency and equity. From an efficiency perspective, the private universities compete among themselves and with public universities to offer quality education to students. The presence of private universities places pressure on public institutions to innovate and improve their own quality. Such a system also enhances equity because private universities in Vietnam operate according to a cost-recovery model. Students are basically paying user fees. Since many students in higher education are from urban areas and of higher socioeconomic status, they should be paying for their education because private returns from higher education in Vietnam tend to be high (Moock, Patrinos, & Venkataraman, 1998; World Bank, 1997, p. 135). Universities such as Van Lang then provide scholarships to poorer students. Highly subsidized public universities lack such equity because, in reality, farmers and workers are helping to subsidize the study of elites in those institutions.

Thus, the policy of the socialist government of Vietnam to foster a mixed system of higher education appears to be wise and sound. Vietnam's long-term economic future depends largely on the quality of its human resources. The country's private universities have an important opportunity to strengthen Vietnam's human resources development. Under the new system of *doi moi* there is no longer a single model for Vietnamese universities such as the one that existed during the period of significant Soviet influence (1945–1986). However, growing U.S and Western influence can be seen in the move toward the adoption of a credit system and the reform of pedagogy to emphasize more student-centered learning approaches. However, the orientation varies significantly from institution to institution, largely dependent on the nature of the institution's leadership and leading faculty members and their prior training and current external relations and international partners.

The Emergence of Distance Learning

In 1993, several distance-learning centers were established at universities such as Hue University, Hanoi Pedagogical University, and Hanoi and Ho Chi Minh City Open Universities. Books, television, video, and radio are the main methods and tools of learning. Hanoi Open University has invested VND 20 billion (U.S.$1.3 million). Currently, over 42,000 students are using distance learning to gain access to higher education. This system has been of major benefit to students residing in remote or mountainous regions.

Despite such successes, it is important to note that poor facilities are the main problems with regard to distance learning. The cost of Internet service is extremely high, and the number of computers is limited. Technology networks are weak, and thus distance learning is still not an attractive option in Vietnam. Vietnam has received some financial support from international organizations and countries—such as Australia, Singapore, and the United States—to help it develop distance learning.

During the next five years, Vietnam is planning to expand its system of higher education with ten additional universities to serve approximately a hundred thousand students. U.S.$25 million will be invested in these facilities and related staff development. The development of Vietnam's national information technology capability in accord with global trends will enhance opportunities for distance learning in Vietnam. Such investments are critical for Vietnam to compete in the new knowledge-based economy and to help transcend the digital divide.

TRENDS AND CHALLENGES

In thinking about the future of Vietnamese universities and system of higher education, it is important to recognize important historical, cultural, and political legacies from the past that may help us to understand both the current problems and future potential of Vietnamese higher education. The first and critically important legacy is that of Chinese civilization and the influence of great philosophical traditions such as Confucianism, Buddhism, and Taoism. For an entire millenium, Vietnam was under the imperial rule of China with its Confucian traditions. There are many elements in Confucianism that create a highly favorable ethos surrounding teachers and learning. In fact, it is hard to think of another country in which teachers are more respected than in Vietnam. Also, in the Confucian tradition, what is important is not a person's native intelligence but how hard an individual has worked to realize his or her intellectual potential. Both these ideals resonate well with motivation and commitment to learning integral to the development of quality higher education.

A second important legacy is Vietnam's long history of battling against natural disasters such as floods and typhoons and struggling against external invaders. Illustrative of the ingenuity of the Vietnamese in their struggle against nature are the huge dykes that protect Hanoi from the potential flooding of the Red River. During the second millennium the Vietnamese repelled the powerful Mongols and defeated attempts by the Sung, Ming, and Manchu emperors of China to restore their control over Vietnam. Later they were successful in their wars of liberation and unification against the French and then the United States. In nearly all these conflicts, the Vietnamese were clearly at a great disadvantage, facing much more powerful and "advanced" foes. In defeating these external enemies, the Vietnamese were noted for their remarkable ingenuity and innovative approaches to warfare. Such traits also seem highly germane for the development of the innovative R&D associated with effective higher education.

A third legacy is that of the French colonial period, lasting for almost a century from 1859 to 1954. The influence and impact of this legacy is multifaceted and complex. Despite the repressive nature of the French colonial regime, it did plant the seeds for a modern system of higher education and a research tradition. Most important and ironic, the French imperial and colonial presence with its dramatic inequalities and racism raised Vietnamese political consciousness and commitment to the Western ideals of both Marxism and the French revolution (McConnell, 1989).

A fourth major influence was that of the Soviet Union and its socialist state-planned system. The major negative aspects in education of the Soviet legacy were narrow overspecialization and ideologically oriented social sciences lacking in modern empirical rigor and methods. Thus, many observers superficially dismiss the Soviet influence as only negative, failing to realize that Russian approaches to science, mathematics, medicine, and educational and linguistic pedagogy had some impressive positive elements.

A fifth legacy relates to Vietnam's special demographic niche resulting from a historically high people-to-land ratio, necessitating the country's historical expansion to the south. In this sense, Vietnam and Japan share an important commonality. Given such an ecological niche, it is imperative to be creative and innovative in the use of limited land space.

The most recent legacy is the introduction of *doi moi* in 1986 and the transformation of the Vietnamese economy from a state-planned system to one of free-market mechanisms. During the past fifteen years, there has been a dramatic expansion of higher education in Vietnam to respond to the needs of the new free-market economy. Vietnam recognizes the dangers and limitations of having an economy overdependent on the availability of abundant supplies of cheap low-skilled labor. Also, Vietnam is keenly aware of the new knowledge-based economy and its growing influence in the twenty-first century. Thus, Vietnam has plans to continue to expand its system of higher education in targeted areas. By 2020, the goal is to have a modern higher education system in place consistent with a knowledge-based economy. By that year, the ratio of students in higher education per 10,000 population should be 300 (compared to the current rate of 117), representing a roughly 3-fold expansion in the number of students that Vietnam's system of higher education serves. By 2010, the target is to have 1.8 million undergraduate students, 38,000 graduate students, and 15,000 Ph.D. students, with the percentage of the labor force holding an undergraduate degree reaching 4 percent. The basic goal is to have the system expand at a rate of 5 percent per year.

The past ten years have seen the emergence of a major private system of higher education in Vietnam and increasing international links and partnerships with institutions of higher education overseas. These trends will certainly continue and facilitate the goal of continuing to expand the system of higher education in Vietnam. Implementing such an expansion will require both diversifying and intensifying financial support for higher education. Other nations with strong Confucian backgrounds such as Taiwan, South Korea, and Japan have demonstrated commitments to support higher education in recent decades. Thus, it seems reasonable to assume that Vietnam will follow a similar pattern.

Many challenges are associated with such a dramatic expansion in higher education. The most critical is the issue of assuring and enhancing quality, defined broadly. It is important to develop and maintain high academic standards, consistent with international norms. Improving the quality of higher education is a complex and difficult challenge (Austin & Chapman, 2002, p. 257). There are also concerns, for example, that in the era of the new free-market economy, the moral character and social responsibility of students may be adversely affected. Another major challenge relates to the universities' capacity to produce R&D of value and use to the private sector.

Another major policy challenge in higher education relates to the future priority given to equity and equality as Vietnam's economy becomes both more market-oriented and prosperous. There has been a major move away from the former system under which all students received scholarships, which has been replaced largely by a new tuition system. Also, with dramatic economic growth in major urban areas such as Ho Chi Minh City and Hanoi, the children of the well-to-do will certainly have the advantage of better access to quality primary and secondary schooling. Reflective of the socialist legacy and its emphasis on equity, funding for a program of support for education in mountainous areas and economically disadvantaged areas has increased from 16 billion dong (U.S.$1.03 million) a year to over 100 billion dong (U.S.$6.43 million) a year after repeated increases (M. H. Pham, 1998, p. 175). The persistence of socialism in Vietnam may help to soften some of the inequalities associated with a modern free-market economic system.

Another key challenge relates to the bureaucratic and legal systems influenced by a legacy of French and Soviet influences. Such bureaucratic and legal rigidities affect the system's flexibility and ability to educate a "new creative class" and allow Vietnamese students to realize their creative potential. Universities critically need both more autonomy and accountability in six major areas: governance, staffing, student recruitment, curricula, assessment, and evaluation.

The balance between the universities' preparation of graduates and labor market needs is another challenging area. Currently there is the anomaly of unemployed university graduates, while important labor market needs are going unmet.

Teekens (2002) notes that Vietnam has not had a brain drain problem. While this is certainly true for those Vietnamese who went abroad for training in places such as the USSR and Eastern European countries, the situation now has changed dramatically, with overseas study now primarily in Western countries such as Australia, France, Canada, and the United States. Another related challenge is to find ways to attract highly educated overseas Vietnamese to return to their homeland to contribute to its development (*Vietnam 2001–2002*, 2002, pp. 45–46). This could also enhance Vietnam's capacity in the area of science and technology.

In February 2003 several high-level administrators of both public and private universities were interviewed about the future of Vietnamese higher education. They emphasized several key issues. First, the quality of higher education is highly dependent on the quality of the graduates of the secondary school system. Thus, reforms at that level are extremely important. Second, the reform of pedagogy toward more student-centered learning at universities is seriously impeded by the lack of adequate library and computer resources. Third, there are inadequate mechanisms to facilitate the sharing of key learning resources such as computer laboratories. This is reflective of general problems of a lack of administrative coordination and articulation among various departments and institutions of higher education. Fourth, it is critically important to develop additional sources of funding for higher education such as seeking budgets from local authorities and providing services (e.g., special English-language courses) that can become profit centers. Fifth, there is the important issue of how Vietnam can move successfully toward the massification of higher education, given existing financial and infrastructure constraints.

CONCLUSION

Vietnam is a country with enormous potential. Its strategic Pacific location in close proximity to three of the world's four largest countries and its own large and growing population provide the country with many special advantages. Vietnam is already one of the world's leading exporters of rice, providing much-needed foreign exchange for the development of the country and its human resources. The country has much as yet unrealized industrial and tourism potential, other valuable sources of future foreign exchange. Vietnam ranked ninth in the world as a travel destination in 2003. The rapidly growing industry of tourism also provides jobs for new university graduates, especially those with good international language skills.

Vietnam was the first country in Southeast Asia to have a university, and it has a long historical legacy and heritage in education. It has also had a long history of relations with foreign countries—China, France, Russia, Eastern Europe, and now Western countries—which has significantly influenced the evolution and shape of Vietnamese higher education. Despite such important outside influences, Vietnam has a determined will to build its own *indigenous system* of higher education, reflective of its history of successful anticolonial resistance against many external invaders. In building its own system, Vietnam has the unusual opportunity to be highly eclectic in drawing upon the best from other diverse systems with which its highly educated citizens are familiar.

The major mission of Vietnam's rapidly expanding indigenous system of higher education is to produce knowledge workers capable of demonstrating creativity, adapting to rapidly changing technologies and labor markets, dealing effectively with peoples of diverse cultures, and at the same time preserving the essential values of the distinctive Vietnamese culture. Certainly the continued development of universities in Vietnam is central to its becoming a major player on the world scene, economically, culturally, and intellectually.

ACKNOWLEDGMENT
We appreciate the research assistance of Laurie Brumm and Hongyi Lan in preparing this chapter.

REFERENCES
Altbach, P. G. (1998). *Comparative higher education: Knowledge, the university, and development.* Greenwich, CT: Ablex.

Altbach, P. G. (Ed.). (1999). *Private Prometheus: Private higher education and development in the 21st century.* Westport, CT: Greenwood.

Altbach, P. G. (2002). Twisted roots: The Western impact on Asian higher education. In P. G. Altbach & V. Selvaratnam (Eds.), *From dependence to autonomy: The development of Asian universities* (pp. 1–21). Newton, MA: Center for International Higher Education, Boston College.

Boothroyd, P., & Pham, X. N. (2000). *Socioeconomic renovation in Viet Nam: The origin, evolution, and impact of doi moi.* Ottawa: International Development Research Centre.

Austin, A., & Chapman, D. (2002). Balancing pressures: Forming partnerships. In D. Chapman & A. Austin (Eds.), *Higher education in the developing world: Changing contexts and institutional responses* (pp. 253–261). Westport, CT: Greenwood.

Do, P. (1998). *Vietnam-image of the community of 54 ethnic groups.* Hanoi, Vietnam: Ethnic Cultures Publishing House.

Duiker, W. J. (2000). *Ho Chi Minh: A life.* New York: Hyperion.

Duong, D. N. (1978). "Education in Vietnam under the French domination." Unpublished Ph.D. diss., Southern Illinois University at Carbondale.

Education in Viet Nam: Trends and differentials. (1996). Hanoi, Vietnam: Statistical Publishing House.

The Education Law of the Socialist Republic of Vietnam (1999). Hanoi, Vietnam: National Assembly.

Education Management Information System Center (2001). *Education statistics.* Ministry of Education and Training.

Glewwe, P. W., & Patrinos, H. (1999). The role of the private sector in education in Vietnam: Evidence from the Vietnam living standards survey. *World Development, 27*(5), 887–902.

Green, C. B. (1973, June 15). *Some current observations, general information and data on higher education in Vietnam.* Saigon, Vietnam: USAID.

Grey, A. (1982). *Saigon: An epic novel of Vietnam.* London: Pan.

Gubry, P. (2000). *Population et développement au Viêt-nam.* Paris: Karthala/CEPED.

Gubry, P. (2001). The population of Vietnam: Its evolution and related issues. Retrieved October 15, 2002, from www.ceped.ined.fr/cepedweb/activite/publi/chro9an. pdf.

Hoang, X. S., & Sloper, D. (1995). An entrepreneurial development: Thang Long University. In D. Sloper & T. C. Le (Eds.), *Higher education in Vietnam: Change and response* (pp. 200–210). Singapore: Institute of Southeast Asian Studies.

Lam, Q. T. (1998). Vietnamese higher education in the "doi moi" period. In *Higher education in transition economies in Asia: Proceedings of the first workshop on strategies and policies in higher education reform in transition economies in Asia* (pp. 88–104). Bangkok, Thailand: UNESCO.

Lam, T. B. (1967). *Patterns of Vietnamese response to foreign intervention, 1858–1900.* New Haven, CT: Southeast Asian Studies, Yale University.

McConnell, S. (1989). *Leftward journey: The education of Vietnamese students in France, 1919–1939.* New Brunswick, NJ: Transaction.

Moock, P. R., Patrinos, H. A., & Venkataraman, M. (1998). *Education and earnings in a transition economy (Vietnam).* Working Papers—Education, No. 5. Washington, DC: World Bank.

Nguyen, D. H. (1948). *Higher education in Viet-Nam from the early French conquest to the Japanese occupation.* New York: School of Education, New York University.

Nguyen Q. T. (1993). *Khoa cu va giao duc Vietnam* (Examinations and education in Vietnam). Hanoi, Vietnam: Van Hoa-Thong Tin.

Nguyen, V. A., & Phan, T. M. (2000, August). Current status of financial policy for education in a new era. *Phat Trien Giao Duc*, 11–12.

Nguyen, V. X. (1995). *Phong trao Duy Tan* (The Duy Tan reform movement). Danang, Vietnam: Danang Publishing House.

Pham, L. H. (2000, December 28). Nang cao chat luong cho cac truong dai hoc dan lap (Increasing the quality of private universities). *Phat Trien Giao Duc*, 6, 28.

Pham, L. H. (2001, April). Kinh nghiem trong day va hoc cua truong Dai Hoc Oregon (Learning and teaching approaches at the University of Oregon). *Sai Gon Giai Phong*, 88, 32.

Pham, M. H. (1998). *Vietnam's education: The current position and future prospects.* Hanoi, Vietnam: The Gio Publishers.

Pham, L. H., & Fry, G. (2002). The emergence of private higher education in Vietnam: Challenges and opportunities. *Educational Research for Policy and Practice 1*, 127–141.

Phan, D. T., & Truong, T. H. (1996). *Cai Cach Ho Quy Ly* (The reform of Ho Quy Ly). Hanoi, Vietnam: Chinh Tri Quoc Publishing House.

Poras, M. (2002). *Mai's America* [Video]. New York: Women Make Movies.

Ronnas, P., & Ramamurthy, B. (Eds.). (2001). *Entrepreneurship in Vietnam: Transformation and dynamics.* Copenhagen: Nordic Institute of Asian Studies.

Sauvageau, P. P. (1996). *Higher education for development: A history of modern higher education in the Socialist Republic of Vietnam.* Unpublished doctoral dissertation, Boston University.

Schramm-Evans, Z. (1996). *A phoenix rising: Impressions of Vietnam.* London: Pandora.

Sinlarat, P. (1997). *Raajngaan kaanpahtiruup kaansygsaa khong prathet Vietnam* (Report on educational reform in Vietnam). Bangkok, Thailand: Office of the National Education Commission.

Sloper, D., & Le, T. C. (1995). *Higher education in Vietnam: Change and response.* Singapore: Institute of Southeast Asian Studies.

Task Force on Higher Education and Society. (2000). The importance of general education. In *Higher education in developing countries: Peril and promise* (pp. 83–90). Washington, DC: World Bank.

Teekens, H. (2002). Thi's story: Growing up in the Mekong Delta and studying abroad: A reflection on international education and development cooperation. In W. Grünzweig & N. Rinehart (Eds.), *Rockin' in Red Square: Critical approaches to international education in the age of cyberculture* (pp. 147–161). Münster, Germany: LIT Verlag.

Tran, Q. T. (2000). *Doi moi giao duc dai hoc* (The reform of higher education). Hanoi, Vietnam: Gioi Moi Publishing House.

Tran, T. V. A., & Le, N. H. (2000). *Women and doi moi.* Hanoi, Vietnam: Woman Publishing House.

Vietnam 2001–2002. (2002). Hanoi, Vietnam: Gioi Publishers.

World Bank. (1997). *Vietnam: Education financing.* Washington, DC: Author.

13

Cambodian Higher Education

Mixed Visions

Pit Chamnan & David Ford

Modern higher education in Cambodia is a relatively recent development and has only existed for about the span of one lifetime, which in
Cambodia is less than about fifty-five years. During that time Cambodia
has been subject to almost every major political ideology: colonialism,
constitutional monarchy, republicanism, communism, socialism, and, finally, the beginnings of democracy. The speed and magnitude of these
changes have dramatically affected all aspects of life in this country.

The main proposition in this chapter is that higher education in Cambodia today is the product of the vision of those in power and that this
vision is still unclear, having undergone radical changes. It will be shown
that this lack of clarity is a result of many factors—including Cambodia's
extraordinarily traumatic recent history, long-standing cultural factors,
current social problems, and various international influences.

Higher education in Cambodia is in a period of turmoil and change.
The history of the sector and the factors pushing it to change are complex. In the past fifty years there have been rapid and radical changes in
political leadership that included a period when the entire education system was destroyed. More recently, international influences and the unregulated growth of the private sector are having increasing effects. Complicating this picture, as in other developing countries in the region, are
tensions between long-held cultural traditions and the requirements of
modernity.

In this chapter, the term *higher education* means formal, postsecondary,
advanced, and "higher" learning skills. We have not, therefore, included

a consideration of technical or vocational education.

Briefly, the higher education sector in Cambodia is comprised of nine public higher education institutions including two semiautonomous public administrative institutions (the Royal University of Agriculture and the University of Medical Sciences), eighteen recognized private higher education institutions, and various other unrecognized higher education institutions of variable quality. Almost all are situated in the capital city, Phnom Penh. The recognized institutions serve an estimated 31,000 students (MoEYS, 2002f), of whom about 75 percent pay fees. However the gross enrollment rate in tertiary education is only 1.2 percent, compared to an average of 20.7 percent in Association of South-East Asian Nations (ASEAN) countries and 5.1 percent in low-income countries worldwide. There is already a strong demand for higher education, and the number of students graduating from secondary school is predicted to quadruple within ten years. The existing system of higher education is clearly too small to meet the development needs of the country (Ahrens & Kemmerer, 2002).

The government has begun the enormous task of administrative decentralization (deconcentration) to transform the largely dysfunctional, highly centralized system of education to a more policy-driven sectorwide system of management that is nothing less than a paradigm shift. The main issues for higher education at present—as discussed in a massive review of the Education Sector Support Program (ESSP) conducted by the Ministry of Education, Youth, and Sport (MoEYS)—were the lack of a legal framework, underfunding, inequitable access, curricula lacking relevance, an absence of research, and the need for quality assurance mechanisms. The main policy direction as stated in the ESSP is toward increasing private-sector participation, with the justification that scarce government funds must be reserved for basic education (MoEYS, 2002b, p. 32). Those who benefit from tertiary education (i.e., institutions, commercial interests, and individuals) are expected to shoulder much of the financial burden. Long-term objectives also include increasing participation of the private sector in the governance, planning, and management of public higher education institutions; the promotion of new forms of higher education, such as distance learning; and increased transparency and accountability. A medium-term objective is to provide operational budgets to higher education institutions through the Priority Action Program (PAP) to reduce costs that are now demanded of students so that access for poor students may be more equitable. A program of scholarships targeted at the very poor is also proposed. The ESSP review also noted that "a substantial proportion of the initial capacity building activities have been achieved" (MoEYS, 2002f, p. 12) as well as "substantially increased budget allocation and education policies that are more pro-poor" (MoEYS, 2002d, pp. 14, 19). Progress on decentralization of budget management was described as "tremendous."

Currently, the Cambodian government is considering a draft legislative framework for higher education that would address many of the system's current weaknesses. It would establish an accreditation process, categories of academic institutions, a system of credit transfer, minimum course requirements, and academic organizational structures, as well as clarifying institutional financing and the role of private higher education institutions. The draft law includes the formation of an Accreditation Committee of Cambodia (ACC) and, if enacted, would enable the release of a World Bank loan to finance staff and facilities upgrading.

While issues are being discussed and problems are being solved "step by step," the starting point for development is extremely low. Due mainly to the loss of almost an entire generation of educated people during the 1970s, even as late as 1995 "the concepts of planning and management and their application to education [were] unknown to the wide majority of [MoEYS] administrators" (Altner, 1999, p. 176). Most of Cambodia's regional neighbors dealt with these issues many years ago, so it is not surprising that Cambodian higher education lags behind in many fields. But this handicap also provides Cambodia with the opportunity of learning from the past experience of other countries.

HISTORICAL PERSPECTIVES

Cambodia's history has shaped the characteristics of the present system of higher education. From ancient times through successive regimes, higher education has performed many different roles according to the vision of those in power.

Precolonial Cambodia

Unfortunately, little evidence remains from this time. Documents written on skin and palm leaves have not survived. There were clearly scholars literate in Sanskrit, astronomers competent enough to record astronomical data, and architects and engineers with advanced skills capable of creating and constructing the magnificent temples of Angkor and irrigation works still evident today. About the only hard evidence is that at least one monastery—Preah Khan, dedicated in the twelfth century during the reign of Jayavaraman VII—had more than a thousand teachers and many more students and was probably "a kind of university" (Jacques & Freeman, 1997, p. 128). But who taught and learned and why, how, and what they learned is largely unknown (Ayres, 1997, p. 37). A Chinese envoy, Zhou Da-Guan, who visited Angkor in the thirteenth century, well after the highest point of Angkorean civilization had passed, provides one of the few descriptions of the time. Referring to the Brahmans who were often high officials, he stated, "I do not know what models they follow, and they have nothing which one could call a school or a place of teaching. It is difficult to know what books they read" (Chandler, 1998, p. 72). The best we can say, then, is that it is possible that some form of higher education existed during the Angkor period.

In the precolonial period after the decline of the Angkorean civilization, there does not seem to have been anything that meets the definition of higher education in the modern sense. Any form of higher education that may have existed during the Angkor period does not seem to have persisted afterward and so has not bequeathed a heritage of higher learning to the present. Traditional education in the post–Angkor period was centered in the village *wat*, or pagoda, and usually occurred during the time when a boy became a novice. It mostly consisted of learning to read and recite religious texts (*satras*), didactic poems (*chbab*), folk tales (*gatiloke*), and epic stories like the *Reamkae*, written on palm leaves, and to develop relevant vocational skills like carpentry. Why higher education did not develop before the mid-twentieth century or at least continue after its possible beginnings in Angkorean times is beyond the scope of this chapter, but it would be an interesting question on which to speculate.

The Colonial Period

In modern times, the first institution to offer higher education in Cambodia was the National Institute of Law, Politics, and Economic Sciences, which was inaugurated in 1947, in the last few years of almost ninety years of French colonial rule. Previously, higher education had only been available to a small elite that studied at French universities in France. By the time of independence in 1953, perhaps only a few hundred Cambodian university students had studied in France (Chandler, 1998, p. 183). Clearly, providing opportunities for higher education to Cambodians was not a priority in the *mission civilisatrice* of the French authorities, who were more concerned with training *functionaires* for the civil service. The Cambodian system of education at the time of independence, based on the French model, was centralized, rigid, and competitive—designed with progression to its higher levels as its goal rather than the provision of relevant education that might have contributed to the economic and social needs of Cambodia. According to one (French) UNESCO adviser, who praised the French model of education: "Cambodia could indeed be regarded as an example [to other developing nations]" (Bilodeau, Pathammavong, & Hong, 1954). But in the opinion of another writer, the Cambodian education system was faced with too many students in crowded schools, taught by too few teachers who were inadequately prepared for their task. They used teaching approaches and methods which were copied from schools in France and which were intended to impart knowledge necessary for administrative assistants to the French colonial civil service (Blaise, 1964, p. 34).

The Postcolonial Period, 1950s and 1960s

Cambodia's independence in 1953 should be seen as part of the wider decolonization in Asia that commenced with the withdrawal of the Japanese presence in Indonesia, Korea, and Taiwan after the Second World War. Independence in India and Pakistan followed in 1947 and was achieved shortly afterward by Burma, Ceylon, the Philippines, and then Cambodia, Laos, and Vietnam. Cambodia's postcolonial leader, Prince Norodom Sihanouk, like other leaders of newly independent nations, was faced with the challenge of expanding and nationalizing the education system as a key factor in the modernization process. It was a time of unprecedented expansion of education systems globally (Coombs, 1969, p. 3), supported by both modernization theory, which assumed that nations developed along a linear progression toward "modern" states like those of North America and Western Europe, and by human capital theory, which suggested that education was an investment in human capital and the principal source of economic growth—"the ultimate basis for the wealth of nations" (Harbison, 1973, p. 3).

Higher education was very much a part of Sihanouk's vision of modernity. Impressed by universities overseas but discounting all expert advice at the time, which recommended sustainable expansion in line with financial capacity, "there is little doubt that foremost in Sihanouk's mind when he announced his policy of tertiary expansion was Cambodia's international prestige" (Ayres, 1997, p. 93). The first university in Cambodia was thus founded in 1960 as the Khmer Royal University (now the Royal University of Phnom Penh) during a period of rapid expansion of tertiary education that showed more concern for quantity than for quality. In 1965 alone, six new higher education institutions were created: the Royal Technical University, the Royal University of Fine Arts, the Royal University of Kompong Cham, the Royal University of Takeo-Kampot, the Royal University of Agricultural Science, and the People's University (MoEYS, 1971). The University of Takeo-Kampot even had a Faculty of Oceanography, despite being more than 50 kilometers from the sea, and a Faculty of Medicine, complete with a hospital, despite having no doctors. "By 1966, 7,360 students were enrolled in Cambodian tertiary institutions" (Ayres, 1997, p. 93). The predictable consequence of this quantitative expansion in the absence of sufficient resources was a decline in quality.

Even though four decades have passed since the demise of the education system created by the French and then expanded by Sihanouk, much of the educational ideology from that time has remained in the minds of present-day administrators who belong to the generation that received its education during the 1960s. On the personal recollection of one of the authors of this chapter, who studied at the time, most of the lecturers were French; they lectured in French; and the degrees were recognized in France. The exams were very difficult and few students passed. The preference of some senior administrators for highly selective exams can still be seen today. In the 2002 grade 12 exam for example, out of 47,122 students only 3 were awarded an A, 28 a B, 435 a C, 4,004 a D, 14,198 an E, and the rest failed (CANEP, 2002). The passing grade was set before the exam and modified slightly afterward but was not standardized for the difficulty of the exam, adjusted for subject differences, or related to available places at tertiary institutions. Attempts to reform the examination system have met with prolonged resistance even though "the French idea of maximising the education of a tiny elite is going out of fashion even in France," according to the coordinator of the Cambodia-Australia National Examinations Project (Quirky Exam Results, 2002, p. 17).

The Lon Nol and Pol Pot Regimes, 1970–1979

By the late 1960s, economic stagnation as a result of economic mismanagement and, especially, the cancellation of American aid in 1963 produced a political crisis that led to a coup d'état by Lon Nol in 1970 and the establishment of the Khmer Republic. For the next five years, the nation was effectively at war. Lon Nol's regime adopted the rhetoric of democracy, whereas the opposition was led by Cambodia's Communists. The war effectively prevented democratic reforms in education that might have begun to address the issues of relevance and decentralization. It was a period of "despondency, rivalry, factionalism, corruption, and . . . for those who supported the Khmer Republic one of defeat" (Ayres, 1997, p. 114). The education system suffered the effects of both human and material destruction, but this was merely a foretaste of the devastation to follow.

During the communist regime of Democratic Kampuchea, from 1975 to 1979 (usually referred to as the Pol Pot time), the entire education system was abolished. Because Cambodia's Westernized formal education system was associated with imperialism and did not form part of the radical agrarian vision of the Khmer Rouge leaders, it was rejected in favor of a more nationalistic vision of self-mastery and self-reliance, in which learning was to cultivate "good political consciousness and followed a Chinese model of half study and half work for material production" (Ayres, 1997, p. 160). Educational buildings, equipment, laboratories, libraries, and other teaching materials and facilities were either abandoned, put to other uses, or destroyed. Furthermore, large numbers of qualified teachers, lecturers, instructors, and intellectuals died or fled overseas. It is estimated that 75 percent of tertiary teachers and 96 percent of university students were killed by the Khmer Rouge (Ministry of Education, 1984, p. 1). In 1979 about three hundred people with postsecondary education remained in Cambodia; many of them later fled the country.

The impact of this devastation for today's institutions of higher education cannot be overstated, even after more than twenty years. An enormous reservoir of knowledge and experience was destroyed. Moreover, by killing the intellectuals in whom traditional educational values resided, the culture of education was also destroyed. The majority of current university lecturers passed through the shattered and dysfunctional remains of the education system after the Khmer Rouge era. Most of them lost family members. Some experienced torture and witnessed violent killings. They can in no way be considered as just another group of ordinary teachers.

Many of those in power now are survivors of thirty years of social disorder and of a very unnatural selection process. The communist Khmer Rouge regime was merely the start of this process. The bourgeoisie, the educated, and the old were particular targets of the Khmer Rouge, who chose as their soldiers those most easily manipulated and least likely to question authority: the uneducated, the young, and the illiterate. The strategies used by those who survived have also contributed to the selection process. One successful survival strategy was to become "a person who knew nothing, heard nothing and said nothing, but worked like a slave" (Prum Sokha 2002). A former primary school director "acted like a crazy man. If they asked me about rice paddies, I told them about coconuts" (Asian Development Bank, 1996, p. 3). A law student escaped to a province where he was not known: "It was very important to keep quiet. I could not even tell my girlfriend" (Asian Development Bank, 1996, p. 3). Many survivors now have an understandable reluctance to share their experiences or to collaborate, and their attitude to political leadership is not surprisingly a mixture of distrust and fear. They are also often extremely resourceful and determined, consistent with having survived one of history's most brutal regimes.

The task of reconstructing the education system that faced the Soviet-backed pro-Vietnamese People's Republic of Kampuchea (PRK) in 1979 was "arguably unparalleled in modern history" (Ayres, 1997, p. 185). Because of a lack of international recognition of the new regime that isolated it from desperately needed development assistance, higher education was restructured following the Soviet model into specialized institutes and faculties, with technical assistance from large numbers of Vietnamese and Russian experts. The socialist vision of the new regime was outlined in decision no. 29 of the Central Committee of the Party about "Problems of Higher and Technical Education," on April 30, 1984: "the main objective of higher education is to provide good political and good technical training . . . following the objectives of socialism" (Clayton, 1995, p. 336). A program of actively removing French influence in education was begun that included decentralization and changing the medium of instruction to Vietnamese and Russian. At first, most of the lecturers were Vietnamese and Russian. The study of French and English was prohibited. But the language barrier, lack of resources, and minimal secondary education received by the students reduced the effectiveness of their instruction. According to a former Ministry of Education official, "quality was a long term project" (Ayres, 1997, p. 202). The function of higher education institutions at the time was mostly to train cadre for automatic employment in the civil service.

The beginnings of a change to a more market-oriented system of higher education can be traced to the Fifth Congress of the Kampuchean People's Revolutionary Party in 1985, when formal recognition was given to the private sector. This was followed by gradual reorientation from a planned economy to a market-driven economy throughout the late 1980s—related to economic liberalization programs in both the Soviet Union (*perestroika*) and Vietnam (*doi moi,* or renovation).

Administrative structures from the socialist PRK regime of the 1980s still persist. Public universities are still controlled centrally by a variety of different ministries—the University of Fine Arts under the Ministry of Culture, the University of Health Sciences under the Ministry of Health, and so on—which results in organizational inefficiencies. Staff at public universities are all state civil servants, and appointments of senior administrators must be approved by their respective ministries. Each tertiary institution decides its own administrative procedures and builds its own relationships with different government ministries in an attempt to compete most successfully for limited resources. This has led to "significant fragmentation in policy and programming and a lack of co-ordination" (Neth & Wakabayashi, 2001). This arrangement has changed somewhat in the last decade after the official shift toward a market economy as faculties with commercial potential have broken away from their public institutions to become semiautonomous institutions, now officially called "public administrative institutions."

Although the socialist PRK regime only lasted for a decade, the problems in trying to change to a more market-oriented system of education in Cambodia were similar to those encountered by other socialist countries. In Poland, for example, the creation of separate institutes with narrow and centrally defined programs hampered adaptation to the labor market; institutions controlled centrally and lacking autonomy were isolated from any form of competition; negative selection of faculty members in which political orientation or personal connections prevailed over substantive criteria prevented reforms in human resource development; staff were lacking motivation due to inadequate salaries; and limited funds were being allocated incorrectly and used inefficiently (Dietl, 1996, p. 10). The parallels with the situation in Cambodia are remarkably close.

Since the signing of the Paris Peace Accords in 1991 and the UN-sponsored election of 1993, relative peace has prevailed in Cambodia. The country has joined the international community, albeit as one of its poorest and smallest members, and has been subject to increasing international influence, some positive and some negative. It is of course part of the process of globalization to which small, poor countries like Cambodia are particularly vulnerable.

International Influences

The debut of Cambodian education on the international stage occurred in 1991 at the National Conference on Education for All (Ayres, 1997, p. 210). The effect on higher education of the adoption of the "education for all" agenda was indirect but significant since it focused scarce resources and donor attention on basic education. The problem of the underfunding of higher education will be discussed later in the section on the "Contemporary Context." Soon after came the unprecedented intervention of the UN transitional authority in Cambodia, which has been praised for its role in facilitating the 1993 elections and (falsely) charged with introducing AIDS into Cambodia. The sudden influx of large numbers of foreigners gave many Cambodians their first glimpse of the outside world—a relatively wealthy, mostly English-speaking world. It also began what became a pattern throughout the 1990s of "international multilateral actors shaping the future direction of the education system" (Ayres, 1997, p. 221).

International influence has taken many forms, including international assistance and membership in international organizations like ASEAN. Linkages with foreign institutions sometimes introduce foreign educational concepts or perspectives that demand compliance with standards favored by foreigners. Cambodians returning from overseas study and the exploding business in Internet outlets are other sources of new ideas. Most recently, Article 3 of the proposed higher education law that was prepared by the MoEYS, with assistance from a team of foreign experts, states:

> There shall be established a legal mechanism for administering the accreditation of higher education for all HEIs to ensure and promote academic quality for greater effectiveness and quality consistent with international standards. (*Royal Kret*, 2002, p. 3)

The importance of the education sector as basic to sustainable economic growth and broader nation building was recognized at the 1993 inaugural meeting of the International Committee on the Reconstruction of Cambodia in Tokyo. Subsequently, several studies of the higher education subsector have all documented the need for strategic reform (Ahrens & Kemmerer, 2002). But the near total destruction of human resources in the education sector during the Khmer Rouge period meant that the task of conducting these studies was dependent on foreign expertise. The studies include a UNESCO-supported MoEYS study (UNESCO, 1994); an Asian Development Bank–supported study (Asian Development Bank, 1994); the National Action Plan (NAP), supported by Australia, the United States, France, and the World Bank, and conducted by the National Higher Education Task Force (NHETF, 1996); and a World Bank–funded study of costs (Zhang, 1997). These internationally sponsored studies have all involved cooperation between Cambodians and international experts who have brought with them foreign concepts of educational practice, policymaking, and planning. The foreign experts were welcomed but have sometimes not been as effective as they could have been for various reasons:

> Funding [was] not forthcoming; there [were] doubts whether the implementation of the plan [was] particularly important; or, nobody in the country with the power to move things along had much to do with the plan's development. (Moock, 2002, p. 60)

Ownership by Cambodians was not the issue in the case of the NAP. In December 1994 the Cambodian government made a request to international donors for help in preparing a "master plan" for higher education. A consortium of donors—mainly AusAID, the World Bank, USAID, the French government, and UNESCO—responded. The process involved two years of extensive participation by Cambodians in seven different working groups, a technical committee, a review task force, and a full-time secretariat. The NAP for higher education that was produced was submitted to the Council of Ministers in April 1997 but was never acted upon—due mainly to the political conflict between the two main political parties but also perhaps because it challenged existing power structures and a long tradition of autocratic decision making (Ayres, 1997, p. 52). This enormous exercise was far from wasted, however. A central concept of the NAP was that the process be more important than the product (Sloper & Le Thac, 1999, p. 15). This was confirmed by a World Bank participant speaking in hindsight five years later:

> Thinking about higher education had been transformed and a broader understanding of the situation elsewhere in the region and of the worldwide trends had been internalized by those involved. This was important for Cambodia, which had been isolated for so long. (Moock, 2002, p. 60)

Diminished financial resources have meant that the education sector has also been dependent on foreign aid for much of its development. Until recent events in East Timor and Afghanistan shifted the world's focus, Cambodia was almost a global metaphor for tragedy and attracted a huge number of nongovernment organizations (NGOs). But aid nowadays is usually conditional on something (e.g., language, ideology, religion), and so NGOs have brought with them not only much-needed capital and technical assistance but also many hidden cultural and ideological assumptions. International standards of management are assumed implicitly and sometimes imposed explicitly when higher education institutions cooperate with international agencies, such as the Asian Development Bank, World Bank, UN agencies, or bilateral donors.

For example, until recently France has been one of the largest bilateral donors to the education sector—for French-language training and for specific faculties and institutes (law, medicine, and technology) that required the use of French. In 1993 when USAID attempted to launch a development project in the Faculty of Law and Economic Science at the Royal University of Phnom Penh, the French government "strenuously objected to any compromise to the development of a jointly integrated academic program and to the use of English" (Hebert, 1999). U.S. government assistance to the former Faculty of Business in the Royal University of Phnom Penh in the form of collaboration with Georgetown University, in Washington D.C., required a change in the medium of instruction from French to English that proved to be "crucial to the whole interinstitutional development scheme" (Hebert, 1999, p. 165). International influence continues to be exerted through language—specifically English, which is becoming increasingly dominant.

Linkages with foreign institutions are forming in both the public and private sectors. These range from genuine partnerships involving staff and student exchanges and mutual recognition of degrees, to franchise agreements involving access to foreign resources via the Internet and visiting foreign lecturers, to donor-funded development projects involving foreign expertise and foreign funds. A lack of credibility of local qualifications has created a perception that "foreign" equals "quality," and a few institutions have taken advantage of this. Due to a lack of regulation in the higher education sector, there are some linkages with unaccredited (in their home country) foreign institutions for the purpose of claiming international recognition that is simply fraudulent. These developments have not yet been evaluated since accurate information, particularly from the private sector, is hard to obtain. But what is clear is that almost the only limitation on the entry of international education providers at present is a lack of customers wealthy enough to pay the fees.

Cambodians have also sometimes been the channel by which international influence has entered the system. This was most dramatic in the 1950s when a small number of Cambodians lucky enough to study in France, among them Saloth Sar, later to be known as Pol Pot, returned with radical socialist ideas. From 1980 to 1994, 4,770 Cambodians returned from studying in socialist countries and a further 1,196 have studied in regional or Western countries since then (MoEYS, 2002d) Fortunately, most have returned. Of the thirty-seven Fulbright scholars who have studied in the United States between 1994 and 2001, all but seven have returned. Cambodians who studied outside the country or attended international seminars and workshops have brought back new ideas and expectations that have challenged the status quo. Some now occupy positions of considerable influence. A group of returned overseas Khmer, most of whom left Cambodia during or just after the Pol Pot era, and subsequently prospered abroad, have returned and created their own university. But young, newly qualified lecturers returning to public institutions from egalitarian Western countries have not always been welcomed by their older, less qualified colleagues in Cambodia's traditional hierarchical society. Some have sought employment elsewhere and contributed to the emergence of the private sector.

Legacies of the Past

How has Cambodia's past influenced the present system of higher education? Perhaps it is easier to say first what the past has not bequeathed to the present—namely, a long tradition of higher learning or a community of intellectuals containing a reservoir of academic values. The first nonlegacy is a consequence of the course of history; the second is a result of systematic extermination. Most of the legacies of the past seem to be presenting the present system with unresolved problems.

Several features of the traditional education of precolonial times persist today. Young women are still disadvantaged by the almost exclusively male environment of the pagoda. Young men from the provinces who want to study at universities in Phnom Penh can board at pagodas in the city; young women cannot. There is still a general preference for educating sons before daughters.

The tradition of oral transmission of Buddhist teachings by the reciting of religious texts can still be found in the teaching styles used in many modern Cambodian classrooms. Rote learning is widespread, and thus students often arrive at university lacking analytical skills or the ability to apply theory to practical real-world situations (McNamara, 1999a, p. 91).

The most obvious structural features of the present higher education system are a legacy of the French colonial period and of the Soviet system introduced after 1979. The centralized, elitist, and competitive French model of education established during the 1950s and 1960s is still the basis of the present system. Some public higher education institutions are still administered by related ministries, but not by the Ministry of Education, in line with the Soviet model adopted during the 1980s. Most private higher education institutions created since the mid-1990s have used an American model of mass higher education. These various models have had an impact on everything from institutional responsibilities, to teaching and learning styles, to the language of instruction.

History has also left its mark on the administrators and staff of higher education institutions. These various models of education are manifest in the thinking of a number of education officials. Many senior administrators retain loyalty to the language and theoretical teaching styles from the 1960s. The effects of the Pol Pot time are still evident in the survivors of that period—in their resourcefulness, determination, and attitudes toward political authority. Massive deficiencies of human resources in higher education also stem from this time. Yet in some parts of society the Pol Pot period has produced a sincere desire for a permanent end to the civil disorder that has devastated Cambodia and a commitment to help rebuild the country.

University staff who trained in the late 1980s and early 1990s and who make up the majority of current university lecturers were taught mostly by Vietnamese or Russian lecturers or studied overseas in socialist countries such as the USSR, East Germany, Vietnam, Bulgaria, Hungary, Czechoslovakia, Poland, and Cuba, where they were expected to learn in a foreign language. There are now university staff members who speak the language of the country in which they trained. But resource deficiencies and the lack of opportunities for further study in Cambodia following the collapse of the Soviet Union and the withdrawal of the Vietnamese have made it difficult for these staff members to develop beyond the levels of skills achieved at that time. The majority of university lecturers currently at public higher education institutions do not hold higher degrees (Task Force on Higher Education and Society, 2002). The need to upgrade their qualifications and make up for the lack of opportunities in the past constitutes one of the system's greatest imperatives.

Donor-funded scholarship schemes have begun to address this problem by sending staff overseas for further study, which has created a growing number of young, overseas-trained lecturers with higher degrees. They are being joined by other expatriate Khmers who left during or just after the Pol Pot time and are now returning, some with higher degrees and a desire to share their good fortune. However, most of the people in both groups are being absorbed by the rapidly expanding private sector outside of higher education, where their advanced skills can be adequately rewarded.

This internal hemorrhage of brain power represents perhaps the most fundamental weakness in the present system of higher education, which also has its roots in the socialist regime of the 1980s, and that is the failure of civil service salary scales to adjust to the transition to a market economy. The socialist dream of collective ownership and control of the means of production, distribution, and exchange created a system of universal salaries, which assumed that all workers would receive an equal share of the nation's wealth. But while privatization has now been embraced and the private sector is becoming increasingly competitive, public institutions are still handicapped by salaries that do not adequately reward merit or give incentives to improve. Private institutions that are financed by student fees and are not part of an accreditation process, however, are not subject to these limitations.

ISSUES AND REALITIES

Many of the challenges currently faced by the Cambodian higher education system have their roots in the last five decades. Recent issues concerning funding, access, and relevance are all modern symptoms of long-term ills. Some long-standing social and cultural traditions are also creating conflicts with the expectations of modernization.

Current Context

The adoption of the "education for all" agenda in 1990, which focused attention on improving primary and secondary education, had wide international and local support. But the agenda seemed to present public higher education institutions with an apparently incompatible set of goals. On the one hand, institutions were expected to modernize and respond to the demands of an emerging market economy; and on the other hand, they were meant to fulfill the government's public responsibility to provide free higher education to the most able students and to accomplish both without significant government support. This was occurring in many countries, as the perception of higher education changed from "public service" to "private good," with a subsequent decline in government funding. Following this decision, tertiary institutions were expected to become increasingly self-funding and to orient their courses to market needs.

In fact, government funding of public higher education institutions in Cambodia has increased recently but remains grossly inadequate. Budget allocations to education in general are already low, compared with those of other low-income countries. Actual disbursements are almost entirely for teacher's civil service salaries (a base salary of only U.S.$48.00 per month). Allocations for renovation and maintenance of facilities are almost nonexistent. Consequently, staff commitment is low, and with teachers being able to make more money working in the private sector, there is an exodus from the public universities.

Public institutions are being forced to generate their own income. The government has recently allowed them to accept fee-paying students above their quota of non-fee-paying students. As mentioned earlier, a Priority Action Program (PAP) has been introduced to provide a reliable operating budget and transparent management of financial resources. But the failure to deliver all of the promised PAP funds, and in a timely manner, has shown that the government is perhaps unwilling or unable (due to use of budgeted funds for other purposes) to grant financial autonomy and still retains tight central control over finances.

Access to higher education institutions is a great problem for rural students, especially for young women. Virtually all higher education institutions are in the capital, Phnom Penh. Entry to higher education institutions requires a pass on the grade 12 exam, which also assumes that students have access to a high school with classes up to grade 12 and the teachers to teach them. But teachers cannot survive on their government salary and so must find a second job or conduct extra classes. Both of these options are almost impossible in the poorer, remote areas. The absence of other incentives for teachers to accept rural postings means that rural schools remain understaffed. Consequently, urban gross enrollment rates in upper-secondary education are thirteen times greater than in rural areas (Deolalikar, 1999, p. 39).

Students in the main urban centers have the advantage of having access to the extra classes that have become necessary for exam success. This is clearly shown in the exam results at grade 12. Phnom Penh constitutes only about 10 percent of the population and yet produces almost

50 percent of grade 12 passes. Another five provinces, mostly around Phnom Penh, produce 30 percent of the passes and the remaining 18 provinces, containing 50 percent of the population, provide only 20 percent of the passes. In the 2002 cohort of grade 12 graduates only 33.4 percent were female (CANEP, 2002). Girls from remote areas in particular are disadvantaged since most families are very reluctant to allow their daughters to stay in Phnom Penh unless they have trusted relatives in the city. There are no government-funded dormitories and few other housing options. Consequently, female students at recognized higher education institutions comprise only about 22 percent of enrollments (MoEYS, 2002a).

Geographic disadvantage is compounded by poverty. More than 90 percent of postsecondary students come from the top two quintiles of the population (40 percent) ranked according to per capita consumer spending (Deolalikar, 1999, p. 39). Students from the poorest quintile of the population have virtually no representation in higher education.

The lack of relevance of the curriculum is a problem that has existed since colonial times. The elitist concept of education from that time can still be seen in higher education in the highly theoretical nature of science courses at all levels. The vast majority of students entering their first year at university have never done a single experiment and are used to rote learning of large amounts of theory. "The emphasis is not on *how* to teach, but on *what* to teach" (Neth & Wakabayashi, 2001, p. 26). Resource deficiencies have obviously contributed to the lack of practical subjects and laboratory courses, but there is still a general preference among university lecturers for theoretical courses. The approach of some lecturers to improving the quality of their courses is to include *more* theory of greater difficulty rather than to improve the relevance for students.

The reform of the curriculum is also affected by underfunding. It is difficult for universities to raise adequate funds to undertake the restructuring of courses. Even through it is now possible to charge fees, there is currently a very poor "match" between academic programs and what employers are looking for in prospective employees.

The National Action Plan of 1997 that summarized the state of academic programs in Cambodia still accurately describes the situation in 2003.

Academic programs in Cambodian higher education are not necessarily related to national development and labour market needs and demands: degree holders from some programs are in surplus and unemployed; and new programs are required for present and future demands. Existing academic programs are not flexible and diversified. Some are not of a higher education level. A revision of academic programs is urgently required to meet social and economic needs, to provide higher education with more flexibility, diversity and access, and to strengthen standards towards regional and international levels. . . . Almost all courses currently given in higher education are limited to presentations of theory. This situation derives mostly from the poor quality and limited number of instructional materials available. There is a crucial need to develop locally-designed and produced higher education instructional materials . . . in a systematic manner. There is also no flexibility in existing academic programs, e.g., transfer of academic credit between higher education and post-secondary institutions is not possible; there are no short-term non-degree programs; and formal higher education study to upgrade people in employment through continuing education or mixed mode learning is not available. (NHETF, 1996, p. 20)

There have been some curriculum developments since the above evaluation. With donor assistance, some well-targeted programs have begun in a few public higher education institutions—such as a bachelor's program in the English language at the Institute of Foreign Languages and tourism and media management programs at the Royal University of Phnom Penh (RUPP). Cost-recovery measures will gradually be implemented—such as introducing student fees instead of government support; some programs have already become self-supporting. At the better private institutions there has been some diversification of curriculum from the commonly offered narrow range of business-related subjects. Programs in civil engineering, electrical engineering, electronics, and architecture are offered, and some instructional materials and reference texts in Khmer are being produced.

Underfunding, inequitable access, and curricula lacking relevance are current issues that affect private and public institutions differently, with consequences for the higher education sector as a whole.

Public and Private Sectors

The latter half of the 1990s saw a confluence of factors that resulted in the appearance of private higher education in Cambodia. Low government teachers' salaries, the return of young overseas-trained Cambodians, ministry intransigence on the introduction of student fees in public institutions (Coyne, 1999, p. 147), a thriving system of private English-language schools, and an increasing demand for postsecondary education combined to provide staff in need of adequate incomes the entrepreneurial experience and the customers to create very profitable opportunities.

The first recognized private higher education institution, Norton University, appeared in December 1996. Its appearance preempted ministry policy, but through a combination of bold entrepreneurial spirit and political influence it succeeded in bypassing restrictive bureaucratic procedures to obtain official recognition directly from the Council of Ministers in September 1997 (McNamara, 1999b). The managing director was a very enterprising twenty-three-year-old student in the Faculty of Law and Economic Sciences. Income from student fees allowed the university to offer staff adequate salaries and thus attract some teachers away from the public institutions. Average growth in enrollments over the first five years of operation was 36 percent.

The door having been opened to a market with many buyers and few regulations, many new private institutions have since appeared. The unregulated growth of the private sector in Cambodian higher education in keeping with the national shift toward a market economy has resulted in mass higher education mostly similar to the North American model (open access and self-selection by students) (Watson, 2002). However, strong government control and inadequate government funding have largely isolated public institutions from market forces, leaving them with little incentive to improve educational quality or change the model they have inherited from the past, although this does not apply to all public institutions.

In 1997 the RUPP Faculty of Business received significant assistance from USAID to upgrade its staff members to the postgraduate level but was faced with competition from the newly formed Norton University, which was able to offer better salaries. The Faculty of Business followed the precedent set by Norton and, in spite of strong opposition from the MoEYS, obtained approval directly from the prime minister to charge student fees and rename the institution the National Institute of Management (NIM) (McNamara, 1999b). Cost recovery via student fees has allowed NIM to retain qualified staff (77 percent with postgraduate training), to construct purpose-built buildings, to open a branch campus in Battambang, and to attract an enrollment of 10,560 students (Iv, 2002, p. 68) that represents almost one-third of all students enrolled in higher education. Some other individual departments within public higher education institutions have also progressed from donor-funded programs to self-sufficiency by introducing student fees (e.g., the Computer Sciences and English Departments at the RUPP).

An increasing number of private higher education institutions are appearing, some recognized and others not. In 2001–2002 alone, the number of institutions more than doubled. But at present the process of recognition of private institutions is very unclear and has little connection with educational quality. A subdecree on the criteria for establishing higher education institutions was passed in July 2002, but the necessary regulations to support it are still needed. Consequently, the quality of these institutions varies from poor to excellent. Some have voluntarily chosen to compete in terms of quality and are already developing in the direction outlined in the proposed legal framework for higher education: Norton University has restructured its faculties to conform with the proposed legislation; Pannasastra University has introduced a foundation year of general education and is presenting all courses in English; the International Institute of Cambodia (IIC) has introduced a "real" system of credit transfer, has almost 100 percent postgraduate-trained staff, and has produced a range of textbooks in Khmer to support their courses.

Other institutions are taking advantage of the huge demand and providing the minimum that will sell. The absence of a legislative framework or accreditation system for higher education has led to a commercialization in most of these private institutions that has tended to narrow the range of courses being offered (most are related to business). The programs are designed to benefit individuals at the expense of producing graduates who might contribute to national development. The model adopted by most private institutions is one that maximizes profits—so access is usually open to all those who have completed high school and can afford the fees. Some faculty members teach as many as forty hours per week, working simultaneously at several institutions, which severely limits the time available for preparation and other teaching-related activities. A small number of private institutions have chosen educational value as the goal of management, but at most institutions, as in other countries, the drive for profit has become an end in itself. There are now almost four times as many students in private higher education institutions as in public institutions (MoEYS, 2002a).

Sociocultural Issues

Cambodia is a small, poor developing country with an ancient culture. It is particularly vulnerable to the powerful forces of globalization. Its values are similar to those of other countries in the region and can generally be described as Confucian in tradition: collectivist, with informal controls and respect and obedience for authoritative leaders (Biggs, 1996). In addition, Colletta (2002) has described the Cambodian cultural values as including indirect communication, a hierarchical social order, fatalistic beliefs, shame-based morality, reverence for the past, and a certainty concerning social codes and structures.

Owing to globalization, however, modernity is usually based on Western concepts. Likewise, the principles of management that form the basis of many donors' expectations also developed in a Western cultural context that generally values direct communication, equality, nonfatalistic beliefs, guilt-based morality, an orientation toward the future, and flexible social codes and structures (Colletta, 2002). According to one writer there has been a "crisis" caused by the "fundamental contradiction between a social environment which celebrated tradition, and therefore upheld the status quo, and an education system which promised modernity and change" (Ayres, 1997, p. 268). But it must be remembered that there are two (or more) sides to any conflict. In spite of the obvious cultural differences some international donors have made little effort to acknowledge this.

> Cambodian education was (and perhaps continues to be) drowning in plans
> (some good, some not so good) that various donors have developed, often in
> isolation from other donors—and sometimes it would seem, in isolation from
> Cambodians. (Moock 2002, p. 60)

The differences between the generally conservative Cambodian values and Western concepts of modernity are obvious and are probably the cause of at least some of the "crisis." For example, Cambodia's hierarchical society shows great respect for age, experience, and authoritative leadership, which has led to public acceptance of decisions from the top levels of government, even those that bypass normal procedures—as in the recognition of Norton University that was mentioned earlier. Modern management, however, usually requires procedure-based decision making. Cambodians' acceptance of decisions from above is based on respect and loyalty but can sometimes depend on personal relationships. People's responses are thus at times changeable and unpredictable, which is the opposite of the assurance that is required of modern quality management. These issues directly affect Cambodia's public universities since they are subject to direct government control with regard to much of their financing and staffing.

Contributing to the current crisis is the weakened state of the national justice system. After almost thirty years of civil disorder, the rule of law is still being established and enforcement is weak. This environment is limiting the effect of market forces that could bring about improvements in the higher education system. When even small numbers of students enter or graduate from institutions by "alternative" means, public opinion concerning the value of the education provided is undermined.

TRENDS AND CHALLENGES

Examining the characteristics of the present system of higher education is relatively easy. Predicting the future is much more difficult. Lessons learned from the past should be able to help inform plans for the future. But forward planning assumes an environment of predictable change and the power to control it. The combination of structural, social, and cultural factors described above have created an environment that is the antithesis of this.

Professional Resistance

The central question for this section is whether the higher education system will be able to respond to student needs and also satisfy the demands of national and social development. In seeking an answer, perhaps the five professional resistance factors, widely acknowledged as inhibiting change in underdeveloped education systems (Beeby, 1966) can provide a conceptual framework through which we can analyze the present situation in Cambodian higher education. These factors are: (1) a lack of clear goals, (2) insufficient understanding and acceptance of the need for reform, (3) the fact that teachers are a product of the system in which they work and in which change is being attempted, (4) the professional isolation of teachers leading to outdated knowledge and practice being taught, and (5) teachers' lack of effectiveness and adaptability.

It is worth noting that the last three of the above five factors relate to teachers, which is not surprising since they are the people who actually deliver the education that the system is supposed to provide. Policies and plans mean nothing if there is no one to teach. They are the vital link in the education system, and yet, as this chapter has discussed, points 3, 4, and 5 above accurately describe the situation of many teachers in Cambodian higher education, the exceptions being those who have been trained abroad and have sufficient language skills to access the international knowledge system.

On the positive side, there does seem to be an acceptance of the need for reform as in point 2. Two participants at a recent conference on accreditation in Cambodian higher education expressed this optimism. In the words of a World Bank representative:

> There is a growing number of young people in the system, many of them trained abroad, who understand quality and are eager to help make it happen. But even "old-timers" have changed—they now know where the system should go or now believe that there is some small chance that these changes will occur within their lifetime." (Moock, 2002, p. 60)

The secretary of state for MoEYS stated: "Our minds are in the future even if we don't have the needed structures and processes to travel there in place yet" (Pok, 2002, p. 171).

But the goals for education, point 1, are still unclear, which is the central contention of this chapter. This is evident in the new policy developments for higher education as outlined recently in the ESSP Forward Plan report:

> Although there has been significant progress on higher education strategy in the past year, long term higher education development needs to be set within a more comprehensive policy framework. The broad purpose would be to clearly define a policy framework for government and private sector roles in higher education. More specific objectives of the study would include strategic options for education financing, while assuring equitable access for the less well off. A third objective would be to examine the scope for introduction of provincial level community colleges, linked to efficient credit transfer and quality assurance mechanisms. (MoEYS, 2002c, p. 21)

More clearly defined policy, diversified funding, more equitable access, decentralization, credit transfer, and quality assurance are laudable goals and there seems to be genuine commitment at the ministry level for such policy-driven reforms. But the realization of the ESSP agenda will hinge on the central government's commitment to direct its actions according to stated policies. At present, there is often considerable difference between stated policy and what actually happens, in the shadow play that is Cambodian public administration.

The extent to which documents like the ESP, ESSP, and Forward Plan Report represent the vision of the government is also not clear. They were "based on an intensive consultation process within the Ministry" (MoEYS, 2002b), but were still mostly written by foreign technical advisers. The need to rely on foreign advisers is a practical reality given devastation of human resources during the past thirty years and the fact that the current generation of administrators is mostly Francophone at a time when English is the dominant international language.

Privatization

The current policy direction is headed toward increasing private-sector participation in the hope that market forces will generate a natural expansion of the system in response to increasing demand. This is also the direction suggested in the proposed law for higher education. But evidence elsewhere has shown that marketization of higher education does not necessarily lead to high quality standards. Speaking of the core qualities that higher education systems need to develop, the Task Force on Higher Education and Society warns that "on its own the market will certainly not develop this kind of system" (2000, p. 15). The need for government support has been recognized. The ESSP states that the government "will assume responsibility for underserved areas" (MoEYS, 2002b, p. 32), but its capacity and commitment to do so remain doubtful. The private sector is at present unregulated and mostly narrowly commercial. This is a dangerous trend with serious consequences for national development. It could lead to a proliferation of courses that require little capital investment at the expense of fields that are vital for expansion and economic growth (e.g., science, technology, and in particular postgraduate research).

The unregulated growth of private institutions could present another danger. Most private institutions have opened within the last few years and are providing a similar narrow range of courses. But there has been little or no growth in foreign investment that could generate jobs in high skills areas like management or information technology, which constitute the majority of courses offered. Parent-clients are mostly not well informed about what constitutes educational quality and are mostly buying the most expensive course they can afford assuming, to the delight of private institutions, that high price correlates with high quality. It is feared that Cambodia's small market will be quickly flooded and result in a large number of frustrated unemployed graduates who have paid dearly for their education. There are precedents for a situation like this in Cambodia during the 1960s (Ayres, 1997, p. 106) and also in a number of Southeast Asian countries, and the consequences were dramatic.

Research Capacity

The lack of research capacity in Cambodia was discussed recently at the Fifth Socio-Cultural Research Congress in Phnom Penh, the annual expansion of which has ironically been hailed as the beginning of a new culture of research. Research is "normally done with the assistance of foreign or expatriate experts" (Hean, 2002) and is mostly "non-academic contract work [that is] only available as grey literature" (Henke, 2002).

This lack of research capacity may stem from deeper cultural traditions in Cambodia. In the traditional teaching style, the teacher leads and students passively follow. Learning without a teacher, which is the essence of research, goes against this tradition. To a certain degree, new styles of teaching are recognized. The terms *student-centered learning* and *learning to learn* are being used (Neth & Wakabayashi, 2001). But for many, the concept of research is as described in a traditional Cambodian poem: "like a blind man left to himself who sets out on his way with no one to take his hand" (Chandler, 1984, p. 275).

But if higher education is like the head of the education system, then research is its brain. Higher education institutions at present are almost entirely teaching institutions. A whole new culture of thinking needs to be created that the private sector is unlikely to attempt since the rewards of research are often intangible and related to national or institutional interests rather than individual benefit. The rewards could be significant, however, if at least a few centers of research could be established to cultivate the most creative minds and encourage innovation. The contribution of such centers would be greater than the new or indigenized knowledge they would create. A small cadre of Cambodian researchers could catalyze new teaching styles and modes of thinking in higher education that could be transferred to secondary and eventually to primary education. Without this creative input at the top, the higher education system is likely to remain of low quality, dependent on foreign textbooks and technical expertise, and unable to produce the highly skilled human resources necessary for industrialization. The rewards can also be tangible. Some of Cambodia's regional neighbors, faced with the same need to diversify funding sources, are generating significant revenue from research contracts (Sloper & Le Thac, 1995).

Policy Framework

Will the new draft law for higher education be the same as the National Action Plan for Higher Education, which was submitted to the government in 1997 but never enacted? Why has there been such a long delay (twelve months, as of February 2002) in enacting the new law and implementing long-recommended, widely supported reform?[1] The delay perhaps indicates the degree of difference between the agendas of the various stakeholder groups. And if the proposed law is not enacted, then it is likely that the public sector and the national interest that it serves will be the main losers. A few private institutions, anticipating the requirements of the new legal framework and accreditation procedures, have already introduced measures to improve and assure the quality of the education they provide. "Change is in the Cambodian air. The Royal Kret (decree) to change universities will go through. If not, Norton will find other ways to get course accreditation and join the international university system" (Parer, 2002).

With the present focus on basic education, higher education is perhaps only in the government's peripheral field of vision. This is not surprising in light of the past half century, during which higher education was considered part of an elitist vision of modernity, a Western imperialist notion, a training ground for socialist cadres in certain ministries, and, more recently, a "private good" and thus the responsibility of those who might benefit from it.

Education systems are rarely the result of an idealized vision by a single group (Archer, 1984, p. 2). However, since most recent developments in higher education have been the product of foreign aid, a bid for escape from central control, or a quick grab for profit (i.e., not policy-driven), it is likely that the final outcomes will be a compromise between the wishes of the major stakeholders: education officials, donors, and powerful, politically connected vested interests. Without a regulatory framework and genuine government support for disadvantaged groups and noncommercial subject areas, higher education could well become a privilege of the rich. The result could be a system that would not produce the human resources with the skills that might benefit Cambodian social and economic development.

CONCLUSION

Cambodian higher education is not yet mature enough to be well known regionally or internationally. Fifty years is a relatively short period for any system of higher education to develop, even without the destruction experienced during the Khmer Rouge regime. In addition, the system has been impelled in radically different directions through French, Russian, and, lately, Western educational models.

Current challenges include trying to maintain the quality of the higher education system while allowing for expansion and privatization. Complicating this situation are the effects of globalization and technological advancement, which are introducing increasing international influence. Nevertheless, the development of new policies and a new legal framework is under way.

In the future, Cambodian higher education will need highly qualified, experienced, strong-willed, and committed human resources. Inevitably, much assistance will be required. The challenge will be to manage that assistance in genuine partnership with Cambodians so that national priorities are maintained. When observed with a long perspective and with an understanding of Cambodia's past, recent progress is encouraging.

NOTE

1. The proposed law for higher education was approved by the Council of Ministers on April 19, 2003, after several amendments were made by the government concerning the membership and governance of the Accreditation Committee of Cambodia (ACC). In the opinion of the World Bank, the changes might result in a lack of independence and professionalism in the committee. However, according to some Cambodians, partly due to the previous destruction of the education system, it is felt that in the initial stages at least, the ACC should still be a government responsibility. This is in line with regional neighbors who also have accreditation committees under government control.

The ACC has already been established and has started to define the roles of each division within the committee. But the lack of experts in the field is a handicap that the committee is facing. It has sent some officials to take relevant courses in neighboring countries so that they can adapt the experience from those countries to the system in Cambodia. However, we cannot be certain how effective the implementation is going to be. Some hold that the roles of MoEYS and the ACC remain unclear. The latest ESSP review has once again reported the need for greater clarity in higher education policy. "The Kret is unclear on the role of the MoEYS in higher education and the independence and professional focus of the ACC" (MoEYS, 2003, p. 6). The issue is still being debated (Ford, 2003, p. 12).

REFERENCES

Ahrens, L., & Kemmerer, F. (2002 January–March). Higher education development. *Cambodia Development Review*, 6(1).

Altner, D. (1999). Building national capacity in education sector management: A UNESCO/UNDP project in Cambodia 1995–98. In D. Sloper (Ed.), *Higher education in Cambodia: The social and educational context for reconstruction* (pp. 173–201). Bangkok, Thailand: UNESCO.

Archer, M. S. (1984). *Social origins of education systems*. London: Sage.

Asian Development Bank. (1994). *Education sector review*. Phnom Penh, Cambodia: Author.

Asian Development Bank. (1996). *Cambodia: Education sector strategy study*. Manila: Author.

Ayres, D. (1997). "Tradition and modernity enmeshed: The educational crisis in Cambodia, 1953–1997." Unpublished Ph.D. diss., University of Sydney.

Beeby, C. E. (1966). *The quality of education in developing countries*. Cambridge, MA: Harvard University Press.

Biggs, J. (1996). Western misperceptions of the Confucian heritage learning culture. In David A. Watkins & John B. Biggs (Eds.), *The Chinese learner: Culture, psychological and contextual influences*. Melbourne, Australia: CERC & ACER.

Bilodeau, C., Pathammavong, S., & Hong, L. Q. (1954). Compulsory education in Vietnam, Cambodia and Laos. *Studies on Compulsory Education*, No. 14.

Blaise, H. (1964). *The process and strategy of institution building: A case study in Cambodia*. Ann Arbor, MI: University Microfilms.

Cambodia Australia National Examinations Project (CANEP). (2002). *Cambodia Australia National Examinations Project: Grade 12 results 2002*. Phnom Penh, Cambodia: Author.

Chandler, D. (1984). Normative poems (*chbab*) and precolonial Cambodian society. *Journal of Southeast Asian Studies*, 15(2), 271–279.

Chandler, D. (1998). *A History of Cambodia* (2nd ed.). Chiang Mai, Thailand: Silkworm Books.

Clayton, T. (1995). *Education and language in education in relation to external intervention in Cambodia, 1620–1989*. Ann Arbor, MI: University Microfilms.

Coletta, C. (2002). *Initial observations on conflict resolution processes and Cambodian culture: Mediation won't work, conciliation has, does and will*. Phnom Penh, Cambodia: East West Management Institute.

Coombs, P. H. (1969). *The world educational crisis*. New York: Oxford University Press.

Coyne, G. (1999). The bachelor of education (TEFL) program: Issues of quality assurance. In D. Sloper (Ed.), *Higher education in Cambodia: The social and educational context for reconstruction* (pp. 144–161). Bangkok, Thailand: UNESCO.

Deolalikar, A. B. (1999). Socioeconomic development in Cambodia. In D. Sloper (Ed.), *Higher education in Cambodia: The social and educational context for reconstruction* (pp. 25–50). Bangkok, Thailand: UNESCO.

Dietl, J. (1996). The dilemma of higher education in an economy in transition: Polish case study. *Higher Education Management*, 8(2), 9–18.

Ford, D. (2003, Fall). Cambodian accreditation: An uncertain beginning. *International Higher Education*, 33, 12–14.

Harbison, F. H. (1973). *Human resources as the wealth of nations.* New York: Oxford University Press.

Hean Sokhom. (2002). "Some challenges of research work in Cambodia." Paper presented at the Fifth Socio-Cultural Research Congress, Phnom Penh, Cambodia.

Hebert, P. (1999). USA assistance to higher education in Cambodia. In D. Sloper (Ed.), *Higher education in Cambodia: The social and educational context for reconstruction* (pp. 163–172). Bangkok, Thailand: UNESCO.

Henke, R. (2002). "Mapping Cambodian research expertise and activities." Paper presented at the Fifth Socio-Cultural Research Congress, Phnom Penh, Cambodia.

Iv, Thong. (2002, July 31–August 2). "Applying the concept of total quality management (TQM) to higher education in Cambodia." Paper presented at the national conference on accreditation in Cambodian higher education, Phnom Penh, Cambodia.

Jacques, C., & Freeman, M. (1997). *Angkor cities and temples.* New York: River Books.

McNamara, V. (1999a). The education system of Cambodia: Framework and characteristics. In D. Sloper (Ed.), *Higher education in Cambodia: The social and educational context for reconstruction* (pp. 67–98). Bangkok, Thailand: UNESCO.

McNamara, V. (1999b). Some profiles of Cambodian higher education institutions: How policies are made. In D. Sloper (Ed.), *Higher education in Cambodia: The social and educational context for reconstruction* (pp. 295–321). Bangkok, Thailand: UNESCO.

Ministry of Education. (1984). *Education in the People's Republic of Kampuchea.* Phnom Penh, Cambodia: Author.

Ministry of Education, Youth, and Sport (MoEYS). (1971, December 27–31). *L'Enseignement superieur et le developpement rapport final du colloque national.* Phnom Penh, Cambodia.

Ministry of Education, Youth, and Sport (MoEYS). (1994). *Rebuilding quality education in Cambodia.* Phnom Penh, Cambodia: UNESCO.

Ministry of Education, Youth, and Sport (MoEYS). (2002a, October). *Education indicators, 1998–02.* Phnom Penh, Cambodia: EMIS Center, Department of Planning.

Ministry of Education, Youth, and Sport (MoEYS). (2002b, August). *Education Sector Support Program.* Phnom Penh, Cambodia: Author.

Ministry of Education, Youth, and Sport (MoEYS). (2002c). *Education Sector Support Program, Forward Plan report.* Phnom Penh, Cambodia: Author.

Ministry of Education, Youth, and Sport (MoEYS). (2002d, August). *Education Sector Support Program review 2002, education sector performance report.* Phnom Penh, Cambodia: Author.

Ministry of Education, Youth, and Sport (MoEYS). (2002e, August). *Education Sector Support Program Review 2002, Forward Plan report.* Phnom Penh, Cambodia: Author.

Ministry of Education, Youth, and Sport (MoEYS). (2002f, August). *Education Sector Support Program review 2002, monitoring and capacity building progress report.* Phnom Penh, Cambodia: Author.

Ministry of Education, Youth, and Sport (MoEYS). (2002g, December). *Number of students sent abroad 1980 to 2002 by year and country.* Scholarship Office CRS. Phnom Penh, Cambodia: Author.

Ministry of Education, Youth, and Sport (MoEYS). (2003, May). *Education sector review 2003, summary report*. Phnom Penh, Cambodia: Author.

Moock, P. K. (2002, July 31–August 2). "Issues identified and recommendations made in Cambodia's National Action Plan for higher education (1997): Progress since then and directions for the future." Paper presented at the national conference on accreditation in Cambodian higher education, Phnom Penh, Cambodia.

National Higher Education Task Force (NHETF). (1996). *The National Action Plan*. Phnom Penh, Cambodia: Author.

Neth, B., & Wakabayashi, M. (2001). *Science and mathematics education development in Cambodia through building higher education systems*. Discussion paper No. 91. Nagoya, Japan: Graduate School of International Development, Nagoya University.

Parer, M. (2002, December). Presentation at Norton University's third annual conference. Retrieved from www.norton-u.com.

Pok Than. (2002, July 31–August 2). *Closing remarks*. Presentation at the national conference on accreditation in Cambodian higher education, Phnom Penh, Cambodia.

Prum Sokha. (2002, December 31). Top government official fulfills dreams of education. *Cambodia Daily*, 13.

Quirky exam results may harm education. (2002, September 16). *Cambodia Daily*, 17.

Royal Kret regarding accreditation of higher education. (2002, May 26). Draft legislation, English translation. Phnom Penh, Kingdom of Cambodia.

Sloper, D., & Le Thac Can. (Eds.). (1995). *Higher education in Vietnam: Change and response* (Chaps. 8 & 9). Singapore: Institute of Southeast Asian Studies.

Task Force on Higher Education and Society. (2000). *Higher education in developing countries: Peril and promise*. Washington, DC: World Bank.

UNESCO. (1994). *Rebuilding quality education in Cambodia*. Phnom Penh, Cambodia: UNESCO.

Watson, K. (2002). Looking west and east: Thailand's academic development. In P. G. Altbach & V. Selvarathnam (Eds.), 2002, *From dependence to autonomy: The development of Asian universities* (pp. 63–95). Newton, MA: Center for International Higher Education, Boston College.

Zhang Minxuan. (1997). *Cost-sharing and higher education in Cambodia*. Phnom Penh, Cambodia: MoEYS and World Bank.

Contributors

Philip G. Altbach is the J. Donald Monan SJ Professor of Higher Education and director of the Center for International Higher Education at Boston College, Chestnut Hill, Massachusetts. He is editor of *The Review of Higher Education*. He is the author of many books on higher education, including *Comparative Higher Education: Knowledge, the University, and Society*, and editor of *The Decline of the Guru: The Academic Profession in Developing Countries, International Higher Education: An Encyclopedia*, as well as other books.

Mochtar Buchori is a member of the Indonesian Parliament. He is a columnist for the *Jakarta Post* and has been deputy chairman of the Indonesian Institute of Sciences, and rector of Muhammadiyah University, as well as other posts. Among his books are *Notes on Education in Indonesia* (2001). He received master's and doctoral degrees from Harvard University and has been a consultant for USAID, UNESCO, and other organizations.

Pit Chamnan is the rector of the Royal University of Phnom Penh, the largest postsecondary institution in Cambodia. He completed his tertiary education in Cambodia in the early 1970s and during the Pol Pot regime became a farmer and cook. He is one of the few educated people who were not executed. He was educated at the Ecole normale superieure in France, and has been rector since 1999.

David Ford is currently an adviser to the Chemistry Department of the Royal University of Phnom Penh. He has worked as a science teacher for twenty-five years in Australia, Malaysia, Zimbabwe, and Cambodia.

Gerald W. Fry is professor of international and intercultural education and director of graduate studies in the Department of Educational Policy and Administration, University of Minnesota. He is an editor of *The Encyclopedia of Modern Asia* (2002) and author of *Synthesis Report: From Crisis to Opportunity, The Challenges of Educational Reform in Thailand* (2002), published by the Asian

Development Bank. In 2000, he was a visiting USIA professor at Van Lang University, Ho Chi Minh City, Vietnam.

Bro. Andrew Gonzalez is vice-president for academics and research at De La Salle University, Manila, Philippines. He has served as secretary (minister) of education in the government of the Philippines and president of De La Salle University. He holds a Ph.D. in linguistics from the University of California, Berkeley.

N. Jayaram is professor and head of the department of research methodology at the Tata Institute of Social Sciences, Mumbai, India. He was formerly professor of sociology at the University of Goa and Bangalore University. He is the managing editor of *Sociological Bulletin* and the editor of *ICSSR Journal of Reviews and Abstracts: Sociology and Social Anthropology*. He has published extensively on the sociology of higher education in India, and his books include *Higher Education and Status Retention, Sociology of Education in India*, and *Social Conflict* (coedited with Satish Saberwal).

Motohisa Kaneko professor of higher education at the University of Tokyo, where he served as director of the Center for Research and Development of Higher Education. He is now director of the Research Center for Basic Academic Competence at Tokyo University. He has served as a consultant for the World Bank and was a visiting assistant professor at the State University of New York at Albany, before joining the Research Institute for Higher Education at Hiroshima University. His academic interests include higher education, economics of education, and development and education, on which he has published extensively.

Molly N. N. Lee is the program specialist in higher education at UNESCO Bangkok. She has been professor of education at the Universiti Sains Malaysia, Penang, where she taught sociology of education and curriculum studies. Her research interests include higher education, teacher education, private education, and educational policy. She is a research fellow at the National Research Institute on Higher Education, Malaysia. She was a Fulbright fellow, a British Council scholarship recipient, and a founding member of the Comparative Education Society Asia and of the Malaysia Educational Research Association.

Sungho H. Lee is professor of higher education at Yonsei University, Seoul, Korea, where he has also served as dean of the Graduate School, dean of the College of Education, and vice president for administration and development. He is a former assistant minister of higher education in the government of the Republic of Korea and served as vice chairman of the Presidential Commission on the 21st Century. He has published widely on Korean higher education and on curriculum issues. Among his books are *Conflict in Korean Higher Education* and *Curriculum Development in Korean Higher Education*.

Abdul Malik is secretary of the Ministry for Research and Technology and is also special aide to the minister for research and technology. He received his undergraduate degree in civil engineering from Bandung Institute of Technology and a Ph.D. in economics from the University of Michigan. He has been on the staff of the National Development Planning Agency (Bappenas) and has been bureau chief for education and religion.

Weifang Min is the executive vice-president of Peking University and dean and on the faculty in the Graduate School of Education. He received his Ph.D. from Stanford University in 1987. Concurrently, he serves as the president of the China National Association for Research on Study Abroad, vice-president of the China National Association of Economics of Education, vice-president of the China Higher Education Research Association, and senior research fellow at the National Center for Education Development Research of China.

Pham Lan Huong is associate professor in the Department of Basic Sciences, Van Lang University, and former director of the International Training Center. She is currently director of the Advanced Technology and Education Consultancy Company. She is former assistant to the rector of the Maritime University. She holds a doctorate from VUT State University, Brno, in the Czech Republic and has been a visiting USIA scholar at the University of Oregon. She is the author of three books and numerous articles on Vietnamese research and education.

Paitoon Sinlarat is associate professor and dean in the Faculty of Education, Chulalongkorn University, Bangkok, Thailand. He serves as president of the Thailand Association of Higher Education. Among his books are *Higher Education in Thailand: Critical Perspectives* and *Foundations of Thai Higher Education*.

Jason Tan is associate professor in Policy and Management Studies at the National Institute of Education, Singapore. He graduated with a Ph.D. in comparative education from the State University of New York at Buffalo. Among the topics on which he has published are the education of the Malay minority in Singapore, school privatization initiatives, and curriculum reform. He is the editor of *Challenges Facing the Singapore Education System Today*.

Toru Umakoshi is professor of higher education in the Graduate School of Obirin University, Tokyo, Japan. He was formerly professor of comparative education at Nagoya University, Japan and served as founding director of the Center for the Studies of Higher Education. He is currently president of the Japan Comparative Education Society. He has written widely on Korean education and comparative education.

Index

Academic freedom, 30, 214, 239; historical perspectives on, 17; in private higher education, 26

Academic profession, 14, 29–30, 48; in Cambodia, 346–347, 351–352, 354–356; in China, 74–76, 81; in India, 93–94, 105; in Indonesia, 261; in Korea, 164, 165–166, 170–171; in Malaysia, 238–241; in Philippines, 287–288, 296; and United States, 258; in Vietnam, 312, 316, 322–323

Access, 28; in Cambodia, 348–349; in China, 79; in East Asia, 20; economic aspects of, 19–21; expansion of, 22–23; in Indonesia, 259–261; in Japan, 130; in Singapore, 188–191; in Philippines, 293–294; and women, 28, 130, 189–190, 229, 260–261, 348. *See also* Enrollment

Accountability, 30, 138, 232

Accreditation, 28–29; in China, 72; in India, 98; in Indonesia, 264–265; in Japan, 138; in Philippines, 292, 296; of private higher education, 45; transnationalization of, 31; in Vietnam, 321–322

Admissions, in Singapore, 183

Affirmative action, 242

Agricultural University (Malaysia), 225

Air and Correspondence University of Korea, 46

Altbach, Philip, 34

Americanization, 18, 165

American university traditions. *See* U.S. academic model

Anglo-American academic model. *See* U.S. academic model

Arabic, 225, 252

ASEAN (Association of Southeast Asian Nations), 36

Asian Development Bank, 294, 343

Asian Institute of Technology (Philippines), 25

Asian Institute of Technology (Thailand), 25

Assumption University (Thailand), 25

Ateneo de Manila University (Philippines), 24, 25

Atma Jaya University (Indonesia), 24

Australia, 31, 104, 106, 179–180, 184, 187, 212, 226, 318, 319, 328, 343

Australian National University, 267

Autonomy, 232; and academic profession, 30; in China, 81; historical perspectives on, 17; in India, 104; in Malaysia, 234–236; and private higher education, 26

Baejac Hakdang (Korea), 147

Bahasa Malaysia, 18, 232

Bangladesh: enrollment, 14; historical perspectives, 15

Beijing Agricultural University, 60

Beijing Chemical Engineering University, 60

Beijing College of Mines, 60